U0756048

小学英语说课与试课
视频课例

主　编　罗晓杰　张　璐　牟金江
副主编　黄锡汝　洪晓翠　赵凯婧
参加编写人员（按照姓氏拼音顺序）

陈丽娜	董方圆	冯心怡	何曦晨	洪晓翠	黄家欣
黄锡汝	姜　俐	李聆梵	李　然	李莞尔	李钰阳
林陈霜	刘　晨	刘　娜	罗晓杰	牟金江	潘金琳
邱梦梦	单　婵	王俊之	项纸陆	谢　冰	谢智莺
徐　速	许　萍	杨金生	杨　艳	姚婷婷	叶欣雨
张丽琼	张　璐	张心如	赵凯婧	周培培	朱温铭

说课视频入口　　　　试课视频入口　　　　课件下载

复旦大學出版社

前　　言

　　"双新"教育改革给广大中小学英语教师带来了机遇,也提出了挑战:深入理解新课程方案和新课程标准,有效使用新教材和新教法,切实提高"教、学、评"一体化的教学设计与实施能力,已经成为一线英语教师专业发展的新要求。在"双新"背景之下,"中小学英语说课与试课丛书"应运而生。

　　除基本的介绍外,该丛书精选了中小学一线优秀教师常见课型的教学设计、说课和试课案例,呈现新课堂改革的创新实践,示范并助力英语教师掌握英语说课和试课的方法与技巧,提高教师"双新"背景下不同课型的教学设计与实施能力,促进中小学英语教师专业发展,提高英语课堂教学质量。

　　该丛书包括《高中英语说课与试课(视频课例)》《初中英语说课与试课(视频课例)》和《小学英语说课与试课(视频课例)》。三本书皆分为基本理论与实践课例两部分。

　　每册书的第一部分(基本理论)为英语学科说课与试课方法,共分两章。第一章"英语学科说课的基本方法"简要介绍了说课的定义,按说课目的和用途,将说课划分为评估型说课和教研型说课;按照有无媒体辅助,将说课划分为有辅助说课和无辅助说课。重点介绍了"五模块"和"三模块"英语说课法的内容框架,同时探讨了说课内容、说课语言和说课行为的优化方案,以及提高说课的科学性、艺术性和互动性的技巧。第二章"英语学科试课的基本方法"界定了试课的定义,根据是否有学生配合,将试课划分为有生试课和无生试课;根据试课目的,将试课划分为教研型试课和展示型试课。重点介绍了讲解、提问、理答和活动组织等试课技巧,同时探讨了教学活动、教学语言和体态语言的优化设计,以及提高试课科学性、艺术性和互动性的技巧。

　　第二部分(实践课例)为英语说课与试课课例。研究团队指导小学、初中、高中一线优秀教师,共同开发了数十个优秀课例,包括词汇课、对话课、听说课、阅读课、语法课和读写课等常见课型。为了更好地助力读者掌握说课和试课的方法与技巧,说课和试课案例都以话语实录的形式呈现,便于教师理解和模仿学习。为了更好地助力教师提高常用课型的教学设计能力,每一个课例还提供了教学设计方案和配套课件(扫码即可下载),为教师提供教学参考。值得一提的是,本书所有课例均基于现行的中小学英语课程标准的教学理念设计,积极践行英语学习活动观,认真贯彻主题意义探究和"教、学、评"一体化。这也是本书的突出特点。

该丛书属于新形态教材,其突出特点是立体和全面。每个课例均配说课和试课视频,读者可以扫码观看学习。该丛书可以作为职前和在职英语教师专业发展的教材,用于高师英语专业学生教师职业技能训练,用于英语教师资格证笔试和面试的备考,也可以用于在职英语教师教育培训或教研竞赛等。

由于编写时间和专业水平有限,疏漏之处在所难免,敬请广大读者斧正。

浙江师范大学　罗晓杰

2023 年 10 月 1 日

目　　录

第一部分

英语学科说课与试课方法

第一章

英语学科说课的基本方法

一、说课的定义

所谓说课,是教师在备课的基础上,面对同行或教研人员等,在规定时间内(10—15分钟)讲述自己将要上的或已上过的某节课的教学设计及其理据。说课教师要用简明、准确、形象、生动的语言(包括体态语言)说明"教什么"(教学内容)和"教谁"(教学对象)、"怎么教"(教学方法)和"为什么这样教"(教学设计的理论依据)。

"教什么"应说清具体教学内容,进行教材分析或语篇研读,明确教学重点难点。"教谁"应说清教学对象及其语言能力水平和思维品质,进行学情分析。"怎么教"应在说教材和说学情的基础上,说清为达成教学目标,如何处理教材,采取何种教法学法,设计哪些教学活动,以及教学活动如何开展、效果如何。"怎么教"重点关注教学过程,要说清教学步骤名称、各环节师生主要活动的组织与调控,展示课堂教学中如何教、学、评。"为什么这样教"应结合"教什么"和"怎么教",说清教学设计与实施的理论依据,具体包括教学目标和教学重点难点确定的理论依据,教学流程和具体教学活动设计的理论依据,教学过程组织与调控的理论依据,等等。

说课要求教师以英语课程标准中的教学与评价建议,语言学、教育学和心理学相关理论为指导,系统阐述自己对教材的语篇研读、对学生已知和未知的了解,对教学重点难点和教学目标的把握,对教学方法和学习方式的选择,对教学活动、作业和板书的设计和安排,以及对课堂教学设计与实施的反思。

说课既是一种教学研究活动,促进教师的专业发展,也是一种评估手段,评估教师的专业素养和职业技能。作为一种教研活动,说课常常回答同行的质疑和建议;作为一种评估手段,说课常常回答专家的提问,接受专家的评价。

虽然说课的总体思路是说明一节课"教什么"和"教谁"、"怎么教"和"为什么这样教",但是,现实中说课一般按照分析教材和学生,陈述教学目标,描述教学过程和效果,说明作业和板书设计,反思教学亮点和问题的顺序进行。

二、说课的类型

从不同的角度可以将说课划分为不同类型。最为常见的是按说课的目的和用途,将说课划分为评估型说课和教研型说课。还有就是按照有无媒体辅助,将说课划分为有辅助说课和无辅助说课。

(一) 评估型说课

英语学科的评估型说课主要用于评估英语教师的教学与教研能力,通常用于在职教师或英语专业师范生的教师技能竞赛,用于英语教师入职考核、职称评定或教师招聘等。此类说课的语言通常为英语。通过说课评估说课者作为英语教师所具备的专业技能和职业技能,评估说课者的英语学科教育教学能力和教育教学理论水平。

一般情况下,评估型说课本身有时间要求,对准备说课的时间也有一定要求,因此,也被称为限时说课,是较为科学的教师综合素质评价手段。就英语学科评估型说课而言,使用英语说课则更能体现说课者的英语教师素质,这是由英语学科的特殊性所决定的。

(二) 教研型说课

教研型说课可以进一步划分为集体备课用的教研型说课、课堂观摩前的教研型说课和课堂观摩后的教研型说课。集体备课用的教研型说课一般使用汉语,其操作程序为:指定1—2人先行说课,然后集体研讨,最后综合各方意见,形成最佳的教学设计方案。课堂观摩前后的教研型说课,其主要目的是为评课研讨活动提供上课和听课不能提供或无法获得的备课信息。课堂观摩前的教研型说课的主要操作程序是说课——上课——评课研讨,参加研讨的教师可以根据教师上课和说课所提供的理论与实践两个方面的信息,把教师课前的主观设想(说课呈现)与课上客观的教学效果(上课呈现)进行比较、分析和研讨。课堂观摩后的教研型说课的主要操作程序是上课——说课——评课研讨,参加研讨的教师可以根据教师的课堂教学实况和课后说课反思展开专题研讨。

(三) 有辅助说课

有辅助说课是指运用多媒体课件进行辅助的英语说课。与无辅助情况下使用英语进行说课相比,有辅助说课可以展示课堂教学的课件和说课的内容,其通过对文本、声音、图像等多种媒体形式的运用,增强了说课内容的直观性,有助于听者想象和推测课堂教学情境。多媒体课件呈现的教学信息,作为教师"说"的有效补充和延伸,弥补了无辅助英语说课不易直接理解的不足。虽然有辅助说课在说课内容上较无辅助说课不会发生大的方向性变化,但由于有了多媒体课件的辅助,说课的内容侧重点及教师的说课行为会产生相应的变化。此外,由于使用多媒体技术,教师增加了课件的设计、制作与使用,如果课件播放和说课语言配合不好、文本信息的选择与呈现量度把握不准,都会影响说课效果。

(四) 无辅助说课

无辅助说课是指按照说课常规要求,教师不借助任何辅助手段,面向同行、教研人员等,说明某节课的教学设计及其理论依据。由于缺少其他媒体辅助,仅使用英语口头分析教材和学情,陈述教学目标和重点难点,介绍教学方法和学习策略,描述教学活动及说明设计意图,无论对说课者的口语表达还是听者的理解,难度都很大——那些不常用的教学术语会增加听者对说课内容的理解难度。因此,使用英语进行无辅助说课,说者应降低英语难度,使用肢体语言辅助,根据现场反馈调整语速,以便与听者的思维保持同步,提高说课的效果。

三、说课的内容和方法

(一) 说课的内容

说课的内容包括说教材、说学生、说教学目标、说重点和难点、说教学思路、说教材处理、说教法学法、说教学媒体、说教学过程、说作业设计、说板书设计、说教学效果等。

教材、学情和教学目标是说课的重要内容。说教材要分析语篇的主题和内容,语篇传递的意义,语篇的文体特征、内容结构和语言特点。分析学情要评估学生关于本课主题的已知与未知,说明学生对所学知识和技能的熟悉和熟练程度,以及完成本课学习任务必备的思维能力等。分析教材和学情有助于明确教学内容的难易度,为重点、难点的确定和教学目标的构建提供依据。说教学目标要在核心素养的框架内,按照英语学习活动观中的学习理解、应用实践和迁移创新的理论框架陈述。教学目标陈述要明确、具体、可观察或可测量,与具体教学内容相关。

教学思路和教学过程是最重要的说课内容。教学过程是教学目标达成的主要途径。教学思路和教学过程的设计除了与教学内容,学生的文化知识、语言能力和思维能力有关,还与教师秉持的教学理念、课堂教学采用的教学模式或教学方法直接相关。说教学思路和教学过程,要说清教学的总体设计思路,说清教学推进过程中各教学活动为何开展、如何开展、效果如何。

说教学思路一般需要列举教学步骤名称,简要介绍各步骤的教学活动组成和内容安排,简要说明各步骤和各活动间的逻辑关系。说清教学思路对于说课而言至关重要。只有说清教学思路,才能让听者领会到说课者匠心独具的教学设计,才能依此判断其教学理念是否先进,教学步骤安排是否合理,教学活动设计是否科学,教学方法的选择和使用是否恰当。

说教学过程要具体说明教学活动如何开展,说清各个教学活动的具体操作流程、完成教学活动所需时间。说教学过程还需要说清各个教学活动的目的是什么,或可能的教学效果如何,说清在教学活动过程中教师如何为学生提供认知支架和情感支架,如何围绕教学目标,突出重点、突破难点地开展教与学的双边活动。

说教学过程重在描述。之所以使用"描述"一词,是因为听者需要根据说课教师的描摹阐述,想象教学活动如何开展及效果如何。描述教学过程,要按照教学活动设计的先后顺序,依次描述具体教学活动的操作过程,说明教学活动如何开始,如何展开、推进和结束。描述教学过程要注意两个要点:一是描述各个教学活动中的师生活动,二是说明教学活动设计的主要意图,必要时还要说明在教学活动过程中生成的问题与对策。具体来说,教师先简要罗列本节课的教学环节,然后按顺序说明各教学环节所包含的教学活动名称,各活动中师生的教与学行为、活动的设计意图和所需时间。说教学过程重在描述教师的言行,例如:教师下达了什么教学指令,问了什么问题,创设了怎样的情境,让学生采用怎样的方式学习和操练;学生说了什么、做了什么、做得怎样;在学生遇到学习困难时,教师如何提供支架、怎样启发诱导、怎样指导学生自主探究、引导学生解决问题;等等。

作业设计和板书设计也是重要的说课内容。作业设计是课堂教学的延伸，是帮助学生巩固所学和迁移创新的重要抓手。板书设计是教师突出重点、突破难点和强化学生记忆的重要手段。说作业设计要求教师说清作业的内容、类型、完成作业的方式、检测或评价作业的方法、设计该作业的意图，以及作业本身的科学性与合理性等。说板书设计要求教师说清板书的主要内容、整体布局及其展开程序，说清板书的设计意图和板书效果。

说教学效果，即说明教学目标的达成情况，是说课不可忽视的内容。在评估型说课中，说预设的教学效果经常与说教学过程相结合，即结合特定教学活动设计，说明该活动的教学效果，而教学亮点则在教学反思部分加以概括。在教研型说课中，反思教学目标的达成情况要说明实际教学效果，即既要反思教学设计与实施过程中的亮点，也要反思实际教学中存在的问题。说教学亮点要求教师将教学设计的突出特色、实际教学中的精彩之处，有选择地呈现给听者。说教学问题要求教师具体说明教学设计或师生互动存在哪些不足之处，或值得商榷的问题，反思教学疏漏之处或效果不佳的根本原因。

（二）说课的方法

1. "五模块"英语说课法

"五模块"英语说课法将英语学科说课的内容划分为五个模块：分析教材和学生、陈述目标和方法、描述过程和效果、说明作业与板书、反思亮点与问题。"五模块"英语说课法打破了以往的线性说课方法，将说课内容加以整合，避免了说课内容的交叉重合。各模块内容要素相对稳定，模块内部内容可以相互融合，以便灵活应对说课时间和内容要求。具体模块及内容要素如下：

模块一：分析教材和学生。该模块主要包括说教材和说学生。说教材主要是分析教材内容，分析教材的地位和作用；说学生主要是分析学生的知识与技能基础，分析学生的学习兴趣和认知风格。分析教材和学生有助于确定重点和难点。

模块二：陈述目标和方法。该模块具体包括说教学目标和说教学方法。教学目标主要是基于对教材和学生的分析确定的。明确教学重点和难点后，再基于学情处理教材和选择教学方法。

模块三：描述过程和效果。该模块主要包括说教学过程（有时只说教学思路）和说教学效果。说教学过程主要是按照时间顺序，说明本节课的教学活动顺序，描述师生互动过程；说教学效果可以从教学设计的出发点说设计意图，或者从教学实施的落脚点说预设的效果。描述过程和效果既要形象生动，又要有理有据，以便听者想象教学过程的实施和理解教学活动设计的理据。根据说课目的和所给说课时间的不同，描述教学过程和教学效果的方法也有所不同。教研型课前说课只需简述教学设计的思路、教学步骤以及设计意图，而教研型课后说课则无需描述教学过程和教学效果，只有评估型说课才要求说课教师描述教学过程。

模块四：说明作业与板书。该模块主要包括说作业设计和说板书设计，说明作业设计和板书设计的意图及其对学生英语学习的促进作用。

模块五：反思亮点与问题。具体包括说教学亮点和说教学问题，一般情况下，评估型说课主要反思教学亮点，教研型说课则二者兼顾。

对于评估型说课而言,分析教材和学生,陈述目标和方法,描述过程和效果,说明作业与板书,反思亮点与问题五个模块都很重要。因为,上述模块内容能够反映出说课者的教学设计与实施能力,以及教育教学理论水平。对于教研型说课而言,陈述目标和方法、反思亮点与问题更为重要。因为听者就在上课现场观摩教学,已经亲眼目睹教学的全过程,对教材与学生也比较了解,执教者说教学目标、教学目标的达成以及对教学效果的反思更能体现和发挥说课在教学研讨中的作用。

2.“三模块”英语说课法

“三模块”英语说课法将说课内容划分为“教学目标定位”“教学目标达成”和“教学效果反思”三个模块。具体模块及内容要素如下:

模块一:教学目标定位。该模块主要包括分析教材和学情、陈述重点难点和教学目标,即基于教材分析和学情分析,确定重点难点和定位教学目标,并加以阐述。

模块二:教学目标达成。该模块主要包括说教学理念或教法学法、说教学设计思路、说教学活动的具体实施过程、说作业设计和板书设计。具体而言,教师要重点围绕教学目标,说明为了突出重点、突破难点和达成教学目标,选择和使用何种教法或学法,进行了怎样的教材处理,按照怎样的教学思路实施教学活动,如何科学利用板书,布置了什么作业,最后说明教师通过什么方法评价目标的达成情况。

模块三:教学效果反思。该模块主要包括说教学效果、说教学亮点、说教学问题和说再教设计。具体而言,教师要反思教学设计所体现的先进教学理念,举例说明教学实施过程中师生互动是否有效,教学目标为何有效达成或效果欠佳,在教本课时会进行怎样的改进。

四、英语学科说课的注意事项

(一) 优化说课内容,提高说课的科学性

提高说课的科学性,可以从甄选说课内容入手。优化说课内容主要关注说课教师的内容选择和内容侧重。说课教师要根据说课类型在内容上有所选择,根据所给时间在内容上有所侧重,有所取舍。例如,根据说课类型和所给说课时间的不同,描述教学过程和教学效果方法也有所不同。教研型说课只需简述教学设计思路、教学步骤和设计意图,无需描述教学过程和教学效果,评估型说课才要求说课教师细致描述教学过程。因此,说课教师要根据不同的说课类型区分主要说课内容和次要说课内容,在关注一般说课内容的同时,又能突出重要的、基本的、关键的内容,做到内容模块间相对完整、主次分明、详略得当,符合该类型说课的目的与要求。

提高说课的科学性,可以从整合说课内容入手。无论是“五模块”英语说课法,还是“三模块”英语说课法,都需要对说课内容进行整合。例如:教材分析可以和学情分析整合,还可以和重点难点、教学目标分析进行整合;说教法学法可以与说教学思路或教学过程整合;说重点难点、说教学效果还可以和教学反思整合;等等。整合说课内容也是为了精简说课内容,避免不必要的重复,从而节省说课时间。

此外,还有一种说课内容的整合形式是将教学重点难点与所有说课内容相整合。模块式英语说课没有将说教学重点难点归到任何一个模块,并非因其不是说课的重点,恰恰相

反,正是因为其非常重要,因此应将其融合到五个模块之中,贯穿说课的全程。具体而言,说课教师可以结合教材和学情分析,说明重难点确定的理据;结合教学目标陈述,明确重点和难点;结合教学过程描述、作业设计和板书设计,说明突出重点和突破难点的活动设计和实施方法;结合教学反思,说明突出重点和突破难点教学的效果。总之,说重点难点是不可或缺的重要说课内容,需要多次与各模块的说课内容融合。

(二) 优化说课语言,提高说课的艺术性

提高说课的艺术性,可以从优化说课语言入手。英语说课的艺术性主要体现在语言的艺术上,说课语言的准确性、生动性和艺术性在很大程度上决定了说课的效果。

1. 关注说课语言的准确性

英语说课必须关注说课教师语言的准确性,要做到语言准确无误。说课语言的准确无误指说课内容无词汇、语法和语用错误,无语音、语调和意群停顿错误,无语篇衔接和语义连贯错误。说课语言的准确性,还表现为说课内容的逻辑性。清晰的条理和严密的逻辑,有助于听者准确理解说课内容。因为无论是对于说课教师,还是听说课的教师,英语都是外语而非母语,边听英语边思考一节课的教学设计并想象其教学效果,需要大脑进行复杂的认知加工。如果说课条理不清,逻辑混乱,说课者不能准确表达,听者很难准确理解说课内容,更不能准确推断教学设计与实施效果,说课效果将大打折扣。

2. 关注说课语言的生动性

英语说课必须关注说课教师语言的生动性,要做到语言形象生动,易于理解。无论教学设计多么科学,说课内容整合多么合理,如果离开了生动形象的语言,都无法达到良好的说课效果。只有当说课教师化枯燥为生动,化抽象为具体,化隐微为显著,化无形为有形,熟练运用形象生动的说课语言时,才能为听者创造课堂教学情境和教学效果的想象空间。只有当说课教师熟练运用生动形象的说课语言,富有激情地分析教材和学情、陈述教学目标与教学思路、描述教学过程与效果、说明作业和板书设计,反思教学亮点与问题时,才会方便听者想象教学活动开展过程和推测教学活动实施效果。说课的语言艺术才会真正体现出来。

3. 关注说课语言的艺术性

英语说课必须关注说课教师语言的艺术性,要做到语言风格独特。说课是在较为正式场合进行的口语表达活动,其语言同时具有书面语和口语的双重特点。例如:说课者在分析教材和学情、陈述教学目标和教法学法时,更关注表达的精确性,故多采用书面语;而描述教学活动和教学效果更需要通俗易懂,最好使用简单、形象、生动传神的口头语言。再如:说课者系统介绍教学设计及其理论依据时,适合采用独白语言;在说教学过程时,可以适当模拟师生对话,帮助听者想象课堂教学情境和推测课堂互动效果。正所谓不同风格的说课语言会给英语说课带来不同的效果。当说课教师恰当地运用各种语言风格,声情并茂地讲述课堂教学设计或描述课堂教学情景时,听者就不仅仅听到和看到说课行为,还会想象到上课的情境,体会到教学艺术和说课艺术的魅力。当说课教师有问有讲,有读有说,用富有变化的语言将听者带入课堂教学中去,听者未进课堂却仿佛身临其境,似乎"看到了"师生的互动,想象出课堂教学效果,那是一种艺术的享受。

（三）优化说课行为，提高说课的互动性

提高说课的互动性，可以从优化说课者的说课行为入手。优化说课行为主要关注说课教师体态语言的使用。说课教师要做到站姿稳健、手势得体、表情自然、目光充满自信、灵活运用体态语言。

1. 站姿与手势

站姿是说课教师重要的体态语言。教师的站立位置因是否有多媒体辅助而略有不同。在进行无辅助说课时，教师站在讲桌与黑板之间较为合适。如此站位，教师可以边说课边板书，口述手写，方便自如，还能随时参阅教材、教案或说课稿。低头可及，既节约时间又快捷方便。在进行多媒体辅助英语说课时，说课教师的站位以不影响听者观看效果为宜。教师最好使用激光笔代替有线鼠标，侧身站立于屏幕边，用余光看屏幕，必要时指点幻灯片内容，避免因需要操控鼠标频繁走动或遮挡听者视线，从而影响视听效果。无论有无媒体辅助说课，教师都不能频繁走动或晃动身体，以免分散听者注意，但也不能固定站立于一处，显得呆滞刻板。教师应该在讲台和黑板之间自然走动，在"微动"中求得放松，灵活自然地运用手势。此外，说课开始前后教师的站姿非常重要。站在讲台上，说课教师应该面向全体听者，先进行自我介绍，导入说课。若使用多媒体辅助说课，说课教师应先做使用多媒体课件的准备，再面向全体听者，微微侧身，开始说课。切忌上讲台就侧身而站，与听者无目光交流就开始说课。

手势是动作变化最快、最多、最大的体态语，具有丰富的表现力。在说课中，适度地运用手势，可以帮助说课教师更准确地传达说课内容，使说课更具说服力和感染力。因此，教师在说课中要善于运用手势，以手势助"说"，增强"说"的效果。教师在说课的过程中，要根据说课内容，适当地运用手势，通过手势的变化来使说课更加自然生动。教师说课时手势应配合说课内容的需要，如在分析教材或描述教学程序时，手势要柔缓舒展，这样可以渲染气氛，把听者带入角色，使之有亲临课堂的感觉；要突出说课的重点时，在讲关键词句处要配合迅速有力的手势；在归纳、总结时，手势应慢慢收拢，使听者感受到说课教师的自信，不能匆匆收势或随意乱挥。与说课内容统一的手势动作，不仅有利于听者对说课者要表达的内容的理解，也能显示出教师的教态美。当然手势的动作要灵活，要自然得体，切忌动作太多太大，细碎烦琐，单一呆板。矫揉造作的手势会让听者觉得眼花缭乱，头晕目眩，影响听的效果。没有手势变化，将双手一直保持在固定位置会给人呆板的印象，压抑语言的表意功能，甚至会让人产生说课教师在背稿子的感觉。

2. 表情与目光

面部表情是说课教师重要的体态语言。说课教师自始至终都要做到面带微笑，轻松自如，表现出对所说课的教学设计充满自信的神态，表现出我知道本节课"教什么""怎么教""为什么这么教"，我知道本节课会取得良好的教学效果。除了通过面部表情展现自信，说课教师还可以运用面部表情有效地调节说课气氛，增强说课效果。配合不同教学内容所表现的情感以及说课语言，及时调整面部表情，表现出或喜或忧的神情，不仅有助于听者理解说课内容，想象课堂教学情景，还能使听者受到感染，获得沉浸式的体验。

目光是最具互动性的体态语言。说课教师要做到目光中充满自信，要善于用目光来传

情达意,表达思想感情,吸引听者注意。说课要注意目光的指向性。说课者不能用语言要求听者认真听讲或集中注意,只能通过目光或手势引导听者。尤其是进行多媒体辅助说课时,说课者有时会希望听者看屏幕上的内容,可以先将自己的目光转移到屏幕上的要点,并用手或激光笔辅助指点,这样就能将听者的注意力带到屏幕上。但说课者的目光不能长时间停留在屏幕上去读课件内容,而应该及时转过身面向听者,必要时再转身指示重点内容,这样能确保随时和听者进行目光交流,把握听者对信息的理解程度。此外,在说课的过程中教师应与听者进行适当的目光交流,根据听者的目光、表情、肢体等非语言反馈信息,判断听者的理解程度,及时调整语速或媒体播放速度,努力营造和谐愉悦的气氛,提高说课的效果。

综上,说课教师的教学语言要与体态语言配合使用,根据不同的说课阶段和说课内容,及时调整站姿、手势和面部表情,使说课更加生动形象,更具说服力和感染力。说课教师还应与听者进行有效的目光交流与互动,及时获取反馈信息,根据听者理解情况调整说课内容和说课策略,保证说课效果。

提高说课的互动性,还可以从优化说课媒体入手。优化说课媒体主要在于优化课件设计及使用。说课课件中,教师可以用表格和流程图来表征说课内容以增强说课的条理性;在时间充裕的情况下,可以在说课课件中将文字、声音、图像,甚至视频等多种信息整合起来,将说课的内容形象化、具体化和立体化,帮助听者理解、想象和推测教学设计、教学情境和教学效果,提高说课效果和效率。

第二章

英语学科试课的基本方法

一、试课的定义

试课,也称模拟试讲或模拟试教,是教师(包括在职教师和师范生)根据预设的课堂教学方案演示模拟课堂教学的过程。根据是否有学生配合,可以将试课划分为有生试课和无生试课。根据目的,可以将试课划分为教研型试课和展示型试课。试课的具体时长受具体科目、教学内容、教学对象、试课目的等诸多因素影响。通常情况下,教研型试课一般没有严格的时间限制;展示型试课时长一般在 10—15 分钟。如果要展示一节课的完整过程,无生试课时长一般为 10—15 分钟,有生试课则可能持续 10—20 分钟。

二、试课的分类

(一) 有生试课

有生试课是指执教者与指定的模拟学生或与充当模拟学生的同伴合作完成的试课。有生试课要求执教者在试课过程中与模拟学生进行真实的师生互动,包括提问、候答、叫答、应答、评价或反馈等一对一的师生互动,以及包括角色扮演、小组讨论、辩论等配对或小组形式的生生互动。

在各级各类教师职业技能竞赛中,无论执教者是在职教师还是师范生,模拟学生通常由竞赛活动的组委会指定安排,一般会安排 4—8 名模拟学生,以方便执教者开展配对活动和小组活动。但在师范生微格教学技能训练或是教育实习中,模拟学生一般为试课者的同伴,具体模拟学生数量没有严格要求,一般 4 人以上即可。如果试课者是在职教师,模拟学生人数则更为灵活。

有生试课在师范生微格教学技能训练、教育实习课前试讲和在职教师公开课磨课中被广泛使用,在重点评估执教者课堂互动能力的教师职业技能竞赛中也被广泛使用。

(二) 无生试课

无生试课是指在没有模拟学生配合的情况下,执教者单独演绎课堂教学过程的试课。

无生试课要求执教者在试课过程中借助语言,配以面部表情和肢体动作,根据预设的教学方案,与假想的学生进行假想的互动,具体教师行为包括提问、候答、叫答、倾听、观察、评价或反馈等一对一的师生互动,以及包括配对和小组活动的组织、实施与评价反馈等生生互动。

无生试课对时间、地点、活动组织等要求不高。该类试课在各级各类教师职业技能竞赛和教师资格证面试、教师招聘和新教师考核中被广泛使用,但在师范生微格教学技能训练、教育实习课前试讲和在职教师公开课磨课中被使用得不多。

(三) 教研型试课

教研型试课旨在检测教学方案设计的合理性和可操作性,诊断课堂教学实施过程中可能存在的问题,供试课教师优化教学设计之用。教研型试课要求执教者在试课前认真备课,在试课过程中模拟与学生的互动,试课后与同伴或独自评估课堂教学效果和教学目标的达成情况,研究教学方案的优化措施。

教研型试课多用于师范生教育实习中的课前试讲,也常用于在职教师各级各类教研活动中公开课前的磨课。二者的区别在于前者通常有同伴模拟学生配合,而后者有无模拟学生则视具体情况而定。但无论哪种类型的教研型试课,其主要目的均为及时发现文本解读、教学设计、活动设置、师生互动中存在的问题,通过试课及课后讨论,优化教学设计,为正式授课做更加充分的准备。

虽然教研型试课在多数情况下有模拟学生,但也可以由执教者单独完成。试课时,执教者可录制视频,事后反复回看录像,进行自我反思或征求他人意见,以达到优化教学设计和提升教学效果的目的。

(四) 展示型试课

展示型试课旨在展示或评估执教者教师专业技能和教师职业技能水平。该类试课一般会限定执教者的备课时间,要求执教者在规定的时间内完成教学设计和课堂教学展示,执教者借助语言和非语言行为,演示教学过程,模拟课堂师生互动,供评委对执教者的教师专业技能和综合素质作出评价。

展示型试课适用于教师资格考试和教师入编考试的面试环节,也常常用于各级各类教师职业技能或教学基本功竞赛,因此也被称为评估型试课。教师资格考试和教师入编考试中使用的展示型试课通常为无生试课,执教者现场抽取题目,根据试题要求在给定时间内,在规定地点进行现场备课和试课。此类试课通常只选取课堂教学某个或某几个环节进行微格教学,时长在10—15分钟,由考官或评委现场打分或点评。各级各类教师职业技能或教学基本功竞赛通常以竞赛形式开展,该类型的展示型试课既可以有模拟学生配合,进行有生试课,也可以由执教者单独完成,进行无生试课;既可以现场试课进行评比,也可以在规定时间内录制视频通过网络进行评比。

近年来,随着教育技术的不断发展,加之新冠疫情的影响,许多教师职业技能竞赛及教学基本功竞赛转为线上进行。线上评比的展示型试课通常由活动主办方在给定时间下发题目,选手在规定时间内撰写教学设计、制作课件和录制试课视频,并按要求上传至指定网络平台,评委通过观看视频评定分数。线上评比的展示型试课教学时长一般为 10—15 分钟,有些竞赛要求有生试课,有些则要求无生试课,教学流程相对完整,视频录制要求一镜到底,不允许后期制作。

三、试课的技巧

(一) 讲解技巧

讲解技巧是最重要的试课技巧。讲解是指教师运用口头语言(主要用英语)向学生展示、说明、解释英语语言知识和文化知识,传授英语学习方法和语言运用规律,促进学生综合语言运用能力和思维品质提升的主要教学行为。

教师可以采用讲解技巧来实现有效讲解,具体包括:使用视听刺激、使用重复和强调、使用专门术语、使用幽默的语言、使用更有活力的引入方式、将要点编号、将讲解与具体经验相联系、将讲解与其他知识相结合、有效运用连接词、定义关键词或概念、形成规则或原理、采用合适的节奏、避免无意识重复、考虑听众、保持流畅、避免遗漏重点内容、举例(包括正例和反例)、插入任务(在适当时机插入相关的学习活动)、建立反馈环(教师暂停讲解,采用提问或布置任务等方法,判断学生是否理解所讲内容)、利用"语言学技巧"(指出讲解中的内容要点或提示教学方向的改变)、在讲解中提出认知要求(从最低认知水平的数据层面转向较高水平的概念层面和最高水平的抽象概念层面)等。

(二) 提问技巧

提问技巧是重要的试课技巧。试课中的提问技巧主要指教师问题设计、提问追问、叫答和候答技巧。

首先,教师的问题设计要有针对性,要做到目的明确,要符合学情,在学生思维活动的疑惑处或阻碍处设计问题,以便激发学生的认知冲突,引发学生思考。问题设计要难度适中,突出重点,适时适度,由浅入深,最好能够形成问题链,促使学生有逻辑地思考问题,循序渐进地理解和掌握所学知识,使提问发挥最好的效果。

其次,教师的提问叫答要面向全体,尽可能给每个学生参与的机会。当问题难度大时,教师应先叫中等生回答,优生补充,学困生重复,以确保大多数学生有足够的时间思考问题和组织语言进行回答。

再次,教师提出较为复杂和难度较大的问题时,要使用候答策略,给学生预留一定的思考时间,在学生回答后不要马上对学生的回答作出评价或者提出另外的问题,让学生有一定的时间深入思考,补充或修改对问题的回答,使其回答更加系统完善。

(三) 理答技巧

理答技巧是重要的试课技巧。教师的理答因学生应答的准确性和完整性的差异而有所不同,常用的教师语言性理答包括激励性理答、诊断性理答、发展性理答、目标性理答。当学生回答问题快速而正确时,教师应该对学生进行激励性理答,具体包括口头认可学生的观点和口头表扬。诊断性理答,即对学生的正确回答进行简单肯定、简单重复、意义重复或提升肯定,对学生的错误回答进行简单否定、纠正否定或引导否定。发展性理答包括:当学生回答正确时继续追问;当学生回答不上或回答说不完整时,转问其他学生;当学生难以回答或不知从何说起时进行探问,将一个问题分解成多个问题逐一发问,或换一种方式提问;当学生思维受阻时逆向发问,引导学生思考自己的回答是否合理,进而明确回答的不足之处。目标性理答通常用于理答的最后阶段,即对学生的回答进行重新组织或概括,给学生一个更加准确、清晰、完整的答案。

(四)活动组织技巧

活动组织技巧是重要的试课技巧。活动组织技巧是指教师在课堂活动组织中使用的呈现、调控、反馈和结束策略。常见呈现技巧包括:指令语言简洁清晰,多个指令间逻辑要严谨,避免遗漏指令;对讨论或角色扮演等活动过程或汇报过程进行示范;对讨论或角色扮演等活动进行组内角色分工,或按照组别分配不同任务,介绍活动规则,指导小组活动技巧,促进组内及组间合作等。常见调控技巧包括:帮助学生梳理活动思路,在学生思路受阻时,通过询问、解释、总结、增加新信息和运用新视角的方式重新解释活动任务;在学生活动任务完成达不到预期时提供建议。常见反馈技巧包括:组织尽可能多的小组呈现结果;鼓励学生参与活动,共同完成任务;适当纠正语言错误或给出提示,必要时提供技巧指导;点评小组展示情况和成员表现;对小组的汇报成果进行总结,给出全面反馈。常见结束技巧包括:关注各组讨论进度,给进度较快的小组提出更高要求或布置新任务;根据课堂实际情况适时结束活动。

四、英语学科试课的注意事项

(一)优化设计教学活动,提高试课的科学性

教学设计是试课的前提和基础,而科学合理的教学设计的前提与基础又是深入的语篇研读和学情分析,合理的目标构建和教材处理,指向目标达成的教学思路、活动设计,板书设计和作业设计,等等。

1. 语篇研读和学情分析

英语教学设计的第一步是进行语篇研读。《义务教育英语课程标准(2022年版)》要求教师要以语篇研读为逻辑起点,开展有效的教学设计,要求教师:对语篇的主题、内容、文体结构、语言特点、作者观点等进行分析;明确主题意义,提炼语篇中的结构化知识,建立文体特征、语言特点等与主题意义的关联,多层次、多角度分析语篇传递的意义,挖掘文化内涵和育人价值,把握教学主线。此外,还要求教师在研读语篇时要重点回答三个基本问题:第一,语篇的主题和内容是什么,即 What 的问题。第二,语篇传递的意义是什么,即 Why 的问题。不论口语语篇,还是书面语篇,都有其特定的交际目的或传递的主题意义,也就是作者或说话人的意图、情感态度或价值取向等。第三,语篇具有什么样的文体特征、内容结构和语言特点,如果语篇配有图片或表格,其传递何种意义或具有何种功能,即 How 的问题。对口语语篇的研读不仅要关注其呈现形式(对话、独白、访谈、指令等),还要关注其语境的正式程度、语言表达方式及功能等。如果呈现形式是对话,则要关注对话场合的正式程度和说话人

的身份,其语言表达方式是随意、直接、客气还是委婉,说话人使用了什么样的交际策略等。对语篇中配图的分析,教师要关注图片中人物或动物的行为、表情、心理状态、色彩搭配,以及场景布局等传递的意义,这些也是构成语篇主题意义的必要成分。关于 Why 和 How 的问题,受教育背景、生活阅历、认知方式等的影响,教师对这些问题的看法不尽相同,一般没有唯一答案,要注重与其他教师交流研讨,相互学习。

学情分析是保证教学设计科学合理的重要条件,是以学生为中心的教学理念在教学设计中的具体落实。《义务教育英语课程标准(2022 年版)》要求教师基于学生对主题的已知与未知,确定教学目标和教学重难点,为设计教与学的活动提供依据。这里的已知和未知主要指语言知识和文化知识。新课标主张在语言学习和文化学习中发展思维,在思维发展中推进语言学习和文化意识的形成和发展。因此,学情分析应从学生的文化知识、语言能力和思维品质三个角度进行。文化知识既包括饮食、服饰、建筑、交通,以及相关发明与创造等物质文化的知识,也包括哲学、科学、历史、语言、文学、艺术、教育,以及价值观、道德修养、审美情趣、劳动意识、社会规约和风俗习惯等非物质文化的知识。学生对与语篇相关文化知识的了解程度,直接影响其对语篇内容及其蕴含的态度和价值观的理解。语言能力指运用语言和非语言知识以及各种策略,参与特定情境下相关主题的语言活动时表现出来的语言理解和表达能力。思维品质指人的思维个性特征,反映学生在理解、分析、比较、推断、批判、评价、创造等方面的层次和水平。学生的文化知识、语言能力和思维品质决定了教学设计的难易度和活动组织的形式,是教学设计必须考虑的重要因素。

2. 目标构建和教材处理

英语教学设计的第二步是进行目标构建和教材处理。教学目标可以划分为单元教学目标和课时教学目标(或语篇教学目标)。单元教学目标一般按照语言能力、文化意识、思维品质和学习能力四个维度的核心素养表现目标构建。课时教学目标可以在核心素养的框架内,按照英语学习活动观中学习理解、应用实践和迁移创新的理论框架构建。一节课的教学目标确定后,再基于具体学情进行教材处理,以确保教学目标有效达成。

构建清晰合理的教学目标,要以学生为行为主体,运用可观察和(或)可测量的行为动词,指出学生经过本课学习后,在具体情境下达成目标的具体表现及表现程度。教学目标的陈述应尽量清晰、可操作、有递升。教学目标表述得越是简洁、明确,教师和学生对目标达成度的把握就会越准确。

教学目标陈述一般由四个部分组成:一是行为主体;二是外显的、能观察到的行为表现;三是这种行为表现的发生条件;四是行为表现程度或标准。行为主体有三种表述形式:(1)"程度副词+主语",如程度较好的学生(学优生)、程度稍弱的学生(学困生)等;(2)"百分比+主语",如 85% 的学生、60% 的学生等;(3)"表示范围的副词+主语",如全体学生、多数学生、少数学生等。行为是指学习者在学习结束后"知道什么"(know)和"能做什么"(can do)。可以使用"了解""理解""领会""知道""交流""表达""讲述""询问""叙述""描述"等行为动词。行为表现的发生条件是学习者完成规定行为时所处的情境,即评价学习结果时,该在哪种情况下评价。条件通常用一个介宾结构表示,如"在教师提示下,能够……""在教师的帮助下或以小组讨论的方式……""通过重复、举例、解释等方式……"等。行为表现程度或标准衡量的是"做得怎么样",通常附在行为动词前后,说明行为的准确性或质量,即行为要达到的水平和程度。例如,"能连贯、流畅地……""能有效地……""能稍做准备后有条理地……"。

教材处理是指教师根据教学目标和学情,对教材进行合理的重组、改编、删减或增加,使之更贴近学生的生活和经历,把教材内容变成教学内容。因为教材的编写过程不可能考虑到不同层次学校和具体某个班级学生的具体情况,因此教师有必要对教材进行处理。经典的教材处理框架是 LARA 方法:L(leave)指略去或删除教材中部分材料,或将其作为课后作业等,不必在课上处理;第一个 A(adapt)指对可用的材料进行适当处理,如调整顺序等,使其服务于本课的教学目标;R(replace)指将教材中必不可少的,但原材料又不十分适合具体课堂教学的材料替换为教材外比较适当的类似材料;第二个 A(add)指教师根据课堂的具体要求增加部分材料。教材处理有助于落实因材施教,体现以学生为中心的教学原则,更好地实现教学目标。

3. 教学过程与活动设计

教学过程设计是指为达成教学目标,教师对其课堂教学过程与行为进行系统规划。教师先要依据教学目标选择教学模式或教学方法,并据此确定教学流程和设计具体教学活动,然后按照一定的教学逻辑组织教学活动。

教学过程与活动设计始于教学思路。教学思路是贯穿整堂课的逻辑线索,是各教学活动展开的时空框架,是达成教学目标的路线图。教学思路是课堂教学中的"序",清晰的教学思路,可以保证教学内容有序组合,由浅入深;保证学习任务之间相互联系,由易到难。有了清晰的教学思路,可以保证各个教学步骤环环相扣,呈现一种循序渐进的教学路径。教学思路设计十分重要,课堂教学的艺术与创新往往就体现在教学思路上。教学思路设计的方法多样,教师可以挖掘教学材料本身的话题和内容线索,也可以遵循教学方法或教学模式展开的逻辑顺序。合乎学情、便于执教的教学思路可以使教学程序更简化,使课堂教学更活泼、更高效。

教学过程设计要做到教学方法、学习方式与教学目标保持一致,每一个教学活动都必须为教学目标服务;教学环节间的设计要有梯度,要有适当的过渡和衔接,有一定的逻辑性,要对各个教学环节进行合理的时间分配。

教学活动设计是教学过程设计的落脚点,是教学设计的重中之重。教学活动设计必须考虑教学活动的目标指向,考虑教学过程中学生的表现、可能遇到的困难及教师的针对性指导和反馈。一节课无论是以语言知识教学为主,还是以语言技能训练为主,教学设计都要适应学习需要,设计能够引导学生思维的"问题链",设计旨在训练学生语言技能的"活动链",设计有助于了解学生学习效果,检查学生知道什么和能做什么的教学评价与反馈。教学活动设计要关注每一个教学活动的名称、教学活动的描述和预期的教学效果。教学活动名称要有概括性,能够揭示教学活动的性质。教学活动的名称可以是动词或动词短语,也可以是名词或动名词短语。教学活动的描述一般以学生为行为主体,具体说明学习内容(学什么)和学习方法(怎么学),同时说明教学活动的设计意图,教学活动实施过程中教师主导作用和学生主体作用如何发挥,教与学的效果,等等。

4. 作业设计与板书设计

作业设计是不可或缺的教学设计内容,因为课外作业是课内教学的延伸和拓展。首先,作业设计要有目的性,要落实教学重点,解决教学难点。其次,作业设计要有选择性,要布置必做作业和选做作业,保证学生在完成复习巩固所学知识技能的基础上,根据个人兴趣和水平完成相应的作业,实施作业布置的隐性分层,满足不同层次学生的学习需求。再次,作业设计要有科学性,难度要以中等学生基本能够独立完成为宜,分量要以大多数学生能够接受为宜。最后,作业设计要明确具体,是必做还是选做,是口头作业还是书面作业,是独立完成还是小组合作,要求当天完成还是在一段时间内完成,必须有清楚的说明。总之,英语教师的作业设计应注意目的性、选择性、科学性,充分发挥课外作业在巩固和发展学生知识与技能中的积极作用。

板书设计也是不可或缺的教学设计内容,因为板书设计合理与否直接影响学生对教师教学意图的理解和对教学重点、难点的把握,直接影响学生的课堂学习效率。科学合理的板书设计,可以条理清楚地展示教学内容,使一节课的重点一目了然,不但能够提高视觉记忆效果,还能引导学生思考,启发学生的高水平创造性思维。首先,板书设计要有计划性和整体性,教师要合理安排板书内容,注意整体布局,要对板书内容出现的先后顺序,文字的详略、大小、去留、布局,以及与语言的配合等作出预设。其次,板书设计要有直观性和示范性,教师要用文字、符号、板画等形式进行书写,工整、规范、美观的板书有助于学生准确理解、迅速记忆,从而达到听觉和视觉结合和强化记忆的效果。再次,板书设计要体现概括性,教师的板书要呈现关键词句,还要能够全面、深刻地揭示教学内容,概括本课重点知识和技能。板书设计还要有条理性,要体现知识结构,以及讲与练的程序,体现教学内容各要素间的逻辑关系,提纲挈领,层次分明。最后,板书设计要有启发性,要巧妙安排并留有余地,使板书能够启发、引导和调节学生的思维,指点迷津。

(二) 优化设计教学语言,提高试课的艺术性

试课是在虚拟课堂中展示课堂教学过程,试课教师要在规定时间内通过讲解、示范、提问、追问、理答等语言手段展现一堂课(有时是一堂课的主要教学环节)的教学过程,因此教师对试课语言进行优化设计至关重要。

首先,试课教师应灵活运用多种讲解技巧,展示、说明、解释语言知识和文化知识,传授英语学习方法和语言运用规律,要做到知识讲解条理清晰,讲解语言形象生动,组合使用多种讲解技巧突出重点和突破难点。其次,试课教师应有效使用提问、理答和课堂活动的组织技巧,充分展示课堂师生互动和生生互动的过程。教师要有澄清问题的意识,使用意义重复等手段,保证学生对问题本身有正确的理解。抛出问题后,教师应根据问题的思维层次预留相应的候答时间,以确保学生有足够的时间思考问题和组织语言回答问题。教师还应根据学生的应答情况进行理答,当学生正确快速回答问题后,应针对学生的表现给予具体的口头表扬;如果学生回答错误,教师可以直接纠错、间接纠错或引导学生自我纠错。如果学生回答得不够完整,教师可以提供认知支架或转问其他学生。最后,试课教师在组织角色扮演,以及全班、配对或小组讨论等活动时,要使用通俗易懂且言简意赅的教学语言,尽量避免与教学活动无关的寒暄话语,有效运用呈现、调控、反馈和结束等课堂教学活动组织策略。总之,教师要优化设计教学语言,清晰地展示教学设计与教学过程,提高试课语言的艺术性,提升试课内容的可理解性。

(三) 优化设计体态语言,提高试课的互动性

试课是面向虚拟的学生或在没有学生的情况下展示课堂教学过程。除了口头试课,教师还要配合使用面部表情和手势等展现一堂课(有时是一堂课的主要教学环节)的师生互动过程,因此试课教师的体态语言的优化设计也十分重要。

具体而言,体态语言是教师通过目光、表情、手势等,与学生交流的一种非语言形式。教师体态语言在组织教学、传递信息、解释说明和表达情感中都具有重要作用,有助于提高教师的课堂教学艺术,营造轻松的课堂氛围,提高学生课堂参与的积极性。对于试课教师而言,体态语言与教学语言相互配合,能够更加形象生动地展示课堂师生互动过程,展示教师的课堂驾驭能力。

作为一种特殊的教学语言,体态语言的使用能充分展示课堂教学的互动性。尤其在没有学生配合的无生试课过程中,试课者需要通过自己的目光、表情和手势等展示其对课堂教学活动的组织和对学生学习行为的反馈。如果试课者能在无生的情况下,通过目光转向、手势指向和身体倾向等进行提问、叫答、倾听、候答、转问和追问,通过竖起大拇指、点头、微笑、注视并配合口头表扬对预设的学生应答进行反馈,通过行间巡视和附身低语等对学生小组活动进行组织和指导,通过扫视全班学生、凝神注视电子屏幕和音响设备等监督学生认真观看视频和聆听音频等,试课的互动性会大大提高。总之,试课教师可以充分利用体态语言配合课堂教学语言,模拟课堂师生互动,活化课堂教学过程,展示教师专业能力和教师职业素质。

第二部分

小学英语说课与试课课例

课例 **1**

PEP B4 U2 What time is it?
（Part A Let's talk）

说课视频

Hello, everyone! I'm Paige. It's my great honor to present my lesson plan for you. I'd like to introduce my teaching from three aspects: learning objectives, learning process and learning effects.

Learning objectives

First, it's very important to analyse the learning material and learners before setting the learning objectives.

The text is from PEP Book 4, Unit 2 *What time is it?* Part A *Let's talk*. The theme of this dialogue is *man and self*, concerning *time arrangement*.

What

This text is a daily dialogue between two students after school. John invites Wu Binbin to play basketball on the playground at 4 o'clock. While they are playing, John asks Binbin the time, and Binbin responds that it's 5 o'clock. After a while, a doorman comes to remind them to go home. John asks Binbin the time again, and Binbin replies that it's 6 o'clock, so they decide to go home.

Why

The dialogue shows how John and Wu Binbin arrange their time, with the purpose of reminding readers to pay attention to time and developing their awareness of cherishing time. Also, the scenario of the two boys forgetting the time because of playing basketball is conducive to guiding readers to organize their time properly and form a good habit of punctuality.

How

It is a common dialogue in students' daily life, of which the plot is simple and easy to

---

① 本说课稿由浙江师范大学外国语学院叶欣雨和温州市沁园小学周培培撰写。

understand. John uses the sentence structure "What time is it (now)?" to ask questions in time order, while Wu Binbin and the doorman mainly use the sentence pattern "It's … o'clock. It's time for/Time to … " as well as words and phrases like "to go to the playground/to go home (for dinner)" to respond and give suggestions. With the help of these useful expressions, students will be able to ask or answer questions about time in their daily life and offer suggestions to others on how to organize their time appropriately.

Now, I'd like to illustrate the analysis of learners. My students are in Grade Four and they are familiar with the topic of time. They have already been equipped with a certain amount of English vocabulary about numbers, which provides the basis for learning today's lesson. However, they have not yet systematically learnt how to ask questions about specific time points and describe what to do at a particular moment, so conversation drills and role-plays need to be organized in this lesson, which could help students acquire the target language effectively during peer cooperation. Moreover, being acute and flexible in thinking, students can sort out factual information quickly and extract the core structure of a dialogue. But they lack profound and critical thinking skills. Therefore, sufficient guidance is of great need to help them understand the thematic meaning of the dialogue and the importance of appropriate time management.

Based on the above analysis, the following learning objectives are set. By the end of this lesson, students will be able to:

1. extract information about time and activities in the dialogue through viewing, listening and speaking, and understand that time differs from places to places due to different time zones on the earth.

2. use the sentence pattern "What time is it? It's … o'clock." to ask and answer questions about time, and then act out the dialogue.

3. make comments on John's behavior and role-play as John's friend to help him make reasonable time arrangements.

4. make a dialogue about time and relevant activities by using the above sentence patterns in a real-life situation, and provide suggestions on time management for others.

Learning process

In this lesson, the Activity-based Approach to English Learning will be adopted, which divides all the learning activities into three categories: learning and understanding, applying and practicing, as well as transferring and innovating, thus enabling students to go through three stages in sequence: Thinking by Learning, Using by Learning, and Creating by Using.

At the first stage, with the help of the chain of questions, students are guided to extract and sort out the basic information of the dialogue and preliminarily perceive and practise the key sentence patterns.

Focusing on Using by Learning, the activities not only require students to role-play and try to imitate the angry Mum, but also need them to think about how to solve real-life problems in a chant.

As for Creating by Using, students are asked to work in groups and offer John advice on time management by making a new dialogue and show their own schedules to the class.

Now, let's move on to the implementation of the lesson.

The first stage, Thinking by Learning, consists of eight activities.

In Activity 1 and Activity 2, students will sing the song "What time is it?" and think about what they have seen in the video. Then, they are asked to observe the time in different countries while learning the new expression "It's … o'clock." These two activities not only create a vibrant atmosphere, but also let students perceive the target language and understand relevant cultural knowledge of the time zone.

In Activity 3, students will view a picture and predict where John and Binbin will go after school. Then they will listen to the dialogue and tick the correct answer on the learning sheet, following which they will check the answer and do role-play. I can assess students' ability to infer information from the picture based on the reasonableness of their guesses. And by observing their choices, I could determine whether they can extract information accurately.

After that, in Activity 4 and Activity 5, students need to view the pictures and guess how John will ask about the time and then listen to the dialogue, check the answer and practise the new expression "What time is it?". Next, the students will be asked to watch the video and choose two right time points. These activities are designed not only to cultivate students' ability to view and infer, but also to develop their listening skills.

Later, in Activity 6, students will check the answer by making a dialogue with their partners with the assistance of a sample dialogue pattern. Through observing their dialogue, I can make sure whether students have mastered the sentence pattern "What time is it? It's … ". I will give them guidance and assessment if necessary.

Activity 7 is Review together. Students will review the dialogue according to the given timeline on the blackboard. Meanwhile, they will learn and employ the new expression "It's time for … " to finish the timeline with more details. Based on their use of the sentence pattern, I can judge whether my students have had a good command of the target language.

In Activity 8, students are required to predict what the doorman will say and then read the dialogue independently to find the answer. Then they need to role-play the doorman and practise the new expression "Time to go home, kids". Throughout the process, guessing the content stimulates students to express themselves and deepens their understanding of the dialogue. Meanwhile, independent reading develops students' ability to access key information. Role-playing enlivens the classroom atmosphere and enables students to further consolidate the sentence pattern "Time to … " when they are trying performing as a doorman with whole emotion. Whether they can find the correct answer and do a vivid role-play can be the measurement of the achievement of the first and the second learning objectives.

In the second stage, Using by Learning, three activities are designed.

Activity 1 is Listen and imitate. Students will listen to the tape and repeat it with correct pronunciation, intonation and rhythm. In this way, they can internalize the language by imitation.

Activity 2 is Do a role-play. To help students understand the characters' language and inner world, I will let them act out the dialogue in groups of three. Then, students are asked to evaluate each other's show according to the checklist.

After that, students will think about the question. Then they listen to the chant, and try to imitate the angry Mum. Whether students can guess reasonably and imitate vividly can help me decide whether the third learning objective has been partially realized.

In the last stage, Creating by Using, there are altogether two activities.

The first one is Discuss and act, which is divided into two parts. Part A is Think and discuss. Students will have an open discussion on the question "If John wants to eat dinner at 6 o'clock, at what time should John go home?". The natural transition from the chant to open questions can encourage them to think about how to solve problems in real life. Part B is Write down and act it out. Students are asked to work in pairs, and write down the reasonable time on the card to generate authentic language expressions. Then they will make a new dialogue about John's new time arrangement. It will pave the way for students to further apply what they have learnt in real life. Whether they correctly use what they have learnt can be observed during the discussion to show that the third learning objective has been achieved.

Activity 2 is Make a dialogue, which is divided into three parts. Part A is Choose a place and write down the time. Students will think about their time arrangement at school or at home, then choose one and write it down on the learning sheet. Part B is Discuss and say. Students will make up dialogues with the new expressions. Then they evaluate their dialogues according to this checklist. In case some students may have difficulties, I will collaborate with a student to set an example. Part C is Act it out. Students will show the new dialogues to the class. I will focus on whether the students use the checklist properly and evaluate the learning effects based on their presentations. In this way, I can cultivate students' ability to use the language they have learnt to solve problems in real life, deepen their understanding of the theme of this lesson, and help them form a correct attitude and value judgment on time arrangement.

After the class, there are two assignments. First, they are required to listen to the dialogue on Page 14 and read it aloud, so they can review today's lesson. The second is to ask students to do a survey and know more about their classmates' time arrangements, which can encourage them to communicate by using the language they have learnt.

As for blackboard design, the core sentence pattern is presented at the top so that students can attach great importance to its correct writing format. Also, the timeline of the dialogue is clearly shown in the middle, from which students can better memorize as well as recall the whole dialogue.

Learning effects

Now, let's take a close look at the merits of this lesson.

The first one can be seen in the presentation of a multi-level question chain focusing on the topic of time all along. Facing these comprehensive questions, students can basically understand the dialogue and achieve teacher-student and student-student interaction. When trying to answer analytical questions, students are inspired to consider how to make proper time management and explore the theme of the dialogue. To solve practical problems, students are guided to express their time arrangement, which will promote their logical thinking, and thus realize the internalization of the thematic meaning beyond the dialogue.

The second one is the integration of teaching, learning, and evaluation. With the help of the checklists, self-evaluation and mutual evaluation are carried out to help students deepen their understanding of the target language and the thematic meaning. Multifaceted evaluation helps students improve autonomous learning ability and ensures effective learning.

That's all for my presentation. Thanks for watching.

试课实录①

试课视频

步骤一　学中思（16分钟）

Activity 1: Enjoy the song

T:　Class begins! Stand up, please! Good morning, boys and girls.

Ss:　(Good morning, teacher!)

T:　It's time for a song! Let's sing together, OK? Here we go! You can shake your body.

Ss:　[sing the song]

T:　Wow! You can sing the song very well. Big hands for yourself. Sit down, please.

Activity 2: Look and say

T:　And kids, from the video, we can see a …?

S1:　(Clock!)

T:　Yes! Follow me. Clock.

Ss:　(Clock.)

T:　Show me your hands! Let's spell together, cl-o-ck, clock.

Ss:　(Cl-o-ck, clock.)

---

① 本试课稿由温州市沁园小学周培培撰写。

T: Yes. Kids, look at the clock. How many numbers can you see? You, please.

S2:   (Twelve.)

T: Yes, there are twelve numbers. Let's read together.

Ss: (One, two, … twelve.)

T: Good job! And we know the time from the clock. Look here! What time is it?

S3:   (It's three o'clock.)

T: Yes. It's three o'clock. Follow me. It's three o'clock.

Ss: (It's three o'clock.)

T: Here! Pay attention. "o" says /ə/. Show me your hands and touch your tummy, /ə/, /ə/, o'clock.

Ss: (/ə/, /ə/, o'clock.)

T: And what time is it in China? You, please!

S4:   (It's four o'clock.)

T: Yes, you're right. It's four o'clock in China. And how about Australia? What time is it now? Tell me together!

Ss: (It's six o'clock.)

T: Yes! It's six o'clock. And the last one, what time is it now?

Ss: (It's eight o'clock.)

T: Yes! It's eight o'clock. Look! Time is different around the world at the same moment. Right?

Ss: (Yes.)

Activity 3: Listen and tick

T: Look! What time is it?

Ss: (It's four o'clock.)

T: Yes. It's four o'clock. [plays the recording of "School is over."] Oh, school is over. Follow me! School is over.

Ss: (School is over.)

T: It's four o'clock. And school is over. So at this time, where will Binbin and John go? Please use the sentence pattern "Let's go to the …".

S5:   (Let's go to the playground.)

T: Good idea! Let's go to the playground. How about you?

S6:   (Let's go to the library.)

T: Good try! Look here! Maybe they will go to the library. Maybe they will go to the playground. Now take out your learning sheet. Let's listen and tick. OK? Here we go.

Ss: [listen to the recording]

T: OK. Time's up. Did you get the answer? You, please!

S7:　（Let's go to the playground. ）

T:　　Is he right?

Ss:　（Yes. ）

T:　　Yes. Big hands for him. Let's go to the playground. Follow me! Let's go to the playground.

Ss:　（Let's go to the playground. ）

T:　　Look here! Let's do a role-play. I have a basketball. I'm John now, and you are Binbin. Are you ready? Hi! School is over. Let's go to the playground.

Ss:　（OK. ）

T:　　I think you are not very happy, Binbin. Let's try it one more time, OK?

Ss:　（OK. ）

T:　　Hi! School is over. Let's go to the playground.

Ss:　（OK. ）

T:　　This time, you are John. I'm Binbin. Please stand up.

Ss:　（Hi! School is over. Let's go to the playground. ）

T:　　OK. Wow! You did a good job. Big hands for yourself.

Activity 4: Listen and answer

T:　　Look here! Where are they?

Ss:　（Playground. ）

T:　　Yes, they are in the playground. But John doesn't know the time. What will John ask? This time, let's listen and answer.

Ss:　[listen to the recording]

T:　　Got the answer? What does John ask? You try.

S8:　（What time is it? ）

T:　　Oh, yes! John asks "What time is it?". Follow me! What time is it?

Ss:　（What time is it? ）

T:　　Group 1! Ready, go!

G1:　（What time is it? ）

T:　　Wow, very good! How about you, Group 2? One, two, three, go!

G2:　（What time is it? ）

T:　　Super! And Group 3, one, two, three, go!

G3:　（What time is it? ）

T:　　Wow, wonderful! John asks … ?

Ss:　（What time is it? ）

Activity 5: Watch and choose

T:　　So what time is it? Do you know? Maybe it's … ?

Ss:　（Five o'clock. ）

T: Maybe it's … ? Oh, it's a little hard. I can help you. Show me your hands first. Five ten! [does the action]

Ss: (Five ten!) [do the action]

T: And maybe it's … ?

Ss: (Six o' clock.)

T: Yes! This time, let's watch the video again and choose the right answer. Please take out your learning sheet. Are you ready? Let's go!

Ss: [watch the video and choose]

Activity 6: Check in pairs

T: OK, kids. Did you get the answer? Before checking with me, please check with your partners first. One is John. The other is Binbin. Here we go!

Ss: [work in pairs]

T: Time's up! Which group can share with us? How about Picture One? G4, please.

G4:   (What time is it? It's five o'clock.)

T: Oh, is it five o'clock?

Ss: (Yes!)

T: Big hands for them. How about Picture Two?

G5:   (What time is it? It's six o'clock.)

T: Is it six o'clock?

Ss: (Yes!)

T: Big hands for them. Let's say it together.

Ss: [look at the blackboard and say the time]

Activity 7: Review together

T: Look! It's four o'clock. And … ?

Ss: (School is over.)

T: Tick-tock, tick-tock, what time is it?

Ss: (It's five o'clock.)

T: It's five o'clock. And it's time for … ?

S9:   (It's time for basketball.)

T: Yes! It's time for basketball. Follow me. It's time for basketball.

Ss: (It's time for basketball.)

T: Tick-tock, tick-tock, what time is it now?

Ss: (It's six o'clock.)

T: Yes! It's six o'clock. And it's time for … ?

S10:   (It's time for dinner.)

T: Yes! It's time for dinner. Let's try together.

Ss: (It's time for dinner.)

Activity 8: Read and find

T: Look! Here comes the doorman! Look at the doorman. Can you guess what does the doorman say? You, please.

S11: (Go home, kids.)

T: Wow! Good job. How about you?

S12: (It's too late.)

T: Wow! I love your idea. Sit down, please. Actually, what does the doorman say? Please open your book and turn to Page 14. Let's read and find the answer.

Ss: [read the dialogue]

T: Did you find the answer? Share with me. You, please.

S13: (Time to go home, kids.)

T: Oh. The doorman says, "Time to go home, kids." Follow me. "Time to go home, kids."

Ss: (Time to go home, kids.)

T: Yes, the doorman says … ?

Ss: (Time to go home, kids.)

T: Now let's listen and repeat together!

Ss: [listen to the recording] (Time to go home, kids.)

T: But I don't think Binbin and John can hear you. Let's say it loudly. OK? Go!

Ss: (Time to go home, kids.)

T: Wow! Who can be the doorman this time? You, please.

S14: (Time to go home, kids.) [acts like the doorman]

T: Good job, doorman. You can speak very loudly.

步骤二 学中用(8 分钟)

Activity 1: Listen and imitate

T: Kids, open your book and turn to Page 14! Fingers ready! Let's listen and read the dialogue.

Ss: [listen and read the dialogue]

T: Wow! You can read it very well.

Activity 2: Do a role-play

T: This time I'm John. Who can be Binbin? Who can be the doorman?

S15 & S16: [raise hands]

T: Thank you. And it's our show time. All of you can judge how many stars can we get according to the checklist. OK? Here we go.

T & S15 & S16: [act out the dialogue]

T: How many stars for us?

Ss: (Three stars.)

T: Thank you so much.

T: And this time it's your turn. Let's work in groups of three, OK?

Ss: [act out the dialogue]

T: Time's up. Which group can come here and show us. OK, you three.

S17 & S18 & S19: [act out the dialogue]

T: Wow, big hands for them. How many stars for them?

Ss: (Three stars.)

T: Yes, I think so. Good job, kids!

Activity 3: Chant together

T: Look here! What time is it now?

Ss: (It's six o'clock.)

T: Yes. It's six o'clock. Where is John?

S20:   (He's in the playground.)

T: Yes! He's in the playground. So can John eat dinner with Mum at six o'clock?

Ss: (No!)

T: Oh! Of course not! Let's listen to Mum.

Ss: [listen to the chant]

T: Look at Mum, mum is very … ?

Ss: (Angry!)

T: Yes, I think so. This time, can you be the angry Mum? Please stand up.

Ss: [chant together]

T: Wow, you are so angry! Sit down, please.

步骤三 用中创(11分钟)

Activity 1: Discuss and act

A: Think and discuss

T: So kids, look here! If John wants to eat dinner at six o'clock, what time should John go home? Let's think about it. For me, I think John should go home at 5:10. How about you? This time let's go back to four o'clock. OK? [runs the video backward]

Ss: [watch the video]

T: What time is it?

Ss: (It's four o'clock.)

B: Write down and act it out

T: It's four o'clock. And this time let's discuss in pairs. You should write down the time on your card, make a new dialogue and act it out.

Ss: [work in pairs]

T:　　OK. Time's up. Which group can share with us?

G6:　 [pair performance]

T:　　Oh, you think John should go home at 5：30. Good boy. You go home early. Good job. So we do different things at different time. Please arrange your time properly!

Activity 2: Make a dialogue

A: Choose a place and write down the time

B: Discuss and say

C: Act it out

T:　　Now we are going to talk about your time, maybe your time at school, maybe your time at home. First, you can choose a place. Then it's time for you to discuss and talk in pairs. After it, pay attention to the checklist to evaluate your dialogue. Finally, act it out with partner in the class. Who can come here and work with me?

S17:　[put hand up]

T:　　Good! Come here!

T & S17:　[act out their dialogue]

T:　　Thank you so much! You've done a good job! Now, it's your time to make your dialogues.

Ss:　　[work in pairs]

T:　　Time's up. Which group can share with us? You two, please!

G7:　　[pair performance]

T:　　Wow, you remember your time. Big hands for them. So much for today.

作业布置

T:　　Here comes our homework. Homework One, listen to the dialogue on Page 14 and read it aloud. Homework Two, do a survey and know more about your classmates' time arrangements. Class is over. Goodbye, kids.

教学设计①

配套课件

（一）语篇研读

本课教学内容选自人教版英语四年级下册第二单元 What time is it? A 部分 Let's talk 板块,该语篇属于"人与自我"主题范畴,内容涉及"时间管理"。

What

本课语篇描述了两位小学生放学后的一段日常对话。John 在下午 4 点邀请 Wu Binbin

---

① 本教学设计由温州市沁园小学周培培撰写。

一起去操场打篮球。其间,John 问 Wu Binbin 现在几点了,Wu Binbin 回应是下午 5 点。过了一会,保安提醒他们该回家了。John 再次询问 Wu Binbin 时间,Wu Binbin 回答是 6 点。两人意识到已经是吃晚饭的时间了,于是决定回家。

Why

该对话体现了 John 和 Wu Binbin 对时间的安排——他们在恰当的时间去操场打篮球,玩耍初期有关注时间;虽然之后因为玩得入迷而忘记了时间,但在保安提醒后立刻意识到应该回家。该语篇可以提醒学生关注时间、珍惜时间,也可通过二人因打篮球而忘记时间这一对话情景引导学生妥善安排时间,养成守时的好习惯。

How

该对话发生在日常生活情景中,情节较为简单,易于理解。John 以"What time is it (now)?"的句型结构,按时间顺序展开提问;Wu Binbin 和保安主要用"It's … o'clock.""It's time for/Time to …"等句型来提问,用"to go to the playground/to go home (for dinner)"等表达做出回应与建议。学生利用这些表述能够在日常生活中询问或回答时间,并向他人提供合理安排时间的建议。

(二)学情分析

本课授课对象为 Z 省某小学四年级学生。他们对"时间"这一话题较为熟悉,且已储备一定量关于数字的英语词汇,这为其学习"时间"的表达奠定了基础。但是他们尚未系统学习有关如何问答具体时间、描述某时刻要做什么事情的对话语篇,因此需要教师创设以句单位为主体的对话练习并组织角色扮演,如要求学生围绕"如何帮助 John 合理安排时间"编写对话,引导学生内化核心语言,在小组合作与同伴互助中开展交流,实现目标语言的有效习得。本班学生思维敏捷、灵活,能够较快捕捉对话中的表层信息,提取对话核心结构。但其思维的深刻性和批判性还有待提升,需要在教师的引导下才能理解对话语篇的深意,明白做好自我时间管理的重要性。

(三)教学目标

通过本课时的学习,学生能够:

1. 在看、听、说的活动中提取并梳理对话中的时间点及开展的活动;初步了解因时区不同,同一时刻不同城市的时间差异;

2. 运用核心句型"What time is it? It's … o'clock."询问或回答他人具体时间,并能分角色表演对话;

3. 简要评价 John 的做法,并发挥想象力,扮演 John 的朋友,帮助其进行合理安排时间;

4. 联系个人实际,运用句型"What time is it? It's … o'clock. It's time for/to …"创编对话,与同伴谈论特定时间及相关活动,为他人提供时间管理的建议。

(四)教学流程

学生在本节课将经历"学习理解""应用实践""迁移创新"三个学习阶段,从"学中思"

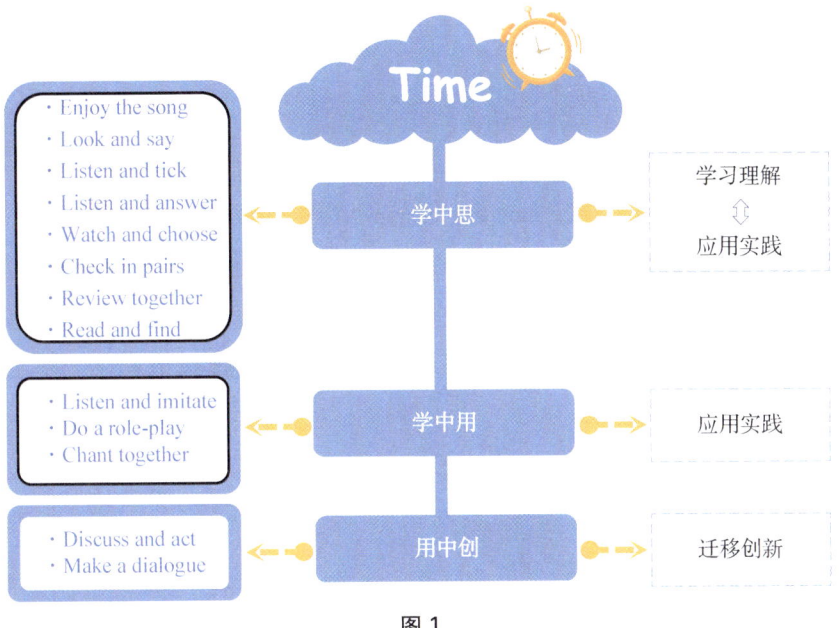

图 1

走向"学中用"，最终达成"用中创"。教师首先利用学习理解与应用实践类活动,助力学生实现"学中思"与"学中用":基于问题链,引导学生通过观看视频、听音频等方式,提取并梳理对话的基本信息,初步感知与操练问答时间所需的核心语言。第二轮应用实践环节更加侧重"学中用",学生不仅需要在对话情境中进行角色扮演并尝试模仿"发怒的妈妈",还将以 chant 方式丰富体验,并过渡到运用语篇核心语言结构思考如何解决现实生活中的问题。为实现"用中创",在迁移创新活动中,学生将联系个人实际,通过小组讨论为 John 提供有关时间管理的建议,并在此基础上以创编对话的方式向全班展示自己的时间和活动安排。

（五）教学过程

步骤一　学中思——获取、梳理核心语言和文化知识（16 分钟）

Activity 1: Enjoy the song（1 min）

Students sing the song "What Time Is It?" with actions and think about what they see in the video.

Lyrics

What Time Is It?

What time is it? (* 4) It's 8 o'clock. It's time to go to school. It's 8 o'clock. It's 9 o'clock. It's 10 o'clock. It's 11 o'clock. It's 12 o'clock. It's 1 o'clock. It's 2 o'clock. It's 3 o'clock. It's time to play the guitar.

What time is it? (* 4) It's 4 o'clock. It's time to sing some more! It's 4 o'clock. It's 5 o'clock. It's 6 o'clock. It's 7 o'clock. It's 8 o'clock. It's time to go to bed. (* 2)

【设计说明】 教师通过节奏欢快的歌曲活跃课堂氛围,调动学生多感官参与学习,帮助其初步感知本课的核心语言。

Activity 2: Look and say (2 mins)

Students observe the time in different countries, like China, the USA, Australia and the UK, and then learn and practise the new expression "It's … o'clock".

图 2

【设计说明】 教师出示时钟(见图2),引导学生在完整的情境中观察不同国家的时间,了解"地球上不同时区在同一时刻的时间是不一样的"这一常识性知识。同时,学生感知并理解核心语言"It's … o'clock."所表达的意义,并在真实交流中掌握这一关键句型。

【效果评价】 教师观察学生使用的语言是否正确,把握学生对所学内容的感知情况。

Activity 3: Listen and tick (3 mins)

Students predict where John and Binbin will go after school according to the main picture of the dialogue, using "Let's go to the …". Then they listen to the dialogue and tick the correct answer on the learning sheet. After checking the answer together, students role-play with the teacher.

图 3

【设计说明】 教师借助看图预测任务(见图3)引发学生思考,培养学生"看"的能力和利用插图信息进行推断预测的能力。学生通过听教材配套的音频资源,整体感知对话内容,提升获取关键信息的能力。

【效果评价】 教师根据学生对地点猜测结果的合理性,评价其利用图片推断信息的能力;观察学生的答案选择情况,判断其能否准确获取信息。

Activity 4: Listen and answer (2 mins)

Students view the pictures and guess how John will ask about the time. Then they listen to the dialogue, check the answer and practise the new expression "What time is it?".

图 4

【设计说明】 教师通过问题引导学生自主回忆并思考如何询问时间,注重培养学生的听力技能。学生通过第二次听教材配套的音频资源,获取和学习关键句型"What time is it?"。

Activity 5: Watch and choose (2 mins)

Students watch the video and choose the right time points from the three given choices (5: 00/5: 10/6: 00) on the learning sheet.

【设计说明】 教师播放教材配套的视频资源,为学生提供更多的视听机会,帮助学生进一步体验和理解对话情境,并获取具体时间信息。

Activity 6: Check in pairs (2 mins)

Students check the answer by making a dialogue about two pictures with partners. A dialogue pattern will be provided.

Dialogue pattern

John: What time is it now?   Binbin: It's …

John: What time is it?   Binbin: It's …

【设计说明】 学生通过与同桌合作,以角色扮演的方式核对所获取的信息,进一步巩固对核心语言的理解和运用,同时提升合作学习的能力。

【效果评价】 教师观察学生在语境中运用核心语言进行交流的情况,根据学生的表现给予指导和评价。

Activity 7: Review together (2 mins)

Students look at the blackboard and review the dialogue according to the timeline. Meanwhile, they learn and use the new expression "It's time for …" to complete the timeline with more details, like "It's 5 o'clock. It's time for basketball." and "It's 6 o'clock. It's time for dinner." etc.

Timeline on the blackboard

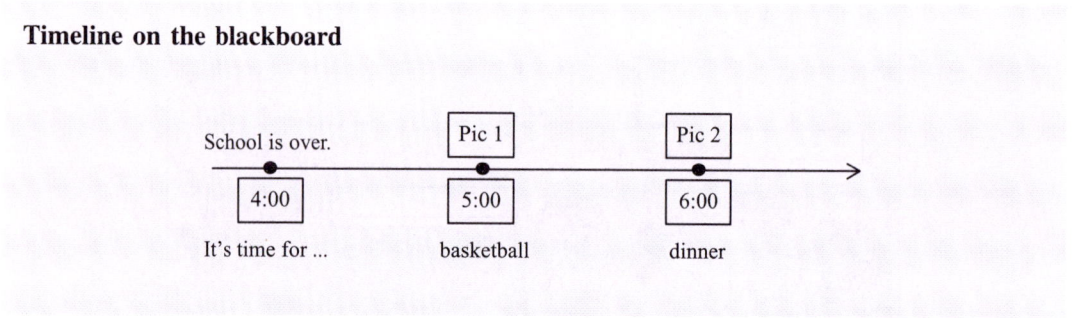

【设计说明】 教师借助板书,通过问答、描述等活动,帮助学生在语境中初步感知"It's time for …"的意思并加以运用,使其逐步内化对话的核心语言。

【效果评价】 教师观察学生能否准确地使用"It's time for …",把握学生对核心语言的理解和内化情况。

Activity 8: Read and find (2 mins)

Students look at the picture of a doorman and predict what the doorman will say. Then they open the book and read the dialogue independently to find the answer. Students role-play as the doorman. Meanwhile, they practise the new expression "Time to go home, kids".

【设计说明】 对保安讲话内容的猜测能够发散学生的思维,激发学生的表达欲望,并加深他们对课文语境的理解。让学生通过打开课本静心阅读,找到答案,提升其在阅读中获取关键信息的能力。扮演保安的活动可进一步巩固学生对"Time to …"这一表达的掌握。同时,表演人物的动作和情绪的环节也让课堂更有趣味。

【效果评价】 教师观察学生能否根据手势猜测保安所说的话,并将之富有情感地演绎出来,根据学生的表现给予必要的提示和反馈。

步骤二 学中用——内化语言,加深理解并初步应用(8分钟)

Activity 1: Listen and imitate (1 min)

Students listen to the tape and repeat with correct pronunciation, intonation and rhythm.

【设计说明】 通过跟读对话内容,引导学生感知和模仿语音、语调与节奏,帮助学生内化所学语言。

Activity 2: Do a role-play（5 mins）

Two students collaborate with the teacher to set an example. Then, students act out the dialogue in groups of three. One will be John, one will be Binbin, and the other one will be the doorman. They evaluate each other's show according to the checklist, "Do they read nicely?" "Do they talk fluently?" and "Do they act vividly?".

Assessment

📖	Read nicely	⭐
💬	Talk fluently	⭐
🏃	Act vividly	⭐

【设计说明】　角色扮演能帮助学生理解人物的语言和内心世界,并做出正确的价值判断。

【效果评价】　教师观察学生能否将角色扮演好,根据学生的表现给予必要的提示和指导。教师观察学生能否从三个方面对其他小组的表演进行评价。

Activity 3: Chant together（2 mins）

Students think about the question "Can John eat dinner with Mum at six o'clock?". Then they listen to the chant, and try to imitate the angry Mum.

6:00

What time is it?　Where is John?
It's 6 o'clock.　John! John! John!
It's time for dinner.　It's six o'clock.
But John's not here.　Six! Six! Six!
　　　　　　　It's time for dinner.
　　　　　　　Time for dinner!
　　　　　　　Come home early!
　　　　　　　Now!

图 5

【设计说明】　教师通过创编的 Chant(见图 5),引导学生体会 John's Mum 的心情,在完整的情境中丰富学生的情感体验,同时再一次复现本课核心句型。

【效果评价】　教师观察学生能否使用正确的语音、语调和表情演绎出 John's Mum 的情感和态度,根据学生的表现给予反馈。

步骤三 用中创——联系实际,运用所学解决生活问题(11分钟)

Activity 1: Discuss and act (4 mins)

A: Think and discuss

Students have an open discussion on the question "If John wants to eat dinner at 6, at what time should John go home?" Then through running the video backward, the teacher take the students back to four o'clock.

B: Write down and act it out

Students work in pairs, and write down the reasonable time on the card. Then they make a new dialogue to show a new time arrangement for John.

图 6

【设计说明】 从 Chant 自然过渡到给 John 提建议这一开放性活动(见图 6),激发学生思考如何解决现实生活中的问题。同时,引导学生和同伴合作,分享合理安排时间的经验,基于个人生活经验与所学语言进行口头产出,在内化核心语言的同时,深化对主题意义的认识,从而为在现实生活中运用所学做铺垫。

【效果评价】 教师观察学生讨论时能否准确运用所学内容进行合理的时间安排,并根据需要给予必要的帮助和指导。

Activity 2: Make a dialogue (7 mins)

A: Choose a place and write down the time

Students think about their time arrangement at school or home, then choose one place and write down the time on the learning sheet.

B: Discuss and say

Students make up a dialogue with their partner using the new expressions "What time is it? It's … ". Then they evaluate their dialogues according to the checklist. In case that some students may have difficulties, the teacher will invite a student to set an example.

C: Act it out

Students show the new dialogue with their partner in the class.

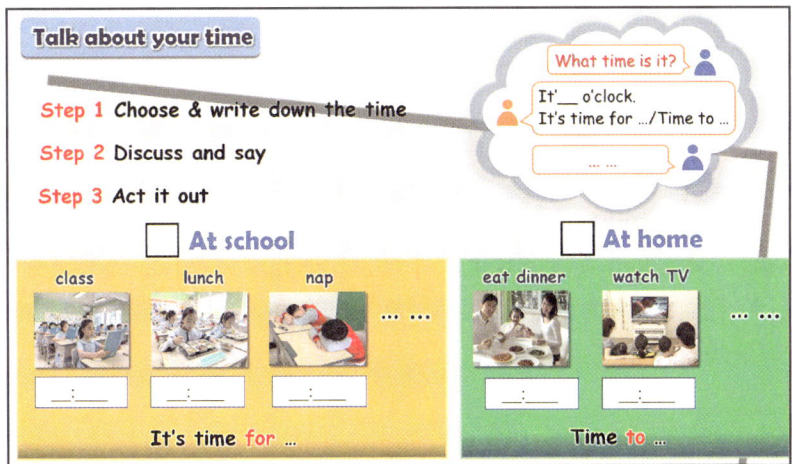

图 7

【设计说明】　通过同伴合作创编对话,描述自己在家或在校的时间安排(见图 7),进行超越语篇、联系实际生活的活动,助学生提升在真实情境中运用所学语言和文化知识解决实际问题的能力,并深化他们对本课主题意义的认识,对时间安排形成正确的态度和价值判断。

【效果评价】　教师观察学生能否在同伴合作中运用所学语言谈论时间及活动安排,同时关注学生是否使用自评表完善对话,并给予指导和鼓励。教师观察学生向全班展示创编对话的情况,评价教与学的成效。

（六）板书设计

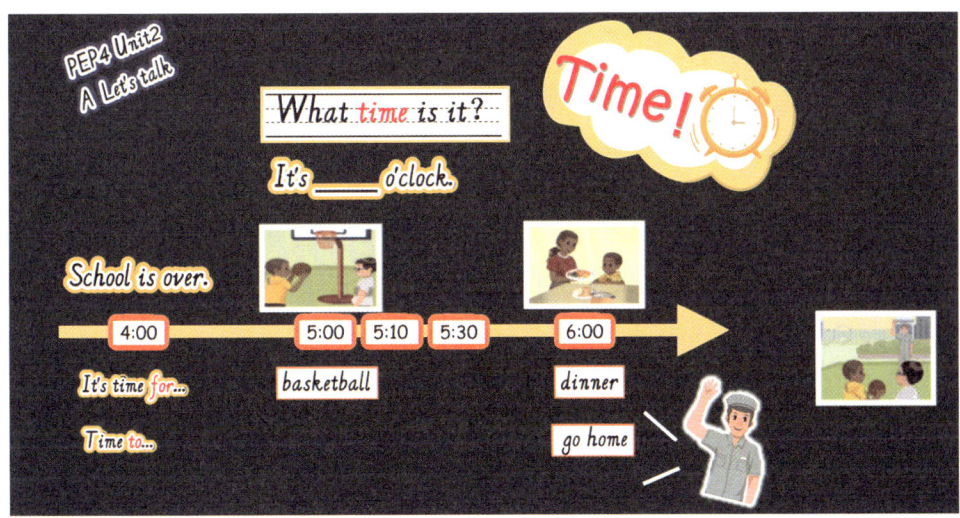

图 8

【设计说明】 板书包括课题名称与课堂要点。首先,板书上方是本节课的核心句型,借助四线三格,学生能关注所学句子的正确书写格式。其次,板书的中间部分以时间轴的方式清晰地呈现了本节对话课的故事发展,包括时间、人物、地点、出现的生词和句型等。借助生成的板书,学生能自主地进行课文的回顾和复述。

(七) 作业设计

★1. Listen to the dialogue on Page 14 and read it aloud.

★★2. Do a survey and know more about your classmates' time arrangements.

【设计说明】 课后作业进行了难度递增的分层设计。一星作业为基础性作业,旨在引导学生及时加深对核心语言的掌握;二星作业为实践性作业,引导学生运用所学语言进行真实的交流,进行合理的时间安排。

(八) 教学反思

本节课是一节对话课,教师基于英语学习活动观,依托问题链,设计不同层次的语用任务,将对话文本与学生的实际生活建立联系,引领学生在真实语境中学会时间的表达方式,并体会到时间管理的重要性。

1. 巧设教学问题链,实现思、用、创一体化

在对话课的教学中,教师应把要求学生理解和掌握的知识转化为问题,使其成为学生思维活动的抓手,通过设计多维度不同层级的进阶式问题,全方位地促进学生语用能力和思维品质的提升。本节课围绕"Time"这一主题,通过理解性问题、分析性问题和真实生活中的问题,形成问题链。教师借助"Where will Binbin and John go?""What will John ask?""What time is it?"等理解性问题,引导学生理解对话的表层意义,并进行基于语篇的主题意义探究,实现"学中思"。紧接着,教师引入 John's Mum,以及"If John eats dinner at 6, what time should John go home?"这一分析性问题,启发学生思考如何合理管理时间,并以创编对话的方式呈现结果,实现"学中用"。随后,教师引导学生围绕主题表述自己的时间安排,促使他们的思维从低阶向高阶稳步发展,实现"用中创"。教师通过巧设教学问题链,引导学生围绕真实情境和真实问题,参与到一系列相互关联的学习活动中,实现思、用、创一体化。

2. 嵌入表现性评价,保障"教、学、评"一体化

在教学过程中,教师要注重落实"教、学、评"一体化,即教师应明确教什么、为什么教、怎么教、怎么评,并建立相互之间的关联。在本节课的教学中,教师借助评价核查表组织学生开展自评和互评,体现以学定教、以教定评,将表现性评价嵌于教学之中,促进学生的英语学习。在角色扮演环节,教师进行示范演绎后,引导学生从语音是否标准、对话是否流利、表演是否生动三个维度开展评价。这不仅实现了"学生能在教师的帮助下分角色表演对话"这一教学目标,同时也体现了教师对学生语用意识和语用能力的培养。在输出活动中,教师通过引导学生从四个方面开展自评,帮助学生结合自身情况,根据评价结果改进学习方法,确保学习真正发生并取得成效。教师通过嵌入表现性评价,及时关注学生语言、文化和思维的协同发展,落实"教、学、评"一体化,发展学生核心素养。

（九）附件

学 习 单

【活动1】Listen and tick（听录音，勾出正确的选项"√"）

【活动2】Watch and choose（看视频，将选项写在括号里）

【活动3】Talk about your time（和同伴分享你的时间安排）

Step 1：Choose a place and write down the time（选择一个地点，并写下你的时间）

Step 2：Discuss and say（讨论不同活动的时间）

Step 3：Act it out（展示对话，加上动作更好哦！）

自我评价

Checklist	Yes	No
Can we talk about the time?		
Can we watch for the time?		
Can we work well with each other?		
Do we know what we need to do at the right time?		

课例 **2**

PEP B8 U4 Then and now
（Part B Read and write）

说课视频

Hi, everyone! I'm Lynn, from the Affiliated Primary School of Wenzhou Experimental Middle School. It's my great honor to present the lesson plan to you. My presentation will cover three aspects, namely, learning objectives, learning process and learning effects. Now, let's come to the first part.

Learning objectives

As we know, the learning objectives are set based on the analysis of learning material and learners. So first, let's look at the learning material of this lesson.

The learning material is from PEP Book 8, Unit 4 *Then and now* Part B *Read and write*, which is the fifth lesson of this unit. The theme of this text is *man and self*, involving *emotions and feelings*.

What

The text is a narrative titled "What a dream!". It tells a dream of Wu Binbin. In the dream, Wu Binbin had a running race with his father and the dog Max, but he couldn't run fast. Then he drank Robin's magic water and ran as fast as a cheetah in his second race with animals. He was about to win the race when he suddenly tripped and fell, realizing it was just a dream. The ups and downs of the plots are formed through the contrast between Wu Binbin's previous and subsequent performances in the races.

Why

By guiding students to understand Wu Binbin's completely different performances in two running races, the teacher promotes students to think about how to run fast in real life and

---

① 本说课稿由温州市实验中学附属小学林陈霜撰写。

realize that "Practice makes perfect". Only by practicing can people fundamentally improve their running speed, which can also be applied to language learning and everything they do.

How

The text could be divided into three parts. The first part is about Wu Binbin's first running race. The second part introduces how Wu Binbin got Robin's help. The third part is about Wu Binbin's second running race. In this text, paragraphs 1 and 3 are similar in structure, both introducing the participants and describing Wu Binbin's performances and feelings in the races. What's more, the text introduces Wu Binbin's dream in the simple past tense with some past tense verbs, including words that students have learnt (*had, were, ran, could, was, said, drank, fell*) and words that they need to understand in the context (*thought, gave, felt, tripped, woke*).

Now, let's take a look at the analysis of learners.

The students are in the sixth grade, and almost all of them have taken part in running races, with the aim to win the race. They are also curious about the topic, "dream", and are willing to share their dreams. Moreover, they are eager to figure out the ending of the story.

Also, having learnt English for nearly four years, the students can read stories with simple plots. They can also utilize reading skills and strategies to acquire key information and understand the main content, but their inferring and reflecting skills need to be improved. Therefore, the teacher should design open-ended questions to invite students to think, express views and exchange feelings on the saying "Practice makes perfect".

What's more, the students have already been able to memorize and spell the past tense forms of some verbs and can use the simple past tense to talk about past events. But they may still find it difficult to compose a complete paragraph by using the simple past tense under the topic "dream". Therefore, some support needs to be provided to improve students' ability to organize texts, thus reducing the difficulty of writing.

Based on the above analysis, the following learning objectives are set to develop students' core competencies. By the end of this lesson, students will be able to:

1. get and sort out the basic information about Wu Binbin's dream, understand the text and form a knowledge structure map.

2. retell the text, complete the dialogue where Wu Binbin shares his dream with his mum and understand the thematic meaning of the text — "Practice makes perfect".

3. write down their own dreams with the help of the structure map and the text.

Learning process

Now let's move on to the description of learning process. In this class, three dreams, namely, "Teacher's dream", "Wu Binbin's dream" and "My dream" are included, where students develop their reading and writing skills and comprehend the thematic meaning of the text.

Now let's come to the first stage, Teacher's Dream. There are two activities.

Activity 1, Look and say. With the help of the special spelling bee in the teacher's dream, students will tell the past tense of corresponding verbs, which can activate their relevant knowledge and pave the way for the following activities. It enables the teacher to know students' mastery of past tense verbs. Activity 2, Think and say. Students will share their opinions about the teacher's dream, which naturally leads to the topic of this lesson.

In the second stage, Wu Binbin's Dream, six activities are designed.

Activity 1, Think and ask. Students will be encouraged to raise questions about Wu Binbin's dream, which cultivates their prediction skills and stimulates their curiosity.

Activity 2, Read the text and answer. Students will read the text quickly and find out the general idea. Through fast reading, they can form an overall perception of the text.

Activity 3, Read Paragraph 1 and answer. Students will read Paragraph 1 about the first race, and answer three questions under the teacher's guidance. In this way, students can develop their skills to get and sort out the key information. Their performance can be observed and corresponding guidance will be given in time.

Unlike what they do in Activity 3, students will learn by themselves in Activity 4. There are four steps.

Step 1, Read, order and match. Students will read Paragraph 3 which talks about the second race, order the pictures and then match them with relevant verbs and phrases. It helps them to learn the core language, which lays a solid foundation for further application. The teacher will observe whether students can complete the ordering and matching tasks in Worksheet 1 to grasp students' understanding of key vocabulary and core language.

Step 2, Let's act. Students will act out what happened in the second race to further understand Paragraph 3 and internalize the language.

Step 3, Read and answer. Students will read Paragraph 3 again and underline the answers to the three same questions as those in the first race by themselves. Then they will finish the Worksheet 2 in groups. Through independent and cooperative learning, students are trained to sort out the key information logically. The teacher will observe whether students can underline the key sentences and whether the information of characters, events and feelings presented in the group presentation is correct and comprehensive, thus judging whether the students can accurately extract the key information.

Step 4, Watch and say. Students will watch a virtual match between the cheetah and Usain Bolt where the cheetah wins the race, and then share their understanding of Wu Binbin's different feelings before and after tripping. The teacher can observe students' description of Wu Binbin's feelings to evaluate their mastery of Paragraph 3, and give hints as well as guidance if needed.

Activity 5, Read Paragraph 2 and answer. Students will try to explain why Wu Binbin suddenly ran like a cheetah with imagination. Then they will read paragraph 2 and find out the answer.

Activity 6, Retell, listen and complete. With the help of the structure map on the blackboard, students will be encouraged to retell Wu Binbin's dream, and complete the dialogue between Mum and Wu Binbin by listening. In this way, further internalization can be expected. The teacher will observe whether the students can complete the retelling with the help of the language scaffoldings presented on the board and fill in the blanks according to the recording, thus judging whether they can internalize what they've learnt. Also, the teacher will give tips and feedback if necessary.

In the third stage, My Dream, two activities are designed.

Activity 1, Think and say. Students will first make a comment on Wu Binbin's dream. Then they will think and share their ways of improving the running speed. In the process, they will realize the thematic meaning of the text, and have a deep understanding of "Practice makes perfect". Next, they will give suggestions on English learning. It promotes students' ability to solve problems and develop their logical thinking. Students' participation in interaction and communication can be observed and necessary feedback will be given.

Activity 2, Think, write and share. Students will first think about their dreams from five aspects based on the text about Wu Binbin's dream. Then they will apply what they've learnt to write down their own dreams. The teacher will observe whether the students' writing covers the above aspects and uses the language learnt, and evaluate the effectiveness of teaching and learning in the context of the students' presentation of their dreams to the class. And the teacher will give guidance when necessary.

Throughout the class, the blackboard design is synchronized with the learning process. As you can see, the topic and main points of this lesson are clearly presented. Students can review and retell the text independently according to the blackboard design.

The assignments are designed from easy to difficult. At Level 1, students are required to listen to Wu Binbin's dream on Page 38 and read it aloud, so they can further consolidate what they've learnt. At Level 2, they need to polish their writing based on the checklist for a better writing.

Learning effects

After introducing the details of this lesson, I'd like to emphasize some uniqueness.

Firstly, questions are designed to develop students' thinking from lower-order to higher-order.

On the basis of analyzing the structure of the text, the teacher designs some questions such as "Who was in the dream?", "What did … do?", "How did … feel?" for the interpretation of the three dreams. In this way, students can build the structure map, and develop their lower-order thinking skills. What's more, a question chain is also designed to help students explore the thematic meaning of the text: "Practice makes perfect". Then students try to solve the problem that the teacher couldn't win the game, which inspires them to tell their dream stories. In the process, students' higher-order thinking skills is gradually improved.

Secondly, activities are designed to develop students' autonomous and cooperative learning skills.

In this lesson, the teacher first consciously guides students to complete the knowledge structure map of the first running race when reading Paragraph 1. Then, students are encouraged to learn by themselves, including reading Paragraph 3, ordering pictures and matching the pictures with corresponding verbs and phrases. After that, students work in groups to complete the key information of the second race in Worksheet 2. Through independent reading, acting and group discussion, the learning objectives could eventually be realized.

That's all for my presentation. Thanks for watching.

试课实录①

试课视频

步骤一　谈论"教师的梦"(4 分钟)

Activity 1: Look and say

T:　Class begins! Good morning, boys and girls.

Ss:　(Good morning, Miss Lin.)

T:　Last night I had a dream. I was in a spelling bee. Look, this is me. It was a special spelling bee. I had to tell the past tense of verbs. Can you help me?

Ss:　(Yes.)

T:　Thank you. Now let's get started. Is.

Ss:　(Was.)

T:　[shows and reads the present tense of verbs]

Ss:　[tell the past tense of corresponding verbs]

T:　Drink tea.

Ss:　(Drank tea.)

T:　Good job! I could win the race. I was so happy. But suddenly, wake, trip, feel, think, give, I didn't know the past tense of these verbs. There was nothing I could do. I was so worried. Oh, no! My trophy! I was so sad.

Activity 2: Think and say

T:　This is my dream. What do you think of my dream?

---

① 本试课稿由温州市实验中学附属小学林陈霜撰写。

S1:　(It's funny.)

S2:　(It's sad.)

S3:　(It's interesting.)

步骤二 研读"Wu Binbin 的梦"(21 分钟)

Activity 1: Think and ask

T:　Funny, sad, interesting, what a dream! This is our friend Wu Binbin. He also had a dream last night. Last night! This is about "When did he have the dream?". Any other questions do you have about his dream?

S4:　(Where was he in the dream?)

S5:　(Who was in the dream?)

S6:　(What did he do in the dream?)

S7:　(What's his dream about?)

S8:　(How did he feel in the dream?)

Activity 2: Read the text and answer

T:　Wow, you have so many questions. First, let's see "What's his dream about?". Everybody, please turn to Page 38, read very quickly and find out the answer. Go!

Ss:　[read the text on Page 38]

T:　Finished? What's his dream about? You, please.

S9:　(It's about the race.)

T:　Right. Can you read this one?

S9:　(Face.) [fails to pronounce it correctly]

T:　Er …

S9:　(Race.)

T:　Much better. Race. Look, this is a … ?

Ss:　(Race.)

T:　This is also a … ?

Ss:　(Race.)

T:　Good job! How many races are there in Wu Binbin's dream?

S10:　(Two.)

T:　Yes, two. How do you know?

S10:　(Wu Binbin had a race with his father and Max. There was a second race.)

T:　Yes, there are two races in Wu Binbin's dream.

Activity 3: Read Paragraph 1 and answer

T:　Now let's see the first race. Look, I have 3 questions for you. Can you read them?

Ss:　(Who was in the race? What did Wu Binbin do? How did Wu Binbin feel?)

T:　Very good! Now everybody, please read Paragraph 1 and try to answer these 3 questions. Remember to underline the key sentences.

Ss:　[read Paragraph 1]

T:　Have you finished?

Ss:　(Yes.)

T:　Now, let's check. Number 1: Who was in the race? You, please.

S11:　(Wu Binbin, his father and Max.)

T:　Good job! How about the second question? What did Wu Binbin do? Could he run fast? You try.

S12:　(No, his father ran very fast, but Wu Binbin could not.)

T:　Yes. He couldn't run fast. Boys and girls, if you were Wu Binbin and you couldn't run fast in the race, what would you do?

S13:　(I would say "Come on, you can do it".)

T:　I see. You are trying to encourage yourself. Good job. Yes, you try.

S14:　(Eat some chocolate.)

T:　Eating some chocolate can give you energy, right? But for Wu Binbin, would these work?

Ss:　(No.)

T:　How do you know? Which sentence? Yes, you try.

S15:　(There was nothing he could do.)

T:　Very good! He could do nothing. Let's listen and read with feelings. [plays the recording of "There was nothing he could do"] Try.

Ss:　(There was nothing he could do.)

T:　Yes, there was nothing he could do. So how did Wu Binbin feel? You, please.

S16:　(He was so worried.)

T:　Right. Wu Binbin was worried. What did he think? You, please.

S17:　(I could run fast at school, why am I so slow now?)

T:　Yes. Here "thought" is from …?

Ss:　(Think.)

T:　Right, let's listen and read. [plays the recording of "I could run fast at school, he thought. Why am I so slow now?"] Try.

Ss:　("I could run fast at school," he thought. "Why am I so slow now?")

Activity 4: Read Paragraph 3 and answer

A: Read, order and match

T:　So this is Wu Binbin's first race. How about his second race? Look, there are 4 pictures. Please read Paragraph 3 and order these pictures. Then try to match the pictures with the following phrases. This tip may help you. Now please take out your worksheet and finish it. OK? Go.

Ss: [read Paragraph 3]

T: Finished? Let's check. Picture 1 is No. …?

S18: (One.)

T: Right, it means …?

S18: (Ran like a cheetah.)

T: Listen. [plays the recording of "ran like a cheetah"] Try.

Ss: (Ran like a cheetah.)

T: Much better. Ran like a cheetah. [reads with actions] This line, please.

L1:   (Ran like a cheetah.) [reads with actions]

T: Ran is from …?

Ss: (Run.)

T: Yes. Picture 2 is No. …?

S19: (Four.)

T: It means …?

S19: (Woke up.)

T: Listen. [plays the recording of "woke up"] Woke up. [reads with actions] Try.

Ss: (Woke up) [read with actions]

T: Very good. Woke is from …?

Ss: (Wake.)

T: Yes. Wake. Picture 3 is No. …?

S20: (Two.)

T: Great! It means …?

S20: (Tripped.) [fails to pronounce it correctly]

T: OK. Boys and girls, can you try to read this one?

S20: (Jumped.)

T: So …?

S20: (Tripped.)

T: Yes. Tripped.

Ss: (Tripped.)

T: And "tripped" is from …?

Ss: (Trip.)

T: Right, but pay attention, there are two "p"s here in "tripped". There are two meanings. Which one is right?

Ss: (绊倒)

T: Very good! The last one. It's No. …?

S21: (Three.)

T: Yes, it means …?

S21: (Fell.)

T:　　Fell is from … ?

S21:　(Fall.)

B: Let's act

T:　　Right. Now let's act out Paragraph 3. I'm the narrator. You are Wu Binbin. Everybody, please stand up.

Ss:　[act out Paragraph 3]

C: Read and answer

T:　　Wow, you are great actors. Sit down, please. You see, in the first race, I have 3 questions. In the second race, I still have the same 3 questions. Step 1, please read Paragraph 3 and underline the key information by yourself. Step 2, please work in groups of four: A and B ask, C answers, and D sticks the answer. Clear? Everybody, this envelope, let's do it.

Ss:　[read and underline by themselves, then work in groups]

T:　　Have you finished? Which group can show us? Come to the front.

G1:　[group performance]

T:　　Thank you. Are they right? Let's check. Number 1: Who was in the race?

Ss:　(Wu Binbin and many animals.)

T:　　Yes. Number 2: What did Wu Binbin do?

Ss:　(Wu Binbin ran like a cheetah. He tripped and fell. He woke up.)

D: Watch and say

T:　　Yes. Here "Wu Binbin ran like a cheetah.", so how fast is a cheetah? Today let's have a PK between the world's fastest man Usain Bolt and a cheetah. Guess who will win?

Ss:　(Usain Bolt.)

T:　　Really? Let's watch the video and find out. [plays the video of a virtual match between Usain Bolt and the cheetah]

T:　　Who wins?

Ss:　(The cheetah.)

T:　　Yeah. If you were Wu Binbin, you could run like a cheetah, how would you feel? You, please.

S22:　(I am so happy. Haha, I'm the fastest boy in the world!)

S23:　(I feel excited. I could win the race!)

T:　　Happy, excited. But suddenly Wu Binbin tripped and fell. Then he woke up. Oh, it was only a dream. Now, how would you feel?

S24:　(I feel disappointed.)

S25:　(I am sad.)

T:　　So here for "How did Wu Binbin feel?", there is more than one answer. Any answer with a reason is OK.

Activity 5: Read Paragraph 2 and answer

T: You see, in the first race, Wu Binbin couldn't run fast. But in the second race, he could run like a cheetah. Amazing, right? But why? Think about it. He was in a DREAM! You, please.

S26: (He had the magic shoes.)

T: Magic shoes? I like your idea. How about you?

S27: (Maybe there was a superman in him.)

T: A superman. Funny. But what really happened? Please read Paragraph 2 and find out the answer.

Ss: [read Paragraph 2]

T: Have you got the answer? Who helped?

S28: (Robin gave him some water. Wu Binbin drank it.)

T: Right. It was Robin. How did Wu Binbin feel? You try.

S29: (I feel great. I can run fast now!)

S30: (I will win the race!)

Activity 6: Retell, listen and complete

T: So this is Wu Binbin's dream. Now look at the blackboard. Let's try to retell it.

Ss: (Wu Binbin had a dream last night. In the first race, he ran with his father and Max. Wu Binbin couldn't run fast. He was worried. Then Robin gave him some water. Wu Binbin drank it and suddenly he felt good. In the second race, there were many animals. Wu Binbin ran like a cheetah. He was so happy. But suddenly he tripped and fell. Then he woke up. It was all a dream. He was sad.)

T: You are such great storytellers. Look, our friend Wu Binbin is telling his mother about the dream. It's on your book, Page 39. Can you try to fill in the blanks?

Ss: [read and fill in the blanks]

T: You don't know some blanks, but it's OK. Let's listen and fill in the blanks.

Ss: [listen to the dialogue and fill in the blanks]

T: Have you finished? Now please read with your partners. Which pair can show us? Yes, you two.

P1: [pair performance]

T: Thank you. What a dream!

步骤三 交流"自己的梦"(10分钟)

Activity 1: Think and say

T: Boys and girls, do you like Wu Binbin's dream?

Ss: (Yes.)

T: What do you think of his dream? You, please.

S31:　(I think it's so interesting.)

T:　　Why? Which part do you think is interesting?

S31:　(Wu Binbin could run like a cheetah. He could run so fast.)

T:　　I see. How about you?

S32:　(I think it's amazing. Robin has this magic water. I wish I could drink that.)

T:　　But mum says "There is no magic water". Boys and girls, if Wu Binbin wants to run faster, what can he do?

S33:　(He can drink Red Bull.)

S34:　(He can eat some chocolate.)

T:　　But will these help a lot? What really should Wu Binbin do?

S35:　(He should run every day.)

Ss:　　(Yes, just run run run.)

T:　　I think so. He should practise, because we know … ?

Ss:　　(Practice makes perfect.)

T:　　Great! You see, in my dream, I couldn't win the spelling bee. I want to learn English well. So what should I do?

S36:　(You should read many English books.)

S37:　(You can watch English movies.)

S38:　(You can "背单词".)

S39:　(You can speak English every day.)

T:　　Thanks for your advice. Like you said, speaking, listening, reading, and reciting words. I should practise. I should learn English every day, because we know … ?

Ss:　　(Practice makes perfect.)

Activity 2: Think, write and share

T:　　Right! In Wu Binbin's dreams, when we talk about dreams, we often talk about …

Ss:　　(When, where, who, what, how.)

T:　　Yes, so first please think about your dreams from these 5 aspects, then write down your dreams. Full content, one star; colorful expression, one star; correct writing, one star. Here we go!

Ss:　　[write about their dreams]

T:　　Finished? Who'd like to share your dream? You, please.

S40:　[shares her dream]

T:　　I like your dream. What a dream! You practised a lot. You made a lot of efforts. Finally, you made it. I'm so happy for you. Thank you.

作业布置

T:　　Boys and girls, you can polish your writing according to the checklist. This is one of your homework. The other one is to listen to Wu Binbin's dream and read it aloud on Page 38. That's all for today's class. Goodbye, everyone.

Ss: （Bye, Miss Lin.）

教学设计①

配套课件

（一）语篇研读

本课教学内容选自人教版英语六年级下册第四单元 Then and now B 部分 Read and write 板块,该语篇属于"人与自我"主题范畴,内容涉及"情绪与情感"。

What

本课语篇为记叙文,标题是"What a dream"。短文讲述了 Wu Binbin 做的一个梦:Wu Binbin 和父亲、小狗 Max 进行了一次跑步比赛,但他怎么都跑不快。接着 Wu Binbin 喝了 Robin 的"神奇水",在第二场与动物们的较量中,他跑得像猎豹一样快。眼看就要赢得比赛,突然他被绊倒了,才意识到这是一场梦。Wu Binbin 在前后比赛中表现的巨大反差,形成了情节的起伏波动,也调动了学生阅读的积极性。

Why

语篇描述了 Wu Binbin 在前后两场跑步比赛中截然不同的表现,教师可以借此引导学生思考在现实生活中跑得快的方法,进而使学生明白"Practice makes perfect",只有不断练习才能真正提高跑步速度的道理。语言学习也是如此,做任何事情都应如此。

How

语篇按照典型的记叙文风格进行叙述,全文分为三个部分:第一部分(第 1 段)是关于 Wu Binbin 的第一场跑步比赛;第二部分(第 2 段)介绍了 Wu Binbin 得到 Robin 的帮助;第三部分(第 3 段)是关于 Wu Binbin 的第二场跑步比赛。语篇脉络清晰,其中第 1 段和第 3 段在结构上相似,都介绍了参赛人员、Wu Binbin 跑步速度和感受的信息。全文使用了一般过去时,涉及较多的动词过去式,包括学生已经学习过的 had、were、ran、could、was、said、drank、fell 等,以及需要学生在本课语境中理解的 thought、gave、felt、tripped、woke 等词。

（二）学情分析

本课授课对象为 Z 省某小学六年级学生,他们几乎都有参与跑步竞赛的经历,希望自己能够跑得更快、赢得比赛,也对"梦"的话题充满好奇,乐于分享自己做过的梦。他们对本课讨论的主题"梦"颇感兴趣,也想了解语篇故事的结局。同时,学生经历近四年的英语学习,可以读懂情节简单的故事语篇,能运用阅读技巧和策略,获取关键信息,理解主要内容,但推

---

① 本教学设计由温州市实验中学附属小学林陈霜撰写。

断能力和反思能力还有待提高。他们对语篇中"Wu Binbin 喝了神奇水,眼看就要赢得比赛却被绊倒,意识到是梦"这一结局颇感意外,却未能意识到这一结局其实在情理之中——现实生活中,要跑得快需经历刻苦训练。教师需借助开放性问题,追问学生"Wu Binbin 如何才能跑得更快",并且反思"梦中教师为何没能赢得比赛",引导学生对语篇蕴含的"熟能生巧"这一人生哲理展开思考、发表看法、交流感受。

此外,学生已掌握部分动词的过去式形式,能运用一般过去时谈论和描述过去发生的事情。但围绕"梦"这一主题,运用一般过去时创编一个完整的语段,对学生来说存在一定困难。因此,教师需要提供图片和语篇结构要点,帮助提升学生的文本组织能力,降低写作难度。

(三)教学目标

通过本课时的学习,学生能够:

1. 通过阅读,获取并梳理 Wu Binbin 的梦的基本信息(时间、地点、人物、事件、感受),理解文本内容,形成知识结构图;

2. 基于知识结构图复述 Wu Binbin 的梦,并将短文转化为对话,内化语言知识,深入理解"熟能生巧"这一语篇主题意义;

3. 借助知识结构图,模仿范文,用连贯的几句话写出自己的"梦",强化"熟能生巧"的意识。

(四)教学流程

教师紧紧围绕"What a dream"这一标题,创设了分别属于教师、Wu Binbin 和学生的三个梦境,学生在经历一个个梦境的过程中,发展读写能力,领悟"Practice makes perfect"的道理。第一阶段为学生谈论"教师的梦"。教师讲述自己梦见在"单词拼写大赛"中遭遇失败的趣味故事,引导学生入境,复习旧知,并为最后读写做好铺垫。第二阶段,教师邀请学生进

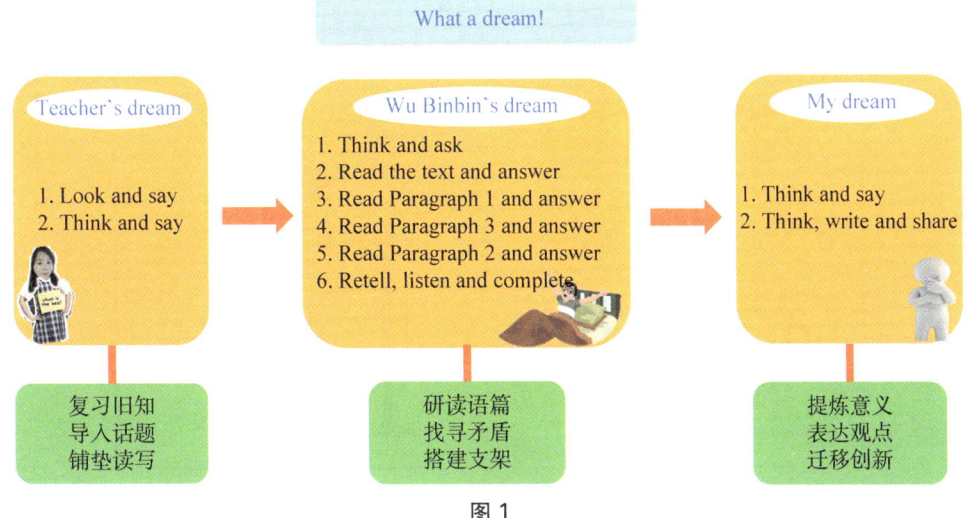

图 1

入"Wu Binbin 的梦",展开对语篇的研读。在本环节,学生先进行读前预测,为阅读热身;初读关于 Wu Binbin 梦的文本,理解主旨大意;后结合问题链细读文本,获取并梳理基本信息,为写作做准备;最后通过复述和听音填空类型的活动,进一步内化语言。第三阶段,学生交流"自己的梦"。此环节中,学生一是需要提炼语篇主题意义,表达个人观点;二是要迁移所学,书写并交流自己做过的梦,实现真实语用。

(五)教学过程

步骤一 谈论"教师的梦"(4 分钟)

Activity 1: Look and say (3 mins)

To help the teacher with the special spelling bee in her dream, students review the past tense of some verbs. Then they get to know the teacher failed the game because she couldn't get all the answers right.

图 2

图 3

图 4

【设计说明】　教师通过引导学生助其完成昨晚梦中别样的"单词拼写大赛"(见图 2、图 3、图 4),激活学生对已学的动词过去式的记忆,为后续阅读与写作活动做好准备。

【效果评价】　教师观察学生的回答是否正确,了解其对动词过去式的掌握情况。

Activity 2: Think and say (1 min)

Students share their thoughts about the teacher's dream.

【设计说明】　通过提问,教师引导学生积极思考并分享观点,并自然地导入本课话题——"梦"。

步骤二　研读"Wu Binbin 的梦"(21 分钟)

Activity 1: Think and ask (1 min)

Students raise questions about Wu Binbin's dream based on the picture and their own experiences.

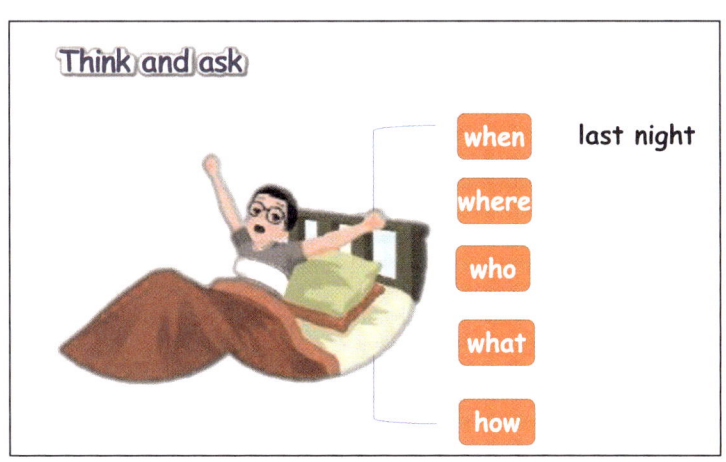

图 5

【设计说明】　教师引导学生基于图片和自己的经历,对文本内容进行提问(见图 5),培养其预测能力,激发其好奇心和求知欲。

Activity 2: Read the text and answer (3 mins)

Students read the text quickly and find out the general idea. Then they learn the new word "race" and find out the answer to "How many races are there in Wu Binbin's dream?".

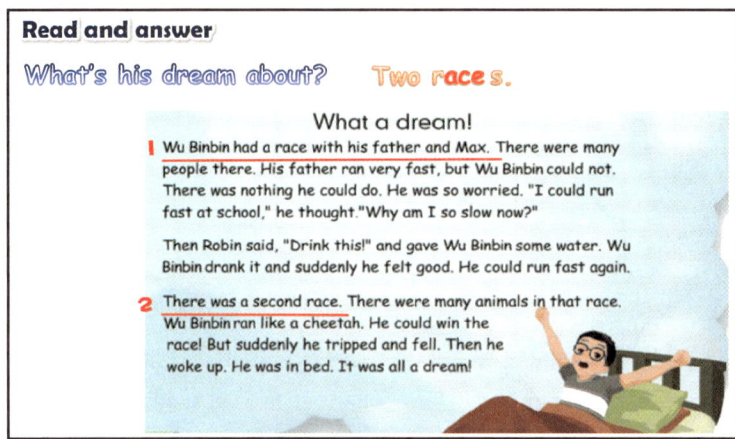

图 6

【设计说明】 通过阅读文本的活动,教师引导学生提炼主旨大意,学习新单词"race"(见图 6),整体感知文本内容。

Activity 3: Read Paragraph 1 and answer (3 mins)

Students read Paragraph 1 (the first race) and answer 3 questions "Who was in the race?", "What did Wu Binbin do?" and "How did Wu Binbin feel?". After knowing "Wu Binbin couldn't run fast", they have an open discussion: If Wu Binbin couldn't run fast, what could he do? Then they learn and further understand the expression "There was nothing he could do".

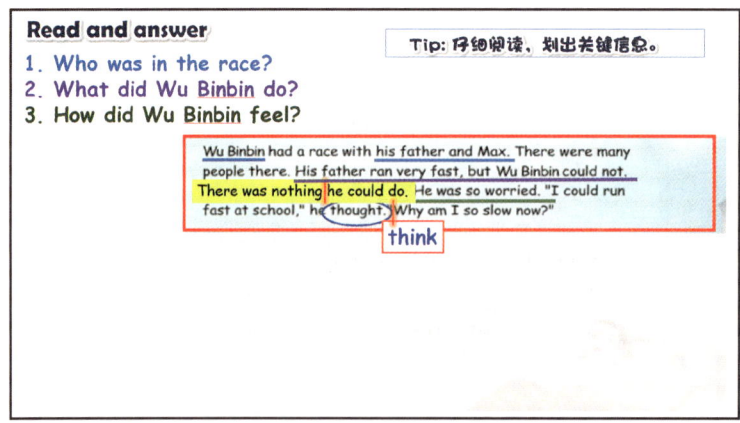

图 7

【设计说明】 通过引导学生阅读文本第一段并回答三个问题(见图 7),教师帮助学生理解文本细节,培养其获取梳理人物、事件、情感等关键信息的能力。通过尝试解决 Wu

Binbin 跑不快的问题,学生能进一步理解"There was nothing he could do"所表达的意义。

【效果评价】 教师观察学生回答问题的表现,判断其获取信息的全面和准确程度。

Activity 4: Read Paragraph 3 and answer (9 mins)

A: Read, order and match

Students read Paragraph 3 (the second race) and order 4 pictures with the help of the tip. Then they match the pictures with relevant verbs or phrases. After that, they check the answers and practise the new expressions "ran like a cheetah", "tripped", "fell" and "woke up".

图 8

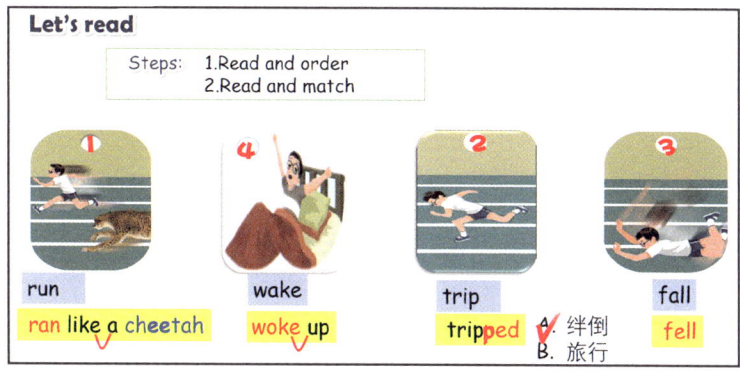

图 9

【设计说明】 通过图片排序、单词词组连线,学生借助提示理解文本第三段(见图8),学习核心词汇(见图9),为进一步在现实生活情境中运用所学做好准备。

【效果评价】 教师观察学生能否完成学习单中的排序、连线任务,把握学生对重点词汇和核心语言的学习情况,必要时提供帮助。

B: Let's act

Students act out what happened while the teacher reads Paragraph 3.

【设计说明】 通过演一演,教师帮助学生深入 Wu Binbin 的角色,运用语言理解意义,增加课堂趣味性。

C: Read and answer

Students first read Paragraph 3 and underline the answers to the same three questions in the first race independently. Then they work in groups of four to finish the Worksheet 2: A and B ask these three questions, C answers them, and D finds out the stickers and sticks them on the worksheet.

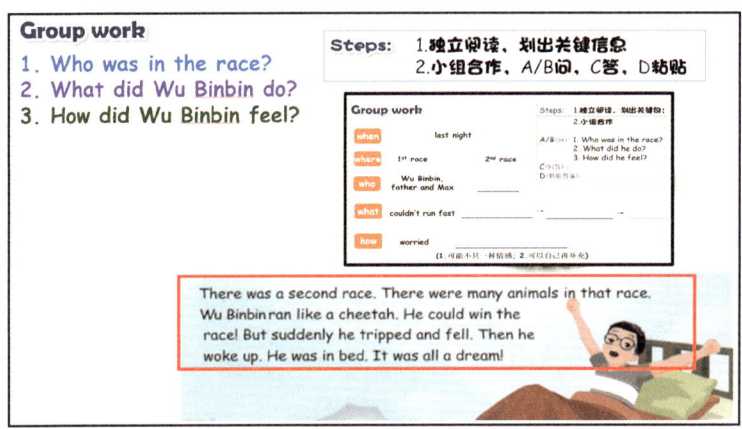

图 10

【设计说明】 学生通过独立阅读文本第三段,思考在学习第一场比赛时回答的三个问题,并标出关键句(见图10)。接着,通过小组合作完成学习单二,梳理并汇报第二场比赛中的人物、事件、情感等信息,提升其在阅读中获取关键信息的能力。

【效果评价】 教师观察学生能否画出关键句,以及在小组展示中所展现的人物、事件、情感等信息是否正确与全面,判断其能否准确获取关键信息。

D: Watch and say

After knowing "Wu Binbin ran like a cheetah", students watch the race between the world's fastest man Usain Bolt and the cheetah, and realize how fast Wu Binbin was in the second race. Then they express their ideas about Wu Binbin's different feelings before and after tripping.

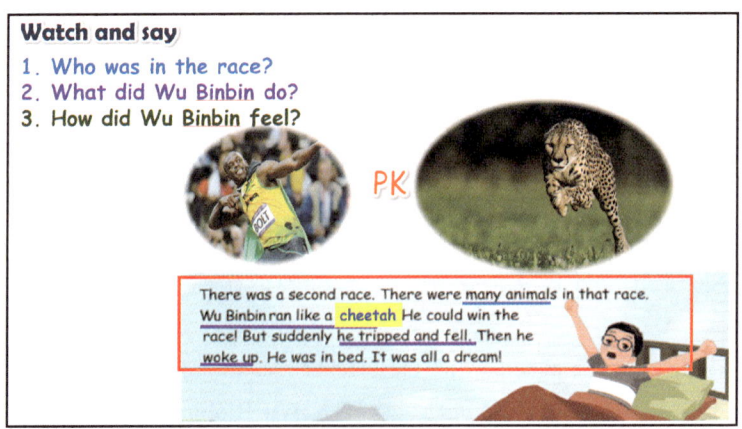

图 11

【设计说明】　通过观看博尔特和猎豹的模拟比赛视频(见图11),学生可以对文中 Wu Binbin 绊倒前后的心情做出判断,加深对课文内容的理解。

【效果评价】　教师根据学生对 Wu Binbin 心情的描述,把握其对所学内容的理解情况,并根据学生的表现给予必要的提示和指导。

Activity 5: Read Paragraph 2 and answer (2 mins)

Students express their ideas about "Why could Wu Binbin suddenly run like a cheetah" with imagination. Then they read Paragraph 2 and find the answer.

【设计说明】　通过大胆猜测 Wu Binbin 突然跑得快的原因,教师引导学生发散思维,激发其表达的欲望。通过阅读文本第二段,教师培养学生在阅读中获取关键信息验证猜测的能力。

Activity 6: Retell, listen and complete (3 mins)

Students retell the dream with the help of the blackboard design. Then they listen to and complete the dialogue between Mum and Wu Binbin.

【设计说明】　教师借助板书引导学生复述文本的主要内容;在根据录音完成 Wu Binbin 和母亲对话的过程中,学生能够进一步内化所学语言。

【效果评价】　教师观察学生能否借助板书呈现的语言支架完成复述,以及能否根据录音完成填空,并根据学生的表现给予必要的提示和反馈。

步骤三　交流"自己的梦"(10 分钟)

Activity 1: Think and say (3 mins)

Students voice their opinions about Wu Binbin's dream. Then they express their ideas about how Wu Binbin could run faster and realize "Practice makes perfect". After that, they give advice on the ways to learn English.

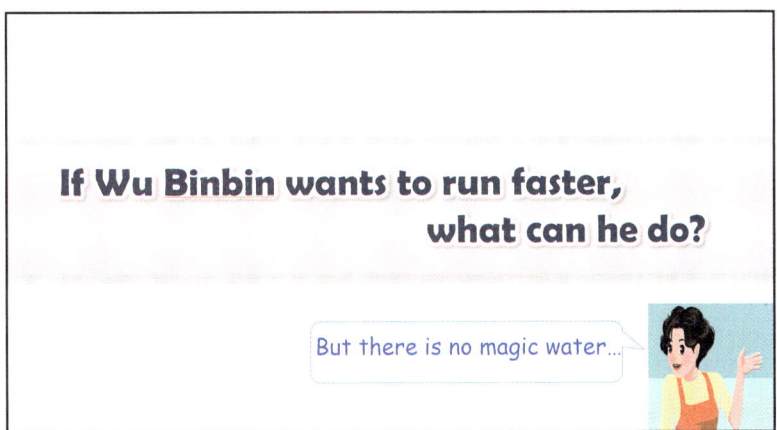

图 12

图 13

【设计说明】 通过评价 Wu Binbin 的梦,学生思考如何才能真正提高跑步速度(图 12),体会语篇背后的隐含意义,树立"熟能生巧"的正确认识。通过思考梦中教师不能赢得比赛的问题解决之法(图 13),培养学生在真实情境中运用所学解决问题的能力。思维从低阶走向高阶,实现主题的内化。

【效果评价】 教师观察学生能否参与互动和交流,并根据需要进行追问或给予鼓励。

Activity 2: Think, write and share (7 mins)

Students think about their dreams from these five aspects. Then write their dreams down and share them with classmates.

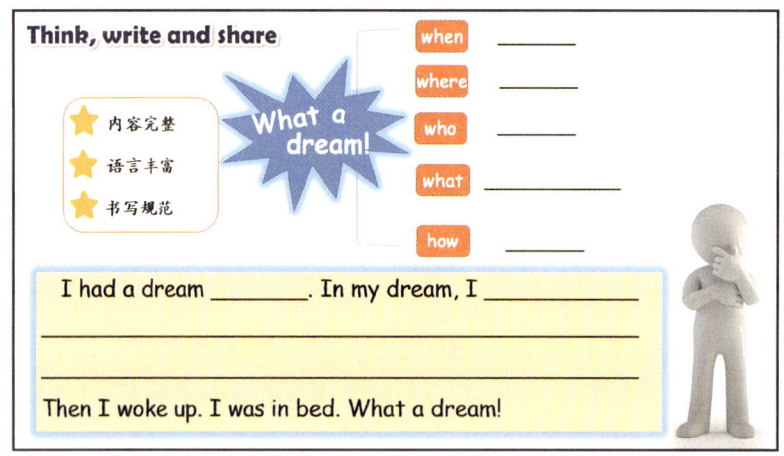

图 14

【设计说明】 教师引导学生参考吴斌斌的梦,按内容要点(when, where, who, what, how)思考自己的梦;综合所学内容,参考评价标准撰写自己的梦并分享,进而实现以读促写(见图 14)。

【效果评价】 教师观察学生的写作内容是否具备以上要点,是否运用了所学语言,必要时给予指导和帮助。教师还可结合学生向全班介绍自己的梦的情况,评估教与学的成效。

(六) 板书设计

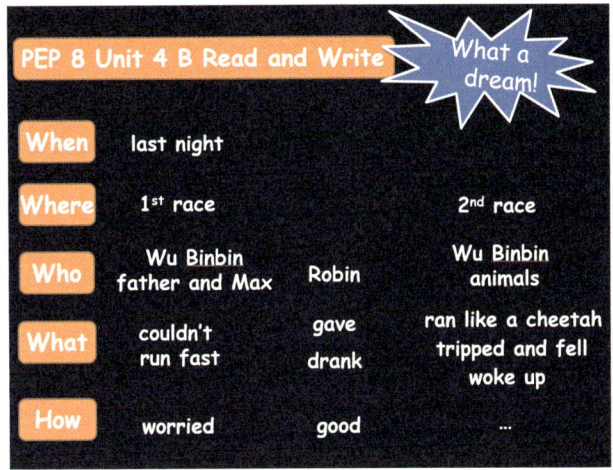

图 15

【设计说明】 板书包括课题名称与课堂要点。教师围绕"What a dream!"这一话题,设计了五个核心问题(时间、地点、人物、事件和心情)。通过对这五个问题的解答,板书呈现了语篇的核心信息与故事的发展过程。板书与教学进程同步,贯穿课堂始终,学生能借助板书厘清文章脉络,自主地进行课文复述。

(七) 作业设计

*1. Listen to Wu Binbin's dream on Page 38 and read it aloud.
**2. Polish your writing according to the checklist.

Checklist	是	否
1. 短文是否包含了 when, where, who, what, how 的具体信息?		
2. 短文是否使用了恰当的句型和丰富的词语?		
3. 短文的书写、拼写、标点是否正确规范?		

【设计说明】 本作业根据星级,进行了难度递增的分层设计:一星作业"课后听读",引导学生进一步理解文本,巩固所学;二星作业"写作润色",旨在提升学生的综合语用能力。学生依据核查表进行自查修改,完善文章,提升作文质量,实现以评促学。

(八) 教学反思

在本节读写课的教学设计中,教师围绕"梦"这一主题,依托语篇,设计了一系列循环递进和相互关联的学习活动,帮助学生建构起一张结构化的"知识网",推动学生对"熟能生巧"主题意义的理解和认识,实现语言学习和课程育人的有机融合。

1. 立足主题语篇结构创设教学问题,发展高阶与低阶协同的思维

问题是思维的起点,也是课堂教学的主动脉,教师在剖析语篇结构的基础上设置问题链,不仅可以突出教学的重难点,还保障了学生思维的连贯性,促进其高低阶思维协同发展。

本课语篇是一则典型的记叙文,主要围绕记叙文的五大核心要素展开。为此,教师为每一个梦境的解读设计了"What's the dream about?" "Where was … in the dream?" "Who was in the dream?" "What did … do?" "How did … feel?"等问题。学生在熟悉问题结构的基础上,可以快速获取、梳理、概括基本的事实性信息,并在脑海中搭建知识结构图,发展低阶思维能力。同时,教师利用故事高潮,即"Wu Binbin 喝了神奇水,跑步如猎豹一样快"的情节与现实情况不相符这一切入点,提出本课的关键问题"There is no magic water. If Wu Binbin wants to run faster, what can he do? Will these really help? What really should Wu Binbin do?"引导学生探究语篇主题意义——熟能生巧。随后,学生从课本走向生活,运用这一道理解决"教师不能赢得拼词大赛"的问题,进而产生讲述自己梦境故事的动力。由此,基于语篇结构生发的关键问题带动学生高阶思维的发展。学生经历三个梦境,其高低阶思维不断互动,最终达成协同发展的效果。

2. 遵循先扶后放原则安排教学活动,打造讲授与探究互融的课堂

本堂课中,教师尝试先扶后放,使教师的讲解或指导与学生的自主或合作学习互融共促,打造民主高效的英语课堂。在阅读文本第一段时,教师有意识地指导学生获取并梳理有关人物、事件、情感等关键信息,完善第一次跑步比赛的知识结构图。接着,教师从"扶"到"放",学生独立阅读文本第三段,完成排序和连线任务,自主地在语境中理解文本、学习核心语言点。然后,学生以小组合作的形式进行阅读,通过自主寻找信息并和同伴分享信息,共同完成学习单上的任务,汇报第二次跑步比赛中的关键信息,内化所学语言。在扶放有度、循序渐进的教学活动中,学生不仅获取了再生性知识,还拥有了经由独立阅读、演绎体验、小组讨论所生成的创生性知识,从而使本节课成为过程和谐、效果显著的高品质课堂。

(九) 附件

学 习 单

Group work

when		last night	

where 1st race 2nd race

who Wu Binbin, father and Max _____

what couldn't run fast _____ → _____ → _____

how worried _____

(1.可能不只一种情感；2.可以自己再补充)

Steps:　1.独立阅读，划出关键句；
　　　　2.小组合作

A/B(问): 1. Who was in the race?
2. What did he do?
3. How did he feel?
C(回答)：
D(粘贴答案)：

课例 3

PEP B2 U3 At the zoo
（Part A Let's talk）

说课视频

Hello, everyone! I am Harper. It's my great honor to present this lesson plan to you. I'd like to introduce the lesson from five aspects, namely learning material and learners, learning objectives, learning process, homework and blackboard design, and learning effects. Now, let's come to the first part.

Learning material and learners

As is known to all, the analysis of learning materials and learners should be the very first concern when setting learning objectives.

The learning material is a dialogue from PEP, Book 2, Unit 3 *At the zoo*, Part A *Let's talk*, which is the first part of this unit. The theme of this dialogue is *man and nature*, concerning *the features of animals*.

What

In this dialogue, the teacher, Miss White, Amy and Zhang Peng see a tall giraffe and a naughty bear in a zoo. However, the absence of an exciting plot is not conducive to students' perceiving the theme, that is, *loving animals*. Therefore, an appropriate supplementary plot is of great necessity.

Why

In this dialogue, the tall, well-behaved mother and baby giraffes and the fat, naughty bear form a striking contrast. It can guide students to observe the differences between them so that students can appreciate the unique features of each animal, thus enhancing their love for animals as well as their awareness of animal protection, and helping them to understand the significance

---

① 本说课稿由温州市临江小学朱温铭撰写。

of visiting zoos courteously by following public rules.

How

To describe animals, Miss White, Amy and Zhang Peng employ diverse language, such as the key sentence patterns, "Look at … It's (so) … (and) …", nouns of animals like "giraffe" and "bear", and adjectives like "tall", "short" and "fat". These expressions will enable students to make up and act out new plots smoothly. Moreover, the characters talk in the present tense, which makes the dialogue easy to understand.

After exploring the learning material, here comes the analysis of learners. My students are in Grade Three. They are familiar with animals and zoos and are curious about animals in the zoo. Also, they are good at observing and are happy to share their observations. These factors contribute to their high motivation for today's learning.

My students have already learnt the sentence patterns "Look at … It is (so) … (and) …" and are able to complete the sentence with the adjectives they have learnt, including "big" "fat" "long", "cute", "funny" and "cool", to describe the characteristics of animals. However, they do not yet understand the surprise and amazement conveyed by these sentence patterns. Therefore, the content of the text needs to be expanded and sufficient language scaffolding needs to be provided to enhance their language understanding.

In addition, my students have strong visualized thinking skills to observe the physical features of animals from different angles, like colors and size. What's more, they can extract information from and make predictions according to the given pictures. However, it is hard for them to divide adjectives into different groups (e. g. color, height, body shape). Therefore, sufficient guidance is of great necessity.

Learning objectives

Based on the above analysis, the following learning objectives are set. By the end of this lesson, students will be able to:

1. grasp the main idea of the dialogue by extracting and combing information about animals as well as their features in the dialogue through viewing, listening and speaking activities.

2. use sentence patterns "Look at … It's (so) … (and) …" to describe the features of animals and then conduct a conversation in the role of animals and visitors.

3. carefully observe the two textbook illustrations and use the core sentence patterns to brainstorm the development of the story, and act out the dialogue in different roles under my guidance.

4. make comments on the bear's action and tell whether it's right or not, discuss with group members to imagine what might happen to the bear if he goes to other areas in the zoo, make up and perform a new story in class.

Learning process

To realize these learning objectives, this lesson will be divided into three stages in accordance with the Activity-based Approach to English Learning, namely, Context Perception, Role Substitution and Story Creation.

In Context Perception, to perceive the context and the target language, students will connect their previous knowledge and experience with the learning process through picture observation and audio-visual combination. Students can understand the context and consolidate the knowledge.

In Role Substitution, students try to switch from the visitors' points of view to the animals' and make up a new dialogue. The internalization and application of linguistic knowledge can be realized.

Lastly, in Story Creation, students are supposed to recreate the story and then act it out. Afterwards, they are asked to create a follow-up story through teamwork, thus generating oral output beyond the original context.

Now, let's have a closer look at how the learning objectives can be realized. I'll elaborate on the whole process from the description of learning activities, the justification of learning activities and the evaluation of learning activities.

In the first stage, Context Perception, five activities are designed.

The first and second activities are Enjoy a song and Look and think. Students will sing a song and observe the pictures to say the names of these parts. While livening up the atmosphere, it encourages students to review the words of animals and further perceive the context. These activities allow students to share their existing personal knowledge and experience of topic. I will observe whether students can participate in interaction and communication and adjust the questioning style to follow up or give encouragement according to the reasonableness of students' guesses about the location.

The next activity is Look and say. Students will look at a picture and predict what Mike will say so that they can view and infer with illustrations. They listen to the dialogue to check the answer and practise the new expression "It's so big", which allows them to recall and perceive the amazement it conveys. I can evaluate the appropriateness of the adjectives used to describe the features of the elephant to judge whether they can extract the information correctly according to the dialogue.

After that, Choose and say and Listen and choose are set. Students choose one animal to discuss with their partners using the sentence patterns and adjectives provided. Then they listen to the dialogue and choose the right answer on the worksheet. Through these activities, students can describe the features of animals and grasp the main idea so as to improve their ability to listen for key information with certain questions in their minds. I will observe whether students can describe the selected animal using the target language and give guidance or encouragement according to students' ability levels. So far, the first learning objective has been achieved.

In the second stage, Role Substitution, five activities are contained.

Activities 1 and 2 are Guess and say and Think and guess. Students predict what characters will say and then check their predictions and imitate the sample dialogue: "Look at that giraffe. Wow! It's so tall." Then students switch the perspective from the visitors' to the animals' and have another discussion about what the animals will probably talk about. It helps students to infer the content of the dialogue and develop their cooperative learning skills. I will keep an eye on the rationality of their predictions and the accuracy of their pronunciation of the sample dialogue. After they complete these two activities, the second learning objective can be achieved to a certain extent.

Next, from Activity 3 to Activity 5, to figure out who is hiding in the grass in the given picture and describe it, students will listen to the rest of the dialogue and watch the corresponding video. After that, they will listen again to mark the tones and imitate the dialogue with correct pronunciation, intonation, and rhythm. Also, imitating the dialogue can help them develop language intuition. Whether students can describe the bear appropriately and imitate the dialogue accurately will be evaluated, then the second learning objective can be fully realized.

In the last stage, Story Creation, there are altogether three activities.

The first one is Read a story, which is divided into three parts. Part A is Guess and enjoy, in which students will guess what the mother giraffe is thinking. Part B is Listen and repeat, in which they will listen to the tape and correctly repeat it with emotions and body movements. Part C is Act out the story, which consists of two performance tasks with different difficulty. Students can choose one according to their ability and act it out in groups of three to achieve output. If they can do the role-play vividly, then the third learning objective can be partially realized. The whole activity cultivates students' ability of prediction and imagination, and also provides students with more audio-visual opportunities. Then, a checklist will be provided for them to evaluate each other's performance from three aspects, including language, performance and innovation.

Activity 2 is Talk and think. Part A is Guess and say. Students will guess what adjective the mother giraffe will use to describe the naughty bear when she sees him teasing her baby, and then compare their opinions with the correct answer, thus perceiving the meaning of the word "naughty". Part B is Chant and say. The funny chant can naturally make students understand the meaning of the new word "naughty". Part C is Think and judge. I will let them judge whether the bear's behavior is right or wrong. The second activity enriches students' vocabulary, strengthens students' language memory and helps students understand the importance of loving and protecting the animals. If students can make the correct choice and reasonable judgment in Part A and Part B, then I can tell the third learning objective has been achieved.

Activity 3 is Make a new story with three parts. Part A is Choose and discuss. Students will choose one animal area and have an open discussion in groups on what the naughty bear will do there in groups, thus making a new story on their own. Then in Part B, Draw and say, students will be asked to draw pictures for the story and make up a dialogue. Part C is Act it out. Students will show the new story to the class. This activity will make it achievable for students to use the language to solve problems and improve their understanding of the thematic meaning and help them form correct attitudes and value judgments. And I will evaluate whether students show a reasonable story to the class. So far, the fourth learning objective will be achieved.

Homework and blackboard design

After the class, there are three assignments for students. Two of them are compulsory. The first is to listen to the dialogue on Page 24 and read it aloud, guiding students to consolidate the target language. The second is to draw an animal they like and talk with their friends, encouraging students to use the language they have learnt to communicate authentically. The last one is optional. They need to act out the story they made and try to take a video. In this way, students' language competence and their creative, communicative, collaborative and choreographic skills will be developed.

As for blackboard design, the sentence patterns, the key words and the lines are presented clearly, enabling students to better memorize and recall what they have learnt.

Learning effects

During the achievement of all the learning objectives, there exist three advantages that I'd like to point out.

Firstly, the skillful combination of viewing and listening activities can activate students' knowledge and experience reserve. Many tasks are based on audio-visual dimension to guide students to achieve output.

Secondly, all learning activities, such as the guessing activities in different stages, are advanced by questions or problems at different levels of thinking, which enables students to acquire the target language and develop their thinking quality.

Thirdly, the full use of the white space between the two pictures in the textbook can encourage students to go beyond the context to carry out transferring and innovating. Students' curiosity and internal drive for innovation will facilitate the transformation of their abilities into literacy.

That's all for my presentation. Thanks for watching!

试课实录①

步骤一　基于语篇,感知语境,学习语言(11分钟)

Activity 1: Enjoy a song

T:　Class begins! Hello, boys and girls.

Ss:　(Hello, teacher!)

T:　Before the class, let's enjoy a song together, OK? You can act with me!

Ss:　[sing the song and act]

T:　Wow! What a lovely song! Big hands for yourself. And what can you see in this song? Do you remember?

S1:　(I can see a monkey.)

T:　Yes. It's short. What else?

S2:　(I can see a cat.)

T:　Good! It runs fast. And we can see a tall … ?

Ss:　(Giraffe!)

T:　Yes, show me your hands! Let's spell together, gi-ra-ffe, giraffe.

Ss:　(Gi-ra-ffe, giraffe.)

Activity 2: Look and think

A: Let's say

T:　Now, please look at the picture carefully. What's that?

S3:　(It's an elephant.)

T:　Yes! What about that?

S4:　(It's a panda.)

T:　You're right! And that?

S5:　(It's a monkey.)

T:　Good! The last one?

S6:　(It's a giraffe.)

T:　Wonderful!

B: Let's think

T:　Wow! So many animals! Where are they? Can you guess? Maybe they are … ?

S7:　(At the zoo.)

T:　Good guess. Now, let's have a look! They are … ?

① 本试课稿由温州市新田园小学邱梦梦撰写。

Ss:　(At the zoo.)

T:　Kids, what other animals can you see at the zoo? Maybe …

S8:　(I can see a rabbit.)

T:　A rabbit! It's so cute. Any more?

S9:　(I can see a tiger.)

T:　Wow! A tiger. What else?

S10:　(A bird.)

T:　Nice try! It's so small. Look! Miss White and the children go to the zoo today. Let's see! What animal do they see first?

Ss:　(Elephant!)

Activity 3: Look and say

T:　Yes, they go to the elephant area first. Look! They are talking about the elephant. Look at that elephant! What will Mike say?

S11:　(Wow! It's big.)

T:　Maybe! And you?

S12:　(Wow! It's tall.)

T:　Now, let's listen and check.

Ss:　[listen to the recording]

T:　Mike says … ?

Ss:　(Wow! It's so big.)

T:　Yes! Mike is so surprised. Wow! It's so big. [does the action] Try again.

Ss:　(Wow! It's so big.) [do the action]

Activity 4: Choose and say

T:　Look! This is a map of the zoo. We can see lots of animals! Which one do you like?

S13:　(I like the monkey.)

T:　Look at that monkey.

S13:　(It's funny.)

T:　Yes! It's small and funny! Now, it's your turn. Choose one animal you like and try to talk about it with your partner. Please use as more words as you can. Here we go!

Ss:　[work in pairs]

T:　Time's up! Which pair can share with us? You two, please.

G1:　(Look at that bird. It's blue and white.)

T:　Wow. You use two words to describe it! Big hands for them! Any volunteers?

G2:　(Look at that tiger. It's so big.)

T:　Nice try!

Activity 5: Listen and choose

T:　　After visiting the elephant area, which area will they go next? Can you guess?

S14: (The panda area.)

T:　　Why?

S15: (It's near the elephant area.)

T:　　Oh, it's near the elephant area. Good! Now, let's listen and choose. Please take out your learning sheet.

Ss:　[listen to the recording]

T:　　Have you got it?

Ss:　(Yes!)

T:　　So they go to the … ?

Ss:　(Giraffe area.)

T:　　You're right!

步骤二　深入语篇,代入角色,应用语言(12 分钟)

Activity 1: Guess and say

T:　　Now, they are in the giraffe area. What are they talking about? Can you guess? Please talk and discuss with your partner! Go!

Ss:　[work in pairs]

T:　　OK, kids. Who can share?

G3:　(Look at that giraffe. It's big and tall.)

T:　　Super! Big hands! Now, let's listen and check!

Ss:　[listen to the recording]

T:　　This time, let's read together! Please pay attention to the linking sounds. Look at that giraffe.

Ss:　(Look at that giraffe.)

T:　　Wow! It's so tall.

Ss:　(Wow! It's so tall.)

T:　　Now, you can practise in pairs.

Ss:　[work in pairs]

Activity 2: Think and guess

T:　　Look! That is the … ?

Ss:　(Mother giraffe.)

T:　　And this is the … ?

Ss:　(Baby giraffe.)

T:　　They see Miss White, Zhang Peng and Amy. What will they talk about? Maybe the mother giraffe will say, "Look at that girl. She's … " You, please.

S16: (She's so short.)

T: I agree! Any different ideas?

S16: (She's so cute.)

T: Yes. Amy is short and cute in giraffe's eyes. Now it's your turn. What will these two giraffes say? Please talk and discuss with your partner! These tips may help you. Let's go!

Ss: [work in pairs]

T: Boys and girls, who can be the two giraffes? OK, this group. Ready? Go!

G4: (Look at that boy. He is so short.)

T: Great! For giraffes, Zhang Peng is so short.

Activity 3: Listen and answer

T: What's that sound? Oh, the grass is moving! Who's there? Can you guess?

S17: (Zoom.)

T: Oh, Zoom is hiding in the grass. Maybe! Let's listen and check the answer.

Ss: [listen to the recording]

T: Haha! Did you get the answer?

Ss: (A bear.)

T: Well done! All of you can get the key words!

Activity 4: Watch and choose

T: But, what's the bear like? Maybe … ?

Ss: (It's short and fat.)

T: Maybe … ?

Ss: (It's tall and fat.)

T: Well, let's watch and choose the answer. Please take out your learning sheet. Are you ready?

Ss: (I'm ready!)

T: Go!

Ss: [watch the video]

T: OK, kids. What's it like? Who can tell me?

S18: (It's short and fat.)

T: Excellent! Follow me. Ha! It's short and fat.

Ss: (Ha! It's short and fat.)

Activity 5: Listen and imitate

T: Boys and girls, please open your books. Let's turn to Page 24! Show me your pen! Let's listen and mark the tones.

Ss: [listen to the recording]

T: Now, let's listen and imitate. Please pay attention to the intonation and tones.

Ss: [listen and read the dialogue]

步骤三 超越语篇,创编故事,活用语言(17 分钟)

Activity 1: Read a new story

A: Guess and enjoy

T: Kids, look at the pictures carefully. There is a question mark! So, the mother giraffe has a question. What is it? Can you guess?

S19:   (Why is the bear here?)

T: Oh, you are the mother giraffe. You will think like this. Look! The mother giraffe wants to know what happened. Is your guess right?

Ss: (Yes./No.)

T: Kids, the bear is running and the baby giraffe is chasing! Why? Can you guess what happened?

S20:   (The baby giraffe doesn't like the bear, so it is chasing the bear away.)

T: Maybe the giraffe doesn't like the bear. Good guess. Anyone else?

S21:   (The bear tricked the giraffe.)

T: I like your guess. Do you want to know what happened in fact?

Ss: (Of course!)

T: Now, let's enjoy the story together.

Ss: [watch the video]

B: Listen and repeat

T: Do you like the story?

Ss: (Yes.)

T: It's so funny, right? Now let's read together and try to use our body language and facial expressions. OK? Let's get started!

Ss: [read the dialogue]

C: Act out the story

T: Now I'm the naughty bear, who can act with me? Who can be the baby giraffe?

S22:   [puts up his hand]

T: Good. It's our show time. All of you can judge how many stars we can get. OK?

T & S22: [act out the dialogue]

T: How many stars can we get?

Ss: (Three stars.)

T: Thank you. Now it's your turn. Let's work in pairs, OK? You can follow the example or make a new one! Choose one task! Go!

Ss: [act out the dialogue]

T: Time's up. Which group can come here and show us? OK, you two.

S23 & S24: [act out the dialogue]

T:　　Wow, big hands for them! They choose task … ?

Ss:　　(Two.)

T:　　How many stars for them?

Ss:　　(Three stars.)

T:　　Yes, I think so. Good job, kids.

Activity 2: Talk and think

A: Guess and say

T:　　We know what happened now. So, if you are the mother giraffe, what will you say?

S25:　(Hey bear! Go away!)

T:　　Oh! You're so angry!

S26:　(Haha. They are so cute.)

T:　　How kind you are! Thank you so much. The mother giraffe says … ?

Ss:　　(Look at that bear. It's so …)

T:　　Follow me! Naughty.

Ss:　　(Naughty.)

T:　　What's the meaning of "naughty"? A or B?

Ss:　　(A.)

T:　　You are right. The bear is so naughty!

B: Chant and say

T:　　Now, let's look at the bear again! What's the bear like? Can you think and tell me?

S27:　(It's short and fat.)

T:　　Good memory. Anything else?

S28:　(It's naughty.)

T:　　Yes, I think so. Now let's enjoy a chant about the bear. And then, let's chant together. OK?

Ss:　　[enjoy the chant and then chant together]

T:　　Do you like the naughty bear?

Ss:　　(No. /Yes.)

C: Think and judge

T:　　Look, is its behavior right?

Ss:　　(No.)

T:　　The naughty bear goes to other areas. Let's look at the pictures and judge! Yes or no. [acts it out] Ready?

Ss:　　(Go!)

T:　　Look at and say "hello" to animals.

Ss:　　(Yes!) [act it out]

T:　Climb trees in the zoo.

Ss:　(No!) [act it out]

T:　Throw rubbish to the animals.

Ss:　(No!) [act it out]

T:　Jump into the animal areas.

Ss:　(No!) [act it out]

T:　Feed the animals.

Ss:　(No!) [act it out]

T:　Can you do these things at the zoo?

Ss:　(No.)

T:　Good! Kids, when we go to the zoo, we should follow the rules and protect the animals.

Activity 3: Make a new story

A: Choose and discuss

T:　Look! We know the story at the giraffe area. Which area will the naughty bear go next? And what will he do? Please choose one area and discuss in groups. Four students in a group! Let's go!

Ss:　[work in groups]

B: Draw and say

T:　Kids, have you finished? Now try to draw some pictures for your story and make up a dialogue for the pictures. You can also draw some stick figures. And then you should write down the key words on your card and act it out.

Ss:　[work in groups]

C: Act it out

T:　OK. Time's up. Which group can share with us? You four, please. Come here!

G5:　[group performance]

T:　Wow, what an interesting story! I like it! Do you like their story?

S29:　(Yes, I do. It's funny.)

T:　Big hands for them!

作业布置

T:　Well, time flies! Here comes our homework. You have to listen to the dialogue on Page 24 and read it aloud. Then draw one animal you like and talk with your friends. Moreover, you can try to act out your story with your partners and make a vlog. So much for today, Bye!

教学设计①

（一）语篇研读

本课教学内容选自人教版英语三年级下册第三单元 At the zoo 的 A 部分 Let's talk 板块，该语篇属于"人与自然"主题范畴，内容涉及"动物的特征"。

What

教材语篇是一段发生在动物园的对话。在动物园游玩时，Miss White 带领 Amy 和 Zhang Peng 参观不同园区。他们先后发现了一只长颈鹿和一只小熊，并谈论它们的外形特点。与语篇匹配的两幅教材情景图显示，小熊先是躲藏在草丛中，后遭小长颈鹿追赶。但是原语篇没有讲述它们之间发生的具体故事。因此，教师利用教材留白自创语篇作为补充，具体内容为：调皮熊在逛动物园时，发现了一只可爱的小长颈鹿，想与之亲近，故用树枝逗它，后遭其追赶落荒而逃。

Why

语篇呈现了 Miss White，Amy 和 Zhang Peng 在动物园游玩的情景，Miss White 让孩子们观察并谈论长颈鹿的特征，随后他们发现了一只被追赶的小熊，并被它又矮又胖的形象逗乐。语篇可以引导学生欣赏不同动物的特别之处，从而增强其热爱动物的情感。此外，语篇呈现调皮熊在动物园捣蛋的情景，可用于引导学生判断调皮熊的游园行为是否得当，使其领悟文明参观动物园与遵守动物园规章制度的意义，从而增强其保护动物的意识。

How

Miss White，Amy 和 Zhang Peng 的简单对话构成了教学语篇的核心内容，谈论动物时涉及的核心语言有"Look at that … It's（so）…（and）…"；介绍动物名称的词汇有 giraffe、bear；描述动物的形容词包括 tall、short、fat。他们在谈论动物特征时使用了一般现在时，对话结构简单，易于理解。

（二）学情分析

本课授课对象为 Z 省某小学三年级学生，他们熟悉动物及动物园相关话题，对动物园里的动物充满好奇，在描述动物的名词、形容词上已有一定储备，且擅长观察不同动物的特征并乐于分享自己的观察结果。同时，本班学生对句型"Look at … It is（so）…（and）…"已有了初步了解，能够使用已学过的形容词，如 big、fat、long、cute、funny、cool 等，将句子补充完整以描述动物特征。但他们尚未理解该句型所传达的惊讶、赞叹之情，且对于不同动物的特征他们有更多内容想表达与交流，需要教师拓展教材语篇内容并提供语言支架来增

---

① 本教学设计由温州市新田园小学邱梦梦撰写。

进其语言理解、丰富其语言表达、促进其语言输出。此外,学生的形象思维能力较好,能够从不同角度观察动物的外形特征,也具有一定推断能力,能够通过图片猜测对话内容。但其逻辑思维能力较弱,需要借助教师的提示进行分类和总结。

(三) 教学目标

通过本课时的学习,学生能够:

1. 在看、听、说的活动中,获取、梳理对话所涉及的动物及其特征,理解对话内容;

2. 在教师的帮助下,仔细观察动物,运用核心句型"Look at that … It's(so)…(and)…"描述动物的特征,并借助人与动物角色转换,进行角色模拟对话交流;

3. 在教师的引导下,仔细观察两幅教材情景图,展开想象,活用核心句型推测留白故事发展,并能分角色表演对话;

4. 分析、评价调皮熊在动物园区的行为是否恰当,在小组内交流并创编调皮熊在其他园区发生的小故事,向全班表演故事。

(四) 教学流程

图1

学生在本节课共经历三个学习阶段。第一阶段为感知语境,教师引导学生通过图片观察、视听结合等方式,将自身知识经验带入学习过程,理解语篇情境并习得核心语言。第二阶段为代入角色,教师引导学生尝试站在动物的角度进行角色扮演,以此加深对语篇的理解并内化所学语言。第三阶段为创编故事,教师引导学生先通过角色扮演的方式再现调皮熊和小长颈鹿发生的小故事,再以小组合作的方式展开讨论并活用所学语言创编新故事,实现超越语篇的输出。

(五) 教学过程

步骤一 基于语篇,感知语境,学习语言(11分钟)

Activity 1: Enjoy a song (1 min)

Students enjoy a song "At the Zoo" with actions and think about what they see in the song.

Lyrics

At the Zoo

Cat is fast. Rat is fat.

See them run. Fun! Fun! Fun!

Monkey is short. Giraffe is tall.

See them play with the ball.

【设计说明】 通过节奏欢快的歌曲,活跃课堂氛围,调动学生参与学习的积极性,并创设情境引出本课时的话题,让学生在情境中初步感知本课时的核心语言。

Activity 2: Look and think (3 mins)

A: Let's say

Students observe the pictures of parts of different animals, like an elephant's ear, a panda's body, a monkey's tail and a giraffe's tail, and then review the names of animals and get ready for the topic.

B: Let's think

Students predict and check where these animals are. Then they think about what other animals they can see at the zoo.

【设计说明】 教师通过呈现动物身体部位的图片,让学生回忆关于动物的单词并猜测这些动物会在哪里,激活旧知。同时引导学生感知本课语境,导入本课时话题"At the zoo",为学生的语言学习做好充分准备。

【效果评价】 教师观察学生能否参与互动和交流,主动分享自己对动物主题已有的知识和经验,并根据学生猜测地点的合理性,调整提问方式,进行追问或给予鼓励。

Activity 3: Look and say (2 mins)

Students observe the picture and guess what Mike will say about the elephant. Then they listen to the dialogue, check the answer and practise the new expression "It's so big".

【设计说明】 通过观察图片中大象的外形特征(见图2),让学生运用已学的 big、fat 等词来形容大象,激活学生已有的知识和经验,建立与语篇之间的关联,培养学生"看"的能力和利用插图信息进行推断的能力。再通过听力任务,使学生感知核心句型"Look at that … It's (so) …"所表达的意义,体会该对话所包含的惊讶、感叹之情,为其学习理解核心语言做好铺垫。

图2

【效果评价】 教师观察学生使用的形容词是否合适,把握学生对所学语言的感知情况。

Activity 4: Choose and say (3 mins)

Students look at the map of the zoo and choose one animal to talk about with partners, and then show the dialogue in class. The dialogue pattern will be provided.

图3

【设计说明】 教师提供句型框架和参考词汇,指导学生观察图片并描述动物的外形特征(见图3),帮助其初步感知与运用核心句型"Look at that ... It's (so) ... (and) ..."来描述动物特征。

【效果评价】 教师观察学生能否使用目标语言描述所选动物,并结合学生的能力水平给予指导或鼓励。

Activity 5: Listen and choose (2 mins)

Students look at the map and predict which area Miss White, Amy and Zhang Peng will go next. Then they listen to the dialogue and choose the right answer on the learning sheet.

Transcript

Miss White: Look! What's that?

Zhang Peng: Wow, it's so tall.

Amy: Yes. It's yellow and brown.

Zhang Peng: Look at that mouth. It's so long.

图 4

【设计说明】 通过看图猜测和听音选择(见图4),教师可以培养学生猜测判断的能力和根据特定问题听取关键信息的能力,引导学生关注目标词汇,如动物名称 giraffe,与描述动物外貌特征的表达,如 tall、yellow and brown、a long mouth 等。

【效果评价】 教师根据学生猜测参观路线的合理性,及时给予指导和反馈;教师观察学生学习单的完成情况,判断其能否准确获取信息。

步骤二 深入语篇,代入角色,应用语言(12分钟)

Activity 1: Guess and say (2 mins)

Students think and guess what Miss White and Zhang Peng are talking about. Then they talk and discuss with partners. At last, they listen to the dialogue, check the answers and do the pattern drills.

【设计说明】 通过观察图片(见图5),教师让学生猜测 Miss White 和 Zhang Peng 之间的对话,引导学生运用所学推测对话内容,促进其进一步内化所学语言;通过同伴合作的方式,帮助学生积极思考,提高合作学习能力;最后,通过听音频,引导学生获取对话信息并操练目标句型"Look at that ... It is (so) ..."。

【效果评价】 教师观察学生猜测对话内容的合理性和运用核心句型进行表达的准确性,必要时提供帮助。

图 5

Activity 2: Think and guess (3 mins)

Students look at the picture and guess what the mother giraffe and the baby giraffe will talk about when they see Miss White, Zhang Peng and Amy. Then they discuss with their partners.

图 6

【设计说明】 通过从游客视角到动物视角的转换(见图6),教师让学生自主想象并猜测对话内容,帮助学生回忆并运用已有语言去架构对话,使其创造性思维能力在有趣的想象活动中得到发展。

【效果评价】 教师观察学生能否转换视角并合理运用语言进行问答与交流,根据学生的表现给予必要的指导和反馈。

Activity 3: Listen and answer (2 mins)

Students look at the moving grass and guess "Who's there?". Then they listen to the dialogue and check the answer.

图 7

【设计说明】 教师通过动画效果激发学生的好奇心(见图7),引导学生带着问题精听教材配套的音频资源,帮助其进一步理解语篇内容并关注到本课"线索"——调皮熊,培养学生获取信息的能力,并为后面的教学活动做好铺垫。

Activity 4: Watch and choose (2 mins)

Students watch the video and choose the right answer (It's short and fat. /It's tall and fat.) to the question "What's it like?" on the learning sheet.

【设计说明】 教师利用教材配套的视频资源,为学生提供视听机会,帮助学生进一步理解对话情境,并获取调皮熊具体的外形特征。

【效果评价】 教师观察学生能否选出正确的答案,根据学生的回答给予提示和指导。

Activity 5: Listen and imitate (3 mins)

Students listen to the tape carefully and try to mark the tones. Then they listen again and repeat the dialogue with correct pronunciation, intonation and rhythm.

【设计说明】 首先,通过听音标记的方式,教师引导学生关注语音、语调与节奏,培养学生"听"的能力和语言感受能力。接着,通过听音跟读,引导学生模仿跟读对话内容,帮助学生内化所学语言。

【效果评价】 教师根据学生朗读对话的情况,确定其模仿能力和语言感受能力,必要时给予指导或鼓励。

步骤三 超越语篇,创编故事,活用语言(17分钟)

Activity 1: Read a new story (7 mins)

A: Guess and enjoy (2 mins)

Students look at the question mark in the picture and guess what the mother giraffe is thinking of. Then they try to find out the reason why the baby giraffe is chasing the running bear and guess what happens. After guessing, they enjoy a new story and check their guess.

图 8

【设计说明】　通过观察教材插图信息(见图 8),学生聚焦图中的问号并思考其含义;然后通过欣赏教师创编的教材留白环节故事"A naughty bear at the zoo",思考推测调皮熊和小长颈鹿之间到底发生了什么有趣的故事。在此过程中,教师不仅培养了学生推测与想象的能力,同时也为学生提供了更多的视听机会。

【效果评价】　教师观察学生能否根据情境展开想象,并根据学生所猜测的故事内容的合理程度,给予必要的提示和指导。

B: Listen and repeat (1 min)

Students listen to the tape and repeat with correct pronunciation, intonation, rhythm, emotions, facial expressions and body movements.

图 9

【设计说明】 通过朗读新编故事(见图9),并模仿角色的表情与肢体动作,学生能感知语音、语调、节奏与情感,在情境中内化所学语言。

【效果评价】 教师观察学生能否深入理解角色,运用正确的表情和肢体动作进行角色扮演,根据学生的表现给予指导或鼓励。

C: Act out the story (4 mins)

Students choose one task and act out the dialogue in pairs. One will be the naughty bear, and the other will be the baby giraffe. They evaluate others' performance from three aspects: Can they read fluently? Can they act vividly? Can they make a new dialogue?

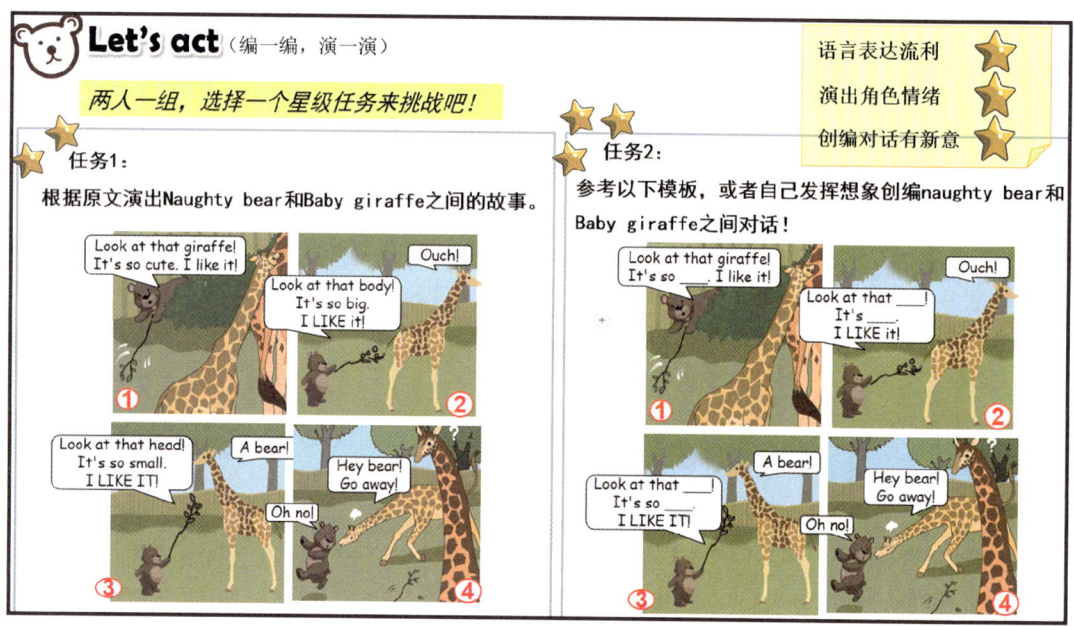

图 10

【设计说明】 教师利用小熊和长颈鹿的头饰与自制的小树枝道具,引导学生进行角色扮演,激发学生表演欲,增加其角色代入感,带动课堂的氛围。其中,教师基于学生的能力水平设置两个不同难度的表演任务(见图10),尊重学生个体的差异性的同时,调动学生的学习积极性。

【效果评价】 教师观察学生能否深入角色进行扮演,能否借助评价标准从不同方面对同伴的表演进行评价,并根据学生的表现给予指导和反馈。

Activity 2: Talk and think (3 mins)

A: Guess and say (1 min)

Students look at the picture and guess what adjective the mother giraffe will use to describe the naughty bear when she sees him teasing her baby. Then students learn the correct answer.

图 11

B: Chant and say（1 min）

Students think about what the bear is like and chant together.

Lyrics

The bear is short.

The bear is fat.

The bear is naughty.

A naughty bear!

C: Think and judge（1 min）

Students look at the pictures where the bear is in different areas at the zoo and judge his behavior. Then they think about the rules at the zoo.

图 12

【设计说明】 通过角色代入的活动（见图11），教师引导学生体会小熊的调皮，理解生词"naughty"的含义，从而拓展和丰富学生的词汇量；并通过自编韵文，活跃课堂氛围，强化学生的语言记忆；再通过观看小熊在参观动物园时的种种行为（见图12），引导学生思考和判断对错，使其懂得游园时要爱护动物的道理。

【效果评价】 教师观察学生能否使用正确的语音、语调和节奏演绎出歌谣，能否对调皮熊在园区的种种行为做出正确的判断，并根据学生的表现给予反馈与引导。

Activity 3: Make a new story (7 mins)

A: Choose and discuss (1 min)

Students think about what the naughty bear will do, and then choose one animal area and discuss the new story in groups of four.

B: Draw and say (3 mins)

Students draw 2 – 4 pictures for the story and make up a dialogue with the expressions "Look at that … It's …". Since time is limited, they can draw some stick figures for the story. In case that some students may have difficulty making up a dialogue, the teacher provides some words and sentence patterns on the learning sheet.

图 13

C: Act it out (3 mins)

Students show the new story in the class.

【设计说明】 通过小组合作创编小熊在其他园区的故事（见图13），教师引导学生进行超越语篇、联系生活的对话活动，培养学生在真实情境中运用所学的语言和文化知识解决问题的能力，深化学生对本课主题意义的认知——树立正确的对待动物的态度，懂得遵守动物园规则。

【效果评价】 教师观察学生在小组合作中运用所学语言讨论故事发展及创作连环画的情况,给予必要的指导和鼓励,并根据学生向全班展示创编对话时的表现,评估教与学的成效。

(六) 板书设计

图 14

【设计说明】 板书包括课题名称与课堂要点。课堂要点可分为四个部分:板书的中间部分是本节课的核心句型,借助四线三格,学生能关注所学句子的正确书写方式。板书左边是参观动物园的路线及相应的生词,清晰地呈现了本节课的故事发展。板书的右边分别列举了有关外形、颜色、性格的形容词,拓展丰富学生的词汇,使其语言表达多样化。板书的下方呈现了各种形态的动物图片,与本课语篇、话题相呼应,有利于学生感知本课主旨。通过生成的板书,学生能自主地进行回顾和复习。

(七) 作业设计

*1. Listen to the dialogue on Page 24 and read it aloud.

**2. Draw an animal you like and talk with friends.

***3. Act out the story "Naughty Bear at the _____ Area" with partners and try to take a vlog.

【设计说明】 作业依据学生的特点分层布置,包括基础性作业和拓展性作业。基础性作业中的一星作业旨在引导学生及时巩固核心语言;二星作业旨在引导学生观察动物,然后用简笔画的方式将其生动形象地展现出来,并运用所学语言进行真实交流。三星作业旨在引导学生通过小组合作完善课上创编的绘本故事,完成表演拍摄,提升其语言表达能力,和创新、交际、协作的能力。

(八) 教学反思

本节课教师以"A naughty bear"作为贯穿整堂课的"线索",结合单元主题"Loving animals",以"A naughty bear at the zoo"这一话题引出本课内容。本课教学通过看、听、说、演等多样的活动,以学为中心,以不断滚动的旧知丰富新知,以层层递进的问题促进思维的发展,以创新有趣的故事激发学习的内驱力,由易到难,循序渐进地发展学生的学习能力。

1. 巧联视听,丰富语言表达

教师在本节课中嵌入多种"看"的活动,使之与"听"的活动紧密结合,借此调动学生已有的知识经验储备,产生知识的"滚雪球"效应,丰富了学生的语言表达。在本节课中,教师首先通过直观的视听歌曲和看图游戏引导学生回忆与本课主题相关的词汇,如动物、颜色、身体部位,以及描述动物特征的形容词等。在学生初步感知并运用核心句型描述动物特征后,教师通过图片、动画效果等视觉刺激,引导学生带着问题精听教材和自编音频资源,并代入角色进行对话表演,促进目标语言的输出。然后,教师提供视听结合的自编故事与动物园里其他动物的图片,给予学生创编对话的语言支架与选择空间,从而进一步丰富和拓展其语言表达。

2. 巧设问题,提高思维品质

教师以教材图示中的问号串联各个教学任务,让学生在思考问题和解决问题的过程中习得目标语言,提高思维品质。教材图示中的问号意在引发学生思考调皮熊和小长颈鹿之间发生的故事并判断调皮熊在动物园的行为是否得当。为了激发学生思考,教师首先通过让学生猜测在教材所给情境中 Miss White 和 Zhang Peng 会谈论什么,引导其运用核心语言去描述动物的特征,并在听力过程中初步感知对话语篇,验证预测。随后,教师利用图标切换视角,引导学生站在动物的角度观察游客,思考两只长颈鹿之间的对话内容,综合运用所学语言描述游客的外貌特征。最后,教师引导学生推测小熊和小鹿之间发生的故事,思考小熊到底做了什么惹怒小鹿,遭受追赶,并反思自己在日常游园时的行为是否得当,从而拓展其思维的深度和广度。

3. 巧用留白,实现创新学习

教师始终以学为中心,利用教材两幅情景图之间的留白空间——A naughty bear at the zoo,推动学生展开迁移创新。教师首先引导学生观察两幅教材情景图中小熊前后动作、表情的变化,激发他们的好奇心来猜测其中发生的故事,帮助学生进行创新,运用目标语言来描述动物的外貌特征,促进其能力向素养的转化。通过视觉、听觉的直观感受和对小鹿外形的多角度描述,学生能够体会到小熊的调皮捣蛋,增强角色代入感。通过模仿跟读留白故事,学生能够巩固对目标语言的掌握。然后,教师指导学生采取同伴合作的方式自主演绎留白小故事,促进其目标语言的内化与拓展。最后,教师引导学生进行小组合作,开放性地讨论调皮熊在动物园还会发生什么小故事,并创编连环画和对话,通过描述不同动物的外形特点来引发学生的创新内驱力,提升学习的乐趣。

（九）附件

学　习　单

091

续 表

三星任务:可以参考以下模板,或者自己发挥想象创编 Naughty bear 和
Baby giraffe 之间对话!

任务:

小组评价:

We can get _____ ★

语言表达流利

演出角色情绪 ★

创编对话有新意 ★

形容词:big, fat, small tall, cute funny, cool, round(圆的), red, yellow, brown, black ....

身体部位:eye, ear, mouth, nose, neck(脖子), leg, body, tail(尾巴)

任务四:编一编,画一画。

四人小组合作,设计 **Naughty bear** 故事,并把它画出来。

小组互评:

You can get _____ ★

语言表达流利

演出角色情绪

创编对话有新意

动物:elephant, tiger, bird, rabbit, monkey, panda, pig, duck …

句型:

Look at the/that/this …

It's (so) … (and …)

身体部位:eye, ear, mouth, nose, body, leg, neck (脖子), tail (尾巴)

I like …

I want to …

Oh no!

Ouch!

形容词:big, fat, small, tall, cute, funny, cool, round (圆的), red, yellow, brown, black …

Sorry.

…

课例 4

PEP B7 U5 What does he do?
(Part B *Let's talk*)

说课视频

Hello, everyone! I'm Jelly. It's my great honor to present my lesson plan here. My presentation will cover three aspects, namely, learning objectives, learning process and learning effects.

Learning objectives

Now, let's come to the first part, learning objectives. As we know, the learning objectives are based on the analysis of learning material and learners. So first of all, let's have a look at the learning material.

The learning material is from PEP Book 7 Unit 5 *What does he do?* Part B *Let's talk*. The theme of this dialogue is *man and society*, concerning *common occupations and people's life*.

What

The learning material is a dialogue between Mike and Xiao Yu on their way home. They talk about Mike's uncle's job, as well as his workplace, ways to go to work and lifestyle. Also, the dialogue conveys the positive idea that "we should study hard and stay healthy".

Why

This text is based on the topic of occupation. The specific information and the positive evaluation of jobs and lives can guide students to understand jobs from different perspectives, and make them think about the meaning of "work hard and stay healthy", thus realizing that they should keep healthy living habits while studying hard.

How

It's a typical dialogue that is closely related to students' daily life. Mike and Xiao Yu use

---

① 本说课稿由温州市仰义第二小学潘金琳撰写。

the present simple tense and the third person singular form when talking about jobs. Meanwhile, the core sentence patterns are "Where does he/she work? He/She works … ", "How does he/she go to work? He/She goes to work … ", and important words and phrases include "fisherman" "police officer" "at sea" "on a boat" "by car" "by bike". These expressions and sentence patterns can help students to describe people's jobs, workplaces and ways to go to work.

Now, it's time to take a closer look at the learners. The students are sixth graders from a common primary school in Z Province. They are familiar with the topic, "jobs", and have their own career expectations. But they don't have chances to deeply talk about this topic in English with their peers. Thus, students show a strong desire to learn.

Moreover, the students can extract and sort out key information purposefully through intensive and extensive listening activities. However, they still have some difficulties refining and summarizing the thematic meaning of the text. The teacher needs to provide some pictures and design appropriate activities, such as asking and answering questions independently.

Also, as students in Grade 6, they have learnt some words and sentence patterns about jobs, places, ways to go to work and daily activities, and they are able to carry out simple communication with others. But students are not proficient in using the third person singular form in the simple present tense to communicate. So multiple rounds of practice should be carried out to promote the internalization and output of the target language.

Based on the above analysis, the following learning objectives are set. By the end of this lesson, students will be able to:

1. extract specific information mentioned in the dialogue like people's jobs, workplaces, ways to go to work and lifestyles, and understand its content through activities like viewing, listening and talking.

2. use the sentence patterns "Where does he/she work? He/She works … ", "How does he/she go to work? He/She goes to work … " to ask and answer questions about the jobs, and then act out the dialogue in the specific context.

3. make comments on the job and lifestyle of Mike's uncle, and realize that it is important to "work hard and stay healthy".

4. make up a dialogue about different jobs in real life with partners by using some sentence patterns.

Learning process

Now let's move on to the description of learning process. In this lesson, the educational values contained in the discourse have been fully explored. Under the guidance of the Activity-based Approach to English Learning, the following four stages are set to carry out the meaningful learning process.

The first stage is Recall and Activate Prior Knowledge.

The aim of this stage is to activate students' background knowledge. Students' attention and interest will be activated and motivated through Sing a song and Let's say. Firstly, students will sing the song "Jobs", and think about the topic of the song. Then they will talk about their dream jobs with the help of pictures and short sentence structures. These two activities help students preliminarily establish the connection between job and self, and lay a good foundation for the following learning process. I can observe how the students express their dream jobs to evaluate their performance.

In the second stage, Perceive and Interpret the Text, four activities are designed.

Activity 1 is Listen, answer and tick. Students will be required to listen to the dialogue twice. For the first time, they will listen and understand the general information by answering the simple question "Who's that man?". For the second time, the students will listen and identify the specific information such as uncle's appearance, job and ways to go to work by ticking out the right answers on the worksheet. It helps students have a better understanding of the new sentence patterns, and also sets up the situation for further study.

The second activity is Look and say. Students will first look at a picture of Mike's uncle from the textbook, then make some description of the picture and have a prediction with short sentences. After that, they will discuss in groups and write down some questions about Mike's uncle on the cards. Some cards of questions will be listed on the blackboard, and then students will read them. In this activity, the picture in the text is fully used to foster students' thinking quality.

Activity 3 is Watch and find. Students will check the questions by watching the video of the dialogue. These questions, the language focus of this lesson, will be left on the blackboard. I will give timely guidance and evaluation according to students' specific answers to the questions.

Activity 4 is Read and say. It aims to help students learn the sentence structures in a communicative context. Students will first read the dialogue aloud to get the right answers to the questions on the blackboard, then work in pairs to check the answers through a short dialogue. The dialogue pattern will be provided. Meanwhile, students will pay attention to the third person singular form while summarizing the information of Mike's uncle. I will observe whether students are able to use the core language in asking and answering questions, and provide the necessary assistance based on their performance.

There are three activities in the third stage, Internalize and Use Language.

Activity 1 is Listen, think and say. Students will get more details about Mike's uncle by looking at the pictures and listening to the text, so that they will think more deeply and express their opinions freely about his job and lifestyle. I can observe whether students can correctly understand the intrinsic meaning of the text and express personal opinions, and give comments as well as feedback if necessary.

After that, students will listen to the tape and repeat it with correct pronunciation, intonation and rhythm. In this way, they can deepen their understanding of the dialogue and internalize the language they have learnt.

Then, students will do a role-play with partners, and they need to evaluate each other's performance according to the checklist from these three aspects. Whether the students will do the role-play according to the requirements of the checklist will be assessed. If not, I will give some hints.

Then here comes the fourth stage, Analyze and Use Language.

In the previous activities, students can get a deep impression about the police officer and fisherman, the jobs mentioned in the dialogue. In the last stage, the context of the activities will return to the real life, allowing students to know more about other jobs. Students will transfer what they have learnt to the real-life context with the help of the sentence structures, which will deepen their understanding of the thematic meaning. Firstly, students will watch a micro-video to get more information about different people's jobs in daily life. After that, students will express their own opinions of the jobs. Then they will discuss and create a new dialogue with partners by using the sentence structures in this lesson and later show the dialogue to the whole class. During the process, students can use the language they have learned to exchange their opinions on their careers. Whether they can create dialogues based on the language and opinions would be assessed, and I will give appropriate assistance according to their performance.

After class, there are two assignments for students. First, they are required to listen to the dialogue on Page 50 and read it aloud. So they can review what they have learnt in this lesson. Second, optionally, students are asked to introduce one person's job, which can encourage them to use the language they have learnt to communicate in real life.

As for blackboard design, the sentence patterns are presented clearly. Key questions written and discussed by students are shown on the left side. On the right side is the answer part, which is about the description and the relevant information of the job. At the bottom, the thematic meaning of this lesson is presented. The content of the blackboard is gradually generated during the learning process, which helps students to learn and use the core language to communicate and express in the context.

Learning effects

In the end, I'd like to highlight the achievement of my lesson.

The first one is the attempt to link listening and viewing. In this lesson, the listening and viewing activities are combined many times, which enables students to extract and sort out the required information more quickly and more accurately and obtain sufficient input of the target language in the context. It can not only enhance students' interest in learning, but also promote their language internalization and help them make adequate preparations for the following meaningful and creative output.

The second highlight is the integration of thinking and speaking. In this lesson, students' "speaking" is generated through different thinking activities, which helps them generate high-quality language output in the language learning spiral. With the help of pictures, students are inspired to recall and predict based on what they have learnt and try to understand the text. Besides, through continuous questions, the teacher guides students to analyze and refine the thematic meaning, and to internalize thematic meaning through communication. In addition, the teacher helps students expand their thinking, express their views and make comments on different people's jobs and lifestyles, thereby promotes their high-quality language output, and helps form a correct attitude and value judgment towards job and life.

That's all for my presentation. Thanks for watching!

试课实录①

试课视频

步骤一　看图说话，回忆与激活旧知（3 分钟）

Activity 1: Sing a song

T:　Hi, boys and girls, let's begin our class. First, let's sing together.

Ss:　[sing the song]

T:　Wow! What a nice song! Tell me, what's the song about?

Ss:　(Jobs.)

T:　It's about jobs. Yes!

Activity 2: Let's say

T:　Boys and girls, look, Binbin wants to be a scientist. Just like his Grandpa, hard-working and great. Amy wants to be a pilot. Just like her father, strong and brave. What about you? What do you want to be? Can you talk about it? You please.

S1:　(I want to be a teacher. Just like my mother, kind and nice.)

T:　Cool! I think you will be a very good teacher. You try.

S2:　(I want to be a doctor. Just like my father, helpful and super.)

T:　Super!

步骤二　听说结合，感知与梳理语篇（13 分钟）

Activity 1: Listen, answer and tick

T:　Boys and girls, different people have different jobs. Look! Mike and Xiao Yu are talking about jobs, too. Look, the question is "who's that man?". Listen carefully!

Ss:　[listen to the recording]

---

① 本试课稿由温州市仰义第二小学潘金琳撰写。

T: Have you got the answers?

S3: (He's Xiao Yu's uncle.)

T: Yes! He is Xiao Yu's uncle. Boys and girls, I have more questions for you. Look! What's he like? What does he do? How does he go to work? With these questions, let's listen again and tick the answers. This task is on your worksheet, Task 1. Take out your pens. Are you ready? Here we go!

T: Finished? Let's check the answers. What's he like? He is … ? You please.

S4: (He's big and tall.)

T: Yes! And what does he do? You try.

S5: (He's a police officer.)

T: Yes, he's a police officer. How does he go to work? Wow, it's a very long sentence for you. Who can have a try? Yes, the girl.

S6: (He goes to work by car.)

T: Excellent! Boys and girls, now, we know Xiao Yu's uncle. Let's talk about him.

T & Ss: (Xiao Yu's uncle is big and tall. He's a police officer. He goes to work by car.)

Activity 2: Look and say

T: Now, we know Xiao Yu's uncle. What about Mike's uncle? Look at the picture, what do you see? You try.

S7: (I see a big fish.)

T: Oh, a big fish. It's very yummy. You try.

S8: (I see Mike's uncle is on the big boat.)

T: Yeah, you have sharp eyes. From the picture, what do you think of Mike's uncle?

S9: (Maybe he's s fisherman.)

T: Maybe he's a fisherman. Good guess!

S10: (I think he likes fish very much. He looks so happy.)

T: Wow, what do you wonder? Do you have questions about Mike's uncle? Now, it's your turn. You can work in groups, and write down one or two questions about Mike's uncle. Look! You get many cards, and you can write down the questions here. OK? Ready? Go!

Ss: [work in groups]

T: Time's up. Boys and girls, look! I've got so many questions from you. Let's take a look.

T & Ss: (How old is he?)

T & Ss: (What does he do?)

T & Ss: (How does he go to work?)

T & Ss: (Where does he work?)

Activity 3: Watch and find

T:　Wow, so many questions. Now, let's watch the video, and try to find out the answers. OK?

Ss:　(OK!)

T:　Here we go!

Ss:　[watch the video]

T:　Now, let's check. The first one, how old is he?

Ss:　(We don't know.)

T:　Not mentioned. OK, let's pass this question. Bye. And what does he do?

Ss:　(He's a fisherman.)

T:　Em, how does he go to work?

Ss:　(By bike.)

T:　By bike? Maybe! And this one, where does he work?

Ss:　(He works at sea, on the boat.)

T:　At sea? On the boat? OK!

Activity 4: Read and say

T:　Now we have three questions here. Let's read and check. This task is on your worksheet, Task 2. Step 1, please read it aloud by yourself. Then Step 2, ask and answer with your partner. Then you will check yes or no. Clear? Here we go!

Ss:　[read alone first, then work in pairs]

T:　Time's up! Any volunteers? Just make a simple dialogue. You two, please.

S11 & S12:　[make the dialogue]

T:　Big hands for them. Boys and girls, are they right? Let's check together.

T:　What does he do?

Ss:　(He's a fisherman.)

T:　Where does he work?

Ss:　(He works at sea.)

T:　Look, he sees lots of fish every day. And also he … ?

Ss:　[listen to the recording]

T:　He works on a boat. So we can say, he works at sea, on a boat. How does he go to work?

Ss:　(He goes to work by bike.)

T:　Now, boys and girls, let's practise together. Boys, you are Mike. Girls, you're Xiao Yu. Let's make a dialogue. Ready? Go!

Ss:　[make the dialogue]

T:　Wow, big hands for yourselves. Great! Now, we know Mike's uncle. Let's talk about him.

T & Ss: (Mike's uncle is a fisherman. He works at sea, on a boat. He goes to work by bike.)

步骤三 由听到演,内化与运用语言(8分钟)

Activity 1: Listen, think and say

T: Look! These are about Mike's uncle. Do you want to know more about him? Let's listen.

Ss: [listen to the recording]

T: Now, what do you think of his job and life? Do you have any ideas? You try.

S13: (He's very hard-working.)

T: Yes! He even works at night. He's very hard-working. And you try.

S14: (He is very healthy.)

T: He has a very healthy life. Boys and girls, Mike and Xiao Yu have the same idea with you. Let's listen.

Ss: [listen to the recording]

T: He works very hard and stays healthy. Try again, work hard and stay healthy.

Ss: (Work hard and stay healthy.)

T: Mike's uncle works very hard and stays healthy. What does Xiao Yu say?

Ss: (We should study hard and stay healthy, too.)

T: We should study hard and stay healthy, too. Why?

Ss: (Mike and Xiao Yu are students.)

T: Yes, because Mike and Xiao Yu are students, and we are students, too. Boys and girls, what else should you do as students? Think about it. You please.

S15: (We should do some sports.)

T: Yes, we should do some sports every day. Good! You please.

S16: (We should eat healthy food.)

T: We should eat healthy food. Great! So as students, we should do some sports, eat healthy food and study hard, then we will have a healthy life. Right?

Ss: (Yes.)

Activity 2: Listen and imitate

T: Boys and girls, now, please open your book, listen and imitate. Ready? Go!

Ss: [listen to the recording and imitate]

T: Boys and girls, pay attention to these sentences. Look! There are many rising tones. Listen carefully.

Ss: [listen to the recording and imitate]

T: Good voices.

Activity 3: Do a role-play

T:　Now, it's your turn. Let's have a role-play. Please act out the dialogue correctly, fluently and vividly, OK? Here we go!

Ss:　[act out the dialogue]

T:　Time's up. Any volunteers? Yes, you two.

S17 & S18:　[act out the dialogue]

T:　Wow, big hands for them. How many stars can they get?

Ss:　(Three stars.)

T:　Three stars? Super!

步骤四　先看后说，分析与活用语言（10 分钟）

Activity 1: Watch and say

T:　Boys and girls, different people have different jobs and lives. Now, let's enjoy a video, and please share your opinions on their lives and jobs. OK? Here we go!

Ss:　[watch a video]

T:　Do you have any ideas about their jobs and lives?

S19:　(Mr Yang works hard and has a super life.)

T:　Yes! What about the others? I want to talk about Mrs Blue's job. Who can talk with me? Any volunteers? You, please. [presents a dialogue] I'm A. You're B. OK?

S20:　(OK.)

T:　Go! Mrs Blue is a scientist.

S20:　(Where does she work?)

T:　She works in a university.

S20:　(How does she go to work?)

T:　She goes to work on foot.

S20:　(She's very hard-working.)

T:　Yes! She works very hard and stays healthy.

Activity 2: Think and talk

T:　What about the others? Boys and girls, now it's your turn. This task is from your worksheet, Task 3. There are two levels for you. Level One, you can choose one person and talk about his or her life and job. Level Two, please talk about one of your family members, and try to say more. Look at the worksheet! There is a sentence bank and a word bank for you, OK? Go!

Ss:　[work in pairs]

T:　Time's up! Who can have a try? You two, please.

S21 & S22:　[perform in pair]

T:　Wow! Big hands for them. Boys and girls, what does his father do?

Ss: (He's a doctor.)

T & Ss: (And he works in the hospital. He goes to work on foot. He has a healthy life. Yes! Big hands for them.)

T: Boys and girls, different people have different jobs and lives, and I hope you study very hard, and make your dream come true. OK?

Ss: (OK!)

作业布置

T: Look! This is your homework. For one star, listen to the dialogue on Page 50 and read it aloud. For two stars, introduce the job of a person around us. It's time to say goodbye. Bye, boys and girls.

Ss: (Bye!)

配套课件

教学设计①

(一) 语篇研读

本课教学内容选自人教版英语六年级上册第五单元 What does he do? B 部分 Let's talk 板块。该语篇属于"人与社会"主题范畴,内容涉及"常见职业与人们的生活"。

What

本课是一节对话课,语篇为小学生日常对话,内容围绕学生与同伴谈论家人的职业、工作地点、出行方式和日常活动展开。Mike 和 Xiao Yu 在回家路上,谈论 Mike 叔叔的职业相关信息及"勤奋工作,健康生活"的积极生活状态,Xiao Yu 表示也要"勤奋学习,健康生活"。

Why

该语篇拓展和延伸了职业这一主题,语篇中的职业具体信息,以及对职业与生活的积极评价等有助于学生从不同角度认识职业,思考"勤奋工作,健康生活"的意义,进而明白在勤奋学习的同时,也要养成健康的生活习惯的道理。

How

该语篇是比较典型的学生日常生活对话。Mike 和 Xiao Yu 在谈论家人职业相关信息时使用了一般现在时,涉及第三人称单数的表达。对话中涉及职业信息交流的核心语言有 "Where does he/she work? He/She works …" "How does he/she go to work? He/She goes to work …";介绍职业、工作地点及出行方式的词汇和短语有 fisherman、police officer、at sea、on a boat、by car、by bike 等。

---

① 本教学设计由温州市仰义第二小学潘金琳撰写。

（二）学情分析

本节课的授课对象为 Z 省某小学六年级学生,他们对"职业"这一话题较为熟悉,有自己的职业期待,但尚未用英语深度学习这一话题,因而对本课时学习内容表现出较强的求知欲。同时,在听力过程中,学生能通过精听与泛听,有目的地提取和梳理语篇关键信息。但他们在提炼和概括语篇主题内容上存在一定困难,教师可通过提供图片、设计学生自主提问与解决等活动,发展他们的思维与认知水平。此外,学生已经积累了一些关于职业、地点、出行方式、日常活动主题的核心词汇与句式,能够与他人开展简单的交流,但尚不能熟练运用一般现在时的第三人称单数形式交流相关职业信息。教师需设计多轮操练活动,帮助学生实现目标语言的内化和输出。

（三）教学目标

通过本课时的学习,学生能够:

1. 在看、听、说活动中,获取 Mike 和 Xiao Yu 在对话中谈到的职业、工作单位、出行方式与人物的生活状态等信息,理解对话内容;

2. 在具体语境中,运用核心句型"Where does he/she work? He/She works …" "How does he/she go to work? He/She goes to work by …"与同伴分角色表演对话;

3. 简要评价对话中 Mike 叔叔的职业及生活状态,感悟"勤奋工作,健康生活"的意义;

4. 与同伴谈论实际生活中不同人物的职业信息及工作、生活状态,以创编对话的方式呈现交流结果,表达观点。

（四）教学流程

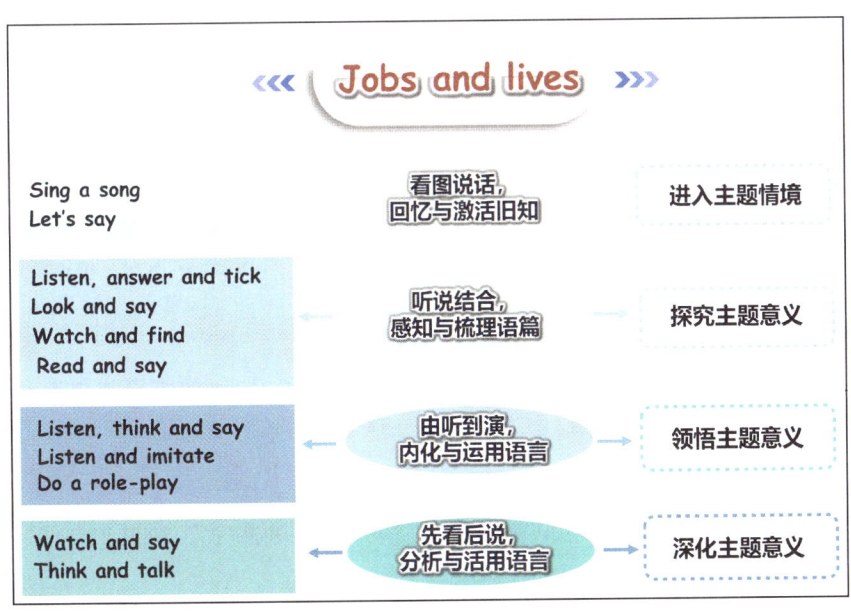

图 1

学生在本节课围绕主题意义的深度探究经历了四个学习阶段。第一阶段,看图说话,回忆与激活旧知。教师通过吟唱歌曲、看图说话等活动,创设了谈论职业的情境,带入本课时的学习主题。第二阶段,听说结合,感知与梳理语篇。教师基于对话语篇,引导学生通过不同层次的听、看、说等活动理解主旨大意,了解 Mike 叔叔的职业及相关信息,形成初步认识,并在语境中逐步学习目标句型。第三阶段,由听到演,内化与运用语言。教师以"听—看"结合的方式输入辅助语篇,通过连续性的问题引导学生进一步分析对话中 Mike 叔叔的职业及生活状态,提炼"勤奋工作,健康生活"的主题意义,加深对语篇的理解;通过深入角色演绎对话,在语境中内化和运用目标语言,进一步领悟主题意义。第四阶段,先看后说,分析与活用语言。学生观看视频,独立思考并简要评价不同人物的职业及生活状态,深化对主题意义的理解;通过与同伴创编对话,联系生活实际,借助语言支架迁移所学,生成对主题的深层认知和价值判断,发展语用能力。

(五)教学过程

步骤一 **看图说话,回忆与激活旧知**(3分钟)

Activity 1: Sing a song (1 min)

Students sing the song "Jobs" and think about the topic of the song.

Lyrics

Jobs

Firefighter, soccer player, teacher, doctor, painter, chef, police officer, astronaut, what do you want to be?

What do you want to be?

I want to be a teacher. Let's learn something fun.

I want to be a soccer player. Let's shoot the ball.

How about you?

I want to be a doctor. I will make you get better.

I want to be a firefighter. I will save you. Wait!

Firefighter, soccer player, teacher, doctor, painter, chef, police officer, astronaut, What do you want to be?

【设计说明】 节奏轻快的歌曲营造了良好的学习氛围,歌曲的主题和内容与 B 部分学习内容非常契合,不仅激活了旧知,也为学生后续学习新内容做好准备。

Activity 2: Let's say (2 mins)

Students talk about their dream jobs with the sentence structure "I want to be a … Just like …, _____ and _____."

I want to be a **scientist**.
Just like my grandpa.
Hard-working and great.

I want to be a **pilot**.
Just like my father.
Strong and brave.

I want to be a ...
Just like ...,
_____ and _____.

writer　　businessman　　coach　　scientist　　...

pilot　police officer　fisherman　postman　teacher　doctor　...
healthy　busy　strong　happy　amazing　super　wonderful　...

图 2

【设计说明】　学生运用所学词汇、句型表达观点,将职业与自我建立初步联系,在教师的引导下尝试谈论自己的理想职业(见图2),为后续学习活动做准备。

【效果评价】　教师观察学生能否运用已学知识,表达自己对理想职业的愿景,并根据学生的表现给予评价。

步骤二　听说结合,感知与梳理语篇(14 分钟)

Activity 1: Listen, answer and tick (4 mins)

Students listen to the dialogue twice. For the first time, they listen and answer the question "Who's that man?". For the second time, they listen and tick the information about Mike's uncle: "What's he like?", "What does he do?", "How does he go to work?".

Transcript

Let's try

Mike:　　Hi, Xiao Yu. Who's that tall man?

Xiao Yu: My uncle.

Mike:　　He's so big. What does he do?

Xiao Yu: He's a police officer.

Mike:　　Cool! How does he go to work? On foot?

Xiao Yu: No. He goes by car. He often takes me to school on his way to work.

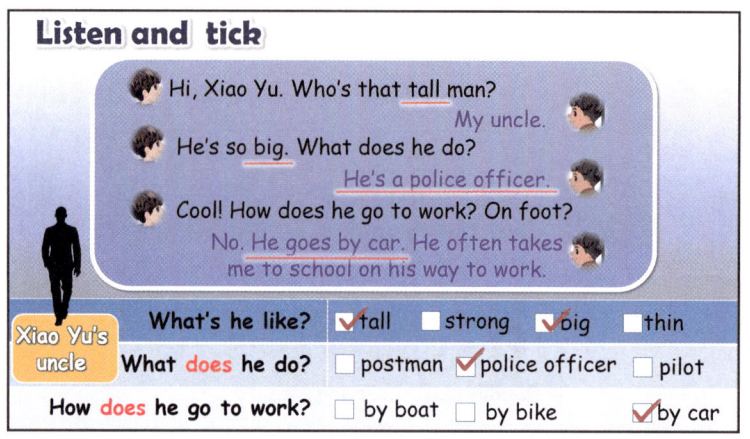

图 3

【设计说明】 学生两次听教材 Let's try 部分的听力内容,从"泛听"到"精听",从大意到细节,逐步理解对话内容,了解 Xiao Yu 叔叔的职业及相关信息。通过听力活动,学生初步感知核心句型"What does he do?"与"How does he go to work?"及其作答方式(见图3)。教师同步生成相应的板书,帮助学生后续运用"He's …""He's a …""He goes to work …"等句型描述人物职业的相关信息。

【效果评价】 教师观察学生完成听力任务的情况,判断学生能否准确获取信息,并给予适当的指导和评价。

Activity 2: Look and say (6 mins)

Students look at the picture of Mike's uncle, and then describe the picture and make predictions with short sentences. Then they discuss in groups, and write down some questions about Mike's uncle on the card. After that, some cards of questions will be listed on the blackboard for students to read.

图 4

【设计说明】 学生首先通过观察图片,获取相关信息;随后思考、推断并提炼其中可能隐含的信息;接着教师引导学生就主题提出疑问,培养其问题意识,激发其学习动机。此活动充分利用了教材图片资源(见图4),引导学生积极思考,提升其思维能力。

【**效果评价**】 教师观察学生观察、推断、提炼图片的相关信息与提出问题的情况,适时给予帮助。

Activity 3: Watch and find (2 mins)

Students watch the video, and then answer the questions on the blackboard.

图5

【**设计说明**】 教师引导学生带着自主提出的问题,通过观看对话视频找到答案,帮助学生理解对话内容,进一步学习核心语言。

【**效果评价**】 教师观察学生回答问题的表现,根据其说出的具体内容,了解其对语篇的理解情况,适时给予指导和评价。

Activity 4: Read and say (2 mins)

Students read the dialogue aloud first, and then work in pairs to check the answers through a short dialogue. After that, boys ask questions and girls answer. In this way, students practise the sentence structures.

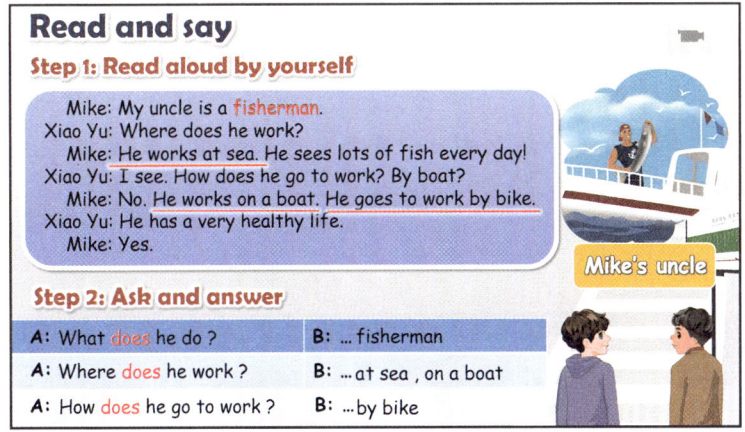

图6

【设计说明】 学生通过大声朗读、同桌问答等形式,在语篇中开展对核心语言的精准学习,为后续语言输出奠定基础(见图6)。

【效果评价】 教师观察学生能否运用核心语言进行问答,并根据学生表现,提供必要帮助。

步骤三 由听到演,内化与运用语言(8分钟)

Activity 1: Listen, think and say (2 mins)

Students listen and look at more pictures of Mike's uncle, and then think about his job and life.

Transcript

Mike's uncle is a fisherman. He's tall and strong. He works at sea, and he works on a boat. He sees lots of fish every day. He can catch big fish. He's hard-working. Sometimes he even works at night. He works on the boat, but he goes to work by bike. He also eats healthy food. And his favorite food is salad.

图 7

【设计说明】 教师补充图片与音频形式的教学资源,挖掘育人价值,使学生深入了解 Mike 叔叔的职业和健康的生活状态,由此引发其进行深度的思考,启发学生在努力学习的同时,保持健康生活(见图7)。

【效果评价】 教师观察学生能否理解语篇的内在涵义,表达个人观点和看法,并根据需要进行追问或给予评价。

Activity 2: Listen and imitate (1 min)

Students listen to the tape and repeat with correct pronunciation, intonation and rhythm.

【设计说明】 通过跟读对话内容的活动,教师引导学生感知和模仿语音、语调和节奏,帮助学生内化所学语言。

Activity 3: Do a role-play (5 mins)

Students act out the dialogue with the partners. Then they evaluate each other's perform-ance from three aspects according to the checklist.

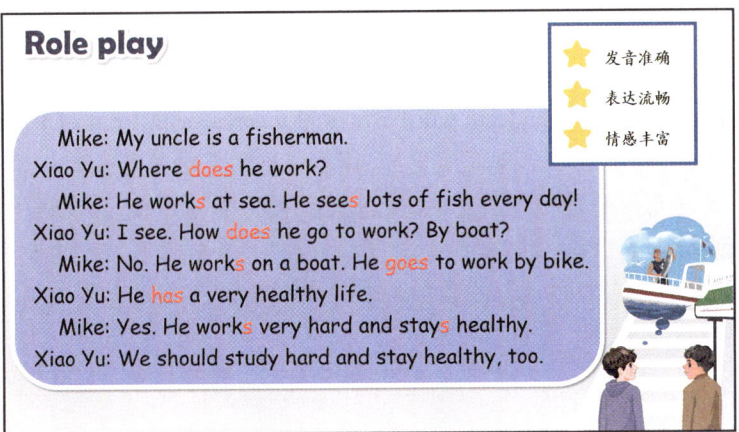

图 8

【设计说明】　该活动引导学生从学习理解过渡到应用实践。学生通过深入角色、表演对话,对主题意义做出正确的理解和判断;同时,在评价标准的帮助下(见图 8)内化目标语言。

【效果评价】　教师观察学生在角色扮演时是否关注三项评价内容,并根据学生的表现给予必要的提示和指导。

步骤四　先看后说,分析与活用语言(10分钟)

Activity 1: Watch and say (4 mins)

Students watch a video about hard-working people like pilots, scientists and coaches, and then share the opinions of their jobs and lives.

图 9

【设计说明】 通过补充视频教学资源,整合本单元 B 部分词汇板块的学习内容,引导学生对不同职业呈现的生活状态做出评价,进一步深入探究单元主题意义,逐渐建构正确的学习观和人生观。

【效果评价】 教师根据学生对内容的回应与反馈,引导学生积极思考并做出正确评价。

Activity 2: Think and talk (6 mins)

Students work in pairs, choose one person or one family member, and talk about his or her job and life. Then one pair of students will be invited to present in front of the class.

【设计说明】 这一活动回归到真实生活,旨在引导学生在真实语境中,借助语言支架进行迁移,创造性地运用所学进行真实交流,体验有意义的学习过程,实现语言学习和课程育人的融合统一(见学习单 Task 3)。

【效果评价】 教师观察学生运用所学语言交流职业相关信息与创编对话汇报的情况,根据学生表现适当给予帮助,评价学习成效。

(六) 板书设计

图 10

【设计说明】 板书包括课题名称和课堂要点。板书左侧是本节课核心句型的提问部分,是先由学生自主讨论、书写,后经教师筛选、修改生成的。板书右侧是核心句型的回答部分,可串联起对人物职业及相关信息的描述。板书下方呈现了本节课的主题意义。板书的设计随着教学推进逐步生成,有助于学生在语境中学习核心语言,并运用核心语言进行交流与表达。

(七) 作业设计

★1. Listen to the dialogue on Page 50 and read it aloud.

★★2. Introduce the job of a person around us.

【设计说明】　根据学生的不同能力水平,本作业呈现了难度递增的两项内容:一星作业为基础性作业,旨在引导学生巩固对本课核心语言的学习;二星为实践性作业,引导学生运用所学进行真实的交流,进一步提升他们的语用能力。

（八）教学反思

本课是一节听说课,教师关注听说技能与策略的指导,通过多层次的学习活动,不断引导学生探究主题意义,内化核心语言,在真实语境中体验有意义的学习过程,实现语言学习和课程育人的有机融合。教师作如下反思:

1. "听—看"结合,丰富可理解性语言输入

本节课中教师多次采用听、看相结合的方式,帮助学生在主题情境中获取充足的核心语言输入,在语境中感知、理解和学习语言,为输出做准备。在 Let's try 的语篇中,教师设计泛听、精听两次听力活动,旨在帮助学生从理解对话大意到理解对话细节,初步感知本课核心语言;在 Let's talk 的语篇中,教师引导学生自主提问,并通过观看对话视频提取目标语言,旨在帮助学生在语境中进一步学习核心语言。此外,本节课的两个补充语篇,分别以"配图听音"和"观看视频"的形式输入,引导学生在整理与归纳核心语言的基础上,运用语言理解意义。视听搭配使学生更加快速、准确地提取、梳理所需信息,促进语言内化,为后续有意义、创新性输出做好充足准备。

2. "思—说"并行,促成高质量的语言输出

本节课中,学生的"说"是在不同层次的思维活动中生成的,教师通过活动设计,助力学生语言使用螺旋上升,生成高质量的语言输出。教师引导学生观察教材图片,获取信息,预测并提出疑问,启发学生基于已知,尝试理解语篇;教师通过连续性问题,引导学生思考补充语篇中呈现的关于 Mike 叔叔的职业与生活状态的信息,启发学生分析、提炼主题意义,并将对主题意义的理解内化于交流表达之中;教师通过呈现不同人物的职业及生活状态,引导学生拓展思维,在分享交流中表达观点,在新的语境中运用所学语言创编对话,促使他们进行高质量的语言输出,同时形成对职业与生活的正确态度和价值判断。

（九）附件

学　习　单

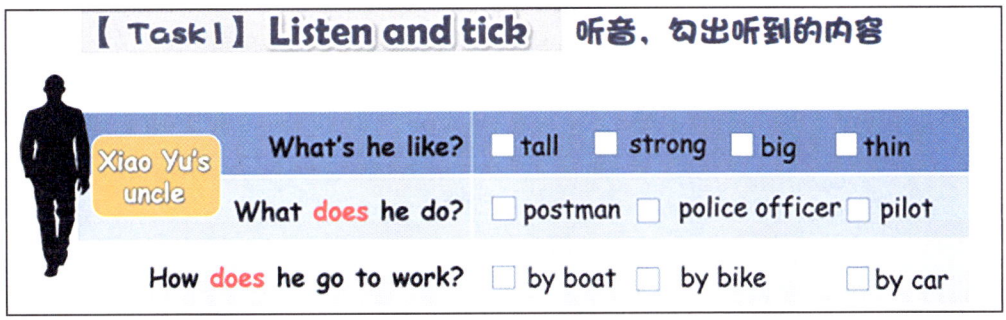

【Task 2】 Read and say

Step 1: Read aloud by yourself 独立朗读、声音要响亮哦

Mike: My uncle is a fisherman.

Xiao Yu: Where does he work?

Mike: He works at sea. He sees lots of fish every day!

Xiao Yu: I see. How does he go to work? By boat?

Mike: No. He works on a boat. He goes to work by bike.

Xiao Yu: He has a very healthy life.

Mike: Yes.

Step 2: Ask and answer 同桌问答,在文中划出关键信息哦

Mike's uncle	A: What does he do ?	B: ...
	A: Where does he work ?	B: ...
	A: How does he go to work ?	B: ...

【Task 3】 Pair work 同桌对话

Pair work

⭐ **Discuss and say**

1.选择一个人物,同桌讨论

2.完成对话,说说他(她)的工作和生活

A: _____ is a ...
B: Where does he/she work ?
A: ...
B: How does he/she go to work ?
A: ...
B: He/She has a very _____ life.
A: Yes! He/She works very hard and stays _____ .

Pair work

⭐⭐ **Think and say**

想一想，说说某个家人的工作与生活

> A: ＿＿＿＿ is a ...
> B: ＿＿＿＿＿＿＿＿?
> A: ...
> B: ＿＿＿＿＿＿＿＿?
> A: ...
> B: He/she has a very ＿＿＿＿ life.
> A: ...

Tips: 除了黑板上的句型，你还可以使用以下单词和句子哦。

Sentence bank

问句: What's he like?/Does he like...?/What are his hobbies? /...

补充语言: That' cool/nice/...　　Sounds great!　　Really?
That's good exercise.
Your＿＿＿ has a very healthy/happy/busy/... life.
We should also study hard and stay healthy.

...

Word bank

fisherman, police officer, teacher, doctor, scientist, businessman, postman, pilot, coach, factory worker, school, hospital, company(公司), office(办公室), university(大学)

...

课例 **5**

PEP B8 U2 Last weekend
（Part A Let's talk）

说课视频

Hello, everyone! I'm Sher from Wenzhou Jianshe Primary School. It's my great honor to present my lesson plan to you. I'd like to share my teaching from three aspects, namely, learning objectives, learning process and learning effects. Now, let's come to the first part.

Learning objectives

Generally speaking, the analysis of learning material and learners are the basis for setting the learning objectives. So first, let's take a close look at the learning material.

It is from PEP, Book 8, Unit 2 *Last weekend* Part A *Let's talk,* which is the first lesson of this unit. The theme is *man and society* as well as *man and self*, concerning *family and family life*.

What

It's a dialogue between a student and his family. As for its content, Mike talks with his grandpa about last weekend on the phone. Grandpa tells Mike that he watched TV and drank tea with Grandma last weekend. Mike tells Grandpa that he cleaned the room, washed the clothes as well as watched TV. Grandpa praises Mike as a good boy.

Why

The atmosphere of the scene in the dialogue is relaxing and warm, providing a good opportunity for readers to understand family life and guiding them to communicate with family members and express their love more often. Students will realize the significance of caring for family and develop the habit of chatting more with their family members in daily life.

---

① 本说课稿由温州市建设小学谢冰撰写。

How

It's a typical dialogue that may take place in students' daily life. The plot is simple and easy to understand. In this dialogue, Mike and his grandpa talk about the activities in the past tense, using the sentence patterns such as "How was your weekend? It was …", "What did you do last weekend? I …", "Did you do anything else? Yes. / No, I…" as well as phrases like "stayed at home" "drank tea" "watched TV" "cleaned my room" and "washed my clothes".

Having explored the learning material, let's come to the analysis of learners. My students are in Grade 6, who are familiar with the topic "weekend". They can easily understand the content of the dialogue, but they don't know much about English afternoon tea. Thus, the teacher needs to provide supplementary materials for them.

During the learning process, after more than three years of English learning, students can not only extract the information they need by listening, viewing and reading, but also use the present tense and the future tense correctly and properly. They have also learnt some verb phrases. So it's easy for them to talk about weekend activities with others. However, this is the first time for them to learn the past tense and use it to ask and answer questions about what they did in the past. So the teacher should leave enough time for students to practise and pay close attention to students' mastery.

However, although they have a sharp mind and are willing to infer and analyze audio-visual materials, their general thinking skills needs to be further improved. They need the teacher's guidance and help to summarize the framework of the dialogue and transfer what they have learnt to practice.

Based on the above analysis, the following learning objectives are set. By the end of this lesson, students will be able to:

1. extract information about last weekend activities in the dialogue through watching and listening, and understand both the content of the dialogue and the culture of English afternoon tea.

2. understand the usage of the past tense and use the sentence patterns to ask and answer questions about last weekend and then act out the dialogue with the help of the teacher.

3. share opinions about Mike's call and realize the significance of caring for family.

4. make up a dialogue about the activities they did last weekend and role-play with partners by using the sentence patterns in a real-life situation.

Learning process

Now let's move on to the description of learning process. In this class, the Activity-based Approach to English Learning is adopted, which divides all the learning activities into the following three categories.

➤ The first stage

In the first stage, to perceive language in the context, there are five activities designed.

As for Activity 1, Sing and say, firstly, students will sing a song, from which they will get the topic of today's lesson. Secondly, they will speak out the phrases about weekend activities based on some pictures and talk about their weekend plans. Then they will find out the differences between "this weekend" and "last weekend". This activity can not only activate the classroom's atmosphere and students' background knowledge of weekend activities, but also help students perceive the past tense by understanding the meaning of "last weekend". I will observe whether students can talk about the weekend plans in the future tense to find out what they have already known about the topic, and give feedback according to their performance.

In Activity 2, Listen and circle, students will listen to the dialogue between Mike and Sarah twice. For the first time, they will circle the right answers on Page 14 and check them by extracting the key sentences in the transcript. For the second time, they will choose the answers to the questions "How was Mike's weekend?" and "What did Mike do?". Then students will learn to read the key words in the text. I will observe whether the students can circle the correct answers in listening to determine whether they can accurately extract information and know to what extent they understand the past tense.

The next activity is Listen and tick. Students will listen to the dialogue between Mike and Grandpa. Firstly, they will listen to the complete dialogue and choose the questions they've heard. Then they will learn to read aloud the questions. Secondly, students will listen to the first part of the dialogue and tick the answers about Grandpa's last weekend, and then they will focus on the second part about Mike's last weekend. Meanwhile, they will learn to read the verb phrases, such as "washed clothes" "stayed at home" and "drank tea". I will observe whether the students can choose the correct answers in listening to judge whether they can identify the questions in the past tense. I will also judge whether they can read these core sentence patterns according to their performance in reading aloud. Then, whether they master the sound and meaning of past tense of different verbs can be seen in the correctness of their answers, and I will give guidance if necessary.

After that, the next activity, Watch and enjoy, asks students to watch a video about the traditional English afternoon tea to know more about it. I will observe whether the students show excitement and expectation after watching the video to judge whether the students have a basic understanding of the culture of English afternoon tea.

The last activity of this stage is Watch, read and underline. Students will try to further understand the text. Firstly, they will watch the complete video and infer "What did Grandma do last weekend?". Secondly, they will underline the verb phrases in the text according to the pictures given, such as "stayed at home" "drank tea" "watched TV" "cleaned my room" and "washed my clothes". I will observe whether students can name the activities Grandma did last weekend to determine whether they can infer information. Also, I will evaluate the extent to which students have internalized the core language and provide timely assistance based on their ability to match the pictures with the text, identify the past tense of verb phrases in the context, and use these phrases to answer my follow-up questions.

The above four activities aim to help students understand the content of the dialogue and the culture of English afternoon tea, perceive the past tense with the questions as well as the verb phrases, and develop their skills to extract information from the text. I will give guidance and feedback according to students' performance during the process.

> **The second stage**

In the second stage, to learn language through exploration, there are three activities contained.

Activity 1 is Do a role-play. Students will practise the key sentence patterns in pairs. A dialogue pattern and some verb phrases will be provided. The next activity is Discuss and find. Students will discuss the changes of the verbs in groups and find the rules by observing, analyzing and summarizing with the help of the teacher. Read aloud and dub is the last activity of this stage. Students will listen to the recording, repeat with correct pronunciation, intonation and rhythm, read alone and then dub it. In this way, students can deepen their understanding of the past tense and internalize the language they have learnt. During the activities, I will observe whether students can give the correct answer about the changes of the verbs and give guidance if necessary. Meanwhile, I will evaluate whether students can act out the dialogue with the self-checklist and read the text correctly, and will offer encouragement and feedback according to their performance.

> **The third stage**

In the last stage, to apply language in dialogue creation, there are three activities contained.

Activity 1 is Think and answer. Students will answer the question "What's Mike like in Grandpa's eyes?" and explain the reasons after fully understanding the text. It aims to enhance their logical thinking skills and make them perceive the significance of caring for family.

The second activity is Watch and say. After watching a video from real life, students will answer these five questions. In this part, students learn how to use the target language to show the caring for family in real-life dialogues and make preparations for the next activity.

In the last activity, students will choose one picture in groups, make a dialogue and then have a role-play in the class. They will evaluate each other's performance according to the checklist. This activity helps students transfer what they've learnt into real-life communication and take the correct attitude towards caring for family. I will evaluate the effect of learning according to students' presentation and the checklist.

After class, there are two assignments for students. First, they are required to listen to the dialogue on Page 14, read aloud and act it out. So they can review what they have learnt in this lesson. The second one is optional. Students need to call their grandparents and then talk about what they did last weekend, which can encourage them to use the language they have learnt to retell what grandparents did last weekend.

As for the blackboard design, the sentence patterns and the past tense verbs are presented clearly, from which students can better memorize and recall what they have learnt in this lesson.

Learning effects

In the end, let us analyze the merits of this lesson.

The first one can be seen in the breakthroughs of the target language. The teacher takes the past tense as the main line to design multi-level activities, in which students break through the difficult language points step by step. In the first stage, students perceive the past tense in the dialogue by extracting the information and understanding the verb phrases. In the second stage, students learn the past tense in the text and consolidate what they've learnt by doing a role-play with the self-checklist and discussing the rules of the simple past tense. In the last stage, students internalize the target language by using the past tense to make a simple dialogue in a real-life situation.

The second highlight is the achievement of the goals of moral education. The teacher guides the students to analyze the text not only in the linguistic level but also in the thematic level, in which students can readily sense the affection among family members and realize the significance of caring for family. Firstly, the teacher guides students to share opinions on Mike's personality with an open question and explore the thematic meaning of the text, from which they can perceive the emotional attitude of caring for family. Secondly, after watching a video from real life, students learn useful ways to show their love and care for others, from which they can develop the awareness of caring for family. Lastly, with a dialogue pattern provided, students are encouraged to transfer the target language in the same way, so as to deeply experience the correct emotional attitude of caring for family.

That's all for my presentation. Thanks for watching.

- - - - - - - - - - - - - - - - - - 试课实录① - - - - - - - - - - - - - - - - - -

试课视频

步骤一 **在语境中, 感知语言**(18 分钟)

Activity 1: Sing and say

T: Good morning, boys and girls. Are you ready for class?

Ss: (Yes!)

———————————

① 本试课稿由温州市建设小学谢冰撰写。

T: OK! First of all, let's enjoy a song. Then tell me what the song is about.

Ss: [sing the song]

T: Have you got the answer?

Ss: (Weekend.)

T: Yes. It's about "weekend". Now let's talk about weekend activities. As for sports, we can … ? Read it together.

Ss: (Do exercises. Play basketball.)

T: As for study, we can … ?

Ss: (Read some books. Do homework.)

T: As for housework, we can …

Ss: (Clean the room. Cook some food. Wash clothes.)

T: Any other fun things?

Ss: (Go shopping. Watch TV. Drink tea. Stay at home.)

T: I'm going to stay at home and cook some delicious food this weekend. How about you? What are you going to do this weekend? Lucy, please.

S1: (I'm going to do homework, wash my clothes and play basketball this weekend.)

T: You have such a good weekend. But today we are going to talk about "last weekend". Follow me. Last weekend.

Ss: (Last weekend.)

T: What does "Last weekend" mean? Please look at the calendar. Today is Friday, March the 19th. We call March the 20th and the 21st "this weekend". We call March the 13rd and the 14th "last weekend". Are you clear?

Ss: (Yes.)

Activity 2: Listen and circle

T: Look! Mike and Sarah are talking about last weekend. Please open your book and turn to Page 14. Let's listen and circle.

Ss: [listen and circle]

T: NO. 1. We choose … ?

Ss: (B.)

T: NO. 2. We choose … ?

Ss: (A.)

T: How do you know? Please read and find.

Ss: [read and find the key sentences]

T: Nancy, please.

S2: (Sarah says, "Tomorrow is Monday. " Mike says, "I'm going to call my grandparents now. ")

T:　Exactly! Sit down, please. How was Mike's weekend? And what did Mike do? Let's listen again and circle.

Ss:　[listen and circle]

T:　NO. 3. We choose … ?

Ss:　(C.)

T:　Yes. It was OK. Follow me "was".

Ss:　(Was.)

T:　NO. 4. We choose … ?

Ss:　(A and B.)

T:　Yes. Follow me "cleaned" "watched".

Ss:　(Cleaned. Watched.)

Activity 3: Listen and tick

T:　Look! Mike is calling his grandpa now. What are they talking about on the phone? Let's listen and tick the questions in this dialogue.

Ss:　[listen and tick]

T:　Have you got the answers? We choose … ?

Ss:　(A. C. F.)

T:　Yes. Please read after me. How was your weekend?

Ss:　(How was your weekend?)

T:　What did you do?

Ss:　(What did you do?)

T:　What did you do last weekend?

Ss:　(What did you do last weekend?)

T:　Did you do anything else?

Ss:　(Did you do anything else?)

T:　How was Grandpa's weekend? What did he do last weekend? Let's listen to the first part of the dialogue and tick the right answers on your learning sheet.

Ss:　[listen and tick]

T:　OK? Lily please.

S3:　(B. It was good. EFH. Grandpa stay at home, watched [/t/] TV and drink tea.)

T:　Follow me. "Stayed". "Drank".

S3:　(Stayed. Drank.)

T:　Can you say it again?

S3:　(Grandpa's weekend was good. He stayed [/d/] at home, watched [/t/] TV and drank [/æ/] tea.)

T:　Well done! Sit down, please. Let's say it together. Grandpa's weekend …

Ss:　(Grandpa's weekend was good. He stayed [/d/] at home, watched [/t/] TV and drank [/æ/] tea.)

T: As we all know, Mike's weekend was OK and he … ?

Ss: He cleaned the room and watched TV.

T: Yes. Did Mike do anything else? Now, let's listen to the second part and tick.

Ss: [listen and tick]

T: Did Mike do anything else?

Ss: Yes.

T: What else did he do? You, please.

S4: (C. Mike washed [/d/] the clothes.)

T: Follow me "washed [/t/]".

Ss: (Washed.)

T: Let's say it together. Mike … ?

Ss: (Mike's weekend was OK. He cleaned the room, washed the clothes and watched TV.)

Activity 4: Watch and enjoy

T: As we all know, Grandpa is in London, the UK. And the custom of drinking afternoon tea is from the UK. But do you know the differences between Chinese tea and English tea? Now, let's have a look.

Ss: [watch the video about English afternoon tea]

T: Now you know how to enjoy the traditional English afternoon tea correctly. Do you want to have a try?

Ss: (Yes.)

T: That must be fun.

Activity 5: Watch, read and underline

T: So much about Mike and Grandpa's weekend. How about Grandma? What did Grandma do last weekend? Let's watch and tick.

Ss: [watch the video and find out the answer]

T: Coco please.

S5: (Grandma stayed at home, watched TV and drank tea.)

T: Good pronunciation! Sit down, please. Now let's look at these pictures and learn more. Please read the dialogue and underline the phrases about these pictures. For example, the first picture is about "stayed at home". Right? Can you finish the other ones?

Ss: [read the text and underline the phrases]

T: About the second picture?

S6: (Drank tea.)

T: Yes. Grandpa drank tea with … ?

S7:　(Grandpa drank tea with Grandma.)

T:　　Yes. With Grandma. How about the third and the fourth pictures?

S8:　(Watched TV.)

T:　　Yes. You know Grandpa watched TV with Grandma. Mike watched TV at home too. What did Mike watch?

S9:　(He watched some children's shows on TV.)

T:　　Yes. Which picture is about children's shows? A or B?

Ss:　[show A with the fingers]

T:　　Of course. We choose A. Did Mike do anything else? Mike says … ?

Ss:　(I cleaned my room and washed my clothes.)

T:　　So the fifth picture is about … ? Read it together.

Ss:　(Cleaned my room.)

T:　　The last one is about … ?

Ss:　(Washed my clothes.)

T:　　Wonderful!

步骤二 在探究中,学习语言(8 分钟)

Activity 1: Do a role-play

T:　　So much for the dialogue. Now let's do a role-play according to this table and evaluate with the checklist. I'm Grandpa. Who wants to be Mike? OK. Jonny, please. How was your weekend, Mike?

S10:　(It was OK.)

T:　　What did you do last weekend?

S10:　(I cleaned my room and washed my clothes.)

T:　　Did you do anything else?

S10:　(Yes. I watched some children's shows.)

T:　　Did we read correctly?

Ss:　(Yes!)

T:　　Did we speak loudly?

Ss:　(Yes!)

T:　　Did we talk fluently?

Ss:　(Yes!)

T:　　So according to the checklist, we've got 3 stars in total. Now it's your turn. Please do a role-play just like this.

Ss:　[do a role-play in pairs]

T:　　Time is up! Who wants to have a try? You two, please.

S11 & S12:　[show the role-play]

T:　How many stars can they get?

Ss:　(2 stars.)

T:　2? Why?

Ss:　(We can't hear what they talked clearly.)

T:　If you can speak more loudly, it will be much better. Sit down, please.

Activity 2: Discuss and find

T:　Now, let's look at these verbs carefully, read them by yourselves and then discuss in groups what you find.

Ss:　[discuss]

T:　Ben please.

S13:　(We find the verbs change.)

T:　Yes. When we talk something in the past, the verbs change. How do they change? You please.

S14:　(Put -ed in the end.)

T:　Yes. Some of them are added with -ed, except "drank". They are called the past tense of the verbs. Do you know the infinitive of the verbs? For example, "stayed" is from "stay".

S15:　("Cleaned" is from "clean".)

S16:　("Watched" is from "watch".)

S17:　("Washed" is from "wash".)

S18:　("Drank" is from "drink".)

T:　Please pay attention to the pronunciation of -ed. Here (stayed/cleaned), -ed is pronounced /d/. But here (watched/washed), it's pronounced /t/. Now read the dialogue again. Can you find any other past tense verbs?

Ss:　[read the text and find the verbs]

S19:　(Was.)

T:　You find "was". It is from … ?

S19:　(Is.)

S20:　(Did.)

T:　You find "did". It's from … ?

S20:　(Do.)

T:　Yes. But sometimes "did" is from "does".

Activity 3: Read aloud and dub

T:　So much about the verbs. Now, it's time to read aloud. Step 1, listen and imitate.

Ss:　[listen and imitate]

T:　Step 2, read aloud by yourselves. Here we go.

Ss:　[read the text by themselves]

T: Step 3, let's dub. These two groups, you are Mike. These two groups, you are Grandpa. Are you clear? Here we go.

Ss: [dub according to the video]

T: Terrific! I like your reading very much.

步骤三 在创编中,运用语言(9分钟)

Activity 1: Think and answer

T: In the text, Grandpa says, "You're a good boy." What's Mike like in Grandpa's eyes?

S21: (Mike is helpful, because he cleaned his room and washed his clothes.)

S22: (Mike is nice, because he made a call to Grandpa and chatted with him.)

T: Mike is nice. I think so! Did you call your grandparents last weekend? Do you often talk with them?

Ss: [Yes. / No.]

T: Some students say YES, but some say NO. To be a nice boy or girl at home. Please often call and talk with your grandparents.

Activity 2: Watch and say

T: Look! Your family is calling your grandparents now. Maybe at this moment, your grandpa is cooking and your grandma is dancing. Maybe at this moment, they are eating breakfast and talking with you. Here is a video. Please watch and find, which picture is the video about, A or B?

Ss: [watch the video and then show B with the fingers]

T: Of course! We choose B. How many roles are there in the video? And who are they?

Ss: (4. Grandpa, Grandma, Mum and I.)

T: Yes. What questions did you hear in the video?

S23: (I heard "How was your weekend? What did you do last weekend? Did you do anything else?")

T: Good memory. Are they nice to each other?

Ss: (Yes.)

Activity 3: Make a dialogue

T: Now let's make a dialogue just like this. Step 1, choose one picture in groups, A or B. Then choose one role, Grandpa, Grandma, father, mother or I. Remember to be a nice boy or girl at home. And pay attention to the checklist. Let's go!

Ss: [choose the picture and roles, then discuss and make dialogues]

T: Time is up! Who wants to have a try? You four, please.

S24 & S25 & S26 & S27: [show the dialogue]

T: Did they speak correctly?

Ss:　（Yes.）

T:　Did they speak loudly?

Ss:　（Yes.）

T:　Did they talk fluently?

Ss:　（Yes.）

T:　Did they act vividly?

Ss:　（Yes.）

T:　Big hands for them! They've got 4 stars in total. Thank you. Sit down, please.

作业布置

T:　Because time is limited, we must stop here. After class, I hope you can listen to the dialogue on Page 14, read aloud and act it out. Do remember to call your grandparents and then talk about their last weekend. Class is over. Bye!

教学设计①

配套课件

（一）语篇研读

本课教学内容选自人教版英语六年级下册第二单元 Last weekend A 部分 Let's talk 板块,属于"人与社会"和"人与自我"主题范畴,内容涉及"家庭与家庭生活"。

What

教学语篇是一则家人间的日常对话,内容围绕 Mike 与 Grandpa 在电话中谈论上周末的活动展开。Mike 给 Grandpa 打电话,问他上周末过得怎么样,做了什么事情。Grandpa 答复他,自己上周末和奶奶在家里一边看电视,一边喝茶。Mike 告诉 Grandpa 自己周末在家除了看电视,还打扫了房间和洗衣服。Grandpa 夸赞 Mike 是好孩子。

Why

Mike 给 Grandpa 打电话问好,主动了解 Grandpa 上周末的生活,并告知 Grandpa 自己上周末的活动,对话轻松,场面温馨。教师可以借此引导学生了解家人生活,多与家人交流与沟通,表达关爱之情。

How

教学语篇是典型的家庭生活情境对话,情节简单,易于理解。该语篇中 Mike 和 Grandpa 谈论上周末活动时使用了一般过去时的语法结构,涉及核心句型如 "How was your weekend? It was … " "What did you do last weekend? I … " "Did you do anything else? Yes./No, I … "等,还使用了介绍周末日常活动的短语,如 stayed at home、drank tea、watched

———————

① 本教学设计由温州市建设小学谢冰撰写。

TV、cleaned my room、washed my clothes 等。

(二) 学情分析

本课授课对象为 Z 省某小学六年级学生,他们对"周末安排"的话题较为熟悉,能快速理解对话谈论的主要活动,但对英式下午茶文化不太了解,需要教师提供补充资料。另外,经过三年的英语学习,学生在一定程度上具备了听音捕捉关键信息、观看视频获取信息、结合图文验证信息的能力,打好了一般现在时和一般将来时的语法基础,储备了相关动词词组,能与他人谈论周末活动。但在本节课中,学生将首次接触一般过去时,并应用该时态询问与回答过去所做之事。因此,教师需要在课堂中为学生留足时间,供学生操练与应用一般过去时,关注学生对这一时态的掌握情况。同时,学生思维敏锐,愿意主动对视听材料展开推理与分析,但其概括能力相对不足,需借助教师的引导与帮助才能提炼对话框架,对语篇内容展开迁移与运用。

(三) 教学目标

通过本课时的学习,学生能够:

1. 在视听活动中,获取对话里谈到的活动信息,理解对话内容,了解英式下午茶文化;

2. 了解一般过去时的基本用法,运用核心句型"How was your weekend? It was …""What did you do last weekend? I …""Did you do anything else? Yes./No, I …"进行询问和回答,并能分角色表演对话;

3. 对 Mike 主动致电长辈的做法发表观点,感悟关心家人的重要性;

4. 在小组内进行角色扮演,简单谈论上周末的活动,以创编对话方式进行交流。

(四) 教学流程

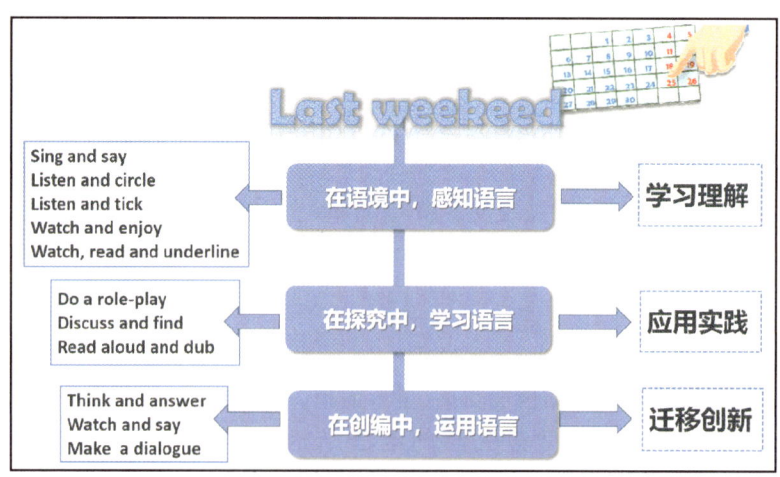

图 1

学生在本节课共经历了三个学习阶段。第一阶段为"感知语言",基于教材 Mike 和 Grandpa 谈论上周末活动的语境,教师引导学生通过唱、说、听、看等方式,初步感知理解一般过去时。第二阶段为"学习语言"，教师引导学生在课文语境中进行角色扮演，进而鼓励学生进行小组讨论，对比分析词形变化规律，学习并巩固一般过去时。第三阶段为"运用语言"，教师创设与 Grandparents 打电话交流上周末生活的情境，引导学生进行小组合作，创编简单对话。学生不仅需要关注语法结构本身，还需将一般过去时初步应用到日常家庭对话中，进而真正内化本节课的目标语言。

（五）教学过程

步骤一　**在语境中，感知语言**（18 分钟）

Activity 1: Sing and say (3 mins)

Students sing the song "Weekend" together. After that, they figure out the phrases about weekend activities based on the pictures and talk about their weekend plan. Then they find out the differences between *this weekend* and *last weekend* by observing the calendar.

Lyrics

Weekend

Oh, my, it's the weekend, a holiday. I'm going to have such fun.

I'm gonna wake up and shake up ready to play all day.

It's Saturday, a holiday. I'm gonna wake up and shake up ready to play all day.

It's Saturday, a holiday. Five days a week, it's working days. Then it's weekend again, weekend again.

Five days a week, it's working days. Then it's weekend again, a holiday. Saturday and Sunday, fun days.

图 2

【设计说明】　教师通过有节奏感的歌曲，活跃课堂气氛，引导学生感知本课主题。教师以思维导图（见图 2）的方式，有序激活学生关于周末活动的已知词汇，引导学生复习将来时态的表达方式,为学习一般过去时的动词词组做好铺垫。教师由 this weekend 引出课题 last weekend,并通过观察日历引导学生理解 last weekend 的意思。

【效果评价】 教师观察学生能否参与交流,能否用一般将来时描述自己的周末活动,了解学生对该主题已有的知识和经验,根据学生的表现给予反馈。

Activity 2: Listen and circle (4 mins)

Students listen to the dialogue between Mike and Sarah about last weekend. Firstly, they circle the right answers on Page 14. After checking the answers, they read the transcript and find out the key sentences. Secondly, they listen again and answer the questions "How was Mike's weekend?" and "What did Mike do?"

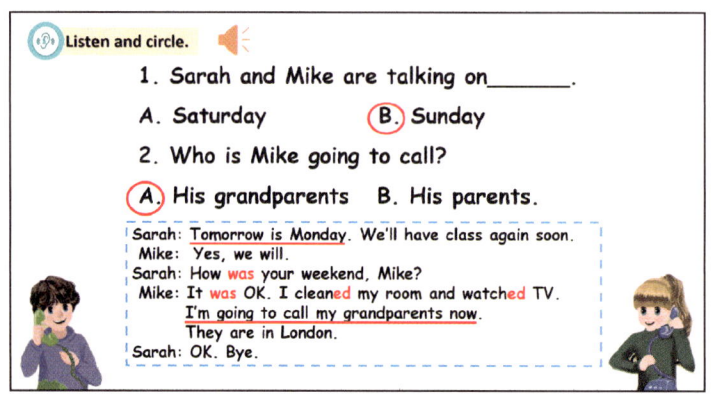

图 3

图 4

【设计说明】 学生一听捕捉关键词,阅读听力材料(见图 3)并搜寻关键句,提升准确获取关键信息的能力,并关注到本节课 Mike 致电 Grandpa 的主情景。二听聚焦核心句型并选择信息(见图 4),对照听力文本整体感知一般过去时的意义。

【效果评价】 教师观察学生能否在听力中勾选出正确答案,判断其能否准确获取信息,把握其对一般过去时的感知程度。

Activity 3: Listen and tick (5 mins)

Students listen to the dialogue between Mike and Grandpa about last weekend. Firstly, they listen to the complete dialogue and choose the questions they've heard. Then they learn to read aloud the questions under the teacher's help. Secondly, students listen to the first part of the dialogue and tick the right answers about Grandpa's last weekend, and then listen to the second part about Mike's.

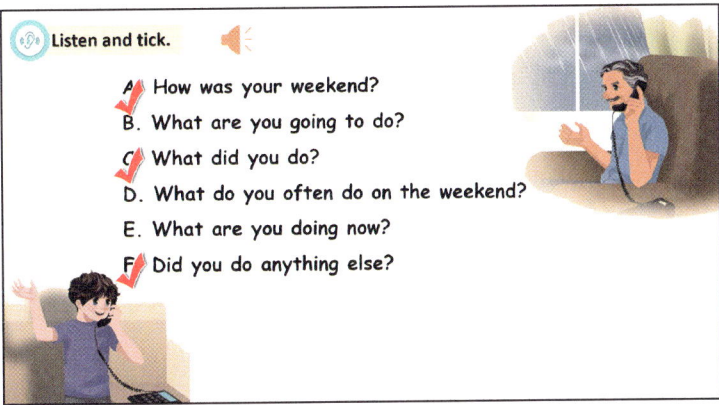

图 5

图 6

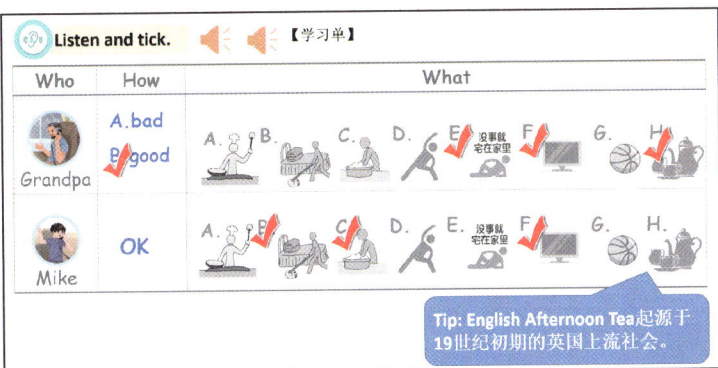

图 7

【设计说明】 第一次泛听捕捉核心问句(见图5),让学生整体感知对话内容。第二次精听捕捉关键信息(见图6、图7),让学生获取 Grandpa 和 Mike 的周末活动细节。在作答的过程中,学生学习理解一般过去时的语法意义和语词发音。在核对答案的过程中,学生在教师的指导下,朗读本课核心问句,初步运用动词过去式进行互动交流。

【效果评价】 教师观察学生能否在听力中选出正确答案,判断其能否准确获取信息;根据学生的跟读表现,判断其能否认读核心问句;根据学生回答的正确性,把握其是否掌握动词过去式的音与义,并给予适时的指导。

Activity 4: Watch and enjoy (1 min)

Students watch a video about traditional English afternoon tea to know more about the ways to enjoy it correctly.

【设计说明】 通过视频,学生了解英国下午茶的相关文化知识。

【效果评价】 教师观察学生观看视频后是否流露出兴奋、期待的神情,判断学生是否初步理解了英国下午茶文化。

Activity 5: Watch, read and underline (5 mins)

Firstly, students watch the video and infer "What did Grandma do last weekend?". Secondly, they underline the verb phrases in the text according to the given pictures (*stayed at home*, *drank tea*, *watched TV*, *cleaned my room*, and *washed my clothes*).

图 8

图 9

【设计说明】　通过观看教材视频,学生推理 Grandma 周末的活动,进一步整体感知对话内容,发展逻辑推理能力;通过图文配对(见图8、图9),学生在教材对话语篇里学习动词过去式的词形和意义。教师采用追问的方式,引导学生运用和内化核心语言。

【效果评价】　教师观察学生能否说出 Grandma 上周末所做的活动,判断其能否通过推理获得信息;根据学生能否进行图文配对、能否在语篇中找出动词过去式词组,以及能否运用词组回答教师的追问,评价其对核心语言的内化程度,并及时提供帮助。

步骤二　**在探究中,学习语言**(8分钟)

Activity 1: Do a role-play (2 mins)

Students practise the key sentences according to the text in pairs. One will be Mike and the other one will be Grandpa. They evaluate each other's performance according to the checklist from three aspects.

图 10

图 11

【设计说明】　通过角色扮演,学生运用动词过去式词组,初步操练核心句型,为下文探究动词过去式的变形规律和进行综合语言输出做好准备。

【效果评价】　教师观察学生能否借助板书和课件呈现的语言支架(见图10)完成角色扮演,把握学生对核心语言的掌握情况,并给予必要的提示和指导。教师观察学生能否借助师生共评和学生互评表(见图11)不断改善学习表现,并及时进行反馈。

Activity 2: Discuss and find (4 mins)

Students discuss in groups and find the changes of the verbs under the teacher's guidance.

图 12

【设计说明】 教师引导学生通过观察分析、小组讨论和交流总结的方式,简单梳理并归纳本课动词过去式的变形规律(见图12),为进一步在真实情境中正确使用动词过去式做好准备。

【效果评价】 教师观察学生能否通过讨论发现动词过去式的变形规律,判断其对所学内容的掌握情况,并适时进行讲解和提示。

Activity 3: Read aloud and dub (2 mins)

Students listen to the recording and repeat with correct pronunciation, intonation and rhythm. After that, they read alud and then dub it.

【设计说明】 通过跟读对话内容,学生模仿语音、语调和节奏,进而独自朗诵并进行角色配音,由此全面内化本课核心语言。

【效果评价】 教师根据学生跟读、自读和角色配音对话的表现,把握其对文本内容的掌握情况,并给予适时的鼓励。

步骤三 在创编中,运用语言(9分钟)

Activity 1: Think and answer (2 mins)

Students answer the question "What's Mike like in Grandpa's eyes?" and explain the reasons after fully understanding the text.

图 13

【设计说明】 学生在教师引导下进行人物评价,训练思维的逻辑性,初步意识到关心家人、多与家人交流的重要性。

【效果评价】 教师观察学生能否做出判断及其判断的逻辑性,引导其进行正确评价。

Activity 2: Watch and say (2 mins)

After watching a video from real life, students answer the following questions: "Which picture is the video about?" "How many roles are there in the video?" "Who are they?" "What questions did you hear in the video?" "Are they nice to each other?".

Transcript

Boy:	Hi, Grandpa. How are you?
Grandpa:	I'm fine. I'm having breakfast with your grandma.
Boy:	How was your weekend?
Grandpa:	It was good.
Boy:	What did you do last weekend?
Grandpa:	I had a big party with my friends near Nanxi River.
Boy:	Sounds great! I want to go with you!
Grandma:	We can go there together on May Day.
Boy:	Oh yeah!
Mum:	How was your weekend, Mum?
Grandma:	It was busy. I cooked delicious food for your father's party.
Mum:	Haha. Please take care of yourself. Did you do anything else?
Grandma:	Yes, I enjoyed the beautiful stars with your father at night!
Mum:	Wow!

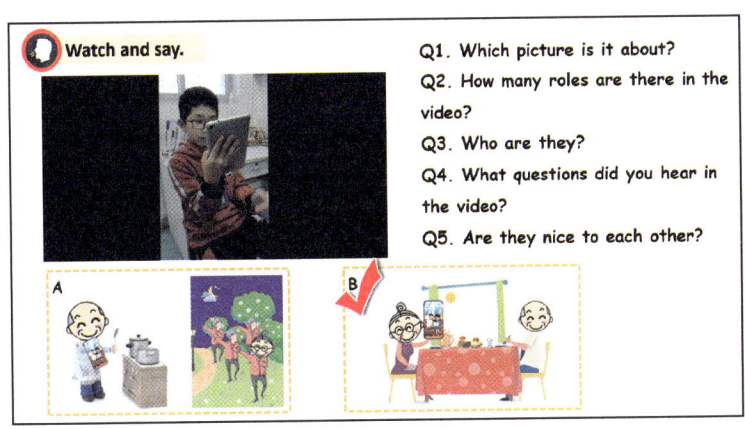

图 14

【设计说明】 学生观看真实的对话视频,通过回答问题来学习如何在真实情境中迁移应用目标语言,表达对家人的关爱之情。这能帮助学生为后续的对话创编活动做好准备。

【效果评价】 教师观察学生的选择及回答情况,判断其是否理解创编对话的基本思路。

Activity 3: Make a dialogue (5 mins)

Students choose one picture in groups, make a dialogue, and then have a role-play. They evaluate each other's show according to the checklist.

图 15   图 16

【设计说明】 学生依托小组合作,选择情境和角色,模拟电话交流,完成交际任务(见图 15),在真实情境中提升创新运用语言的能力,深化关心家人的情感体验,形成文化品格。

【效果评价】 教师观察学生向全班呈现的对话成果及评价表现(见图 16),把握教与学的成效。

(六) 板书设计

图 17

【设计说明】 板书包括标题和内容要点。左边部分是本课的核心句型,随着教学活动的展开逐句呈现,形成本节课语言输出的重要支架。右边部分呈现了本节课涉及的动词及其过去式。该板书有助于学生把握和复习本课重难点。

（七）作业设计

★1. Listen to the dialogue on Page 14, read aloud and act it out.

★★2. Call your grandparents, talk about their last weekend, and then fill in the table according to your conversation.

课后挑战	
课后给你的爷爷或奶奶或外公或外婆打一个电话,你能说说他们上周末都做了一些什么吗?	My grandpa's/grandma's weekend was_____. He/She_____.

【设计说明】　教师设计难度递增的分层作业:一星作业为基础性作业,旨在引导学生通过听、读和表演教材文本,巩固对核心语言的掌握,提升语言能力;二星作业为实践性作业,鼓励学生课后给 Grandparents 打电话,聊聊家常,并借助语言支架进行转述,进而引导学生在真实情境中运用所学语言,培育其关心长辈的美德。

（八）教学反思

本节课是一节对话课,教师围绕"周末生活"展开多层次的教学活动。教师首先引导学生基于情境初步学习一般过去时的发音、形式、意义和用法,进而在真实情境中运用目标语言进行交流,树立关心家人的品格。纵观本课,教师作如下反思:

1. 深入对话情境,实现语言难点的层层突破

本节对话课教师以一般过去时为主线,设计了多层次的学习活动,旨在引导学生在课文情境和真实生活情境中,循序渐进地突破一般过去时这一重难点。在"感知语言"阶段,学生通过视听活动获取信息,图文对照,语义明确,在课文情境中整体感知理解一般过去时。在"学习语言"阶段,学生通过角色扮演进行初步语用,通过小组讨论分析词形变化规律,学习理解动词过去式。在"运用语言"阶段,通过创编真实情境中的简单对话,学生不仅关注语法本身,还将一般过去时应用到了日常交流中,真正内化了核心目标语言。

2. 挖掘对话内涵,实现主题意义的育人目标

在本节对话课中,教师在引导学生剖析对话语篇时,并不停滞于语言知识层面,还带领学生洞察语篇所揭示的家人之间的温情,更有呼吁学生关爱家人、多与家人沟通交流。首先,教师以开放性问题为导向,引导学生评价 Mike 的人物品格,初步体会与认知关心家人的情感态度。然后,在对话环节,教师以学生的视频为范例,引导学生深入感悟与理解如何通过日常对话表达对家人的关爱,培养关心家人的意识和习惯。最后,教师以对话语篇为依托,引导学生综合运用语言,在行动中深刻体验关心家人之情,实现主题意义的育人目标。

（九）附件

学 习 单

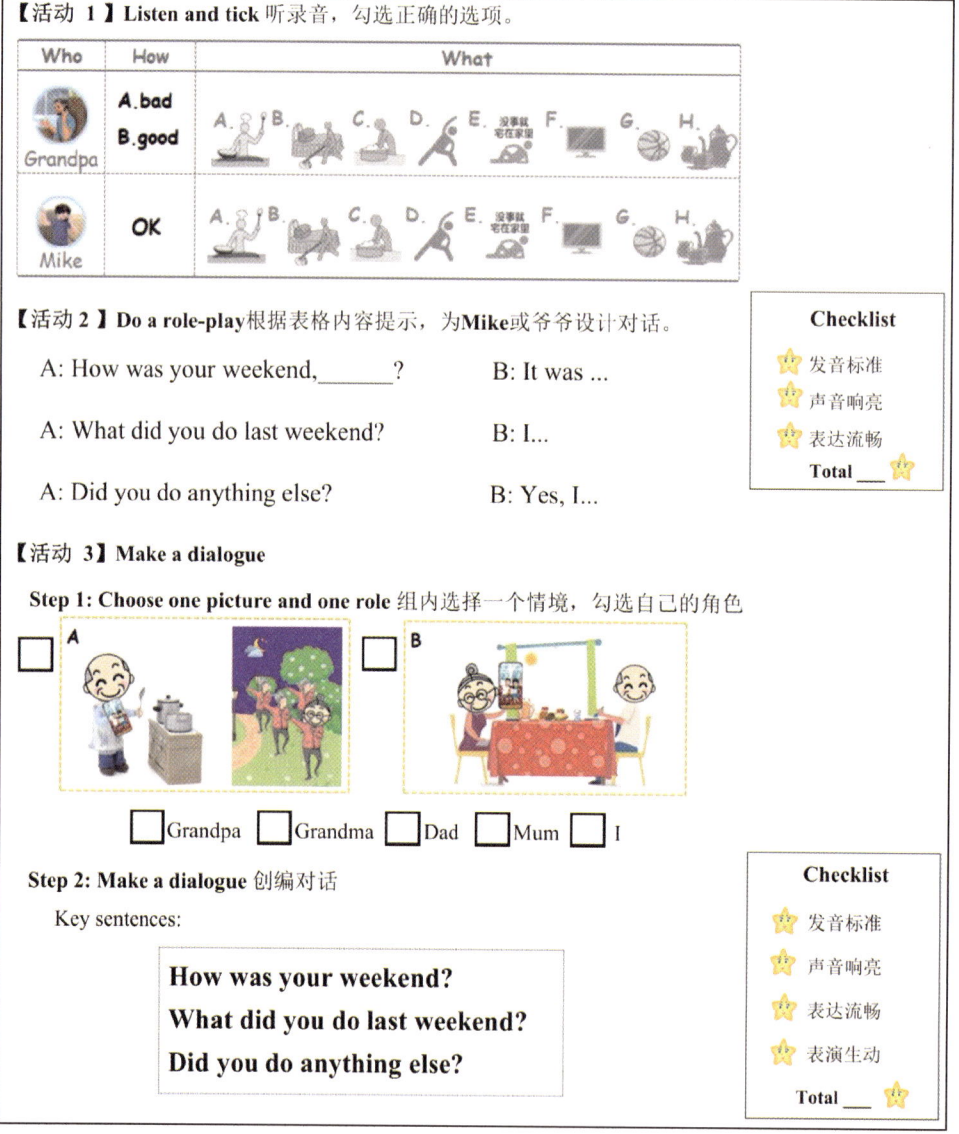

【活动 1】**Listen and tick** 听录音，勾选正确的选项。

【活动 2】**Do a role-play** 根据表格内容提示，为 **Mike** 或爷爷设计对话。

A: How was your weekend,_____?   B: It was ...

A: What did you do last weekend?   B: I...

A: Did you do anything else?   B: Yes, I...

Checklist

⭐ 发音标准

⭐ 声音响亮

⭐ 表达流畅

Total ___ ⭐

【活动 3】**Make a dialogue**

Step 1: Choose one picture and one role 组内选择一个情境，勾选自己的角色

☐ A   ☐ B

☐Grandpa ☐Grandma ☐Dad ☐Mum ☐I

Step 2: Make a dialogue 创编对话

Key sentences:

> **How was your weekend?**
>
> **What did you do last weekend?**
>
> **Did you do anything else?**

Checklist

⭐ 发音标准

⭐ 声音响亮

⭐ 表达流畅

⭐ 表演生动

Total ___ ⭐

课例 6

PEP B6 U5 Whose dog is it?
(Part B Let's learn)

说课视频

Hello, everyone! I'm Shan Chan from No. 1 Experimental Primary School Affiliated to Wenzhou University. It's my great honor to present my lesson plan for you. I will analyze my lesson plan from the following three aspects: learning objectives, learning process and learning effects. Now, let's move on to the first part.

Learning objectives

Generally speaking, the analysis of learning materials and learners is the basis for learning objectives. So first, let's take a close look.

The learning material is from PEP Book 6 Unit 5 *Whose dog is it?* Part B *Let's learn*. The theme of this context is *man and nature*, concerning *love for animals* and *observation of animals*.

What

It is a vocabulary lesson. The textbook gives the present participle forms of six common verbs and two dialogues describing animal actions. The text is a daily conversation among primary school students. Chen Jie and her friends are talking about what animals are doing. Chen Jie likes animals very much and hopes that her classmates can help her complete the vlog and record the cute moments of animals. In order to help students to learn vocabulary based on the text, I also restructure the text through adding a telephone conversation between Chen Jie and Sam. On the phone, Chen Jie learns that Fido has fallen asleep after playing naughtily in the park, so she rushes to the park.

Why

The love for animals inspires Chen Jie to make a vlog about animals and share it with

---

① 本说课稿由温州大学附属第一实验小学单婵撰写。

137

others. By learning how to make a vlog, students will observe animals more carefully, and be friendly to and take care of animals in real life. Inviting students to make the vlog together can prompt students to observe the animals carefully and be friendly to them.

How

Restructuring the text based on the previous vocabulary and conversation lessons in this unit makes it easier for students to understand. The text is in present continuous tense, using present participles. These words involve the core linguistic knowledge in terms of sound, form, meaning and use. In addition, the core sentence patterns in this lesson include "Is he drinking water? No, he isn't. He's eating." and "Are these rabbits eating? No. They're playing with each other."

Then, here comes the analysis of learners. Students in this lesson are the fifth graders from a primary school in Zhejiang Province. "Talking about the animals in daily life" is one of the most popular topics among students in Grade 5. They are curious about the animals and are willing to get close to animals and observe their behaviors.

Also, students have previously learnt about animals, and have a basic knowledge of the original pronunciation and meaning of the common verbs, such as "climb", "eat", "drink", "sleep", "jump", and "play". What's more, in the conversation lesson in Part B of this unit, students have been introduced to the structure of the singular third person present progressive tense and have some understanding of the present participle form of verbs. But they still have difficulty in pronouncing the verbs correctly and memorizing the deformation rules for changing verbs to present participle. This requires the teacher to create real-life contexts for language comprehension and use from the original content of the textbook and to add specific content to expand the opportunities for students to practise and use the syntax.

Based on the above analysis, the following learning objectives are set. By the end of this lesson, students will be able to:

1. understand the meaning of present participle through listening, speaking and viewing.

2. talk about what animals are doing by using present participles correctly, and properly use the deformation rules for changing verbs to present participle.

3. apply "The … is/are …" and "It's/They're so …" in talking about the activities of animals, and perceive and internalize the function of present continuous tense.

4. present the project of observing animals by creating a vlog, express their love for animals, and encourage others to take care of animals.

Learning process

Now let me introduce the learning process. In this class, the Activity-based Approach to English Learning and the Whole Language Approach are adopted, which help divide all the learning activities into the following three categories, Complete Input, Dynamic Interactive

Activities and Complete Output.

In the first stage, Complete Input, three activities are designed.

In the first activity, students will enjoy the vlog "What's Fido doing?" and review the story and vocabulary in the previous conversation lesson. This can activate their background knowledge like some vocabulary and core sentence patterns, which makes it easier for them to learn new vocabulary.

In Activity 2, in order to present the main task of today's lesson, students are guided to know the basic elements of a vlog like "a title, moments, subtitles and narrations".

Then the next activity is Think and guess. Students will use "Is Fido … ?" to predict what Fido is doing now. It helps to cultivate students' logical thinking by stimulating students to think and guess. I will observe whether the students are able to complete the spelling of present participles to determine whether they can initially understand the meanings of the present participles according to the original form of the verbs.

In the second stage, Dynamic Interactive Activities, there are eight activities.

Activity 1 is Listen and answer. Students are going to listen to the text for the first time and get the general idea by choosing the right answer to the key question *"What are they talking about?"*. I will focus on whether the students can think, predict and get the general idea. If necessary, I will give guidance and support.

In Activity 2, Listen and tick, students will listen to the dialogue again and tick what Fido is doing. They will also check the answer and practise the target vocabulary.

In Activity 3, Read and match, students are required to read the dialogues on the learning sheet, match the moments with each dialogue and circle these present participles. They will have a further focus on the sounds, forms and meanings of the target vocabulary by circling them in the text.

In the above two learning activities, I will observe whether students can tick the correct words, match the words with the pictures correctly, and circle the present participles to grasp the effectiveness and difficulties of the process where students match the form and meaning, and provide guidance if necessary.

After that, in Activity 4, Let's spell, I will set examples and encourage students to infer the spelling rules. Students will be able to discover and transfer rules, and practise spelling the present participles in pairs. I will observe whether students can spell the words correctly to evaluate the extent to which they have mastered the sounds and forms of the core vocabulary. And by observing students' attitudes and learning outcomes during cooperative learning, I will give guidance and evaluation.

Next, the activities focus on reading and writing skills of the vocabulary. I adapt the *Let's play* part in the textbook and students will be asked to make sentences according to the moments. I will observe whether students can accurately write the vocabulary with beautiful handwriting.

In Activity 6, the students will try to classify the words into groups and conclude the rules of the deformation. Through group cooperation, students will be guided to discover and summarize the rules, and understand the grammatical meaning of the present continuous tense as well. I can give feedback according to their performance.

Activity 7 is Listen and answer. Students will take a closer look at the main page. Then they will guess what the rabbits are doing with the expression "*Are these rabbits … ?*". After that, they will listen to the dialogue and answer the question.

In the last activity of the second stage, students will read the dialogue and learn the core sentence patterns. And they will solve the difficult phrase "each other" through picture matching. By following the dialogue, students can perceive and imitate pronunciation and intonation, thus internalizing the core language. I will check if the students can read correctly, fluently and vividly. I will give advice when necessary.

In the last stage, Complete Output, there are three activities contained.

The first one is Ask and answer, which is divided into two parts. Part A is Pair-work. I will create an information gap between the roles. Students will look at Sam's and Chen Jie's photos and ask and answer in pairs. What's more, they will talk about animals' characteristics with the expressions *"It's so … /They're so … "*. Part B is Act it out. Students are invited to act out as Chen Jie and Sam in the class. This activity will fully stimulate students' interest in learning and let them further use the target language in real settings. I will observe whether the students can act out the dialogue between Chen Jie and Sam using correct language, pronunciation and intonation, and give feedback and guidance according to their performance.

Activity 2 is Make a new vlog, which is also divided into two parts. Part A is Present an example. A student will present an example on the blackboard with his/her partner's help. Part B is Choose, write and say. Students will work in groups, fill out the sentences on the cards, match the moments with subtitles. At last, they will retell it to the whole class. It can not only cultivate students' skills of group work and cooperation, but it also meets each student's own learning needs. I will observe whether the students accurately use what they have learnt in the discussion to make a reasonable vlog, especially focusing on providing help they may need in choosing sentences. I will give guidance when necessary.

The last activity is Look and enjoy. Students will enjoy a vlog from other students. It will bring students a complete learning experience, and motivate them to create theirs after class.

After class, there are two assignments for students. First, they are required to read the words and dialogue on Page 53. So they can review what they have learnt in this lesson. The second one is practical. Students are asked to make a new vlog in groups with the sentences *"… is/are_____ing. They're so … "*.

The blackboard design includes the title of the topic and the key points of the class. At the top of the blackboard are the core sentence patterns of this lesson. The second half of the blackboard lists the core vocabulary, which is divided into three groups by students and tagged with the rules.

Learning effects

Now, I'd like to highlight the learning effects.

The first one can be text-based vocabulary teaching and learning.

Teaching and learning vocabulary in specific texts outweighs traditional vocabulary teaching. By using Whole Language Approach, students can understand and apply the vocabulary better, as well as improve their reading skills. In this lesson, first of all, I restructure a context and present the complete text for students. Then, all the learning activities are closely related to the text, which help students acquire the target vocabulary and explore the theme more deeply. Finally, students are encouraged to use what they have learnt to create new texts like describing animals in real life. In this way, both the language and learning strategies can be internalized gradually, together with students' love for animals, which strengthens the value of education.

The second highlight is promoting vocabulary learning based on Whole Language Approach. The Whole Language Approach considers text as the smallest unit of foreign language teaching. Teachers should help students develop their language competence and thinking capacity through the Complete Input, Dynamic Interactive Activities, and Complete Output. In this lesson, all the vocabulary learning activities are based on the whole text, guiding students to learn vocabulary as a whole so as to achieve complete output. Through the task of making subtitles and narrating the vlog, and making their own vlogs after class, students produce complete oral output in real-life context.

That's all for my presentation. Thanks for watching.

试课实录①

试课视频

 步骤一　激活旧知，整体输入（5分钟）

Activity 1: Enjoy a vlog

T:　Good morning, boys and girls. Today, we're going to learn PEP 6 Unit 5 Part B Let's learn.

Ss:　(Good morning, teacher!)

T:　First, let's listen and enjoy a vlog. Everybody, stand up! Let's sing and do it together.

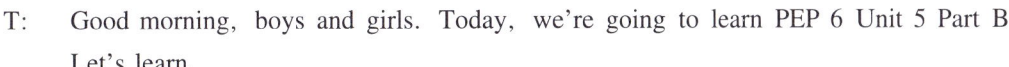

① 本试课稿由温州大学附属第一实验小学单婵撰写。

Ss: [enjoy the vlog and do it together]

T: Good! Sit down, please. Do you like the vlog?

Ss: (Yes!)

Activity 2: How to make a vlog

T: Chen Jie likes the vlog, too. So, she wants to learn how to make it. Look, a vlog has … ?

Ss: (A title, moments, subtitles and narrations.)

T: Yes. Chen Jie wants to make a vlog about pets. Do you want to help her?

Ss: (Yes!)

T: Let's make Part 1 first. It's about Chen Jie's pet, Fido.

Activity 3: Think and guess

T: Listen, Sam and Fido are in the park. Time flies. Chen Jie is very worried. She's guessing "Is Fido _____ ing?" I guess it is "Is Fido drinking?". Who can guess too?

S1: (Is Fido playing?)

S2: (Is Fido running?)

S3: (Is Fido sleeping?)

S4: (Is Fido eating?)

步骤二 听说结合,整体互动(20分钟)

Activity 1: Listen and answer

T: Good guess! Now, let's listen and find out what they are talking about. A, Where is Fido? Or B, What is Fido doing? Are you ready? Go!

Ss: [listen to the recording]

T: OK. Which one is right? Let's say together.

Ss: (B.)

T: Great! It's about … ?

Ss: What is Fido doing?

Activity 2: Listen and tick

T: Now, boys and girls, let's listen to the dialogue carefully and tell me what Fido is doing. Maybe Fido is … ?

Ss: (Playing, running, climbing, jumping, dancing or sleeping.)

T: Good. Please take out your worksheet. Look at Part 1. Let's listen.

Ss: [listen to the recording]

T: Now, let's check. Is Fido playing?

S5: (Yes, he is. And he is running.)

T:　　Is Fido jumping?

S6:　（Yes, he is.）

T:　　Is Fido climbing?

S7:　（Yes, he is.）

T:　　Is Fido dancing?

S8:　（No, he isn't.）

T:　　Is Fido sleeping?

S9:　（Yes, he is.）

Activity 3: Read and match

T:　　Now, let's read the dialogues together. Here are some moments. Which moment matches Dialogue 1?

Ss:　（Moment A.）

T:　　You're right. Please match other moments by yourself. And circle the words with "ing" like this. [acts it out]

Ss:　[read and match]

T:　　Have you finished? Let's check. Which moment matches Dialogue 2?

S10:　（Moment C.）

T:　　Which word can help you?

S10:　（Running.）

T:　　Wonderful! And next?

S11:　（Moment B. Climbing.）

T:　　Excellent! How about this one?

S12:　（Moment E. Jumping.）

T:　　And the last one. Together!

Ss:　（Moment D. Sleeping.）

Activity 4: Let's spell

T:　　You are doing so well! Just now, we've circled so many words with "ing". Do you know how to spell them? Show me your hands. Let's try. Look at the red part. "ing" makes the sound /ɪŋ/. /kl/, /aɪ/, /m/, /ɪŋ/…

Ss:　（/kl/, /aɪ/, /m/, /ɪŋ/. /ˈklaɪmɪŋ/）. [spell "climbing" with gesture]

T:　　Good job! Pay attention to the letter "b". It's a silent "b". Try again.

Ss:　（/ˈklaɪmɪŋ/.）

T:　　Great. Try one more. /rʌ/, /nɪŋ/ …

Ss:　（/ˈrʌnɪŋ/.）[spell "running" with gesture]

T:　　Nice try! Now, you know the rules. Can you spell the other words with your partners?

Ss:　（Yes.）

Ss: [spell in pairs]

T: Well, let's have a try.

Ss: [read the words]

Activity 5: Look, write and say

T: Look! We have the moments now. Can you help Chen Jie to finish the subtitles?

S13:   (Yes. Fido is climbing the tree.)

T: Well done! [makes a writing presentation over the projector] And next?

S14:   (Fido and Sam are playing with the ball.)

T: Wonderful! Can you finish the other subtitles by yourselves? Don't forget to do the narrations for the vlog. It's on your work sheet. Part 3. Go! Let's check the others. Moment 3 … ?

S15:   (Fido is running on the grass.)

T: How do you spell "running"?

S15:   (R-u-n-n-i-n-g.)

T: Right. Don't forget to double the letter "n". Next … ?

S16:   (Fido is jumping on Sam's head. J-u-m-p-i-n-g.)

T: You did a great job. Next … ?

S17:   (Fido is sleeping on Chen Jie's leg. S-l-e-e-p-i-n-g.)

Activity 6: Check and classify

T: Alright, boys and girls, we've learnt the words with "ing". Do they have rules? Can you classify them into three groups and tell me the rules? You can discuss with your partners first.

Ss: [discuss and classify the words]

T: Which group wants to try here?[invites a group of students to present in front of the class] Let's check. Group 1.

Ss: (They add "ing" directly at the ends of the words.)

T: Group 2.

Ss: (They double the last letter of the word and then add "ing".)

T: Group 3. We say bye-bye to … ?

Ss: (We say bye-bye to "e" and then add "ing".)

T: Wow, you are so smart! See? The yellow parts of the sentences. What do you know from them?

Ss: (Be + v. -ing.)

T: Correct! When we talk about something that is happening, we can use "be" and the "ing" form of the verbs. OK?

Ss: (OK.)

Activity 7: Listen and answer

T:　Kids, now let's help Chen Jie to make the second part of the vlog, about more pets. Look, are there more pets at the park?

S18:　(Yes. There are some rabbits at the park.)

T:　You've got it! What are they doing? You can guess like this "Are these rabbits … ?"

S19:　(Are these rabbits running?)

S20:　(Are these rabbits playing?)

S21:　(Are these rabbits eating?)

T:　Good guess! Let's listen and answer.

Ss:　[listen to the recording]

T:　Are these rabbits sleeping?

Ss:　(No, they aren't.)

T:　Are these rabbits playing?

Ss:　(Yes, they are.)

T:　Well done! Let's check the dialogue.

Activity 8: Read and check

T:　Read the dialogue and tell me. Which sentences can help you?

Ss:　[read the dialogue]

T:　Who knows?

S22:　(Are these rabbits eating? No, they are playing with each other.)

T:　Good. Read after me "each other". What does it mean? Which picture is right?

Ss:　[look at the pictures]

S23:　(Picture B is right.)

T:　Why do you think so?

S24:　(Because there are two rabbits. They play together.)

T:　You are so smart! Let's read the sentence one more time.

T & Ss:　(No, they are playing with each other.)

T:　What are the rabbits playing? Maybe … ?

Ss:　[look at the pictures] Maybe they are jumping. They are playing with the ball. They are sleeping.

T:　So cute! Now let's watch and follow the video. Please imitate the pronounciation and intonation.

Ss:　[watch and follow the video]

步骤三　真实运用，整体输出（10 分钟）

Activity 1: Ask and answer

T:　Now, Chen Jie wants to make a vlog about more pets. But there's something wrong with her camera. Sam's camera is OK. I have Sam's camera. Who wants to be Chen Jie and ask me some questions? You please.

S25:   (Is the cat climbing?)

T: Yes, it's climbing the tree. It's so naughty. Who else wants to give it a try? You please.

S26:   (Are the pigs drinking?)

T: No. They are eating. They're so cute. Good job! Now, two students work in pairs. Ready, go.

Ss: [Work in pairs]

T: Which pair want to show? You two please.

P1:   [pair performance]

T: Wow, wonderful!

Activity 2: Make a new vlog

T: Look! We have so many moments. Let's make Part 3 together. First, let's choose a moment.

S27:   (The chick.)

T: The chick? OK. What is the chick doing?

S27:   (It's running.)

T: How's the chick?

S28:   (It's so lovely.)

T: Great! [sticks and writes on the blackboard] Look, when you're writing, please write nicely. Work in groups of four. Choose the moment, fill out the sentences, and then act it out. Are you ready? Let's go!

Ss: (Yes!) [work in groups]

T: OK. Which group wants to come up and share your vlog?

G1:   [put their hands up]

T: This group, welcome!

G1:   [group performance]

T: Good job! Thank you.

Activity 3: Look and enjoy

T: Do you want to make a real vlog?

Ss: (Yes!)

T: Here's an example. Let's enjoy.

Ss: [enjoy a vlog]

作业布置

T: OK. Today's homework. Read the words and dialogue on Page 53. Make a mind-

map of *v.* -ing. And make your own vlog. Goodbye, boys and girls.

Ss: (Goodbye, teacher.)

教学设计①

（一）语篇研读

本课教学内容选自人教版英语五年级下册第五单元 Whose dog is it? B 部分 Let's learn 板块,该语篇属于"人与自然"主题范畴,内容涉及"关爱动物,观察动物"。

What

本课是一节词汇课,教材呈现了六个常见动词的现在分词与两组描述动物动作的对话。语篇为小学生日常对话,内容围绕 Chen Jie 和小伙伴们谈论小动物正在做的事情展开。Chen Jie 非常喜欢小动物,希望同学们帮助她一起完成 vlog,记录小动物的可爱瞬间。为了使学生立足语篇学习词汇,教师还基于教材文本进行了语篇再构,增加了 Chen Jie 与 Sam 通电话的内容。在电话中,Chen Jie 得知 Fido 在公园里调皮玩耍之后睡着了,于是她赶到了公园。

Why

Chen Jie 对小动物的喜爱让她萌生了用 vlog 记录精彩瞬间的想法,并想要与同学们分享。教师通过邀请同学们一起学习制作关于小动物的 vlog,能够促使学生在生活中更加细致地观察小动物,更加友好地与小动物相处,热爱身边的小动物。

How

教师基于本单元 B 部分对话课和词汇课的语境再构语篇,使语篇内容丰富又易于学生理解。Chen Jie 与同伴们的对话,均使用了现在进行时,如 eating、drinking、sleeping、jumping、playing。这些词涉及了动词现在分词的音、形、义、用等核心语言知识点。此外,本课的核心句型有"Is he drinking water? No, he isn't. He's eating."与"Are these rabbits eating? No. They're playing with each other."。

（二）学情分析

本课授课对象为 Z 省某小学五年级学生。"谈论生活中的小动物"是小学生感兴趣的话题。五年级学生普遍对身边的动物充满好奇心,愿意亲近动物,观察动物的动作行为,对身边小动物的特性有一定了解。此前,他们已经多次接触有关动物主题的学习内容,基本掌握了常用动词 climb、eat、drink、sleep、jump、play 的原形、发音与词义。在本单元 B 部分的对话课中,学生已初步感知单数第三人称的现在进行时句法结构,对于动词现在分词的形式也有一定了解,但仍未熟练掌握其发音与变形规则。这需要教师从教材原有语

---

① 本教学设计由温州大学附属第一实验小学单婵撰写。

篇内容出发,创设语言理解与运用的真实情境和补充特定内容,为学生提供操练与使用句法的机会。

(三)教学目标

通过本课时的学习,学生能够:

1. 在听、说、看的活动中,理解动词现在分词的含义;

2. 正确运用动词现在分词谈论小动物正在做的事情,初步掌握动词现在分词的变形规律;

3. 运用句型"The … is/are …""It's/They're so …"与同伴谈论小动物的活动,体会并内化现在进行时的表达功能;

4. 以创编 vlog 的形式呈现观察小动物的成果,抒发对小动物的热爱,呼吁他人关注小动物。

(四)教学流程

本课在整体外语教学理念指引下展开活动设计,教师秉持"整进整出"的思路,设计了以"制作一个动物行为的 vlog"的任务,教学强调整体输入、整体互动、整体输出。第一阶段为"激活旧知,整体输入",教师首先呈现一项有关小狗 Fido 的 vlog,激活学生在 A 部分对话课中的故事语境,激发学生运用 vlog 记录身边小动物行为的欲望,熟悉本节课的目标任务。第二阶段为"听说结合,整体互动"阶段,教师在本环节设计了多类型的视听说活动,让学生在理解 Fido 和 rabbits 动作的过程中完成句型和目标词汇在音、形、义、用四维度上的操练,为后续学生独立制作 vlog 打下基础。最后的"真实语用,整体输出"阶段,教师将延伸语言运用的情境,引导学生通过小组合作的形式,灵活运用所学知识,选择制作自己喜欢的 vlog 素材,实现语言知识的迁移与运用。

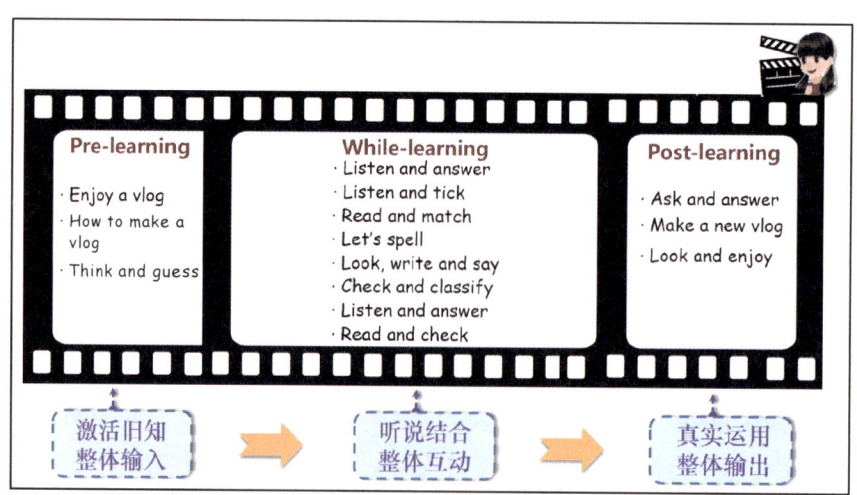

图 1

（五）教学过程

步骤一　激活旧知，整体输入（5分钟）

Activity 1: Enjoy a vlog（1min）

Students enjoy the vlog "What's Fido Doing?" and review the story and vocabulary of Unit 5.

Lyrics

What's Fido Doing?

Sam: Hello, hello. Is Fido eating? Can I play with him?

Chen Jie: No, he isn't. No, he isn't. He is sleeping. Sorry.

Sam: Hello, hello. Is Fido drinking? Can I play with him?

Chen Jie: No, he isn't. No, he isn't. He is sleeping. Sorry.

Sam: Hello, hello. Is Fido playing? Can I play with him?

Chen Jie: Yes, he is. Yes, he is. He is playing. You can come and play with him.

Sam: Hurray!

【设计说明】　滚动呈现 B 部分对话课的语篇，作为学生学习词汇的起点和语言依托，激活学生已习得的词汇 eating、drinking、sleeping 和核心句型"Is he drinking water? No, he isn't. He's eating"。

Activity 2: How to make a vlog（1min）

Students get to know the meaning of making a vlog and the basic elements of a vlog, including title, moments, subtitles and narrations. The teacher presents the main task of today's lesson.

图2

149

【设计说明】 教师引导学生理解制作 vlog 可以记录有意义的瞬间与人分享,帮助学生了解一个 vlog 包含的基本元素(见图 2),提出本课的语用任务——帮助 Chen Jie 完成关于小动物的 vlog,让学生明确学习目标,带着期待进入新课程的学习。

教师讲解 vlog 的构成并明确本课任务。在此过程中,学生了解 vlog 的基本要素并理解制作 vlog、记录瞬间,并与人分享的重要意义,带着帮助 Chen Jie 完成关于小动物的 vlog 的期待进入课堂。

【效果评价】 教师观察学生的回答,判断其能否明确本课的语用任务并适时给予帮助。

Activity 3: Think and guess (3 mins)

Students review the short dialogue of Part A *Let's talk* and predict what Fido is doing now, like "Is Fido … ?".

图 3

【设计说明】 教师引导学生回顾 B 部分对话课的情境(见图 3),带领学生走进本课情境,鼓励其合理推测 Fido 正在做什么,激活学生已知的动词现在分词,为下一步的活动作铺垫。

【效果评价】 教师观察学生是否能够补全动词的现在分词,判断其是否能根据动词原形初步理解动词现在分词的含义。

步骤二 听说结合,整体互动(20 分钟)

Activity 1: Listen and answer (2 mins)

Students listen to the text for the first time. And then get to know the general idea by choosing the key question "What are they talking about?".

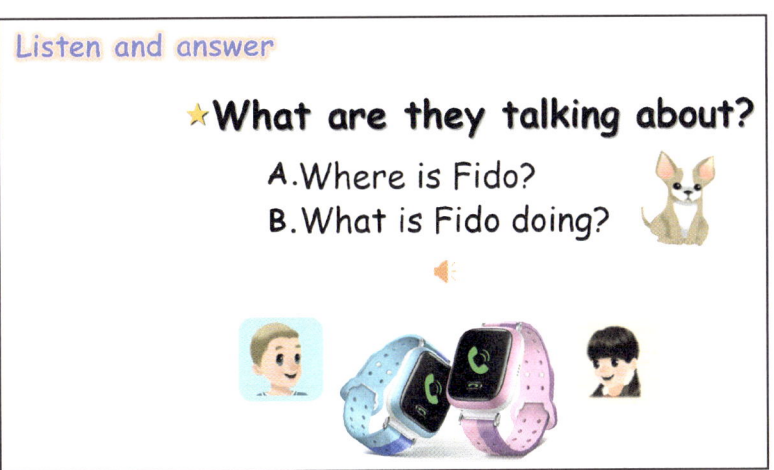

图4

【设计说明】　教师引导学生初听语篇,勾选概括语篇主旨大意的关键问题(见图4)。教师通过激发学生对对话的思考与猜测,培养学生的逻辑思维能力。

【效果评价】　教师观察学生能否正确勾选出语篇主旨大意的关键问题,判断其能否在情境中思考与猜测,并准确获取信息,必要时给予及时的引导。

Activity 2: Listen and tick (4 mins)

Having known the general idea of the text, students listen to the text again and tick out what Fido is doing. Check the answer and practise the present participles "playing", "running", "climbing", "jumping", "dancing" and "sleeping". Review the sentence patterns of "Is Fido …? Yes, he is./No, he isn't. He is …".

Transcript

Chen Jie: Hi, Sam. What are you doing now?

Sam: I'm playing with Fido in the park.

Chen Jie: OK. Is Fido running everywhere?

Sam: Yes, he is.

Chen Jie: Is he tired?

Sam: No. He is climbing the tree now. Oh, no!

Chen Jie: What's wrong?

Sam: He is jumping on my head! Oh, I'm tired!

　　(*Chen Jie is in the park.*)

Chen Jie: Oh, Fido is sleeping!

图5

【设计说明】 学生第二次听语篇,勾选出相关的单词(见图5)。通过复现对话课的句型,带动目标词汇的学习。在校对的过程中,教师引导学生在语篇中初步感知词汇的音和形。

Activity 3: Read and match (3 mins)

Students read the dialogues on the learning sheet. Match the moments with each short dialogue and circle the present participles.

图6

【设计说明】 引导学生通过图文配对(见图6),在语篇中理解和感受词汇的意义,整体学习词汇。让学生以圈出核心词汇的方式,进一步聚焦目标词汇的音、形和义。

【效果评价】 在活动2和活动3中,教师通过观察学生是否能勾选出相关单词,能否将单词与图片正确配对,以及能否圈出动词的现在分词,来及时了解学生"形"与"义"配对学习的成效与困难,进行具体、有针对性的指导。

Activity 4: Let's spell (2 mins)

Students try to spell the words with the support of gestures. They are encouraged to infer and practise the spelling rules of the present participles in pairs.

图7

【设计说明】　学生借助手势法尝试拼读单词,掌握词汇的音与形;接着,通过合作学习感知、体验、发现、迁移动词现在分词的规律(见图7)。

【效果评价】　教师通过观察学生能否正确拼读单词,评价学生对核心词汇"音"和"形"的掌握成效;并通过观察学生在合作学习时的学习态度和学习成果,给予指导和评价。

Activity 5: Look, write and say (3 mins)

According to the moments, students make up the sentences with the present participles, and meanwhile, extend the sentences with the phrases like with the ball, on the grass, on Sam's head, etc.

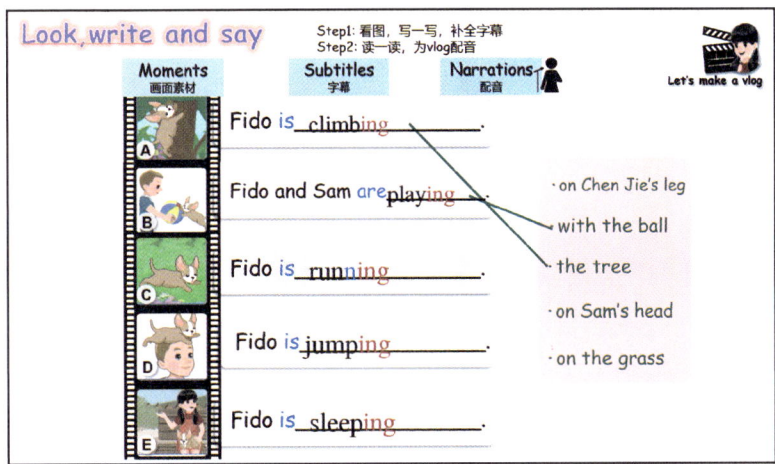

图8

【设计说明】 活动围绕词汇的读写技能开展。教师改编课本 Let's play 部分(见图8),鼓励学生根据语篇造句,操练句型并运用词汇,实现词汇从听说到读写的过渡,全面巩固了对目标词汇的学习。

【效果评价】 教师观察学生的书写,判断其能否在语境中正确拼写目标词汇,掌握四线格的正确书写,并适时给予鼓励。

Activity 6: Check and classify (2 mins)

Students discuss and try to classify the words into some groups, conclude the rules of the transformation and understand the grammatical meaning of Present Continuous Tense.

【设计说明】 教师引导学生通过小组合作发现动词变现在分词的规律,通过将单词分类来总结规律,理解现在进行时的语法意义,进而发展学生的语法规则的概括能力。

【效果评价】 教师观察学生能否根据已有的学习经验总结和概括语法规律,根据学生在概括语法规则时遇到的困难给予必要的提示。

Activity 7: Listen and answer (1 min)

Students look at the main page and find other pets. Guess what the rabbits are doing with the sentence pattern "Are these rabbits … ?". Then listen to the dialogue and answer the question.

图9

【设计说明】 教师利用单元主情境图作为语境的过渡,并通过听前预测活动(见图9),唤起学生表达的欲望。学生结合已知,在情境中运用本课的目标语言,练习使用句型"Are these rabbits … ?"。

Activity 8: Read and check (3 mins)

Students read the dialogue and check. Focus on the expression "Are these rabbits eating? No, they aren't."

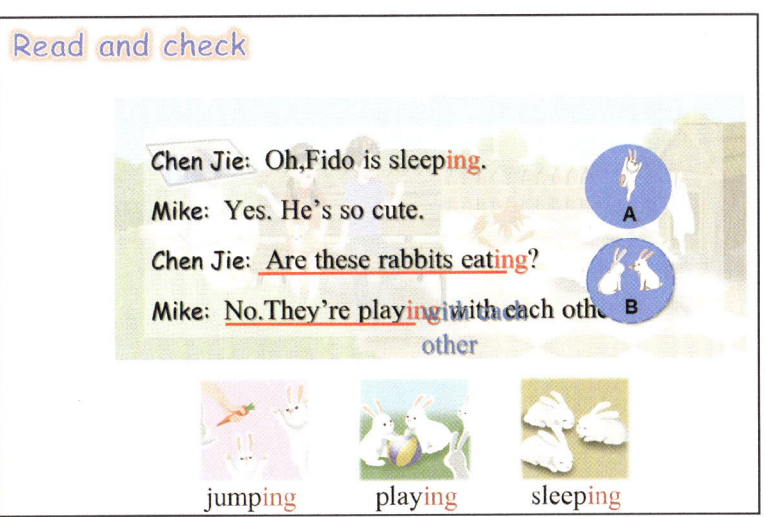

图 10

【设计说明】　学生带着问题读对话，在获取信息的过程中学习核心句型；通过图片配对，解决重难点词组"each other"（见图10）；通过跟读对话内容，感知和模仿语音和语调，内化所学语言。

【效果评价】　教师观察学生能否准确朗读重难点语言，掌握正确的语音语调，把握学生对核心语言的学习和内化情况，必要时进行纠正或调整练习次数。

步骤三　真实运用，整体输出（10分钟）

Activity 1: Ask and answer（4 mins）

Students look at Sam's photos. Ask and answer in pairs to see what the other animals are doing in the park. And talk about their characteristics with the expressions "It's so… / They're so… ". Some of the pairs will be invited to present their dialogue in front of the class.

图 11

【设计说明】 教师通过"Chen Jie 相机坏了,询问 Sam 拍的照片中小动物正在做什么"这一情节,让角色之间产生了信息差(见图 11)。学生根据模糊的图片,运用核心句型和核心词汇完成问答。本活动充分激发了学生的学习乐趣,让学生在真实情境中进一步运用所学语言。

【效果评价】 教师观察学生能否使用正确的语言、语音、语调演绎出 Chen Jie 和 Sam 的对话,根据学生的表现给予指导与评价。

Activity 2: Make a new vlog (5 mins)

Students work in groups of four. They choose the moments (pictures) and fill out the sentences (subtitles) on the cards. Then they match the moments with subtitles. At last, they narrate the vlog (narrations) together. One of the groups will show to the whole class and the other students will evaluate their performance.

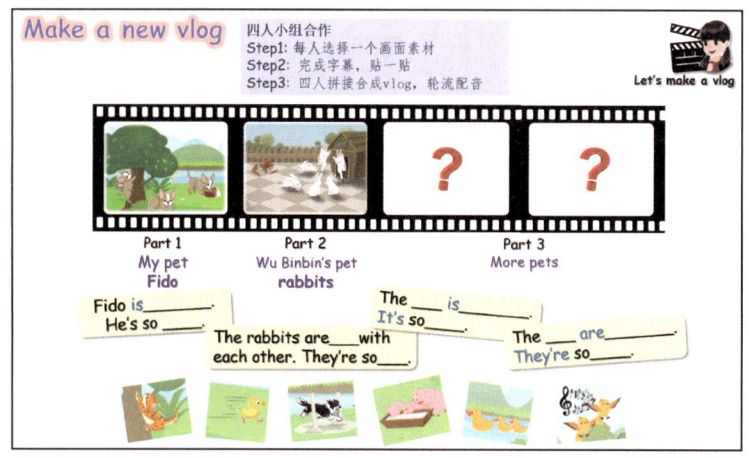

图 12

【设计说明】 学生根据自己的喜好选择学习素材(见图 12),发挥想象力,挖掘内心的真实情感,综合运用目标语言。通过小组活动完成不同难度的任务,每位学生都能在互助中迁移所学语言,在活动中增强运用语言的自信,体验英语学习带来的成就感。

【效果评价】 教师观察学生是否能正确运用所学内容制作 vlog,尤其关注学生在单复数句型的选择上是否存在困难,根据需要给出必要指导和评价。

Activity 3: Look and enjoy (1 min)

Students appreciate a vlog, which gives them a complete picture of today's learning.

【设计说明】 呈现本节课的语用任务成果,给学生带来完整的学习体验感,激发学生课后继续创作的动力。迁移与运用不应仅止于课堂,更应延伸到课后生活中。

(六) 作业设计

★1. Read the words and dialogue on Page 53.

★★2. Make a vlog in groups with the words and sentences on Page 53. The vlog should include more than 4 pets. And it should be in 3 minutes.

【设计说明】　本作业进行了难度递增的分层设计：一星作业为基础性作业,旨在引导学生及时巩固核心语言的学习;二星作业为实践性作业,引导学生运用所学语言完成真实的语用任务,自主创作 vlog。

（七）板书设计

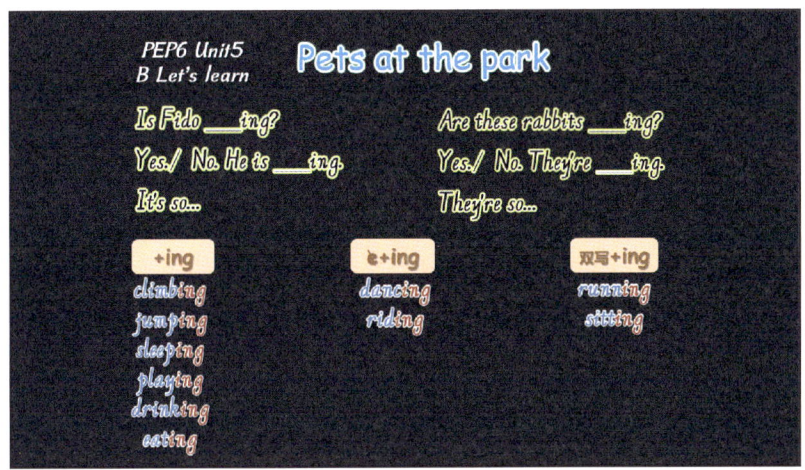

图 13

【设计说明】　板书包括课题名称与课堂要点。板书上方是本节课的核心句型,分成左右两组,学生能关注到单复数句型的不同。板书下半部分罗列了本课核心词汇及其相应的动词变化规律,它们由学生分类排列成三组。板书的生成让本节课的脉络可视化,使本课重难点一目了然,有助于学生进一步复习巩固和拓展运用。

（八）教学反思

本节课是一节词汇课,教师围绕主题意义,创设语用任务,引导学生联系真实生活、在真实语境中学习目标词汇,鼓励学生关爱动物。在课堂中,学生经历"激活旧知,整体输入——听说结合,整体互动——真实运用,整体输出"的学习过程。课后,教师作如下反思:

1. 基于语篇意识,优化词汇学习

传统词汇教学脱离语境,呈零星片断式,基于语篇意识开展词汇情境教学的模式与策略能够很好地弥补这一不足之处。从整体出发,有助于学生更好地理解词汇、运用词汇,同时提高英语阅读能力。本课时延续本单元 B 部分对话课的情境,围绕"Pets at the park"这一主题,以语篇为依托展开教学活动。首先,教师在课堂伊始创设语境,基于学生已知整体呈现语篇。而后,在语篇中开展学习活动,帮助学生在学习语篇的过程中习得目标词汇,更加深入地探究主题意义。最后,鼓励学生运用所学知识创编语篇,用目标语言描述实际生活中的小动物,逐步实现对语言知识和学习策略的内化,同时激发学生对小动物的热爱之情,从而在潜移默化中实现育人目标。

2. 依托整体教学,推进词汇学习

　　整体外语教学理念提出语篇是外语教学的最小单位,教师应以语篇为依托,在帮助学生发展语言能力的同时,通过整体输入、整体互动、整体输出等方式促进学生思维品质的全面提升。本课中,教师基于语篇设计词汇学习活动,如"listen and answer""listen and tick""read and match""let's spell"等,引导学生整体学习词汇,掌握核心词汇的音、义、形,从而实现整体输入。通过整合教材中 Let's play 这一部分的内容,拓展语用任务的文本语篇,学生为 Chen Jie's vlog 中的 Fido 部分配字幕和配音,在这一过程中开展整体学习,实现了在语境中书写词汇、主动探究、发现规则、迁移拓展的目标,落实词汇的读写技能。课后作业,即制作属于自己的 vlog,可鼓励学生在真实语境中积极进行整体输出,表达对小动物的喜爱之情,且在此过程中,学生的语言综合运用能力也能得到提升。

(九) 附件

学 习 单

【活动1】Listen and tick(听一听,用"√"选出你听到 Fido 正在做的事)

【活动2】Read and choose

(阅读对话,将对话与图片所对应的带字母图片配对。记得圈出带有 ing 的单词哦!)

【活动3】Let's write（Step1: 看图，补全句子，写一写。Step2: 读一读，为 vlog 配音）

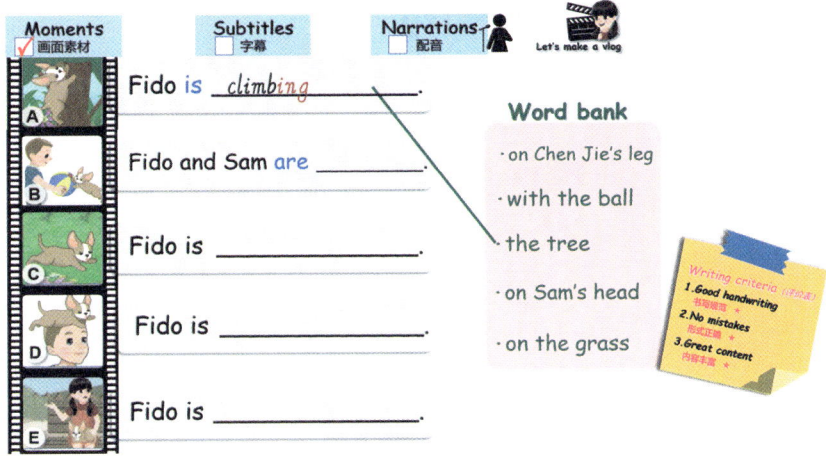

【活动4】Ask and answer

（同桌合作，看自己的学习单，进行问答。要注意单复数哦!）

Student A：

你是 Chen Jie，你的相机坏了，看不清画面。请用以下句型向同桌 Sam 提问，了解画面信息。

Student B：

你是 Sam，你朋友 Chen Jie 的相机坏了，看不清画面。请用以下句型回答她的问题。

课例 **7**

PEP B6 U4 When is the art show?
（Part C Story time）

说课视频

Hello, everyone! I'm Yami from Wenzhou Qinyuan Primary School. It's my great honor to present my lesson plan here. My presentation will cover the following three aspects, namely, learning objectives, learning process and learning effects.

Learning objectives

Now, let's start with the first part. Generally speaking, the analysis of learning material and learners are the basis for the establishment of learning objectives. So first, let's take a close look at the learning material.

The learning material is from PEP Book 6 Unit 4 *When is the art show?* Part C *Story time*. The theme is *man and self*, involving *self-arrangement of learning and living*.

What

It's a story about Zoom. In order to pass the singing test, he refuses the invitations from his friends and practises his song every day. At last, because of his efforts, he gets good grades.

Why

After reading the story, readers will realize that "Practice makes perfect". They will also understand self-improvement comes with not only the courage to refuse temptation, but also patience, persistence, and the efforts to practise.

How

This is a typical dialogue between Zoom and his friends. Through the conversations and pictures in the text, some key words of the unit such as *April 30th*, *May 1st* and *May 2nd* are presented. The text also uses future tense, and some core sentence patterns, including "Will

---

① 本说课稿由温州市沁园小学杨艳撰写。

160

you … ?", "I want to practise the song" and "Practice makes perfect". Students can use key phrases including *come to the party*, *play football*, and *watch TV*.

Now, let's come to the analysis of learners.

Students in Grade 5 have been learning English for more than two years. They are familiar with the English expressions of dates and daily activities. They have also acquired many verb phrases. However, they have little awareness of combining dates with activities when making a plan. In addition, although students are able to have a single round of dialogue with others by using simple future tense, it is difficult for most of them to extract, analyze and summarize the key information of the text and infer the meaning of the theme when the story is composed of multiple rounds of dialogues.

To overcome these difficulties, on the one hand, students need tools provided by the teacher like learning sheets, short video clips, pictures and skillful blackboard design to distinguish different meanings and pragmatic functions of words, such as "practise" and "practice", and sort out the content and organizational structure of the story in chronological order. On the other hand, the teacher needs to help students turn applying and practicing activities into transferring and innovating activities through implementing some learning activities that can inspire students' thinking such as inquiring about the details of the story, designing a title for the story and doing a role-play.

Based on the above analysis, the following learning objectives are set. By the end of this lesson, students will be able to:

1. extract and comb the activities between Zoom and his friends in the story according to the dates and chronological development.

2. apply the key words and sentence patterns into asking and answering questions, filling in the information table and acting out the story with the help of the teacher.

3. evaluate Zoom's behavior in order to explore the meaning of "Practice makes perfect.", make up and show a new ending of the story.

Learning process

Now let's move on to the description of teaching procedures. In this class, the Activity-based Approach to English Learning is adopted, which divides all the learning activities into the following three stages: Learn and understand what Zoom will do before the test; Infer and analyze whether Zoom can pass the singing test; Imagine and create what Zoom will do before swimming.

In the first stage, Learn and understand what Zoom will do before the test, seven activities are designed.

In Activity one, Sing and chant, there are two steps. First, students will sing a song that can activate their interests and quickly recall their previous knowledge of verb phrases together. Secondly, students will chant with me together. They will be required to review the expressions of dates and daily activities. They will also perceive the target language of this lesson. Then, Activity two is Think and ask. Students will appreciate a picture from the textbook and raise questions with when, where, what and how. It will improve their ability to think logically. I can observe whether the students can effectively ask and answer the questions based on what they don't know and what they want to know.

The third activity is Watch and choose. Students are required to watch the video of the whole story and find out what Zoom worries about. They can understand the whole story while watching, cultivating their skills to extract key information.

After that, in Activity four, Listen and answer, students will listen to the first paragraph and find out the date of the singing test as well as what Zoom can't do well. Finally, students will predict what Zoom will do before the singing test with reason. The listening and predicting tasks cultivate students' comprehension and inference skills. It also improves their thinking quality.

In the fifth activity, Watch and answer, students will watch the second part of the video and find out whether Zoom will go out with his friends or not. In this way, they will further explore the story and dig out the significance of the theme by second watching.

Next, students are asked to finish four tasks on the learning sheet, read and match the pictures with the sentences, circle out the dates and underline the activities Zoom may do, fill out the information table, and discuss with partners about the reason why Zoom says "Sorry, I can't". Through these tasks above, students can further experience and understand the situation of the dialogue, and obtain specific information. What's more, students can further consolidate the language and develop the ability of cooperative learning. I can observe their communication in the context, and give guidance as well as feedback according to their performance.

In the last activity of the first stage, Listen and imitate, students will listen to the tape and repeat it correctly. In this way, they can perceive and imitate pronunciation, intonation and stress to internalize the language they have learnt.

In the second stage, Infer and analyze why Zoom can pass the singing test, there are three activities contained.

Activity one is Do a role-play. To help students understand the characters' language and inner world, and make correct value judgments, I will ask them to act out the dialogue in groups of four, to evaluate each other's show according to the checklist including accuracy, fluency and vividness, and to find the differences between "practice" and "practise" through discussion in groups. I will observe whether students can go deep into the role-play, and then give hints and guidance if necessary.

After that, in Activity two, Look and guess, students will observe the picture and predict whether Zoom can pass the singing test or not and what Miss Bird says. Their logical thinking can be developed in a real-life situation. I will assess students' ability to use contextual clues to infer the content of a conversation by observing whether they can make reasonable guesses about the content of the subsequent conversation.

The third activity is Read and find. Students will be asked to answer three questions, "Why is Zoom happy now?", "Why can Zoom sing well?" and "Why does practice make Zoom sing well?". Then students will be asked to find the famous saying in the story. Through three continuous questions, students will be guided to think deeply about the theme behind the story, that is, "Practice makes perfect".

The last stage, Imagine and create what Zoom will do before swimming, includes three activities.

The first one is to Discuss and write. Students will discuss what Zoom is like, and then write down the title for the cover of the story. It improves students' ability to summarize, analyze and think critically.

Activity two is Look and say. Students will observe the picture and predict the ending of the story. It will encourage students to make a new story.

The last activity is Make a new story and act. There are two steps. First, students will discuss in groups and fill in the table. Second, students will make up a new story and act it out. Students can consolidate core vocabulary and sentence patterns by completing tables and making dialogues, and improve their cooperative learning skills. By continuing the story of Zoom's swimming, students again appreciate the importance of "Practice makes perfect". and develop the ability to transfer and innovate. I will observe students' presentations, and evaluate the effects of teaching and learning. In this way, I can cultivate students' ability to use the language they have learnt to solve practical problems.

After class, there are two layered assignments for students. First, at Level A, they are required to finish the story chart. The second one, at Level B, is to act out the story with friends, which can encourage them to communicate with the language they have learnt.

As for the blackboard design, there are three main parts. The sentence pattern is on the left side of the blackboard. The key words and verb phrases are presented in a table which is in the middle of the blackboard. The changes in Zoom's ability and mood are at the top of the table. The blackboard design enables students to have a better understanding of and to think logically about today's story.

Learning effects

To sum up, there are two highlights in my lesson.

In terms of the teaching design and implementation, I adhere to the student-oriented concept and provide students with open experience, which stimulates students' interest in participating and learning. In Let's chant, students interact with me in a cheerful rhythm. In Do a role-play, students directly feel the change of Zoom's singing through acting. In Think and write, students are motivated to learn initially through writing a title for the story. In Make a new story and act, students enjoy making up the story in groups, which stimulates their creativity and develops their innovative thinking. During the whole teaching process, I guide students to dig deeply into the story and encourage them to be persistent like Zoom in daily life, in which students can feel the fun of the story class.

Secondly, I generate three "main questions" and connect the activities with specific stages. The "main questions" are interlinked and progressive, which promotes students to deeply explore the thematic meaning, that is, "Practice makes perfect". The three questions: "What will Zoom do before the singing test?", "Can Zoom pass the singing test?" and "What will Zoom do before swimming?" contribute to the exploration of the story, helping students understand the text comprehensively and apply what they have learnt into practice.

That's all for my presentation. Thanks for your watching.

试课实录①

试课视频

步骤一 探究语篇，感知理解（20分钟）

Activity 1: Sing and chant

A: Let's sing

T: Hello, boys and girls. Are you ready for the class? Stand up. Let's sing and dance.

Ss: [sing and dance]

T: Good job, boys and girls!

B: Let's chant

T: Look! Who is he?

Ss: (He's Zoom.)

T: Yes, he's our old friend, Zoom. Today we are going to learn a story about Zoom. First, let's enjoy a chant. If you like it, please join me.

Ss: [chant with the teacher]

T: Wonderful, boys and girls. What date can you find?

S1:   (I find May 1st, May 2nd, … and May 6th.)

T: Well done. Zoom is very busy every day.

Activity 2: Think and ask

T: Let's see today's characters. Look! Who are they?

S2:   (They are Zoom, Zip, Rabbit, Cat and Miss Bird.)

T: Can you ask some questions with when, where, what and how?

S3:   (When is it?)

T: When?

S4:   (It's April 30th.)

---

① 本试课稿由温州市沁园小学杨艳撰写。

T:　　Yes. Read after me. April 30th. Any other questions?

S5:　 (Where are they?)

T:　　They are in the …?

S6:　 (They're in the music room.)

T:　　How about what?

S7:　 (What are they doing?)

S8:　 (They are having a music class.)

S9:　 (How is Zoom?)

T:　　Look at Zoom. Is he happy? No?

S10: (He is sad.)

S11: (He is worried.)

Activity 3: Watch and choose

T:　　Yes. He is worried. What does Zoom worry about this time? Does he worry about food or the singing test? Now let's watch the video and answer the question.

Ss:　 [watch the video]

T:　　Who got the answer?

S12: (He worries about the singing test.)

T:　　Yes.

Activity 4: Listen and answer

T:　　Now listen to the dialogue again. And answer more questions. Question 1: When will be the singing test? Question 2: What can't Zoom do well? OK? Ready? Go.

Ss:　 [listen to the recording]

S13: (The singing test will be on May 4th.)

T:　　Right. What can't Zoom do well? Don't worry. Let's listen again. Focus on what he can't do well.

Ss:　 [listen to the recording]

S14: He can't sing well.

T:　　Yes, Zoom can't sing well. He says …?

Ss:　 (I can't sing well.)

T:　　So his friend comforts him. Let's listen and read.

Ss:　 [listen to the recording] (Don't worry.)

T:　　Who can be worried Zoom? And all of us are Zip.

S15: [puts up his hand]

T:　　Good. Are you ready? Go!

S15: (I can't sing well.)

T & Ss: (Don't worry.)

T:　　Well done! The singing test will be on May 4th. But the worried Zoom can't sing well. What will Zoom do before the singing test? Maybe you can try with "I will…"

S16: (I will ask the teacher for help.)

S17: (I will go to the concert.)

S18: (I will sing every day.)

Activity 5: Watch and answer

T: What will happen to Zoom? Let's watch the video and answer the question. Will friends ask Zoom to go out or maybe they will sing with Zoom?

Ss: [watch the video]

T: Who can tell me the answer?

S19: (They will ask Zoom out.)

T: Yes.

Activity 6: Read and write

A: Read and match

T: Will Zoom go out with his friends? Let's find out. Look at these pictures and read these sentences carefully. We'll do the matching. Take out your learning sheet. Let's do it.

Ss: [match]

T: Who can tell me the answer? Picture 1 is?

S20: (B.)

T: Listen and read.

Ss: [listen and read] (Will you come to the party? Today is Rabbit's birthday.)

T: Picture 2 is?

S21: (C.)

T: Try.

Ss: [listen and read] (Will you play football with me after lunch?)

T: Picture 3? Tell me together.

Ss: (A.)

T: Listen and read.

Ss: [listen and read] (Let's watch TV together. The show is very funny!)

T: Good job, boys and girls.

B: Circle and underline

T: Look at this picture. Can you find the date?

S22: (May 1st.)

T: Yes, May 1st. Let me circle the date. And what activity may Zoom do?

S23: (Come to the party.)

T: Right. Let me underline. So how about the other two pictures? Let's fill in the table. First, circle the date, and then underline the activity.

C: Read and fill in

T:　Take out your learning sheet. Read and fill in the table with the information you got.

Ss:　[read and fill in the blank]

T:　Now let's check the answer. On May 1st, Zip asks, "will you … ?"

Ss:　(Come to the party?)

T:　Will Zoom come to the party?

Ss:　(No!)

T:　What does Zoom say? Let's listen.

Ss:　[listen to the audio]

T:　Let's read together.

T & Ss: Sorry, I can't.

T:　Now, let's check in pairs. One is Zoom, one is Zip or Cat. Check with your partner. Ready? Go!

Ss:　[check the answer in pairs]

T:　Time's up. Who can try? It's May 2nd.

G1:　(Will you play football? Sorry, I can't.)

T:　Are they right?

Ss:　Yes.

T:　It's May 3rd. Who can try?

G2:　(Will you watch TV? Sorry, I can't.)

D: Read and discuss

T:　Why does Zoom say "Sorry, I can't."? Open your book. Turn to Page 45. Read Pictures 2, 3 and 4. You can discuss with your partner. Why does Zoom say "Sorry"? You can tell me the key words as well.

Ss:　[read and discuss in pairs]

T:　Have you found it? You please.

S24:　(He wants to practise his song.)

T:　Yes. Zoom says, "I want to practise my song." Follow me. Practise.

Ss:　(Practise.)

T:　Run a train. This group, please.

Ss:　[read one by one]

T:　Good job. Follow me. Practise my song.

Ss:　(Practise my song.)

T:　I want to practise my song.

Ss:　(I want to practise my song.)

T:　Wonderful. How can Zoom practise the song? Maybe he can practise the song at home. Maybe he can …

S25:　(He can practise the song at school.)

S26: (He can practise the song in the morning.)

S27: (He can practise the song every day.)

Activity 7: Listen and imitate

T:　　Let's listen and imitate.

Ss:　　[listen and imitate]

T:　　Perfect!

步骤二　进入角色,交流实践(7 分钟)

Activity 1: Do a role-play

A: Let's act

T:　　Boys and girls, now let's do the role-play. I'm Zoom. Who can be Zip? Who can be Cat and Rabbit?

S28 & S29 & S20: [puts up their hands up one by one]

T:　　Good! At last, let's see how many stars we can get. Three. Two. One.

T & S28 & S29 & S30: [do the role-play]

T:　　How many stars can we get?

Ss:　　(Three.)

T:　　Thank you so much. Big hands for us. Now it's your turn. Four students work in a group. One is Zoom, one is Zip, one is Cat and one is Rabbit.

Ss:　　[work in groups]

T:　　OK. Who can come here? Your group please. Three. Two. One.

Ss:　　(Action.)

G3:　　[perform]

T:　　Big hands for them. How many stars can they get?

Ss:　　(Three.)

B: Think and discuss

T:　　Look! There are two [ˈpræktɪs]. One is ended with "se" and one is ended with "ce". Can you tell me the difference? You can discuss in groups.

Ss:　　[work in groups]

T:　　Who can try?

S31:　　(Practise is a verb. And practice is a noun.)

T:　　Smart. The one with "se" is a verb. The one with "ce" is a noun.

Activity 2: Look and guess

T:　　Look at this picture! Does Zoom pass the singing test?

Ss:　　(Yes, he does.)

T:　　How do you know?

S32:　　(Because Zoom looks happy.)

S33: （Because Miss Bird thumbs up.）

T:　Nice try! And what does Miss Bird say? Let's watch the video and tell me the answer.

Ss:　［watch the video］

T:　Miss Bird says …？

S34: （Good job, Zoom!）

T:　And Zoom answers …？

Ss:　（Thank you, Miss Bird!）

Activity 3: Read and find

T:　At first, Zoom is worried. But now he is very happy. Why?

S35: （Because he can sing well now.）

T:　Why can he sing well now?

S36: （Because he practises every day.）

T:　Why does practice make Zoom sing well? Now open your book, turn to Page 45, and read by yourself loudly. And then find the famous saying in this story. You can discuss with your groupmates.

Ss:　［read and discuss in groups］

T:　Who can try?

S37: （Practice makes perfect.）

T:　Yes. Practice makes perfect. Read after me.

Ss:　（Practice makes perfect.）

T:　Wonderful. At first, Zoom can't sing well. He practises every day. Because he knows practice makes perfect. And practice also makes he happy.

步骤三　续编故事,迁移创新（8分钟）

Activity 1: Discuss and write

T:　What do you think of Zoom?

S38: （He's busy.）

S39: （He's patient.）

T:　Yes. Maybe he's hard-working. Maybe he's smart. In my opinion, he's hard-working. It may be a good title for my story. It's your turn. Take out your learning sheet, write down your title for the story and your name as well.

Ss:　［write the title and the name］

Activity 2: Look and say

T:　Will Zoom go out with his friends after the singing test?

Ss:　（Yes.）

T:　What does Cat say? I'll …？

Ss:　（Go swimming.）

T:　　Tonight. Right. What does Zoom say? Let's listen and repeat.

Ss:　 [listen and repeat] (Of course.)

T:　　Now we are Cat. Who can be Zoom?

S40: [puts up his hand]

T & Ss: (I'll go swimming tonight. Will you go?)

S40: (Of course.)

T:　　I don't think you are happy enough. I think you should be happier. Now I'm Cat. All of you are Zoom. I'll go swimming tonight. Will you go?

Ss:　 (Of course.)

T:　　Wonderful! What will happen that night? Let's watch the video.

Ss:　 [watch the video]

Activity 3: Make a new story and act

T:　　What will Zoom do these days? Let's make a new story for Zoom. Step 1, discuss in group and fill in the table on your learning sheet. Step 2, act it out and show to us. Here are the phrase bank and sentence bank for you. Take out your learning sheet. Go!

Ss:　 [work in groups]

T:　　Time is up. Who can come here? Your group please. Three. Two. One.

Ss:　 (Action.)

G4:　[group performance]

T:　　Big hands. How many stars can they get?

Ss:　 (Three.)

T:　　Wonderful! Dear kids, when you need practice, try your best; when you want to play, have fun.

作业布置

T:　　Today's homework. Finish the story chart. And also you can act out the story with your friends. Class is over. Goodbye, everyone.

Ss:　 (Goodbye, teacher!)

配套课件

教学设计①

（一）语篇研读

　　本课教学内容选自人教版英语五年级下册第四单元 When is the art show? Part C Story time 板块，该语篇属于"人与自我"主题范畴，内容涉及"学习与生活的自我管理"。

———————————————

① 本教学设计由温州市沁园小学杨艳撰写。

170

What

该语篇为对话型故事语篇,清晰地呈现了故事的起因、经过和结果。主人公 Zoom 为了通过歌唱测试,多次拒绝好友邀请,坚持每天练习唱歌,最终在考试中取得好成绩。

Why

该语篇通过描述 Zoom 拒绝好友邀请并坚持每天练习唱歌的情景,阐释了“熟能生巧”的深刻含义。教师可以利用该语篇使学生明白做事要专心致志、心无旁骛。如果要实现自我提升,不仅需要拒绝诱惑的勇气,还需要刻苦学习的毅力和坚持不懈的信念。

How

本课语篇内容是 Zoom 和好朋友的对话。故事图片清晰呈现了本单元核心短语,如 April 30th、May 1st、May 2nd 等。故事中的人物在发出邀请时使用了一般将来时,涉及的核心句型包括“Will you … ?”“I want to practise the song. ”“Practice makes perfect. ”等;动词短语包括“come to the party”“play football”“watch TV”“practise the song”等。

（二）学情分析

本课授课对象为 Z 省某小学五年级学生。该年段是学生自我管理与规划意识养成的关键时期,在趣味故事的阅读中开展“学习与生活的自我管理”主题教学能够有效激发学生的学习动机。两年多的英语课程学习后,学生已经熟悉了日期与日常活动的英语表达方式,有一定的动词词组储备,但尚未形成结合日期规划活动的意识。此外,学生虽已能够初步运用一般将来时与他人进行单轮对话交流,但本课时所要理解的故事语篇由多轮对话构成,故提取、梳理和归纳该语篇关键信息和推断主题意义对多数学生而言会比较困难。一方面,教师需要提供学习单、短视频、图片、板书等工具,帮助学生区分核心词汇如 practise 和 practice 的内涵及语用方式,按故事发展的时间顺序整理语篇内容及组织结构;另一方面,教师还需以追问故事细节、为故事拟标题、角色扮演等启迪思维的活动,帮助学生在深挖主题意义的基础上,由学习理解走向应用实践与初步的迁移创新。

（三）教学目标

通过本课时的学习,学生能够:

1. 按照日期和故事发展顺序,获取并梳理故事中 Zoom 和他的朋友们开展的活动;

2. 在教师的帮助下,运用核心词汇和重点句型询问和回答,填写故事信息表,并分角色表演故事内容;

3. 简要评价故事中 Zoom 的做法,思考“Practice makes perfect. ”的深层寓意;在此基础上,小组合作创编故事的结局,并向全班汇报表演。

（四）教学流程

本节课中,教师将跟随 Zoom 所经历的“唱歌测试前、通过唱歌测试、测试后将要做的事”三个阶段设计相应教学情境,引导学生学习。在由“ What will Zoom do before the singing test?”这一问题引导的第一阶段,教师主要围绕语篇结构和核心语言,设计阶梯式

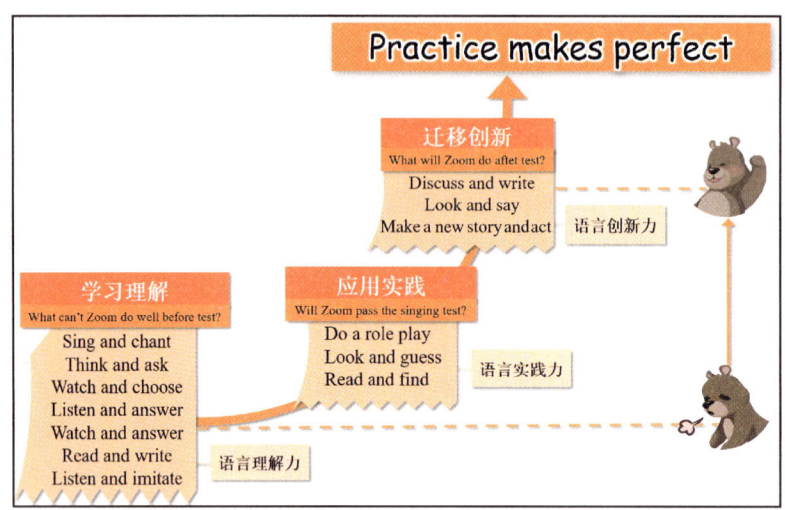

图 1

问题,让学生通过跟音诵读、看图预测、听音回答等活动获取与梳理故事语篇的基本信息,建构对语篇知识的理解力。在以"Will Zoom pass the singing test?"为主要问题的第二阶段,教师将引导学生借助语言支架尝试角色扮演,在具身表现中感知故事冲突,推测 Zoom 是否通过考试和 Miss Bird 可能会说的话,学生在交流中提升语言的表达力。到了第三阶段,师生将围绕"What will Zoom do before swimming?"这一关键问题展开讨论,学生从拟写故事名、思考语篇蕴含的主题意义,到以小组为单位,想象与续编故事,逐步发展语言的创新力。

(五) 教学过程

步骤一 探究语篇,感知理解(20 分钟)

Activity 1: Sing and chant (3 mins)

A. Let's sing

Students sing the song "What Can You Do?" with actions and review the verb phrases.

> **Lyrics**
>
> What Can You Do?
>
> How about you? What can you do? Jump, I can jump. Swim, I can swim. Ride a bike, I can ride a bike. Sing a song, I can sing a song.
>
> How about you? What can you do?

【设计说明】 通过有节奏的歌曲,活跃课堂气氛,激发学生学习兴趣,并激活相关的动词短语。

B. Let's chant

Students watch the video and chant with the teacher. Then they find out the dates in the video.

Text

T: Hello! Everybody! This is Zoom. He's very busy just like you.

T: May 1st.	Ss: A happy day.
T: Will you come to the party today?	Ss: Party, party, come to the party.
T: May 2nd.	Ss: A healthy day.
T: Will you play football today?	Ss: Football, football, play football.
T: May 3rd.	Ss: A funny day.
T: Will you watch TV shows today?	Ss: TV shows, TV shows, watch TV shows.
T: May 4th.	Ss: A great day.
T: Will you go swimming today?	Ss: Swimming, swimming, go swimming.
T: May 5th.	Ss: A wonderful day.
T: Will you go shopping today?	Ss: Shopping, shopping, go shopping.
T: May 6th!	Ss: Hooray!
T: Let's have a big dinner today.	Ss: Hooray!

【设计说明】 教师通过自编 Chant，引出故事主人公 Zoom，同时激活学生对已学的动词短语与日期表达的记忆，将前期语言储备迁移和运用到本课，为故事情节发展埋下伏笔。

【效果评价】 教师观察学生在 Chant 中说出的具体内容，了解其对动词短语的整体把握情况。教师根据学生的回答，了解其对日期表达的熟练程度。

Activity 2: Think and ask（2 mins）

According to the picture, students try to ask some questions with "when" "where" "what" and "how".

图 2

【设计说明】 学生针对图片(见图2)进行思考和提问,提升问题意识,提高逻辑推理能力和信息搜索能力。

【效果评价】 教师观察学生是否能根据已有的知识和经验对图片进行有效提问,必要时给予引导或鼓励。

Activity 3: Watch and choose (2 mins)

Students watch the video and find out what Zoom worries about.

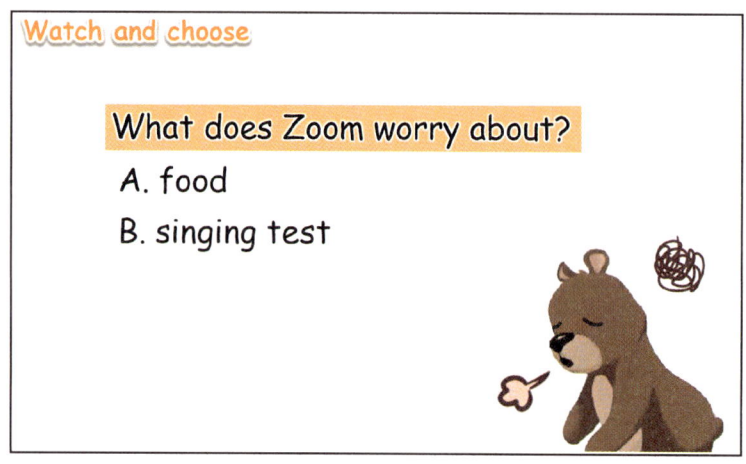

图3

【设计说明】 通过观看完整的视频,学生整体感知故事情节和主旨大意。教师引导学生带着疑问(见图3)走进故事探寻答案,这有助于培养学生准确获取、梳理和记录关键信息的能力。

Activity 4: Listen and answer (3 mins)

Students listen to the recording and find out the date of the singing test. Then they listen again and find out what Zoom can't do well. Finally, students predict what Zoom will do before the singing test.

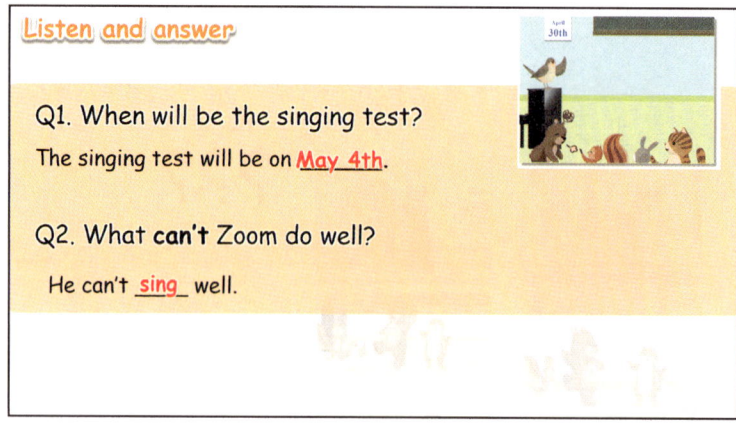

图4

174

　　【设计说明】　学生两次带着问题听故事的录音(见图4),从整体到细节,逐步理解对话内容,把握故事关键信息,运用句型"I will …",并结合已有知识合理预测 Zoom 在唱歌测试前会做些什么。听力任务和预测任务能有效提升学生的理解与推断能力,提高思维品质。

　　【效果评价】　教师观察学生对三个问题的回答情况,根据需要给予必要的指导和评价。

Activity 5: Watch and answer（2 mins）

Students watch the video and choose the answer to the question "What will happen?"

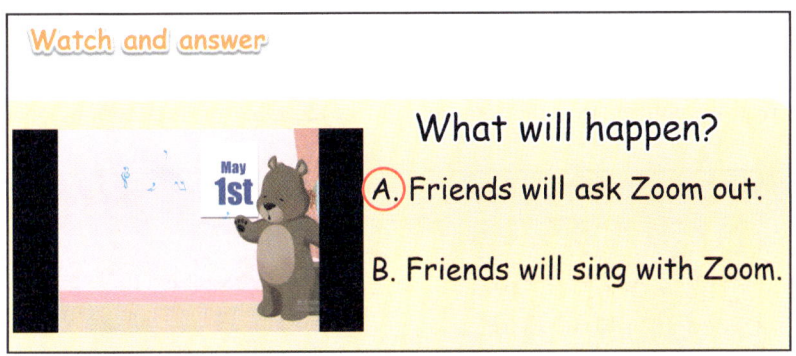

图5

　　【设计说明】　学生再次带着问题(见图5)观看视频,深入理解故事的情节发展,探究主题意义。

　　【效果评价】　教师观察学生能否在观看视频后选择正确的答案,根据需要给予必要的指导和评价。

Activity 6: Read and write（3 mins）

A. Read and match

Students look at pictures and read the sentences carefully. Then they match the pictures with the sentences.

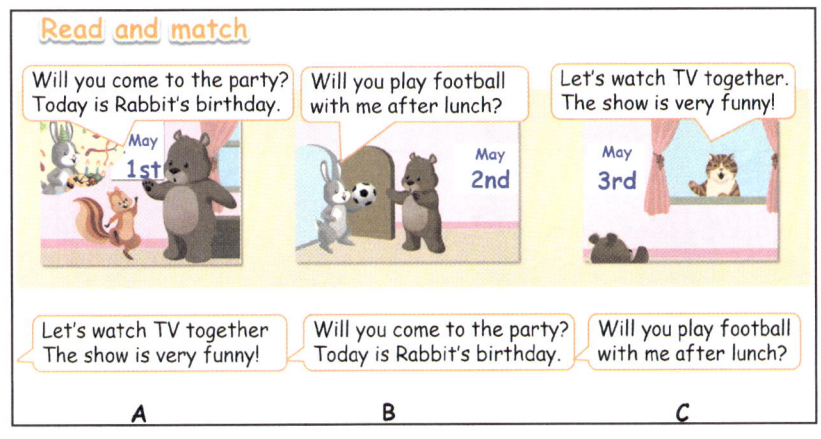

图6

【设计说明】 通过观察图片和细读句子(见图6),培养学生"看"和"读"的能力,引导学生梳理出故事中的冲突,逐步理解对话内容。

【效果评价】 教师观察学生回答问题的表现,了解其对故事内容的掌握情况。

B. Circle and underline

Students circle out the date of each picture first, and then underline the activities Zoom may do.

【设计说明】 学生在教师的引导下,再一次观察图片并细读句子,圈出日期和动词词组,完成对故事核心语言的初步学习。

【效果评价】 教师观察学生完成的情况,适时给予鼓励与评价,必要时提供帮助。

C. Read and fill in

Students read the information they got and fill in the table on the learning sheet.

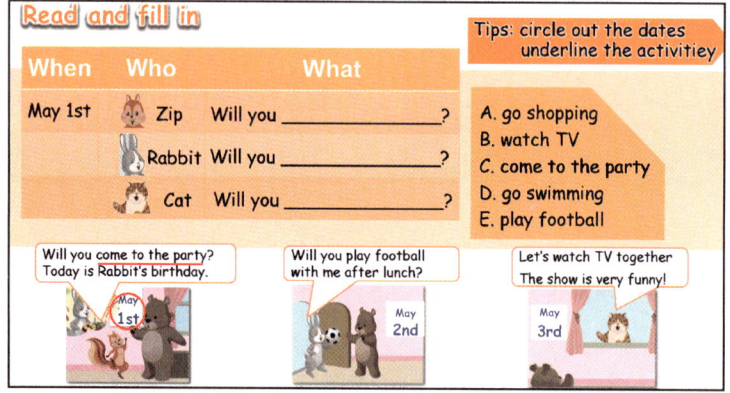

图 7

【设计说明】 学生在教师的引导下,将上一环节得到的信息填入学习单的表格中(见图7),并借助语言支架校对答案,在提升理解与判断能力的同时,内化目标语言。

【效果评价】 教师观察学生完成活动的情况,及时校对答案和给予评价。

D. Read and discuss

Students read the story (picture 2 – 4) by themselves, and then discuss with partners about the reason why Zoom says "Sorry, I can't". Finally, they try to make sentences about how Zoom practises the song.

图 8

【设计说明】　通过细读课文图二至图四的对话，以及同桌讨论 Zoom 拒绝好友（见图8）的活动，学生在情境中挖掘主题意义，理解和运用句型"I want to practise the song"，逐步突破本节课难点。

【效果评价】　教师观察学生进行同桌讨论与回答问题的表现，了解其对故事主题的理解，以及对 practise 的掌握程度，并适时给予指导。

Activity 7: Listen and imitate (2 mins)

Students read after the recording and imitate the pronunciation, intonation and stress.

【设计说明】　学生听录音跟读课文时，通过模仿语音语调，体会角色情感，进一步理解对话内容，为语言输出奠定基础。

【效果评价】　教师根据学生跟读对话的情况，适时给予指导和鼓励。

步骤二　进入角色，交流实践（7分钟）

Activity 1: Do a role-play (4 mins)

A.　Let's act

After the teacher's demonstration, students play the roles in groups of four and act them out in the class. Then they get assessments from the teacher and other students.

Performing Checklist	
1. Can you act as worried as Zoom?	☆
2. Can you act without book?	☆
3. Can you act vividly?	☆
Total stars	___ ☆

图 9

【设计说明】　在角色扮演中，学生根据对故事的掌握程度和对角色的理解，自主协商分配角色，体验角色的真实性和学习的趣味性。这不仅能培养其小组合作意识，而且能引导学生在归纳与整理核心语言的基础上，应用内化语言，为后面进行真实表达做好准备。

【效果评价】　教师观察学生能否借助板书呈现的语言支架完成角色扮演，并给予必要的提示和指导。教师和其他同学根据评价表（见图9）对表演小组的表现给予评价和鼓励。

B.　Think and discuss

Students discuss in pairs and find the difference between "practice" and "practise".

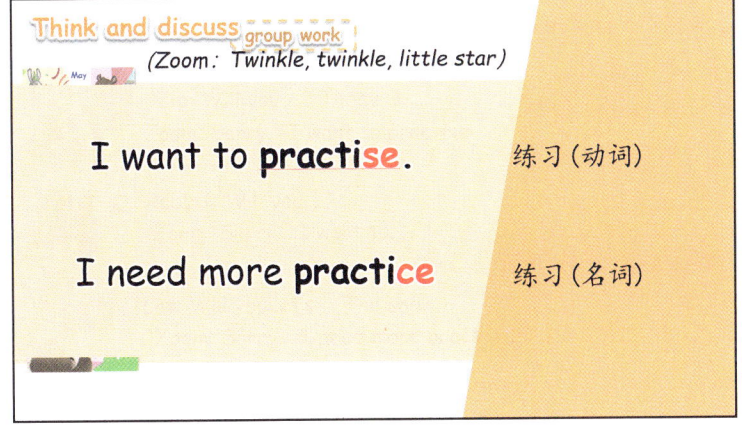

图 10

177

【设计说明】 学生在情境中推断"practice"和"practise"(见图 10)在意义与用法上的区别。

【效果评价】 教师观察学生的选择,判断其区分、理解"practice"和"practise"的准确度。

Activity 2: Look and guess (1 min)

Students observe the picture and guess whether Zoom passes the singing test or not and what Miss bird may say. Then they watch the rest of the video and find the answer.

图 11

【设计说明】 通过观察图片中的细节(见图 11),学生猜测 Zoom 是否通过考试以及 Miss Bird 可能会说的话,发展其逻辑思维能力。

【效果评价】 教师通过观察学生能否合理猜测后续对话内容,评价其利用情境线索推断对话内容的能力。

Activity 3: Read and find (2 mins)

Students find out the famous saying "Practice makes perfect." through answering three questions "Why is Zoom happy now?", "Why can he sing well now?" and "Why does practice make Zoom sing well?", and read the whole story and discuss in groups.

【设计说明】 教师通过三个连续性的问题,引导学生深入思考语篇的主题意义"熟能生巧",同时自然过渡到迁移创新类活动。

【效果评价】 教师观察学生能否在小组讨论中提到关于主题意义的关键信息,根据情况给予必要的指导。

步骤三 续编故事,迁移创新(8 分钟)

Activity 1: Discuss and write (2 mins)

Students discuss about what Zoom is like, and then they think of a title for the cover of the story and write it down on the learning sheet.

图 12

【设计说明】 通过为语篇起标题的活动(见图 12)提升学生的概括分析能力,培养其辩证思维能力。

【效果评价】 教师观察学生讨论和拟写标题的情况,给予必要的提示和指导。

Activity 2: Look and say (1 min)

Students observe the picture, answer the question "Will Zoom go swimming with friends after the singing test?", and guess the ending of the story.

图 13

【设计说明】 学生根据自己的观察,猜测故事结局与对话内容(见图 13),为续编故事做准备。

Activity 3: Make a new story and act (5 mins)

After watching a video about Zoom who can't swim that night, students discuss in groups about what Zoom will do before the next swimming day. Students choose three dates and activities to fill in the table. Then they make a new story about how Zoom practises swimming and act it out.

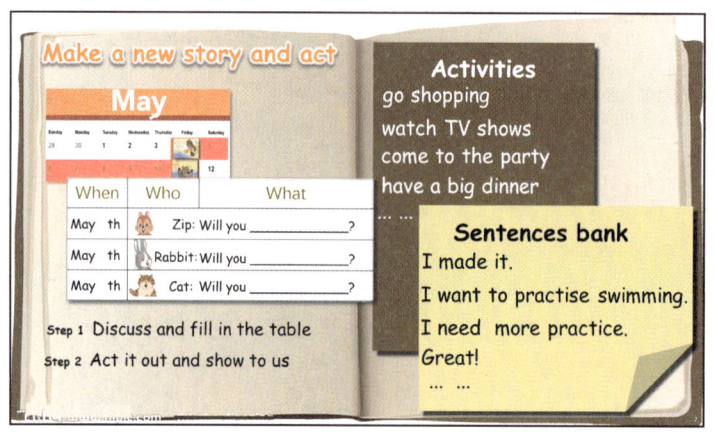

图14

【设计说明】 学生完成表格并进行对话(见图14),从而巩固核心词汇和句型,提升合作能力。通过续编 Zoom 游泳的故事,学生不仅能再次体会到"熟能生巧"的重要性,发展迁移创新能力,还能培养运用所学语言解决实际问题的能力。

【效果评价】 教师观察学生小组讨论和小组展示续编故事的情况,根据需要给予必要指导。

(六) 作业设计

*1. Finish the story chart.

**2. Act out the story with friends.

【设计说明】 本作业设计依据学生特点而分层布置:一星作业中的 story chart 旨在巩固课上学习的核心语言,便于课后表演;二星作业旨在引导学生从学习理解活动过渡到应用实践活动,促进学生语言的真实运用,并提升学生的合作能力。

(七) 板书设计

图15

【设计说明】　板书包括课题名称和课堂要点。课堂要点可分为三个部分：板书左边是重难点词句"I want to …"和"practise my song"。板书正中间为 when，who 和 what 对应的日期、人物和核心动词词组，清晰地呈现了故事发展过程。板书上半部分是 Zoom 心情和能力的变化。该板书的设计能帮助学生复习巩固所学知识，学生深化对主题的理解并形成正确的价值观，促进其核心素养综合表现目标的达成。

（八）教学反思

本节课是一节故事课，教师通过多层次的教学活动，深度挖掘语篇的内涵和趣味性，引导学生在学习活动中主动思考，有条理地表达自己的观点，并联系生活反思自我。

1. 以生为本，开放体验鼓励学生参与

教师在教学设计与实施过程中始终秉持以生为本的理念，为学生提供开放体验与具身感悟的空间，调动学生的学习兴趣，提高学习参与度。在 Let's chant 环节，学生在欢快的节奏里与教师进行互动，在滚动复习旧知的同时感知本课的核心语言，提升学习兴趣。在 Do a role-play 环节，学生在完整语境中直观感受 Zoom 唱歌水平变化的经历，并通过深入故事角色感受语篇内容的趣味性，深刻领会"Practice makes perfect."的主题意义。在 Think and write 环节，教师引导学生根据自身理解和感悟，为故事拟写标题，激发学生学习的主动性，使学生乐于表达。在 Make a new story and act 环节，学生以小组为单位，讨论并续编故事，充分发挥创造力，发展创新思维。在整个教学过程中，教师引导学生深挖语篇主题意义，激励其在日常学习生活中也要像 Zoom 一样有毅力，同时使学生深深地感受到故事课的乐趣所在。

2. 以出为入，主线问题促进意义探究

教师根据不同阅读阶段希望学生达成的目的，生成三个"主线问题"，串联起特定阶段的活动，主线问题环环相扣，层层递进，推动学生对主题意义展开深度探索。本节课需探究的主题意义为"Practice makes perfect."，因此，教师首先设计第一个主线问题"What will Zoom do before the singing test?"，引导学生理解故事语篇的主要情节和基本信息，即"Zoom can't sing well."，掌握"April 30th、May 1st、come to the party、play football"等核心词汇和"Will you …? I want to practise my song."等核心句型。其次，教师设计第二个主线问题"Can Zoom pass the singing test?"。为回答这一问题，学生需要在感知故事冲突中推断 Zoom 能否通过唱歌测试，这能锻炼他们分析和推理语篇的能力，帮助他们感悟语篇蕴含的主题意义。为了促进学生内化与迁移所学知识，教师在读后环节提出第三个问题"What will Zoom do before swimming?"。围绕这一问题，学生将综合运用已学知识和对主题意义的把握，续编不会游泳的 Zoom 去游泳的故事，从而实现"Practice makes perfect."这一主题意义的迁移。

(九) 附件

学 习 单

PEP 6 U4 Story

_____ Zoom

Made by_____

【学习内容】	PEP6U4 Story Practice makes perfect
【学习目标】	1. 学生能够复习巩固句型：The singing test will be on May 4th; I can't... I wantto... 。
	2. 学生能够理解角色，朗读并演绎整个故事。
	3. 学生能懂得故事的含义，理解熟能生巧的意义。

【学习过程】	
学习内容链接：P45	**Story**

Activity 1 Read and match (看视频，图文配对)

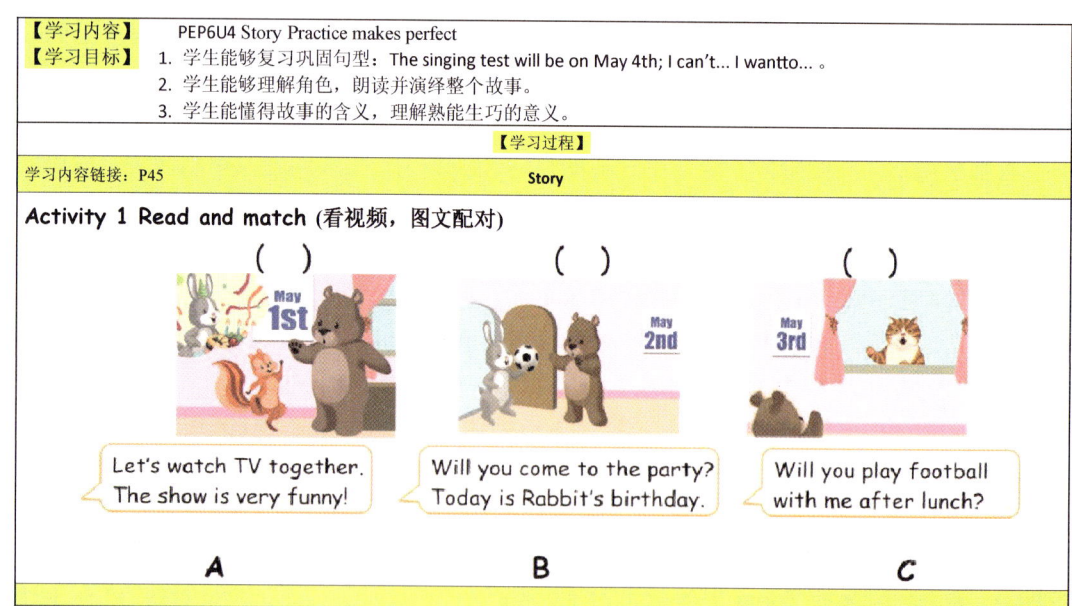

Story Chart
PEP6 U4 Story

Story title: _____　　**Main character:** _____

Event:	_____ ⟹ _____
Feeling:	☺ ⟹ ☺

When	Who	What
May 1st	Zip:	Will you _____?
_____	Rabbit:	Will you _____?
_____	Cat:	Will you _____?

What
A. go shopping
B. watch TV
C. come to the party
D. go swimming
E. play football

Tips: circle out the date and underline the activity

圈出上页图中的日期，划出好友邀请 Zoom 参加的活动并完成表格；同桌讨论，Zoom 是否会同意好友的邀请。

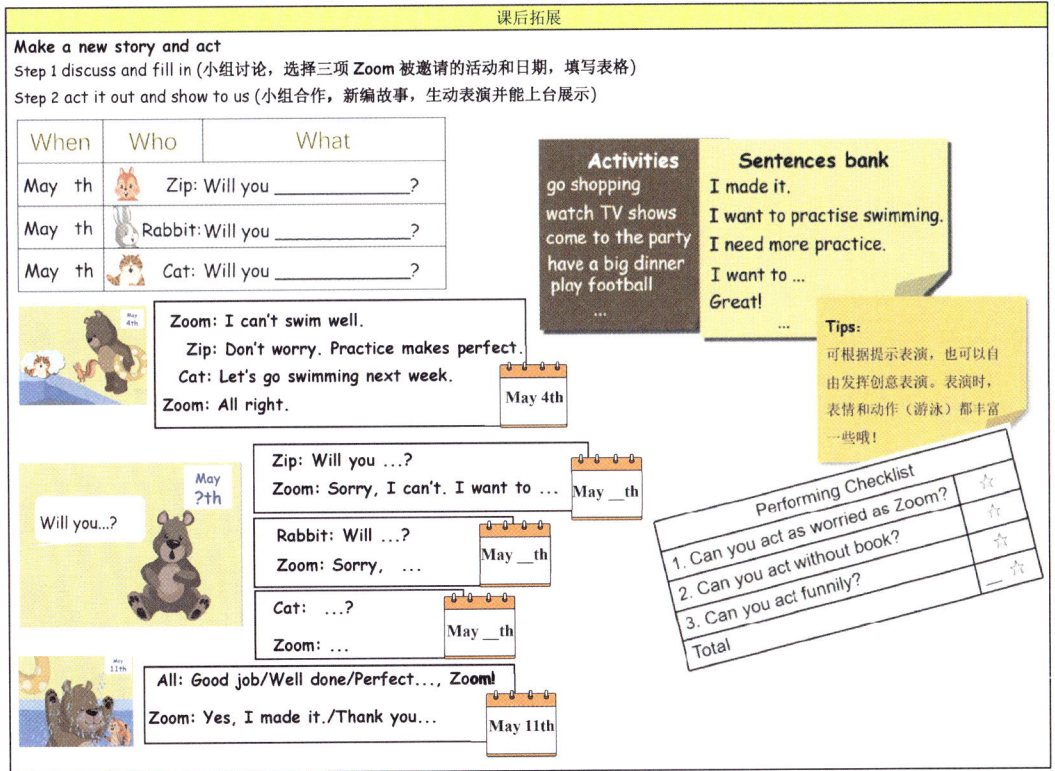

课后拓展

Make a new story and act

Step 1 discuss and fill in (小组讨论，选择三项 Zoom 被邀请的活动和日期，填写表格)

Step 2 act it out and show to us (小组合作，新编故事，生动表演并能上台展示)

When	Who	What
May　th	Zip:	Will you _____?
May　th	Rabbit:	Will you _____?
May　th	Cat:	Will you _____?

Activities
go shopping
watch TV shows
come to the party
have a big dinner
play football
...

Sentences bank
I made it.
I want to practise swimming.
I need more practice.
I want to ...
Great!
...

Tips:
可根据提示表演，也可以自由发挥创意表演。表演时，表情和动作（游泳）都丰富一些哦！

May 4th
Zoom: I can't swim well.
Zip: Don't worry. Practice makes perfect.
Cat: Let's go swimming next week.
Zoom: All right.
May 4th

May ?th
Will you...?

Zip: Will you ...?
Zoom: Sorry, I can't. I want to ... May __th

Rabbit: Will ...?
Zoom: Sorry, ... May __th

Cat: ...?
Zoom: ... May __th

All: Good job/Well done/Perfect..., Zoom!
Zoom: Yes, I made it./Thank you...
May 11th

Performing Checklist
1. Can you act as worried as Zoom?　☆
2. Can you act without book?　☆
3. Can you act funnily?　☆
Total　☆

183

课例 **8**

PEP B3 U1 My classroom
（Part A Let's learn）

说课视频

Hello, everyone! My name's Judy. I am from Wenzhou Xintianyuan Primary School. It's my great honor to present my lesson plan to you. Now, I'd like to introduce the lesson from three aspects, namely, learning objectives, learning process and learning effects.

Learning objectives

Now, let's come to the first part.

Generally speaking, the analysis of learning material and learners is of great importance for the establishment of learning objectives. So first, let's take a close look at the learning material.

The learning material is from PEP, Book 3, Unit 1 *My classroom*, Part A *Let's learn*, which is the second period of this unit and is a vocabulary lesson. The theme of this lesson is *man and society*, concerning *school environment and facilities*.

What

This learning material is a conversation between Zoom and Zip, who are going to the new classroom and are talking about some facilities in it, like a blackboard, windows, lights, chairs, desks and so on.

Why

In this lesson, the everyday dialogue between Zoom and Zip about the facilities and objects in the classroom conveys the message of "knowing, cherishing and decorating the learning environment", which will guide students to appreciate the joy of learning with their peers in the classroom and to inspire their love of school life.

---

① 本说课稿由温州市新田园小学李聆梵撰写。

How

In this lesson, the illustration of objects in a classroom helps to present the sentence patterns simply and clearly, like the question "What's in the classroom?" and the corresponding answers, such as "One blackboard", "One TV", "Many desks and chairs", as well as words and phrases like "picture", "door", "light", "blackboard", "window", "classroom", "desk" and "chair".

Now, here comes the analysis of learners. My students are in Grade Four.

As is known to us all, the classroom is students' daily learning place, and they are in contact with the facilities and objects in the classroom almost every day, so they are interested in the theme and are highly motivated to learn the corresponding English expressions.

In addition, as fourth graders, they are at the stage of transition from image thinking to abstract thinking. At this time, they are good at imitating. Meanwhile, after more than a year of English learning, they have already accumulated vocabulary such as desk, chair and classroom. With a little guidance and practice in a familiar context, they can quickly memorize new vocabulary, such as window, blackboard and light, and understand the key sentence pattern "What's in the classroom?".

However, the immature state of abstract thinking will limit their ability to reflect and evaluate. In addition, they have difficulty in matching core vocabulary and corresponding quantifiers when answering the question, "What's in the classroom?". Also, they have difficulty perceiving the thematic meaning of "knowing, cherishing and decorating the learning environment" by themselves.

In view of this, when designing learning activities, I need to take into consideration the integration of sound, form and meaning of words, highlighting the correspondence between form and meaning. In this way, students can know the collocation of certain words. Besides, through imitating the character's actions, students can gradually understand the thematic meaning beyond words and dialogues.

Based on the above analysis, the following learning objectives are set. By the end of this lesson, students will be able to:

1. master the name of classroom facilities, like classroom, window, blackboard, light, picture and door in two ways, sound and form, and then finish the To-do list.

2. use the sentence pattern "What's in the classroom? I see a/an …" to talk about their classroom and enjoy the process of cooperative learning.

3. make brief comments on the behavior of Zoom and Zip and give suggestions on cleaning the classroom, expressing their love for the learning environment.

Learning process

Now let's see how the above learning objectives can be realized in the learning process. According to the theme of this lesson *school environment and facilities*, I have designed three sub-situations: *To know the classroom, To cherish the classroom* and *To decorate the classroom*, which lead students to experience the following three stages, including Knowing by Spelling, Understanding by Role-playing, and Applying by Creating.

Firstly, in Knowing by Spelling, students are asked to use words to name the classroom and facilities. Meanwhile, through the combination of audio and visual resources, they can understand the meaning of keywords and master their spelling in two ways: sound and form.

Secondly, in Understanding by Role-playing, students are supposed to use sentences to describe the classroom and facilities so that they can be aware of the importance of cherishing the classroom.

Lastly, in Applying by Creating, students are encouraged to make new dialogues about their decoration plans, thus developing their pragmatic competence.

Next, I'd like to explain how my students can gradually achieve all the learning activities in detail. The explanation will be developed in the following aspects, namely, Why to learn, How to learn, and How to evaluate.

In the first stage, Knowing by Spelling, there are five activities designed.

The first one is a TPR (Total Physical Response) activity. All the students will sing a rap and involve themselves in acting it out, which will arouse their interest and help them get a basic understanding of this lesson.

In the second activity, students can get interested in what's in the classroom by viewing a picture and guessing. This activity can activate what they have learnt before. In this activity, whether they can say each word correctly will be checked.

In the third activity, students need to listen to and watch how I pronounce each word and then tick items they have just seen in the video. This activity can improve their ability to extract information and promote their further perception of the main content, *My classroom.* If my students can tick the right items, we'll move on to the next activity.

In the fourth activity, students are required to match words with items in the picture. To lower the difficulty, I will demonstrate the first matching and then ask students finish the rest of them. When making matching, students can gradually understand the meaning of each word, and I can observe their performance in this activity to evaluate to what extent they can relate pronunciation with meaning.

The fifth activity is Let's spell. Students learn natural spelling, deduce the pronunciation of new words according to the pronunciation of known words, and master the pronunciation of new words in the context. For example, I will present "oar", which says /ɔːr/, and then following my pronunciation, students will work in pairs and pronounce from "oar", "roar" to "blackboard". This activity activates students' existing schemas. It encourages students to spell words and try to work out the correct pronunciation through pair work. I will evaluate students' performance through whether they can cooperate with each other and spell new words correctly according to the pronunciation of known words.

In the second stage, Understanding by Role-playing, there are altogether two activities designed.

The first activity is Listen and write. Students will listen to the tape and fill in the missing letters on the four lines grid. During the process of making the whole sentence complete, students are able to consolidate their mastery of the words that they have learnt. By observing their performance during listening and writing, I will be able to evaluate whether they have mastered the pronunciation and meaning of each word.

In Activity 2, at first, students are going to watch the video about how Zoom decorates classroom disorderly. Then, students will imitate Zoom's actions and act out in pairs. By imitating Zoom and Zip's conversation and actions, students will fully practise the target sentence patterns and vocabulary. I will evaluate their performance according to how correctly they use the sentence patterns as well as vocabulary and how vividly they present the plot.

In the last stage, Applying by Creating, there is one activity that contains three tasks. Initially, students review when and where Zoom and Zip have a party. Then, by appreciating the pictures, their interest in having a party will be ignited. Having already been equipped with necessary sentence patterns and vocabulary, students will be asked to choose one from the pictures provided, talk in groups about how to decorate the classroom and then act it out. In this way, students can not only reinforce sentence patterns and vocabulary, but also deepen their understanding of today's lesson. Meanwhile, their ability to use the language to solve problems in real life can be improved, and so can the correct habits and attitudes toward classroom arrangement.

After the class, there are two assignments for students. First, they are required to listen to and read the words and sentences on Page 5, through which they can review what they've learnt today. Then, they are supposed to finish the list of classroom decoration, thus practicing using words and sentences to arrange their classroom properly.

Now let's take a look at the blackboard design. There are some pictures and word cards clearly presented on the blackboard. When students learn how to write words correctly, I can turn back each word card and unveil the four lines grid hidden behind it. With the help of the blackboard design, students can learn more about how to write the words and recall what they have learnt today.

Learning effects

To sum up, there are two highlights I'd like to point out.

The first one is connecting the teaching focus of this lesson with the theme of this unit. I have created a real situation for students to master the words step by step and use the target language in real life from ease to difficulty. Specifically, during the stage of learning new words, a series of activities are designed to enable students to understand the meaning of each word. From perceiving the meaning as well as the phonic features through guessing and video-watching, to understanding the meaning through matching, and finally to internalizing the meaning as well as usage through talking, students will gradually have a good command of the target language.

The second one is using two cartoon characters, Zoom and Zip, to set up multiple sub-situations and organize the teaching structure. Specifically, in this lesson, I have involved two cartoon characters in three scenes: Outside the classroom, Inside the classroom as well as Clean and decorate the classroom. By finishing tasks in each teaching scene, students can gradually reach the goal of making a plan to decorate the classroom for the party. The use of cute cartoon characters stimulates students' desire to learn the target language, thus enhancing their classroom engagement. In addition, the contextual setting of "use what you have learnt to help the cartoon characters" is in line with students' psychological expectations and helps to stir up their enthusiasm for applying the target language.

That's all for my presentation. Thanks for watching.

试课实录①

试课视频

步骤一 由音识词——了解教室(17分钟)

Activity 1: Let's rap

T: Hi, everyone! It's very happy to see you. I'm Kiki. Today let's have a rap, OK? Now, everybody stands up, follow me. Move your body. Ready?

T: Hey, hey, this is Kiki. Here is a rap for you and I hope you like it, too. We are going to have a party. Play with me. Ready? Follow me! Turn on the light!

Ss: (Turn on!)

T: Turn on the light!

Ss: (Turn on!)

T: Put up the stars!

Ss: (Put up!)

T: Put up the stars!

Ss: (Put up!)

T: You are so cool. Let's have a party! Party!

Ss: (Party!)

T: Party!

Ss: (Party!)

T: Are you ready?

Ss: (Yes!)

---

① 本试课稿由温州市蒲鞋市小学李钰阳撰写。

T:　Wow! Thank you. You are good rappers. Sit down, please. So today, we are going to have a party with our friends. So first, let's make a party plan. See? It's the time and it's the place. So please tell me, where is the party?

Ss:　(It's in the classroom.)

Activity 2: Let's guess

T:　Bingo! Everyone, read after me. Class, class, room, room. Classroom, classroom. It is a classroom. We are going to have a party in the classroom. Look, this is the classroom. What's in the classroom? Now, boys and girls, read after me. What's in the classroom?

Ss:　(What's in the classroom?)

T:　So what's in the classroom? You please.

S1:　(Desks and chairs?)

T:　Yes. Maybe some desks and chairs, right? More?

S2:　(Some lights?)

T:　Excellent!

Activity 3: Let's tick

T:　Look at these things. Are all the things in the classroom? Maybe we can watch a video and tick out the things in the classroom. Now, take out your learning sheet, Task 1. Are you ready? Go! [plays the video]

Ss:　[watch a video and tick]

T:　Have you finished? OK, can tell me what's in the classroom? You please.

S3:　(The window. The picture. The blackboard. The light. The door.)

T:　You are so clever. There are so many things in the classroom.

Activity 4: Let's match

T:　So this is the classroom. Look, Zoom and Zip are talking about the classroom. Zoom says, "Look at the window, it's so clean. " Now, can you tell me where the window is? Can you match the word with the picture? Yes. You please.

S4:　(Number 5.)

T:　Yes. It's number 5. Good! Now, I want you to read the dialogue and match the words with the pictures. OK, here we go.

Ss:　[read and match]

T:　OK. Who can come here and match on the blackboard? Yes. Can you? Come up!

S5:　[match on the blackboard]

T:　Look, is she right?

Ss:　(Yes.)

T:　Very good. OK. Now, please check by yourself.

Ss:　[check with the blackboard]

Activity 5: Let's spell

T: Finished? Boys and girls, look at this word "roar", can you read it?

S6:   (Roar.)

T: Good, so we know "oar" says /ɔː/. How about this word?

S7:   (Black.)

T: Yes. So, put them together. Now can you read this one?

S8:   (Blackboard.)

T: Nice! The words we know can help us read these new words. Now, please work in pairs. Read these words first, then read the new words. Understand?

Ss: [read in pairs]

T: Finished? Well, let's check them one by one. This group, who can read them?

S9:   (Yellow. Window.)

T: Nice! How about the second group?

S10:   (Roar. Blackboard.)

T: Good! What about this group?

S11:   (Nature. Picture.)

T: Right! And the fourth one. You please.

S12:   (Floor. Door.)

T: Perfect! And the last one? Say together.

Ss: (Night. Light.)

T: OK. Now, open your English book. Show me your finger. Let's listen, point and read. Go!

步骤二 表演解词——爱护教室(8分钟)

Activity 1: Let's listen and write

Ss: [listen and follow]

T: Look, Zoom and Zip stand here. Then, what will they do? Just stay outside or get into the classroom? Let's have a look. Look at the picture. Zoom and Zip get into the classroom but Zoom is so naughty. Can we see the list now?

Ss: (No!)

T: Oh, I'm so sorry. Without the list, they can't decorate the classroom well. But some letters are missing. Boys and girls, can you help them?

Ss: (Yes!)

T: Well first, let's listen to the tape and finish the first sentence. Can you do it?

Ss: (Yes.)

Ss: [listen and write]

T: Good job! Let's help Zoom. Listen to the tape and fill in all the blanks.

Ss: [listen and fill in all the blanks]

T: Now, let's check them one by one! The second one, the missing letter is …?

S13: (Letter "i".)

T: Yes, how about the third one?

S14: (It's "igh".)

T: You are so smart. The fourth one and the last one?

S15: (The fourth one is "oor", and the last one is "ow".)

Activity 2: Let's act and do

T: Yes! You guys did a good job! Now we can see the decoration list clearly. With this list, Zoom is so happy. He says, "So easy, I can do it!" But, can Zoom really do it? Let's enjoy some pictures.

Ss: [enjoy the pictures]

T: Oh my god! What did Zoom do? Now I am Zoom. I turn on the light. I turn off the light! So so funny! Can you be Zoom? Everybody, stand up! Let's follow Zoom, say and act!

Ss: [say and act]

T: Wow! So interesting! Here are more pictures. Now, work in pairs. Choose one picture you like. Let's act!

Ss: [work in pairs and act]

T: Thank you, my little Zoom and Zip! You are so active! Zoom did so many things in the classroom. But do you think the classroom is beautiful now?

Ss: (No! It's not beautiful!)

T: Right. So can you help Zoom and Zip and make our classroom beautiful?

Ss: (Yes.)

T: Yes. Now everybody stand up. Now, let's do it. [plays a video]

Ss: [read after the video]

步骤三 创编用词——美化教室(15 分钟)

Activity: Let's decorate

T: Thank you boys and girls. You guys are so helpful! The classroom is so clean! We can have a party now. But how to decorate the classroom for a party? First, let's enjoy some pictures about parties.

Ss: [enjoy some pictures]

T: Wow, we can have so many kinds of parties in the classroom! Now let's decorate the classroom! Take out your learning sheet. Please work in groups of four. Step 1, choose one party you like. Step 2, talk about how to decorate the classroom for the party. Are you clear? Let's do it!

Ss:	[work in groups]
T:	Well, time's up! Which group can share your list?
Ss:	(Let me try!)
T:	Good! You four come here and share your list.
S16:	(What's in the classroom?)
S17:	(I see a light. I can turn on the light.)
S18:	(I see a blackboard. I can draw on the blackboard.)
S19:	(I see a window. I can put up the apple balloons on the window.)
S16 & S17 & S18 & S19:	(Let's do it! GO! GO! GO!)
T:	Excellent! I bet your classroom must be very beautiful and interesting! Thank you. Sit down please.

作业布置

T:	So after class, you can finish your list and talk about it. It's your homework. Of course, you should listen to the words and sentences on Page 5 and read them aloud. OK?
Ss:	(OK!)
T:	Class is over. Bye-bye!

教学设计①

配套课件

(一) 语篇研读

本课教学内容选自人教版英语四年级上册第一单元 My classroom A 部分 Let's learn 板块,该语篇属于"人与社会"主题范畴,内容涉及"校园环境与设施"。

What

语篇是一段发生在 Zip 和 Zoom 之间的对话。两只小动物去看新教室并站在教室外谈论,后因好奇心驱使翻窗进入教室并将教室弄得乱七八糟,最后小动物和孩子们共同努力,将教室清扫干净并装扮起来。在"为举办派对装扮教室"的具体情境中,Zip 和 Zoom 讨论了教室内的黑板、门窗、电灯、课桌椅等设施和教室的装扮方式。

Why

该语篇利用 Zoom 与 Zip 的日常对话,讨论了教室内的设施与物品。文本传递了"了解、爱护与美化学习场所"的信息。教师可以利用语篇对话所传递的意义,引导学生体会在教室里与同伴学习和活动的乐趣,激发对校园生活的热爱。

---

① 本教学设计由温州市蒲鞋市小学李钰阳撰写。

How

对话涉及核心问句"What's in the classroom?"及其相应回答,如"One blackboard""One TV"和"Many desks and chairs"等。除对话语篇外,教材还提供了一张体现教室内设施与物品的插图,以便学生掌握本单元核心词汇: picture、door、light、blackboard、window、classroom、desk、chair 等。

(二) 学情分析

本节课的授课对象为 Z 省某小学四年级学生。在学习动机层面,学生每天在教室学习,与教室内的设施与物品接触,有掌握对应的英语表达的强烈动机。同时,四年级的学生正处于由形象思维向抽象思维过渡的阶段,但学生的抽象思维还不成熟,反思与评价能力有限,需要教师搭建支架,引导学生深入思考。此外,学生的模仿能力强,经过一年多的英语学习,已经积累了 desk、chair、classroom 等主题词汇。在熟悉的话题语境下,教师稍加引导并提供操练机会,学生便能快速记忆 window、blackboard、light 等新词汇,理解核心问句"What's in the classroom?"。但他们在回答核心问句,即搭配核心词汇与量词时往往有失准确性,也很难主动领悟词汇与对话背后所传递的"了解、爱护与美化教室"这一主题意义。鉴于此,教师在设计活动时要兼顾音、形、义,突出词形与词义,让学生能知晓其与其他词的搭配方式,在动作模仿等过程中感悟语词所构成的对话文本背后所蕴含的深刻内涵。

(三) 教学目标

通过本课时的学习,学生能够:

1. 在看、听、说活动中,掌握核心词汇的音与形,如 classroom、window、blackboard、light、picture、door,并完成 to-do list;

2. 熟练运用核心句型"What's in the classroom? I see a/an ... ",展开询问和回答,了解学习场所,体会在教室里与同伴学习和活动的乐趣;

3. 简要评价 Zoom 和 Zip 的做法,并发挥想象力帮助他们整理教室,进而产生对学习场所的爱护之情。

(四) 教学流程

在本节课中,围绕"教室及其设施"这一主题,教师创设了"了解教室""爱护教室""美化教室"三项意义递进的学习子情境,并引导学生依次经历"由音识词""表演解词""创编用词"三个学习阶段。第一阶段为"由音识词",意在让学生在情境中了解并以词为单位表达有关教室及其内部的设施。其间,学生跟随 Zoom 和 Zip,通过说唱、预测、看视频勾词汇、词图配对、自然拼读等活动,主要从音与形两方面理解并巩固学习场所内陈设的英文表达。第二阶段为"表演解词",学生完成听音填词和角色扮演,模仿朗读这些由名词与动词词组搭配生成的句子,明确语篇体裁并体会爱护教室的意义及重要性。第三阶段为"创编用词",学生通过运用本节课所学词汇、词组和句式,讨论教室装扮计划,创编相关对话,表达个性化的装扮想法,达成发展语用能力的最终目的。

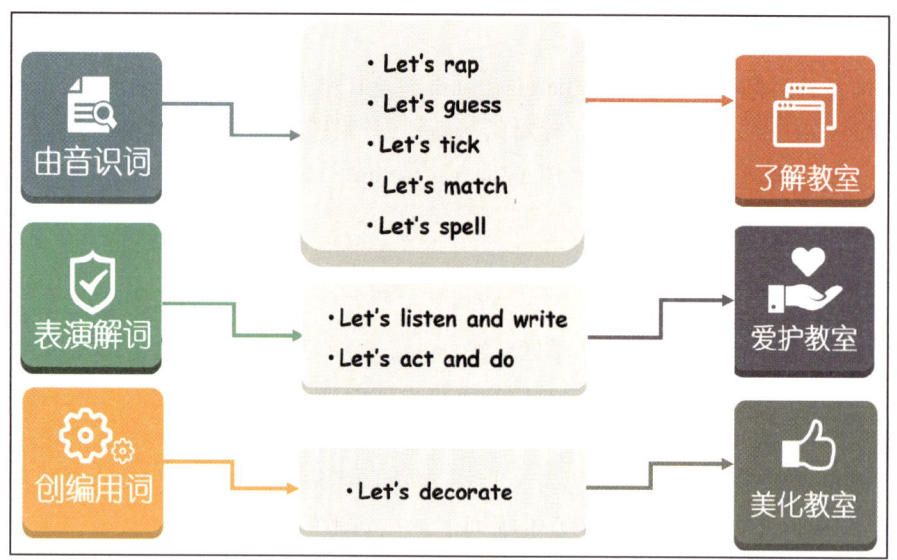

图 1

（五）教学过程

步骤一 由音识词——了解教室（17分钟）

Activity 1：Let's rap （2 mins）

Students rap with the teacher. It contains the key sentence patterns and words that will be learnt in this lesson.

Lyrics：

Hey，hey，this is Kiki. Here is a rap for you. Hope you like it too.

We are going to have a party. Play with me.

Ready？Follow me.

Turn on the light. Turn on！

Put up the stars. Put up！

You are so cool！Let's have a party！

Party！Party！Party！Party！

Are you ready？

Yes！

【设计说明】 将本节课的教学核心词汇与句型融入节奏轻快的说唱中，充分调动学生说和演的兴趣，同时使其初步感知本课的重难点句型，为后续的学习活动做好铺垫。

【效果评价】 教师观察学生是否全情投入到与教师的互动当中，判断学生学习英语的热情是否被激发，并进行相应的引导与评价。

Activity 2: Let's guess（3 mins）

Students learn the key sentence "What's in the classroom?" and predict what may exist in the classroom by looking at the pictures.

图 2

【设计说明】　通过看图预测（见图 2），发展学生"看"的能力，激活学生的思维，引发其对故事的兴趣和学习动机，降低后期学习难度。

【效果评价】　教师根据学生对教室内物品的猜测情况，评价其结合所给图片和已知信息进行推断的能力；教师观察学生的回答，检测学生对于教室内物品已有的词汇储备。

Activity 3: Let's tick（3 mins）

Students watch the video about the classroom and tick out the items in the classroom.

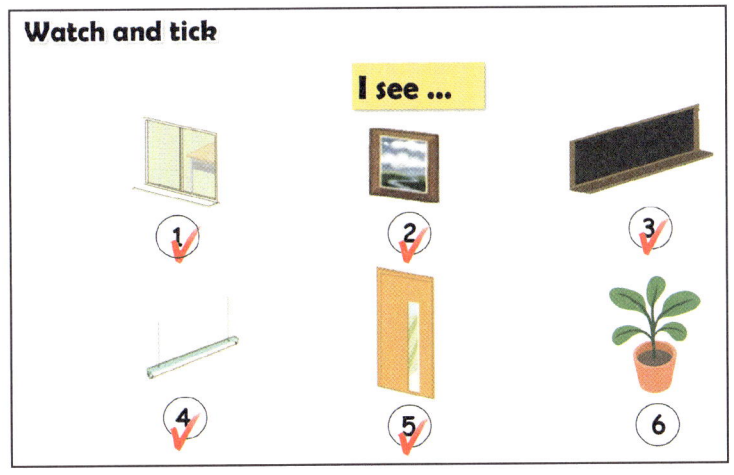

图 3

【设计说明】　通过看视频勾词的活动，发展学生提取关键信息的能力（见图 3），促进学生对学习内容的进一步感知。在观看视频勾选物品前，教师引导学生先看图片并专注听音，初步感知目标词汇的发音，由此降低任务难度。

【效果评价】 教师观察学生看视频勾选单词的情况,评价学生从视频中提取关键信息的能力。

Activity 4: Let's match (4 mins)

Students read the dialogue and match the words with the objects in the pictures.

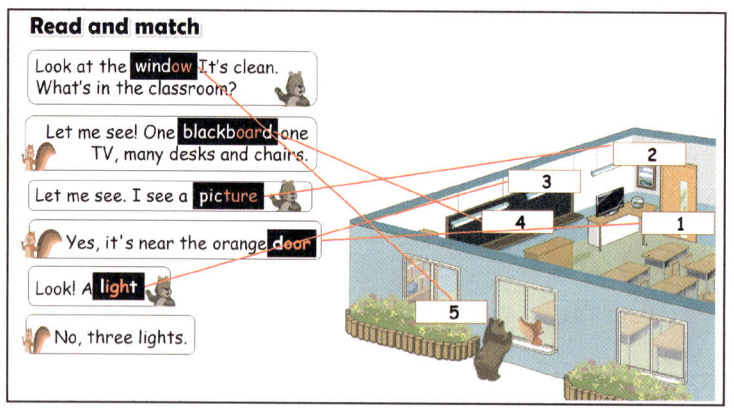

图 4

【设计说明】 通过配对活动,学生能够在语境中充分理解词义(见图4)。教师首先以"window"为例进行示范——带领学生将该单词与代表"窗户"的数字5连线。接着由学生们自主完成剩余单词和图片的配对。

【效果评价】 教师观察学生能否正确将单词和图片连接起来,把握学生对核心词汇的掌握情况。

Activity 5: Let's spell (5 mins)

Students learn phonics, deduce the pronunciation of new words according to the old ones, and master the pronunciation of new words in the context. Then, students listen to the tape and read after it.

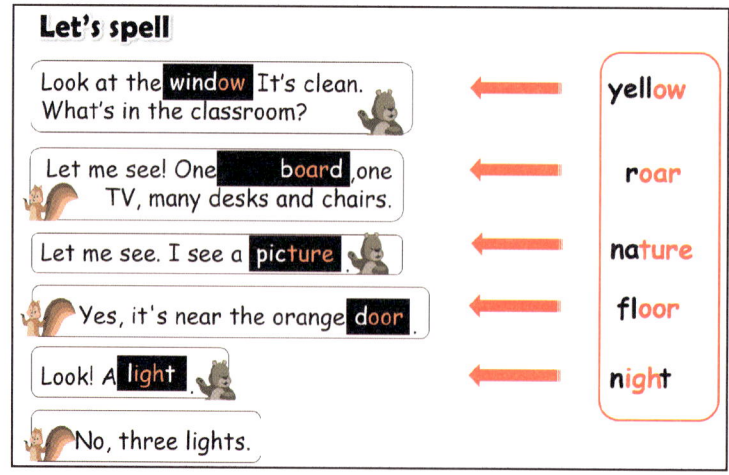

图 5

【设计说明】　通过推导式拼读,从已知过渡到未知,培养学生的自主学习能力(见图 5)。教师首先呈现发音组合"oar",并通过自然拼读法教授其发音。然后,引导学生通过 roar 的发音推导出 blackboard 的发音,帮助学生实现从词到词的发音迁移。接着,再以同样的方式处理 window 的发音。教师示范后,呈现其他帮助发音的词汇,由学生两两合作,根据已知词汇的发音推导出新词的发音。

【效果评价】　教师通过观察学生与同伴合作拼读的情况,判断学生是否理解推导式自然拼读,是否掌握了举一反三的单词拼读本领。

步骤二　表演解词——爱护教室(8 分钟)

Activity 1: Let's listen and write (3 mins)

Students listen to the tape and fill in the missing letters on the four lines grid according to the pronunciation of the words to complete the sentence.

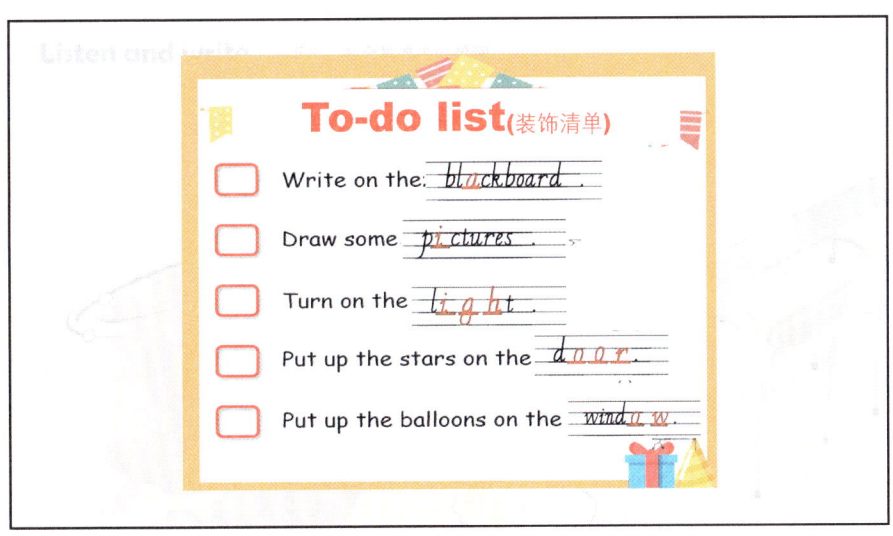

图 6

【设计说明】　听音补词的活动促使学生巩固所学单词(见图 6)。学生通过欣赏图片,知道了 Zoom 和 Zip 两只动物进入教室,打翻颜料桶,弄脏了 party plan,并遮盖了关键词汇的部分字母。接着,学生通过听音,拼写出被遮盖的字母。在完成听和写的活动的同时,学生对"How to decorate the classroom for a party?",即装扮教室的方式,有了初步感知,这也为开展产出活动奠定了基础。

【效果评价】　教师观察学生能否在听力中完成补词,以此考查学生对单词的音与形的掌握。

Activity 2: Let's act and do (5 mins)

Students imitate Zoom and Zip's language and actions to practise the target sentence patterns and words. Then students follow the video and make the classroom more beautiful.

图 7

【设计说明】 此活动可以帮助学生巩固所学的关键词汇和句型(见图7),促使学生感受词汇的文体意义与情感意义,为后面的情感升华做准备。首先,学生观看 Zoom 在教室里胡乱装扮的图片。接着,学生尝试模仿 Zoom 开灯和挂气球的动作,操练目标句型和词汇。随后,学生与同桌合作,在四幅 Zoom 调皮捣蛋的场景中任选一副进行自主模仿。最后,教师播放一个视频,引导学生学习如何帮助捣蛋的 Zoom 把教室清理干净。

【效果评价】 教师观察学生能否深入人物进行角色扮演,根据学生的表现给予必要的提示和指导。

步骤三 创编用词——美化教室(15 分钟)

Activity: Let's decorate (15mins)

Firstly, students enjoy some pictures about parties. Then they work in groups, choose one party they like, and talk about the way of dressing up the classroom for the party by using the key words like "window", "blackboard", "light", "picture" and "door", and the core sentence patterns like "What's in the classroom?", "I see a/an … I can …". Finally, they do role-plays in the front of the class.

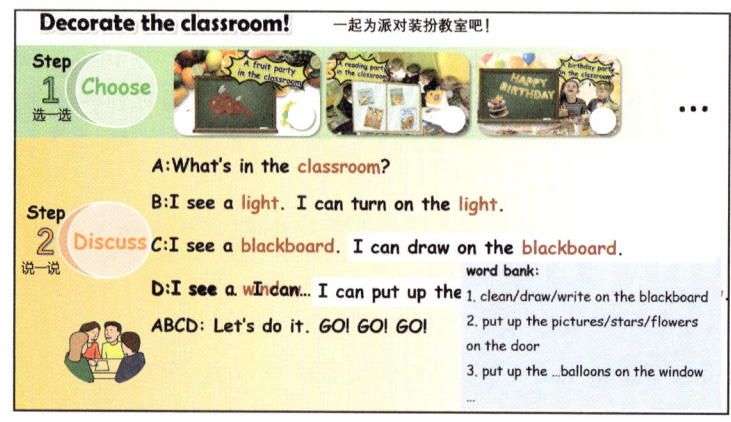

图 8

【设计说明】　该活动促使学生在真实情境中运用所学的词汇和句型,例如 window、blackboard、light、picture、door,以及"What's in the classroom?" "I see a/an … I can …"等,达到了语用的目的(见图8)。学生欣赏几组主题派对的照片,选择心仪的主题,思考装扮方式,并在小组内运用所学语言展开讨论后,上台进行表演展示。讨论和展示的过程可以帮助学生更好地了解学习场所,体会在教室里与同伴活动的乐趣。

【效果评价】　教师观察学生向全班展示创编对话的情况,并根据学生的表现给予必要的提示和指导,评价教与学的成效。

(六) 作业设计

*1. Listen to the words and sentences and read them aloud on Page 5.

**2. Finish your list and talk about your list.

【设计说明】　本作业依据学生的学习特点而设计。首先要求学生巩固课堂所学,对目标词汇和句型有更深层次的掌握。在巩固所学内容后,要求学生将课堂所学运用到真实情境中,达到语用的目的。

(七) 板书设计

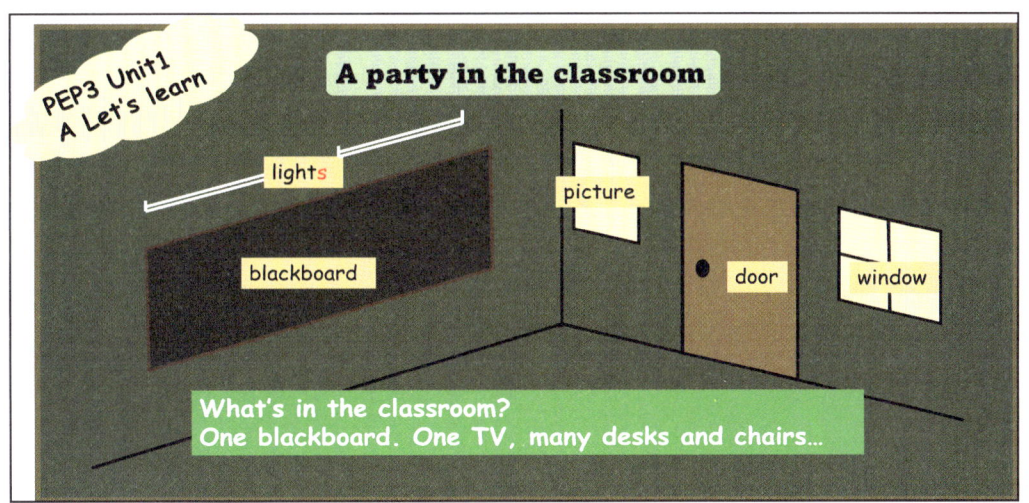

图9

【设计说明】　板书包括课题名称与课堂要点,随着学生学习任务的推进自然生成(见图9)。板书的中间部分以简笔画的方式清晰地呈现了核心词汇的词义,包括教室内的设施及物品。板书下方为本节课的核心句型。通过自然生成的板书,学生能够自主进行课堂内容的回顾和复述。

(八) 教学反思

本课是一节词汇课,教师围绕主题意义,借助不同层次的语用任务,使学生将词汇学习与实际生活经验联系起来,引领学生在真实语境中学会教室物品的表达和教室的装扮方式。纵观整节课,学生既学会了语言,也发展了能力,教师作如下反思:

1. 立足单元立意,锚定教学重点,提升词汇教学站位

与脱离语境、机械训练单词读音与形式的传统教学思路不同,教师从单元教学的主题意义——"了解、爱护和美化学习场所"出发,将学生词汇学习的重心从零散记忆词汇转移到关注词语的使用形式与意义上来。学生首先通过预测教室物品,回忆本课核心名词,根据已知单词的发音推导出新词发音的方式,在选词、拼读、配对等活动中达到"了解教室"的目的。随后,学生在"为派对装扮教室"的情境引导下,观看 Zoom 在教室里胡乱装扮的视频,借用上一环节所学的名词及相关动词词组,模仿 Zoom 开灯和挂气球等调皮捣蛋行为,进而意识到爱护学习场所的重要性。最后,学生围绕"How to decorate your classroom for a party?",综合运用所学,创编关于如何美化教室的对话。由此可见,本节课词汇教学的重心与单元立意相呼应,能够推动学生由机械记忆单词走向思考如何在真实情境中使用词汇,保障学生综合掌握词汇的音、形、义。

2. 巧用人物主线,关联教学情境,高效探究主题意义

推动教学内容结构化是有效教学的前提。在备课过程中,教师观察到 Zoom 和 Zip 两只小动物的形象一直贯穿于单元内容之中,故借用这两个形象,创设相关联的子情境,将零散的语篇内容合理串联起来。在本节课中,教师设计了两只小动物"窗户外参观教室、进入教室并弄乱教室、清扫及装扮教室"三大情境。教师从事件之间的因果关系出发,设计 party plan,明确学生本堂课的最终任务为"为派对装扮教室"。起初,Zoom 和 Zip 对教室充满好奇,想去看看教室里有什么。在 Zoom 和 Zip 的好奇中,学生对学习内容有了初步的感知。随后调皮捣蛋的 Zoom 进入教室,打翻颜料桶,弄脏了 plan,学生在这样的情境下尝试补全单词,两只小动物的角色也愈发深入人心。教师设计的模仿表演活动鼓励学生模仿 Zoom 调皮捣蛋的形象,增添了课堂趣味。伴随着学习情境由"日常生活中的派对设施"到"被弄乱的教室",再回归到"为派对装扮教室",学生脑海中的词汇语义网也得以丰富。与此同时,学生能体会在教室里与同伴学习和活动的乐趣,感受到对校园生活的热爱,其对主题意义的探究也逐渐加深。

(九) 附件

学 习 单

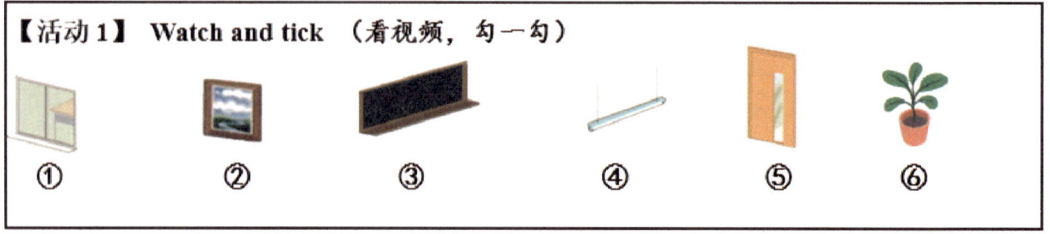

【活动1】 Watch and tick （看视频，勾一勾）
① ② ③ ④ ⑤ ⑥

【活动2】 **Read and match（读对话，连一连）**

Look at the window It's clean.
What's in the classroom?

Let me see! One blackboard , one
TV, many desks and chairs.

Let me see. I see a picture

Yes, it's near the orange door

Look! A light

No, three lights.

【活动3】 **Listen and write（听一听，写一写）**

Decoration list(装饰清单)

☐ Write on the bl___ckboard. Party·

☐ Draw some p___ctures.

☐ Turn on the l___t.

☐ Put up the stars on the d___.

☐ Put up the balloons on the wind___.

Party Plan

Let's decorate the classroom!

步骤1: 勾选一个喜欢的派对。

(　　) Fruit party　　　　(　　) Reading party　　　　(　　) Birthday party

步骤2: 四人分别扮演角色 ABCD，说一说如何装扮教室（用上小语库里的句子，也可以有更多发挥哦！）

A: What's in the classroom?

B: I see a light. I can turn on the light.

C: I see a blackboard. I can ...

D: I see a window/door. I can ....

ABCD: Let's do it! GO! GO! GO!

Sentence bank (小语库)

1. clean/draw/write on the blackboard

2. put up the pictures/stars/flowers on the door

3. put up... balloons on the window

...

课例 9

PEP B3 U2 My schoolbag
（Part A Let's spell）

说课实录①

说课视频

Hello, everyone! This is Kate. It's my great honor to share this spelling lesson plan with you. Now, I'd like to introduce it in the following five aspects: learning material and learners, learning objectives, learning process, homework and blackboard design, and learning effects.

Learning material and learners

At the very beginning, I'd like to elaborate on how I set the learning objectives. In order to set clear and reasonable learning objectives, the analysis of learning material and learners is crucial. Therefore, let's begin with the learning material.

The learning material is from PEP, Book 3, Unit 2 *My Schoolbag*, Part A *Let's spell*. The theme of this text is *man and self*, concerning *the surrounding environment and things*.

What

By combining the kite element from the chant in the textbook with the picture book *Five Pies*, this lesson tells the story of Nini, a pig who loves to play with kites and eat pies. To get the five pies, Nini opens the yard door by differentiating between "big", "five", "six", "nine", "pig" and "ice", writes the words "five", "six", "big" and "kite" on his way to the pies, and finally steals the pies.

Why

In this story, in order to get the pies, Nini should complete some situational tasks with "i-e" pronunciation rules, which provide students with rich resources for learning the pronunciation rule of the letter "i" in the open syllable. Various activities such as storytelling, chanting, and

---

① 本说课稿由温州市临江小学徐速撰写。

spelling contests will help students to better master the pronunciation rules.

How

As a typical picture book story, this text clearly depicts how Nini gets the pies. And the focus of learning activities gradually transits from words with "i" in stressed closed syllables, to words with the letter "i" in open syllables. The story highlights the pronunciation of /ɪ/ in stressed closed syllables and /aɪ/ in open syllables in the context, reinforcing the phonetic and morphological correspondence between the pronunciation and the word.

After taking a close look at the learning material, let's focus on the learners. My students are in Grade Four from Z province. They are familiar with reading picture books, but there is a challenge for them to use phonics to overcome reading difficulties. Therefore, they have high learning motivation in this lesson.

Besides, students have also accumulated some basic phonics rules, but it is the first time they have learnt the pronunciation of the letter "i" in open syllables. Therefore, more attention should be paid to enable students to further clarify pronunciation rules through meaningful drills.

Learning objectives

Based on the above analysis, the following learning objectives are set. By the end of this lesson, students will be able to:

1. learn how to pronounce the letter "i" in open syllables by observing and imitating words that match the "i-e" pronunciation rule, such as "like", "kite", "five", "nine", "rice" etc. , and find the corresponding word when hearing it.

2. establish and deepen the understanding of the phonetic and morphological correspondence between /aɪ/ and the "i-e" structure by analyzing and generalizing.

3. apply the rules to differentiate and pronounce the letter "i" in open-and closed-syllable words in extended reading, thus enhancing their spelling fluency.

4. internalize and utilize the pronunciation rules of "i-e" in the new context through group reading, and perceive the wisdom and cuteness of Nini.

Learning process

According to the learning progress and situation construction, this lesson is divided into three stages, including Review and Activation; Deduction, Segmentation and Synthesis; Transfer and Application.

In the first stage, I will use an audio-visual activity to help students recall the rules for pronouncing "i" in stressed closed syllables and to introduce the main character of the picture book. In the second stage, I am going to guide students to learn and practise the pronunciation rules of "i" in open syllables through a series of phonological activities such as phonetic deduction, phonetic synthesis, phonetic disambiguation and word writing. In the third stage, students are supposed to flexibly apply the pronunciation rules of "i" in open and closed syllables to break through the spelling difficulties and read the picture book independently.

Now, let me explain in detail how the above learning objectives will be achieved in three aspects, the description, the justification and the evaluation of learning activities.

Here comes the first stage, Review and Activation. In Activity 1, Review the learnt phoneme, students will enjoy the song *The Sound of i* and try to sing along. Then they will read words "in", "thin" and "gift" to notice the phoneme /ɪ/ (*i*). Based on this, students add the missing letters according to different pronunciations. This engages students' multiple senses in learning and activates their previous knowledge — the pronunciation of "i" in stressed closed syllables. To meet the main character Nini, students will listen to Nini's monologue and choose his name. After that, students will look at the pictures and talk about what Nini can do, and then choose the right kite for him after listening to a chant. The gradient difficulty of the task helps students naturally perceive the pronunciation of "i" in open syllables for the first time. During the process, students' proficiency in phoneme extraction can be reflected by their reaction speed. So far, the first learning objective have been realized.

In the second stage, there are four activities that contribute to the construction of this situation. Firstly, here is Find the new phoneme. Students will be asked to find out the same pronunciation and the letter combination "i-e" in the chant. Then they will infer the pronunciation of the letter combination. After that, they will watch a video to check their inference, through which they undergo self-evaluation. Also, the results of students' evaluation can offer me feedback on whether they can connect the sound of a word with its spelling. These three steps are closely integrated to achieve comprehensive words learning, which center on pronunciation and are accompanied by spelling and meaning.

Then, there comes Blend the phonemes. After seeing an example of blending phonemes, students will try to blend phonemes into words like "like", "kite", "five", "nine" and "rice" by using letter magnets, and then blend more words with their partners. In this activity, from four letters to five, there is a step-wise increase in difficulty. With the help of my vivid body language and training aids, abstract phoneme blending is visualized and becomes understandable. Besides, the core phonics skill, blending, is hierarchically practised through group cooperation and self-work. With the growing familiarity with words in the picture book, reading difficulty is also reduced. Students' mastery of phoneme synthesis can be reflected by their reaction speed and accuracy of spelling.

Now, let's move on to Activity 3, Segment the phonemes. In this activity, students can help Nini open the lock to get the pies by segmenting the phonemes. Words including "big" "fine", "six", "nice", "pig" and "ice" will be displayed on the screen. Later, students will listen and classify these words as the group of /ɪ/ or the group of /aɪ/, and then conclude the corresponding pronunciation rules. After that, they will be asked to listen and number the words as a way of checking. This activity aims to subtly deepen the situational connection between the picture book and the textbook, helping students to transfer knowledge while making the task less complicated. If students can classify the words correctly and draw the above conclusion, we can move on to the next activity.

Activity 4 is Spell and write the words. After unlocking the door, Nini encounters a new trouble, and students are supposed to write down words to help Nini surmount the obstacle and get the pies. Students will listen to me and spell the word I say. Then, they need to listen and write down the words on their books. To ensure the quality of their writing, I will first check two students' writing with the whole class and then ask students to check and pay attention to their writing. Words spelling is a practical application of pronunciation rules and also the premise of writing. If students can write accurately and neatly, the second learning objective will be fully achieved.

In the third stage, three activities are designed. The first one is Read for general idea. Students will read the story and answer the question "Can Nini get the pies?". This picture book provides a real-life situation that ignites students' interest in employing the pronunciation rules. And I can check students' understanding by observing their choices.

Later, in the second activity, Read, imitate and understand, students will be asked to read the story, check their pronounciation in groups of four and better their pronounciation. And then, students can try to understand the meaning of two new words, swipe and hide, by choosing the right one for the blanks in two sentences. Learning phonetics in stories can help students avoid simply pursuing the accuracy of the pronunciations of words at the expense of semantics and context. I can evaluate students' internalization by observing whether they can read out the story fluently or not.

The third activity is Read and spell more. I will summarize the story by giving the source of the story and introduce the book series. And then I encourage the students to read them after class, which is one of the after-class assignments for students with higher levels of language competence.

After completing all activities in this stage, the third and fourth learning objectives will be realized.

Homework and blackboard design

As for the homework, two assignments are designed for students with different levels of language competence. The assignment at level 1 is designed to help students master the core learning content of this lesson. Students are required to read the chant in this lesson and write more words fitting the rule of "i-e". Second, at level 2, students can try to challenge themselves to use the new rules to read other books in the reading list, which is to train students' ability of applying and transferring.

In regard to the blackboard design, it is divided into three parts. The left side of the blackboard is for students' background knowledge, which reviews the phoneme /ɪ/ (*i*). The middle part is the focus of this lesson, using magnetic letters to show the process of spelling, which clears learning barriers. The right side presents the learning situation with the picture book, through which every stage and activity is naturally connected.

Learning effects

To sum up, all the learning objectives will be achieved and satisfactory effects will be made. And I'd like to point out the uniqueness that contributes to the success of this lesson.

Firstly, the combination of the picture book and the textbook creates a vivid situation for students to perceive, learn, and apply the knowledge. From words to discourse, the deepening of language input and progressive task chain provide a coherent language learning environment, which improves the vitality of teaching and learning effectiveness.

Secondly, the emphasis on the integration of sound, spelling and meaning is closely connected with learning strategies so as to trigger students' motivation to spell and improve their independent spelling skills.

That's all for my presentation. Thanks for watching.

试课实录①

试课视频

步骤一　复习与激活(8 分钟)

Activity: Review the learnt phoneme

T:　Class begins! Good morning, everyone.

Ss:　(Good morning, teacher!)

T:　Today we're going to learn PEP 3 Unit 2 A *Let's spell*. First, let's enjoy a song together. And tell me, what does "i" say? OK?

Ss:　[enjoy the song]

T:　So, what does "i" say?

Ss:　(/ɪ/)

T:　That's right, "i" says /ɪ/. Can you say more words with letter "i"? [presents three words on the slide]

Ss:　(In. Thin. Gift.)

T:　/ɪ/, /ɪ/, "i". Who can spell "six"? You try.

S1:　(S-i-x.)

---

① 本试课稿由温州市蒲鞋市小学张丽琼撰写。

T:　　Good job! How about "milk"? You please.

S2:　　(M-i-l-k.)

T:　　Excellent! How about "fish"? Together!

Ss:　　(F-i-s-h.)

T:　　Bingo! Now look, what can you see?

Ss:　　(A pig!)

T:　　Yes, it's a pig. Look at the pig. What's his name? A. Nini. B. Nono. Listen and tell me.

Ss:　　[listen]

T:　　So, A or B?

Ss:　　(Nini.)

T:　　That's right. It's Nini. Nini can fly a kite. Look, which one is his kite? A or B? Listen to the chant and choose.

Ss:　　[listen and choose]

T:　　So, A or B? You try.

S3:　　(B.)

T:　　That's right. The kite with the big number nine. Now, let's chant together with Nini, OK?

Ss:　　[chant]

步骤二 推导、拆分与合成(18 分钟)

Activity 1: Find the new phoneme

T:　　Let's read these words one more time.

Ss:　　(Nice, kite, nine, like, fine.)

T:　　Which sound do you hear most? You try.

S4:　　(/aɪ/.)

T:　　Look at these words. Which letters do you see most?

S5:　　("i-e")

T:　　It is i-e. So what's the sound of "i-e"? Can you guess?

Ss:　　("i-e" says /aɪ/.)

T:　　"i-e"? You sure? Now, let's check. [plays a video]

Activity 2: Blend the phonemes

T:　　"i-e", /aɪ/. OK, look here and spell together with me. B-i-e, /baɪ/. P-i-e, /paɪ/. N-i-e, /naɪ/. Now, please work in groups of four, take out your letter magnets and try to spell. OK? Let's go.

Ss:　　[work in groups]

T:　　OK, time's up! Let's spell these words with me. /l/-/aɪ/-/k/→like. Together, one two go! /l/-/aɪ/-/k/→like.

Ss:　　　(/l/-/aɪ/-/k/→like.)

T:　　　The second one, together! /k/-/aɪ/-/t/→kite. Together! /k/-/aɪ/-/t/→kite.

Ss:　　　(/k/-/aɪ/-/t/→kite.)

T:　　　The third one, who can try? You please.

S6:　　　(/f/-/aɪ/-/v/→five.)

T:　　　Good job! This one, who can try? You please.

S7:　　　(/n/-/aɪ/-/n/→nine.)

T:　　　Yes. /n/-/aɪ/-/n/→nine. Last one. Together! One, two, go!

Ss:　　　(/r/-/aɪ/-/s/→rice.)

T:　　　OK, let's read these words together with our fingers.

Ss:　　　(/l/-/aɪ/-/k/→like, /k/-/aɪ/-/t/→kite, /f/-/aɪ/-/v/→five, /n/-/aɪ/-/n/→
　　　　　nine, /r/-/aɪ/-/s/→rice.)

T:　　　Excellent! Now let's spell more words. Please work in pairs. Try to spell these four-
　　　　　letter words. OK?

Ss:　　　[work in pairs]

T:　　　OK, time's up. Which group can try? The first one. You two, have a try!

P1:　　　(Five.)

T:　　　Bingo! Five. The second one. You two.

P2:　　　(Bite.)

T:　　　Bite, good job! The third one. You two.

P3:　　　(Hide.)

T:　　　Hide, good job! The fourth one. You two.

P4:　　　(Mile.)

T:　　　Excellent! Mile. The last one. You two.

P5:　　　(Wipe.)

T:　　　Good job! Wipe. Now, please challenge yourselves and try to spell these five-letter
　　　　　words. The first one, who can try? You please.

S8:　　　(Smile.)

T:　　　Mile, smile. Excellent! The second one. Who can try? You please.

S9:　　　(Swipe.)

T:　　　Wipe, swipe. Good job! Big hands for them.

T:　　　What can you see now?

Ss:　　　(Five pies.)

T:　　　Where are the pies?

Ss:　　　(In the house.)

T:　　　Yes, they are in the house. Remember, who likes pies?

Ss:　　　(Nini.)

T:　Yes, Nini. Can Nini get the pies?

Ss:　(No.)

T:　Let's help Nini together. OK?

Ss:　(OK.)

Activity 3: Segment the phonemes

T:　Here is your task. First, let's read these words together.

Ss:　(Big, fine, six, nice, pig, ice.)

T:　Now, tell me. Which words have the sound of /aɪ/? You please.

S10:　(Fine, nice, ice.)

T:　Bingo! Which words have the sound of /ɪ/? You try.

S11:　(Big, six, pig.)

T:　Good job! Now please listen and number these words.

Ss:　[listen and number]

T:　Have you finished? Check with me.

Ss:　[check their answers]

T:　Are you right?

Ss:　(Yes!)

T:　Good job! You know the difference between /aɪ/ and /ɪ/ .

Activity 4: Spell and write words

T:　Now here comes more tasks. Let's see if you can spell. Take out your letter magnets. Now let's have a spelling competition. Work in groups of four. Listen to my words and spell them. If you have finished, please hands up. Let's see who is the first.

T:　OK, first one. Kite. OK. Group 1.

G1:　[spell the word]

T:　Good job! Second one. Big.

G2 & G3:　[spell the word]

T:　Oh, Group 2 and Group 3. Excellent. The third one. Six.

G7:　[spell the word]

T:　Group 7. Good job! Last one. Five.

G4 & G5:　[spell the word]

T:　Group 5 and Group 4. Excellent! Now let's try to write them down. Take out your books, and turn to Page 16. Listen and write.

Ss:　[listen and write]

T:　Have you finished? Let's check with Li Ming's and Xiaoyang's. Look at Li Ming's and Xiaoyang's writing. Are they right?

Ss:　(Yes.)

T:　Bingo! Pay attention to your writing. Please write them correctly and beautifully.

步骤三　迁移与运用(9分钟)

Activity 1: Read for general idea

T:　Look at Nini! Can he get the pies? Let's watch and find it out.

Ss:　[watch]

T:　Can Nini get the pies?

Ss:　(Yes, he can.)

T:　That's right. See, the swine smiles.

Activity 2: Imitate and fill in

T:　Look at these pictures. Please work in groups of four. First, read it by yourself. Second, check in groups of four. Work together and read it better. OK, let's go.

Ss:　[read and work in groups]

T:　OK, let's have a try. First one, which group can read? You four.

G5:　(The swine.)

T:　Good! This one. You four.

G6:　(Bite, bite, bite.)

T:　Good job! This one, who can try? You four.

G7:　(The swine smiles.)

T:　Good job! This one. You four.

G8:　(The swine swipes the five pies.)

T:　Excellent! Last one. You four, have a try.

G9:　(The swine hides by a pile of pies.)

T:　OK. Good job! Let's read the whole story all together.

Ss:　[read the story]

T:　I see, you can read the story of *Five Pies*. In the story, we can find these two words: "swipe" and "hide". What do they mean? Can you choose the right word for each sentence? First one, you please.

S16:　(The swine hides by a big crib.)

T:　Excellent! Second one, you try.

S17:　(The swine swipes the five pies.)

T:　Good job!

Activity 3: Read and spell more

T:　Look, luckily Nini gets the pies. What a lovely and interesting story! Actually, it's from "Now I'm Reading!". It is a set of books. And you can find more similar stories like *Pig Sits*, *Pig Jigs* and *Mice On Ice*. You can read them after class.

作业布置

T: Here comes your homework. Challenge yourself to use the new rule to read other books in the reading list. Don't forget to read the chant in this class and write more words fitting the rule of "i-e". So much for today. Goodbye everyone.

配套课件

教学设计①

(一)语篇研读

本课教学内容选自人教版英语四年级上册第二单元 My schoolbag A 部分 Let's spell 板块,该语篇属于"人与自我"主题范畴,内容涉及"身边的事物与环境"。

What

本课将教材配套音频 chant 中印着数字九(nine)的风筝(kite)的部分与绘本 *Five Pies* 进行衔接。该绘本讲述了一只爱玩风筝、爱吃派的小猪 Nini 的故事。热爱吃派的小猪 Nini 偶然发现了窗上的五个派,通过区分 big、five、six、nine、pig、ice 的发音打开院门,在写出单词 five、six、big、kite 后成功溜进院子,偷吃了派。

Why

在该绘本中,小猪 Nini 为了吃到派,要完成含"i-e"的词汇直拼任务,如 like、kite、five、nice、rice 等,为"i"的开音节直拼学习提供了拼读资源。小猪 Nini 的故事描述、chant、拼读比赛等任务有助于学生掌握见词能读、听音能写的直拼技能。

How

该绘本故事清晰地描绘出小猪 Nini 偷派的情境,教学材料涉及了如 swine、hide、swipe、five、bite、smile、big、six、pig 等包含 i 的闭音节与开音节的词汇。故事在小猪 Nini 偷派的情境中凸显了"i"的发音规则,即在重读闭音节中发 /ɪ/ 和在开音节中发 /aɪ/,并强化了二者的音、形对应关系。

(二)学情分析

本课授课对象为 Z 省某小学四年级学生。他们对绘本阅读较为熟悉,期待借助直拼技能突破阅读难点,因而对融合直拼和阅读的课堂充满兴趣,具有较高的学习动机。此外,通过对本册第一单元和三年级两册英文课本的 Let's spell 板块的学习,学生已积累了 21 个辅音字母的基本发音、5 个元音字母在闭音节中的发音与"a"在开音节中的发音等,并初步掌握了基本的拼读技巧。但是本节课是学生首次接触"i"在开音节中的发音,因此教师需要注重创造多形式、富有挑战的学习活动,让学生通过有意义的操练,进一步理清发音规则。

---

① 本教学设计由温州市蒲鞋市小学张丽琼撰写。

(三) 教学目标

通过本课时的学习,学生能够:

1. 通过观察与认读符合"i-e"发音规则的单词如 like、kite、five、nine、rice 等,做到听音能说;

2. 通过梳理与概括,建立并深化"i-e"的音形对应关系,做到见词能读;

3. 通过区分"i"在开、闭音节单词中的直拼规则,在拓展阅读中运用并深化对相关规则的领悟,做到能拼会写,提高拼读的流利度;

4. 通过小组朗读绘本故事,在新的语境中内化与应用"i-e"发音规则,感受小猪的机智与可爱。

(四) 教学流程

在本节课中,学生将经历三个学习阶段,即复习与激活,推导、拆分与合成,迁移与运用。在第一阶段教师通过视听活动,帮助学生回忆与提取"i"在重读闭音节中的发音规则,并引出绘本人物。在第二阶段,教师引导学生借助音视频资源,推导"i"在开音节单词中的发音规律,通过整体绘本故事的推进,在语音任务中进一步进行拼音合成和拆音辨析操练,强化"i"在开音节中的发音规律并与"i"在重读闭音节中的发音规律进行区分。在第三阶段,学生灵活运用"i"的发音规则,自主阅读绘本,突破拼读难点,提升阅读体验,激发学生后续借助拼读技巧尝试自主阅读的兴趣。

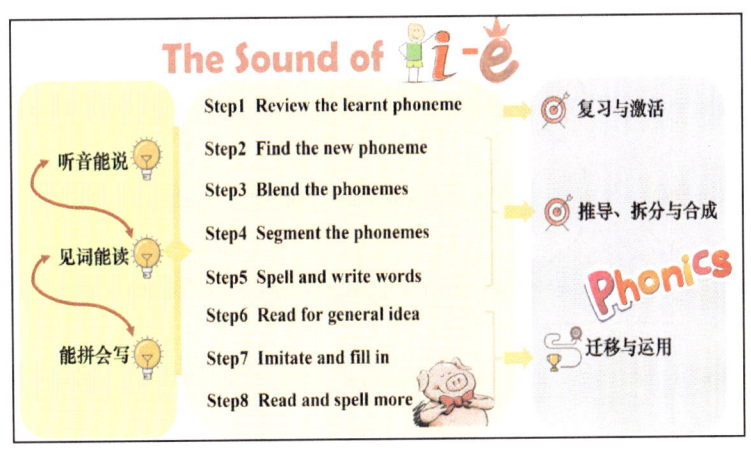

图 1

(五) 教学过程

步骤一 **复习与激活**(8 分钟)

Activity: Review the learned phoneme (8 mins)

Students enjoy the song *The Sound of "i"*. And then they review some CVC words and summarize the sound of "i" in closed syllables. Students meet the main character "Nini" in the picture book within two steps. First, students listen to Nini's monologue and choose his name. Second, students look at the pictures and choose the right kite for him after listening to a chant. And at last, students chant together with Nini.

Lyrics

"i" is a vowel, a letter in the alphabet. (∗4) /I/ (∗16). I saw a pig, pig, pig, pig, pig, pig, pig, pig, pig. It was big, big, big, big, big, big, big, big, big. It wanted to sit, sit, sit, sit, sit, sit, sit, sit, sit. On a hill, hill, hill, hill, hill, hill, hill, hill, hill.

Transcript

Hello, I'm Nini. I like pies very much. But I can't make pies. Guess what I can do? Ha-ha, I can fly a kite.

Chant

See the nice new kite. With the big number nine. Do you like the nice new kite? Yes, it is very fine.

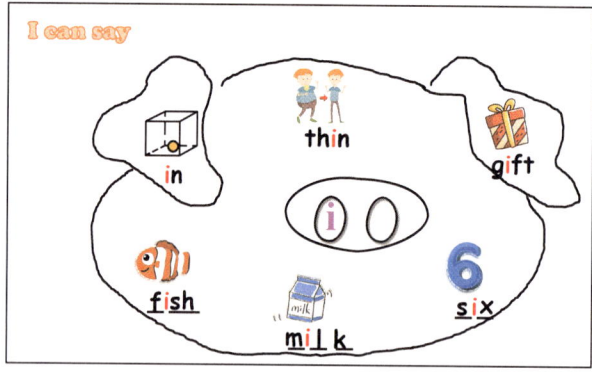

图 2

图 3

214

【设计说明】　首先,通过富有节奏感的歌曲欣赏,教师调动学生多感官回顾"i"发/ɪ/的知识点(见图2)。而后,教师以故事人物Nini为连接点,串联起绘本 Five Pies 和课本中的chant。紧接着的听音选名活动强化了学生对"i"闭音节音形关系的理解,看图说话活动则拉近了学生和人物的距离(见图3)。最后的chant教学帮助学生对含"i-e"的单词进行了第一次自然朗读。

【效果评价】　教师观察学生是否理解人物独白和chant语境,判断其能否在情境中捕获相关语音信息,并根据学生回答的情况给予肯定、鼓励或引导。

步骤二　推导、拆分与合成(18分钟)

Activity 1: Find the new phoneme (3 mins)

Students find the new phoneme in Nini's chant by 4 steps. First, students find the same sound in these words. Second, students find the same letter combination in these words. Third, students infer the sound of the same letter combination. Finally, students watch the video to check their inference.

图4

【设计说明】　借助单词的音和形,教师引导学生通过对音的关注,引起对形的观察,从而推导字母组合的发音(见图4),最后通过视频进行自我检验并总结规则。三个环节步步相扣且富有体验性,实现了以语音为中心,音、形、义三位一体的综合单词认读学习。

【效果评价】　教师观察学生对信息的获取和整合情况;同时注意教学过程中学生学习是否遵循语音先导原则,即是否能通过语音输入激发学生对规则的思考。

Activity 2: Blend the phonemes (5 mins)

Students watch the teacher blend the phonemes into words, such as n-i-n-e, follow the teacher to spell these words, and then try to blend the letter magnets into "like", "kite", "five", "rice" in groups of four. After that, students try to work in pairs and spell some four-letter words and five-letter words.

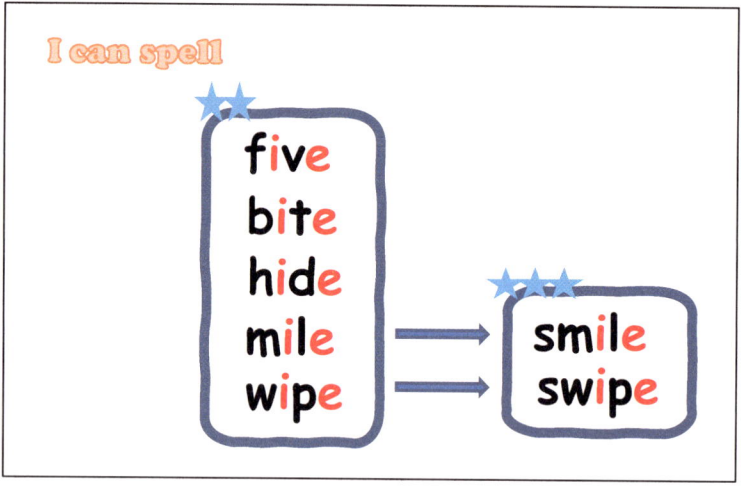

图 5

【设计说明】 通过在黑板上拼字母磁贴和拼读音素,教师帮助学生感知初阶的具象化音素合成。通过丰富的肢体语言示范拼读单词,如"/l/(左手拇指)-/aɪ/(左手食指)-/k/(左手中指)→like(三指收拢合并)",引导学生掌握进阶的抽象化音素合成。通过组内合作和自我挑战,教师带领学生分层次操练核心拼读技巧 Blending(见图5)。拼读单词基本取自绘本 *Five Pies*,为后续绘本阅读降低了难度。

Activity 3: Segment the phonemes (7 mins)

To help Nini open the lock to get the pies, students need to finish a task. First, students read some words and classify them into the group of /ɪ/ or the group of /aɪ/. Then, students listen and number these words, and check the answer with the teacher's answer.

图 6

【设计说明】　随着故事从 Nini 喜欢派发展到 Nini 预备拿到派,教学引出更多绘本情境,巧妙融合教学内容。通过根据音素将单词归类,教师引导学生注意"i"的闭音节和开音节发音规则(见图6),帮助学生在潜移默化中习得新知。

Activity 4: Spell and write words (3 mins)

Students practise spelling the phonemes in the spelling game: The teacher speaks out the words "big" "five" "six" "kite", and students spell the word with letter magnets in groups of four.

Students listen and try to write the correct words to help Nini to get the pies. Teacher checks the writing on the blackboard together with the whole class.

图 7

【设计说明】　设在感悟规则的活动后的拼词游戏,既是对规则的实际运用,又为其后的书写活动搭了台阶,在活跃课堂气氛的同时帮助学生进行有效学习。通过集体校对,教师能带领学生进一步落实拼写的目标,并引导学生关注书写的正确与美观。

【效果评价】　教师观察学生是否做到正确书写和规范书写,提醒学生注意书写美观。

步骤三　迁移与运用(9 分钟)

Activity 1: Read for general idea (2 mins)

Students read the story to find the answer to the question "Can Nini get the pies?".

Transcript:

The swine. The swine hides by a pile of pies. The swine swipes the five pies. Bite, bite, bite. The swine smiles.

图8

【设计说明】 故事学习本身是学龄儿童最喜闻乐见的学习方式之一,有助于激发学生参与的兴趣和表达的欲望。改编绘本(见图8)中含有多个 i 的开音节单词,如 swine、hide、swipe 等,它们给学生提供了充分运用本课所学发音规则的舞台。

Activity 2: Imitate and fill in (5 mins)

Students read the story, check the pronunciation in groups of four and better their pronunciation. Then, students try to understand the difficult words "swipe" and "hide" by choosing the right word for each sentence.

Sentence 1: The fine pig _____ by a pile of pies.

Sentence 2: The fine pig _____ five pies.

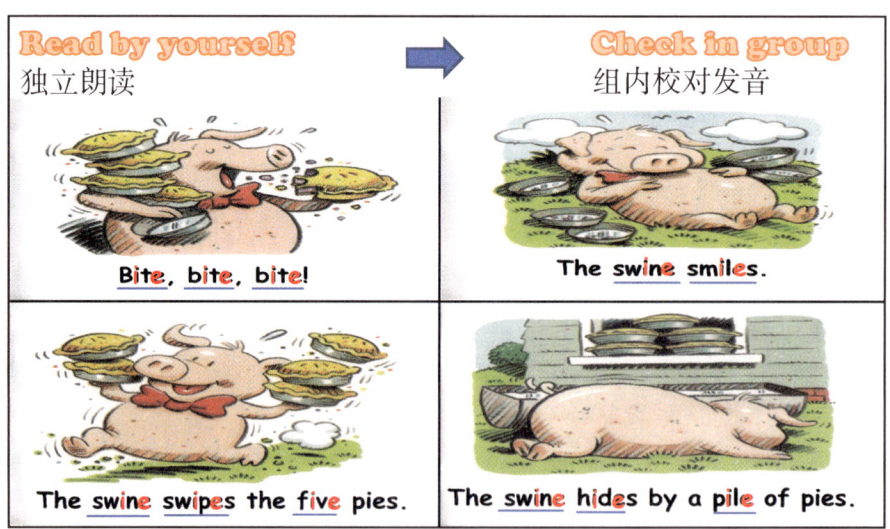

图9

【设计说明】 在故事中学习语音能避免学生单纯追求读音的准确性而忽视语义和语境,并与语调和语流相结合。通过引导学生从自学到互学(见图9),教师既能检验本堂课的学习成效,又能帮助学生感受故事中的情感,满足其学习成就感,并在情感上有所收获。

【效果评价】　教师观察学生是否能顺利地朗读绘本故事,把握学生对直拼技巧的学习和内化情况。

Activity 3: Read and spell more (2 mins)

Teacher summarizes the whole story by giving the source of the story—*Five Pies*, introduces similar stories from the series "Now I'm Reading!", and then encourages students to read after class.

【设计说明】　教师总结故事内容,自然引出相关书籍,鼓励学生开展课后阅读,丰富了课后作业。

(六) 作业设计

★1. Read the chant in this class and write more words fitting the rule of "i-e".

★★2. Challenge yourself to use the new rule to read other books in the reading list.

【设计说明】　本作业设计依据学生的分层特点而布置:一星作业旨在夯实基础,利用chant 和分类练习针对性地锻炼学生单词认读能力、记忆能力和阅读能力,符合自然拼读的两大学习目标;两星作业旨在运用与提升,让学生运用所学语音技巧突破阅读难点,进而提升阅读能力,让学有余力的学生进一步发展拼读和阅读能力。作业设置由简入难,有梯度性,有助于激发学生的学习兴趣和学习动力,帮助学生突破最近发展区。

(七) 板书设计

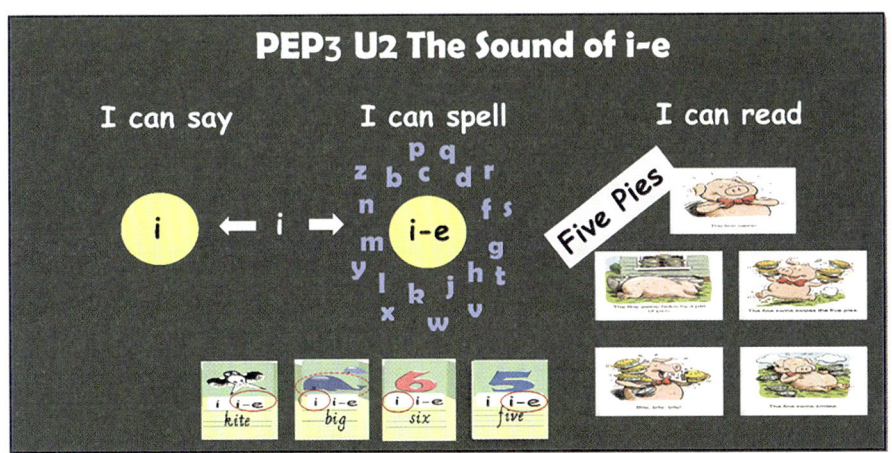

图 10

【设计说明】　板书包括标题与课堂要点。课堂要点分为"会说""会拼""会读"3个部分:板书左边复习了"i"在重读闭音节中发音的旧知,引导学生"会说";中间部分展现了借助磁力字母进行拼读,进而突破课堂拼、说、写三个难点的内容,引导学生"会拼",是板书的重点;板书右边是绘本中的不同的情境,贯穿课堂教学各个环节,指引学生走向"会读"。这样的板书设计,有助于学生区分字母"i"的两种常见发音,条理清晰地学习拼读并将拼读技能用于阅读。

（八）教学反思

本节课是一堂直拼课,聚焦从学习语境与学习策略两方面来帮助学生实现知识意义的自主建构,主要凸显为三点:听、拼、读。通过听的活动,学生关注语音,思考发音规则,做到听音能说、见词能读。通过拼写的活动,学生在实践中运用拼读策略,施展拼读技巧,做到能拼会写。通过读的活动,学生在情境中进一步运用直拼规则。

1. 词、句、篇融合创设语境,激发直接拼读动力

教师借助绘本 Five Pies,融合教材内容,为学生的拼读学习提供了充分的词、句、篇的整体输入。在"复习与激活"的环节,教师设置听音选名、看图说话等活动初步创建故事语境。在"推导、拆分与合成"的环节,教师借助任务链,丰富小猪偷派过程中的故事内容,拓展故事语境。最后教师通过设问,引起学生对偷派结果的好奇,进行迁移与阅读,完成整体故事情境建构。教师通过融合教材与绘本,基于所创设的故事情境,促使学生在整体情境中进行拼读学习与操练,再从认识拼读规则到运用规则进行拓展阅读,进而产生想要拼读更多语篇内容的动力。

2. 音、形、义一体发展策略,提升自主拼读能力

拼读教学注重对学生学习策略的渗透和引导。教师通过提供音、形、义三位一体的活动,帮助学生获取直接拼读的有效策略,进而提升学生自主拼读的能力。在语音先导原则下,教师通过提出像"Which sound do you hear most?"和"Which letters make this sound?"这样的问题,引导学生关注"i"的拼读,建立其音形对应关系,从而达到听音能说的目标。学生通过观察板书上的字母拼读,进行拆音、拼音练习,建立"i-e"结构与音的关系,即音形对应策略,达成能拼会写的目标。学生通过在具体语境中运用拼读规则进行语篇阅读,即以拼促读策略,避免单纯追求读音的准确性而忽视语义和语境、语调和语流的结合,进一步夯实拼读能力。

（九）附件

The fine swine.

The fine swine hides by a pile
of pies.

The fine swine swipes the five pies.

Bite, bite, bite!

The fine swine smiles.

课例 **10**

Oxford English 5A M2 U3
Moving home
（Look and say）

说课视

Hello, everyone! I'm Taylor. It's my great honor to share my lesson plan with you. Now, I'd like to introduce my plan from following aspects, namely, learning material and learners, learning objectives, learning process, homework and blackboard design, and learning effects. Now, let's come to the first part.

Learning material and learners

In order to set clear and reasonable learning objectives, the analysis of learning material and learners should be conducted first.

The learning material is from Shanghai Oxford English 5A Module 2 Unit 3 *Moving home,* Look and say, which is the first part of this unit. The theme of this dialogue is *man and self*, concerning *family and family life*.

What

It's a dialogue between Dad and Sally. As for the main content, it's their talk about the living room, the study and the garden in their new home from different aspects such as the lights, the noise and the supporting garden. In the dialogue, they show their affection for the new home and the reasons why they like it.

Why

By means of the dialogue between Dad and Sally, the author expresses the factors that should be considered when choosing a new home. The dialogue also shows that the Chens think about and care for each other. Through this discourse, I can let students express what their

_____

① 本说课稿由温州市瓯江小学谢智鸯和温州市瓯江小学姚婷婷撰写。

favourite room is and why they like it and lead them to think about their family, appreciate the warmth of their family and finally care more about their own family and family members.

How

It's a typical dialogue of a family's daily life, with a simple structure and understandable content. In this dialogue, Dad and Sally talk about their new home in the present tense, using the sentence patterns like "Which …?" and "Why …?" to ask for information, and "I like …", "Because it is …", "I can … (with …)" to answer the questions. The words of direction like "east", "south", "west", "north", "face" are also used in this dialogue.

Now, let's turn to the analysis of the learners. The students are in Grade 5. They are familiar with the topic *family and family life*. When it comes to their homes, they are eager to talk about them. After learning English for two years, they have learnt the vocabulary concerning activities, rooms and feelings. What's more, they can talk with others in the present tense, which provides the basis of carrying out the activities smoothly. But it is difficult for the students to talk about their own homes and the rooms they like. Thus, I should carry out different activities to enable them to talk.

To further develop the students' higher-order thinking skills, analyzing and evaluating activities based on their understanding of the basic information of the dialogue should be designed.

Learning objectives

Based on the above analysis, the following learning objectives are set. By the end of this lesson, students will be able to:

1. extract and sort out the information about rooms, activities and feelings in the dialogue and understand the dialogue.

2. use the key expressions like "Which …?", "Why …?", "Because it is …" and "I can …" in the role-play to describe the room they like and the reasons why they like it.

3. give the reason why family members like the room, feel the happiness of being with family members and enhance the awareness of loving family and family members.

Learning process

Now let's move on to the description of learning process. In this class, the Activity-based Approach to English learning is adopted, which divides all the learning activities into the following three stages.

The first stage leads to today's topic and helps review what the students have learnt in the previous units. Therefore, there are two activities designed.

In Activity 1, Enjoy a song, students will sing the song "In My Home" and think about how many rooms there are in the song and what they are. This activity can not only help them to review the knowledge they have learnt, but also lead into today's topic "home" naturally and smoothly.

In Activity 2, Review and check, I check the homework and students say more words about activities, rooms and feelings. After that, students are asked to use the words to fill out the sentence structure "I can … in the … . , so … !" in order to perceive the key words and main sentences. I will observe whether the students can share their thoughts.

The second stage is about understanding the passage and promoting internalization. There are eight activities contained.

Activity 1 is Listen and answer. Students listen to the material and have a discussion on the questions: "Does Sally like her old home? Does Mrs Chen like the new home? And why?" By listening to the first material, students can know the reason why Sally doesn't like their old home. By listening to the second material and answering whether Mrs Chen likes the new home and why, students will be able to perceive the key words and main sentences, which pave the way for speech output. In this activity, I can know whether they can grasp the context and general ideas by observing their answers to the questions.

Activity 2 is Watch, tick and match. Students will watch a video, tick and match the answers to "Are they happy with the new home? Which rooms do they like?" with the help of the pictures and phrases. These two general questions can lead students to perceive the key words and main sentences in the passage, which can also develop their ability to attain, extract and record the key information. Through this activity, I will observe their choices and judge whether they can extract the information correctly.

The third activity is Listen, spell and report. Part A is Listen and answer. Students listen to the dialogue and find the reason why Sally likes the living room. Part B is Spell and pronounce. Students are asked to look at a picture of directions and learn the pronunciation of the new words "east" "south" "west" "north" and grasp the different meanings of the word "face". With the help of the picture, they can know the new words intuitively. Part C is Review and summarize. Students consolidate what they have learnt and give a report. Then read it together. With the help of phonological rules, students can learn the pronunciation, spelling and meaning of the new words in group work. I can provide help and encoragement to students if they have difficulty in understanding and spelling these words or giving relevant words.

The fourth activity is Read and discuss. At first, students read Dad's answers, which are disordered. Then they are required to order Dad's answers according to Sally's questions on the worksheet. I will observe and evaluate their ability of getting information according to the clues. After that, students will brainstorm on the question "What can Dad also do in the study?" and are asked to make up a dialogue with the expressions given in pairs to consider what else they can do in the study in their daily life. This can not only strengthen their feelings of experiences, but can also help them practise the key sentences in this lesson.

In Activity 5, by reading the dialogue by themselves, looking for the answers and checking the answers in groups with the expressions "Peter and Paul are … ", "They like … ", "Because it's … ", "They can … " and "So … !", students will think about the reasons why Peter and Paul like their new home independently, which helps improve their ability to get key information and develop their thinking. Whether they can give the reasons why Peter and Paul like their new home can help me to assess whether they can understand the aspects people consider when choosing suitable homes. Through observing, I can know what they have learnt and what difficulties they have met, and then give guidance and feedback specifically and timely.

In order to help them to internalize what they have learnt today, in Activity 6, Listen and imitate, students will listen to the tape and repeat with correct pronunciation, intonation and tones. I can give guidance and encouragement according to their performance.

In Activity 7, Do a role-play, students can choose different practice patterns to act out the dialogue. One will be Sally and the other Dad. Then students evaluate each other's performance from three aspects. I provide different tasks for students at different levels. This not only reduces the difficulty for the students who are not very good at English, but also meets the demand of the students who do well in English. I will observe whether they can use the sentence patterns correctly and evaluate each other according to the checklist, and then give necessary guidance and feedback according to their performance.

In Activity 8, Watch and say, in order to think deeply about home, students are required to watch a video about Sally's grandma's home and discuss it together. I will observe whether the students can develop a right attitude towards home and develop their thinking through interaction and discussion.

The last stage is about making up a dialogue and sublimating the topic. There are two activities contained.

The first one is Draw and display. Students will display the picture of their own homes which they drew before class. Then they will introduce their homes in groups and make a dialogue according to given expressions. At last, some students will be invited to show in the class. In this way, they can not only have a deep understanding of the subject and internalize the core language, but promote their problem-solving skills by using the language and cultural knowledge in real life. I will observe them making the dialogue and make sure they have indeed learnt something effectively.

The second activity is about enjoying a warm and sweet video about students' home life. Watching the video of students' daily life at home is a good way to strengthen their sense of participation.

Homework and blackboard design

After the class, there are two assignments for students. First, they are required to listen and read the dialogue on Page 27. So, they can review what they have learnt in this lesson. Then, they should draw and write about the topic of "I love my home". In this way, they can perform deep learning.

As for blackboard design, it includes the title and key points of this lesson. Three key questions "Are you happy with …? Which room do you like? Why?" are shown on the top. While the answers are presented clearly in the middle, and the meaning is presented next to it. In this way, students can better memorize and recall what they have learnt.

Learning effects

Now, I'd like to emphasize something special that makes this lesson a successful one.

First, in order to develop students' communicative skills, I set different situations, which can lead students from learning in the textbook to learning in the real life. With the help of three different situations, students' thinking can be developed. By comparing different homes, students can find out the warmth of a home and the warmth of the care and love among family members, and cherish their home and families more deeply.

The second shining point is using various rounds of assessment to cultivate students' independent learning capability. By checking their homework, students assess the body of knowledge they have about "home", which arouses their interest in exploring the unknown. In While-learning, for example, based on students' answers to two questions "Are they happy with the new home?" and "Why do they like it?", I can evaluate students' comprehension of the discourse. Meanwhile, group assessment makes students fully participate in class. What's more, in Post-learning, my evaluation is not bound to a single criterion. I not only attach great importance to students' individualized development and good qualities, but also promote their transferring and innovating ability.

That's all for my presentation. Thanks for watching.

试课视频

试课实录①

步骤一 引入主题,激活旧知(4分钟)

Activity 1: Enjoy a song

T: Hello, boys and girls. Are you ready for the class?

Ss: (Yes, we are ready.)

T: Before class, let's enjoy a song. And think about the question: How many rooms can you hear and what are they? OK? Now let's listen.

Ss: [enjoy the song]

T: Boys and girls, how many rooms can you hear? You please.

---

① 本试课稿由温州市鹿城区瓯江小学谢智莺撰写。

S1:　(Five rooms.)

T:　Yes! And what are they?

S1:　(Bathroom, bedroom, living room, kitchen and dining room.)

T:　Class, do you agree with him?

Ss:　(Yes.)

Activity 2: Review and check

T:　Now let's check the answers and read them together.

Ss:　(Bathroom, bedroom, living room, kitchen and dining room.)

T:　Great! So there are different rooms in our houses. What can we do in these rooms and how do we feel? This time please take out the worksheet you have finished before class. Now let's check your homework.

Ss:　(OK.)

T:　First, activities, I say sleep. Can you say more words? This train please.

Train 1: (…)

T:　Good! And feelings, I say warm. How about yours? This train please.

Train 2: (…)

T:　Nice! Now let's say like this: I can sleep in the bedroom, so warm! And what's your sentence? The last boy.

S2:　(I can read books in the study, so quiet.)

T:　Good sentence.

步骤二　理解加工, 初步应用(23 分钟)

Activity 1: Listen and answer

T:　Boys and girls, look, who are they?

Ss:　(They are the Chens.)

T:　Yes, you're right. They are Mr. Chen, Peter, Paul and Sally. They have a home too, but does Sally like their home? Now let's listen to the material and answer the question.

Ss:　[listen to the audio material]

T:　Boys and girls, does Sally like her home?

Ss:　(No, she doesn't.)

T:　Yes! Sally thinks they really need a new home. So a few months later, the Chens move to a new home. Look, this is the Chens' new home, and how is the new home? Now let's listen to Mrs. Chen, and tell me: Does Mrs. Chen like the new home?

Ss:　[listen to the audio material]

T:　Class, does Mrs. Chen like their new home?

Ss: (Yes, she does.)

T: Why? Read after me: why.

Ss: (Why.)

T: You can answer like this: Because … Follow me: because.

Ss: (Because.)

T: Group 1, try.

G1:   (Because.)

T: Group 2.

G2:   (Because.)

T: Group 3.

G3:   (Because.)

T: Group 4.

G4:   (Because.)

T: Well done! Now answer my question, why does Mrs. Chen like the new home?

S3:   (Because it's very big and nice.)

Activity 2: Watch, tick and match

T: Good. So we know Mrs. Chen likes the new home. But how about the other family members? Are they happy with their new home too? Now let's watch a video, tick and match the answers. Before watching the video, I have two questions for you. Q1: Are they happy with their new home? Q2: Which room do they like? Read after me. Which room do they like?

Ss: (Which room do they like?)

T: Now let's watch.

Ss: [watch the video]

T: Are they happy with their new home?

S4:   (Yes, they are.)

T: Which room do they like? You please.

S5:   (Sally likes the living room. Dad likes the study. Peter and Paul like the garden.)

T: Very good. Now look at the blackboard. Let's say together.

T & Ss: (Sally likes the living room. Dad likes the study. Peter and Paul like the garden.)

Activity 3: Listen, spell and report

A: Listen and answer

T: Why does Sally like the living room? Let's listen to Sally. And answer this question.

Ss: [listen to the recording]

T: Have you got the answer? You please.

S6:   (Because it's so big. And it faces south. There is a lot of sunshine.)

T:　　Great!

B: Spell and pronounce

T:　　Now focus on these two words "faces south". What does "south" mean? Look, what's this?

Ss:　（It's a compass.）

T:　　You are right. Here "S" means south. How about other words?

Ss:　（West, north, east.）

T:　　Nice! Now can you read the words more correctly? First, I'll give you some tips. Look at these words. How to read them?

T & Ss:　（Mouth, house, south.）

T:　　Boys and girls, can you read the rest of the new words according to these tips in groups. It's your time. Go!

Ss:　［work in groups］

T:　　Stop here. Now which group can have a try? You group, please.

G1:　（Wet, best, west.）

T:　　Awesome! This group.

G2:　（Short, horse, north.）

T:　　Good! Last group.

G3:　（Read, eat, east.）

T:　　Very good! Big hands! We know Sally likes the living room, because it faces south. And what does the word "face" mean? A or B? Which one is right?

Ss:　（B.）

T:　　Absolutely! It's B. Because it faces south, there's a lot of sunshine.

C: Review and summarize

T:　　Now look at the blackboard. We know Sally is happy with the new home. Which room does Sally like?

Ss:　（Sally likes the living room.）

T:　　Why?

Ss:　（Because it's so big. And it faces south. There is a lot of sunshine.）

T:　　Yes! It's so warm.

Activity 4: Read and discuss

A: Read and order

T:　　Sally loves her home. And how about Dad? If you are Sally, what can you ask? Who can try? You please.

S7:　（Which room do you like, Dad? Why?）

T:　　Good questions. Look. These are Sally's questions. Let's read them together.

Ss:　［read the questions］

T: And these are Dad's answers. But they are disordered. Please order Dad's answers according to Sally's questions on your worksheet. And then ask and answer in pairs.

Ss: [order the answers on the worksheet, and then work in pairs]

T: Stop here. Who can have a try? You two, please.

S8 & S9: [pair performance]

T: Look, these are their answers. Do you agree with them?

Ss: (Yes!)

T: Right. Look at the blackboard. So we know … ?

Ss: [look at the blackboard and say]

B: Make up a dialogue

T: Great! Now let's think about the question: What can Dad also do in the study? Work in pairs and make up a dialogue with the expressions given. It's your time. Go!

Ss: [work in pairs]

T: Time's up. Any volunteers? You two, please.

S10 & S11: [pair performance]

T: Good job!

Activity 5: Read and say

T: So Dad loves their new home too. Now listen to Dad. What's Dad's question?

Ss: [listen to the recording] (Where are Peter and Paul?)

T: Yes! Where are they? Can you guess? Maybe they're in the … ? You please.

S12: (Maybe they are in the bedroom.)

T: Good guess! How about you?

S13: (Maybe they are in the garden, because they like the garden.)

T: Well done! This time, please open your book and turn to Page 27. Read alone and find the answers. Then check the answers in groups by using these expressions. Got it? Go!

Ss: [Read the dialogue, and then check in groups.]

T: Which group will have a try? This group, please.

G1: (Peter and Paul like the garden, because it's nice. They can play in the garden all day.)

T: Good try! Look at the blackboard. Let's say together.

T/Ss: (Peter and Paul are happy with the new home. They like the garden, because it's nice. They can play all day. So happy!)

Activity 6: Listen and imitate

T: So Peter and Paul love their new home too. Now let's listen and imitate some key sentences. Meanwhile, please pay attention to the pronunciation, intonation and tones.

Ss:　[listen and imitate]

Activity 7: Do a role-play

T:　Well done! Next, let's do a role-play. You can choose different practice patterns to act out the dialogue. Now I'm Sally. Who can be Dad? This boy. Come here please.

T/S14:　[act out the dialogue]

T:　How many stars can we get?

Ss:　(Three stars.)

T:　Thank you so much. And this time it's your turn. Go!

Ss:　[act out the dialogue]

T:　Time's up. Which group can come here and act it out for us? OK, you two.

S15 & S16:　[act out the dialogue]

T:　How many stars for them?

Ss:　(Three stars.)

T:　Wow, big hands for them.

Activity 8: Watch and say

T:　Now we know the Chens all love their new home. But how about their grandparents' home? Do they love their grandparents' home? Why? Let's listen to Sally, Peter and Paul.

Ss:　[watch the video]

T:　Do Sally, Peter and Paul like their grandparents' home?

Ss:　(Yes, they do.)

T:　But how is their grandparents' home?

Ss:　(It's small and old.)

T:　Yes. Then why do they still love their grandparents' home? You please.

S17:　(Because they love the time they spend together with their grandparents.)

T:　Yes, because they love the time they spend together with their grandparents.

步骤三　创编对话,升华情感(8分钟)

Activity 1: Draw and display

T:　So class, maybe your home is old, maybe your home is not big enough, but never mind. If you spend lots of time there helping each other and sharing happiness together, you can get a lot of love from your home and family. That's why we always love our families. Now I want to know your home. Can you share with us? Before class, you were asked to draw some pictures of your home floor plan. Look! These are your home floor plans. This time, let's do group work. Step 1, describe your home. Step 2, share your home in groups and try to make a new dialogue. Step 3, I'll ask some of you to come here, and show your home. Now it's your time.

Ss:　[work in groups and then pairs]

T:　Time's up. Which pair can have a try? You two, come here please.

S18 & S19: [pair performance]

T:　Wow, big hands for them. And you two, have a try.

S20 & S21: [pair performance]

T:　Good job! Big hands!

Activity 2: Enjoy a video

T:　Boys and girls, there's a video about your family life. Let's enjoy!

Ss:　[watch the video]

T:　Wow, so many pictures here. Look, what's this word?

Ss:　(Home.)

T:　Yes, it's home. Do you love your home?

Ss:　(Yes, we do.)

T:　Of course. And me too. Because where there's a family, there's a home.

作业布置

T:　Here comes our homework. The first one, listen to the dialogue on Page 27 and read it out. The second one, draw your home and describe it under the topic of "I love my home". So much for today. Goodbye, boys and girls.

教学设计①

配套课件

(一) 语篇研读

本课教学内容选自上海牛津版五年级上册第二模块第三单元 Moving home 的 Look and say 板块,该语篇属于"人与自我"主题范畴,内容涉及"家庭与家庭生活"。

What

本课语篇是 the Chens 搬家后,Sally 与 Dad 在新家中的日常对话。他们从采光、噪音、配套花园等角度谈论对新家起居室、书房和花园的看法,描述了对新家的喜爱之情并阐述理由。

Why

语篇通过 Dad 和 Sally 的对话,传递出选择家庭住所需要考虑的因素,以及家人之间相

――――――――――――

① 本教学设计由温州市瓯江小学谢智莺撰写。

互考虑与关心的温暖情感。该语篇可用于引导学生思考自己的家庭,发现家的温馨,进而更加爱护自己的家人与家庭。

How

该语篇是家人间典型的日常生活对话,结构简单,易于理解。Dad 和 Sally 谈论新家时使用了一般现在时,涉及的核心语言有"Which … ?""Why … ?"等用以询问信息的特殊疑问句,"I like … ""Because it is … ""I can …（with … ）"等作为回应及表明缘由的句型,以及 east、south、west、north、face 等表示方位的词汇。

（二）学情分析

本课授课对象为 Z 省某小学五年级学生。在认知风格方面,他们对"家庭与家庭生活"主题很熟悉,且"有话可说"。经过几年的英语学习之后,学生已具备了运用"活动""房间""感受"等话题下的相关词汇的能力,能够用一般现在时与他人交流。但他们尚未具备连句成段和以对话的形式与他人交流自己的家的能力,需要教师提供"听、看、读、画、演"等多元活动,帮助学生形成对话语篇意识,达到"有话能说"的效果。此外,尽管学生的高阶思维能力已得到初步发展,但其思维的深刻性和批判性较弱,需要教师设计分析评价类型的活动,帮助其理解对话语篇基本信息,实践运用核心词句,推动学生的思维从低层级的记忆、理解与应用走向分析、评价乃至更高层级的迁移创新,充分践行英语学习活动观,落实学科育人要求。

（三）教学目标

通过本课时的学习,学生能够:

1. 在听、看、说的活动中,获取与梳理家庭成员谈话中提到的房间、活动和感受等信息,理解对话内容;

2. 以角色扮演的方式,运用核心句型"Which … ?""Why … ?""I like … ""Because it is … ""I can …（with … ）"等谈论家中喜欢的房间,并阐明理由;

3. 简要给出家人喜欢某个房间的理由,从中感受家庭的温暖与和家人在一起的美好,懂得爱家、爱家人。

（四）教学流程

学生在本节课共经历三个学习阶段。第一阶段,学生在教师引导下通过听歌、说词语与校对前置性作业来复习旧知、激活已知词汇、感知理解"房间""活动""感受"等话题下的核心词汇与句型。第二阶段,教师引导学生通过听、看、说的活动获取和梳理信息,通过听一听、勾一勾、连一连、拼一拼等活动来落实、巩固核心语言。第三阶段,在教师设置的真实情境中,学生自己动手设计"心目中的家",并通过创编对话进行语言的运用和拓展,创造性地输出语言。

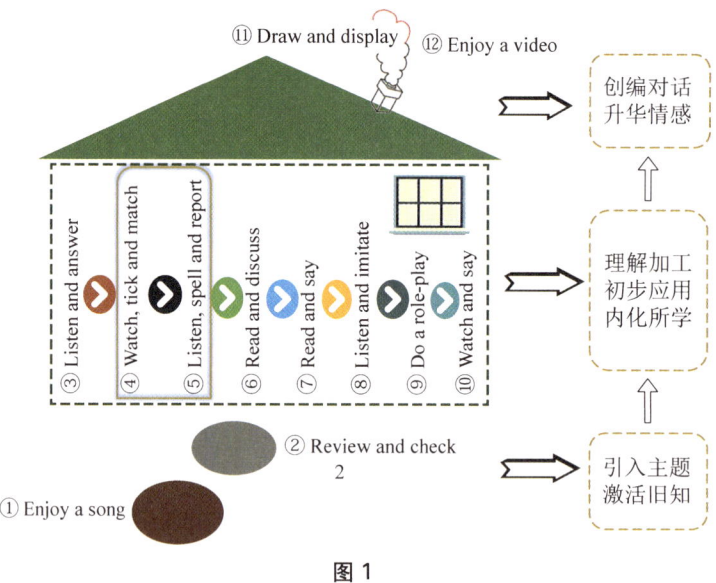

图 1

（五）教学过程

步骤一 引入主题，激活旧知(4分钟)

Activity 1: Enjoy a song (2 mins)

Students enjoy the song "In My Home" and think about how many rooms are there in the song and what they are.

Lyrics

In My Home

I take a bath in the bathroom. In the bathroom, in the bathroom. I take a bath in the bathroom. Where do you go to sleep? I go to sleep in the bedroom. In the bedroom, in the bedroom. I go to sleep in the bedroom. Where do you watch TV? I watch TV in the living room. In the living room, in the living room. I watch TV in the living room. Where do you cook your dinner? I cook my dinner in the kitchen. In the kitchen, in the kitchen. I cook my dinner in the kitchen. Where do you eat your dinner? I eat my dinner in my dining room. In my dining room, in my dining room. I eat my dinner in my dining room. Where do you park your car? I park my car in the garage. In the garage, in the garage. I park my car in the garage. I park my bike there, too.

【设计说明】 用节奏轻快的歌曲复习旧知，导入新课，自然且顺利地引出本节课话题"home"。

Activity 2: Review and check (2 mins)

Students show their homework and say more words about activities, rooms and feelings. Then use the words to make sentences "I can … in the … , so … !"

图 2

【设计说明】 教师利用前置性作业创设情境(见图 2),激发学生兴趣,引导其感知核心语言,评估自身关于本节课已有的知识储备,为后续学习做好铺垫。

【效果评价】 教师观察学生能否参与互动和交流,主动分享个人对该主题已有的知识和经验,并适时进行指导和反馈。

步骤二 理解加工,初步应用(23 分钟)

Activity 1: Listen and answer (3 mins)

Students listen to the audio material and have a discussion on the questions: Does Sally like their old home? Does Mrs Chen like the new home? And why?

Transcript

Sally:

I'm Sally. This is my home. There are seven rooms in it. We have a big living room, but it faces north, we can't get a lot of sunshine. We do almost everything in our bedrooms. Dad likes reading, but we don't have a room for reading or working. Our kitchen is also too small, mum always cooks for a long time. Peter and Paul like playing outside, but our home is too far away from the park. I think we really need a new home.

Transcript

Mrs Chen:

I'm Mrs. Chen. We have a new home. There are three bedrooms, a living room, a dining room, a kitchen, a study and two bathrooms in my home. It's a home with a beautiful garden. The living room and Sally's bedroom face south, there's a lot of sunshine. We can watch TV and play in it. The study faces east, it's quiet. We can work and read books there. The kitchen faces north. It's big and clean. We can cook a lot of food there. And there are two bedrooms facing west. They're quiet. I'm happy with my new home.

【设计说明】 教师利用第一个自创听力材料引出 the Chens 搬家的原因,为下文 the Chens 搬入新家所发生的对话做好铺垫。利用第二个自创听力材料,引导学生初步感知核心短语和句型,为语言产出做准备。

【效果评价】 教师观察学生回答问题的表现,了解其对听力中的语境及其大意的掌握情况,并根据学生的回答及时评价。

Activity 2: Watch, tick and match (2 mins)

Students read two general questions: "Are they happy with the new home? Which room do they like?". Then they watch the video, tick and match the right answers on the worksheet.

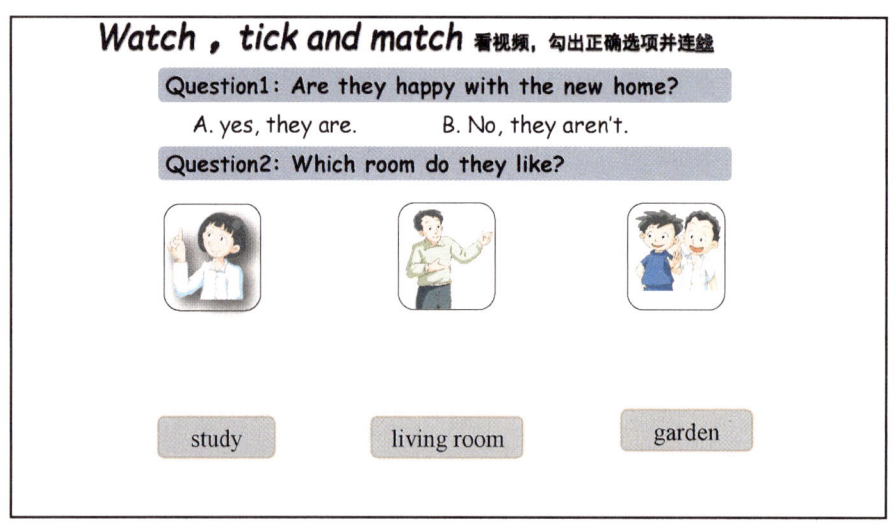

图 3

【设计说明】 在概括性问题的驱动下(见图 3),教师引导学生通过看视频感知语境以及语境中的核心短语和句型,从而提升学生准确获取、梳理和记录关键信息的能力。

【效果评价】 教师观察学生的选择,判断其能否准确获取信息,并根据学生的回答情况调整问题难度。

Activity 3: Listen, spell and report (5 mins)

A: Listen and answer

Students listen to the recording and find the answer to this question: Why does Sally like the living room?

B: Spell and pronounce

Students look at a picture of directions, and learn the pronunciation of the new words "east", "south", "west" and "north" in groups and grasp a different meaning of the word "face".

C: Review and summarize(Sally's part)

Students review what they have learnt and make a summary.

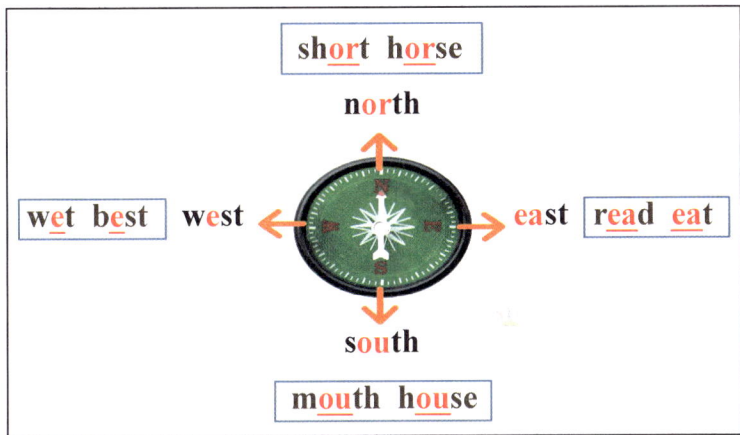

图 4

图 5

【设计说明】 教师通过呈现图片,让学生在小组合作中借助发音规律理解单词的音、形、义(见图 4)。这有利于学生形象地理解方位词,掌握 face 的另一层含义,感受房间朝向与阳光的关系。接着,让学生整理归纳 Sally 部分的逻辑表达,进而提升其获取信息的能力(见图 5)。

【效果评价】 教师根据学生理解词汇、拼读单词和拓展词汇的情况,及时提供帮助与评价。

Activity 4: Read and discuss（4 mins）

A：Read and order

Students order Dad's answers（in disorder）according to Sally's questions on the worksheet.

B：Make up a dialogue

Students brainstorm on the question "What can Dad also do in the study?". And then work in pairs and make up a dialogue with the expressions given.

图 6

图 7

【设计说明】 教师借助提示（见图6）与开放性问题（见图7）引导学生排列顺序，联系生活，主动思考，操练语言。

【效果评价】 教师观察学生能否独立思考和探究，评价其利用线索推断信息的能力，并给予必要的指导。

Activity 5: Read and say（2 mins）

Students read the dialogue by themselves and find the answers. Then they check the answers in groups by using the expressions presented on the slide to complete the passage with more details.

图 8

【设计说明】　教师引导学生通过小组合作,自主思考 Peter 和 Paul 喜欢新家的理由(见图 8)。这有利于提高学生获取关键信息的能力,发展学生的思维能力,并帮助教师评估学生对语篇的深度理解情况。

【效果评价】　教师通过观察学生在上述学习活动中的表现,及时了解学生的学习难点,并据此进行具体的、有针对性的指导,给予及时的评价。

Activity 6: Listen and imitate（1 min）

Students listen to the tape and repeat with correct pronunciation, intonation and tones.

【设计说明】　教师引导学生通过跟读,深入理解对话内容,内化所学语言,为后续输出奠定基础。

【效果评价】　教师根据学生朗读对话的情况,给予指导或评价。

Activity 7: Do a role-play（3 mins）

Students choose different practice patterns to act out the dialogue in pairs. One will be Sally and the other will be Dad. Then students may evaluate each other's performance from three aspects: Do we read/talk correctly? Do we read/talk loudly and fluently? Do we read/talk with emotion?

图 9

【设计说明】 教师根据学生的能力,给予了不同难度的任务选择(见图9),从而降低"学困生"的学习难度,满足"学优生"扩大知识面的需求,适应学生的兴趣和差异。

【效果评价】 教师观察学生角色扮演以及同伴互评的表现,给予必要的指导与评价。

Activity 8: Watch and say (3 mins)

Students watch a video about Sally's grandparents' home. Then have a discussion: What do they think of their grandparents' home? Do they like their grandparents' home? And why?

Transcript

Sally:

This is my grandparents' home. The living room is very small. The floor is old, the TV is old and the sofa is old too. But it's really clean and tidy. I can play chess with my grandpa. And I can watch TV with my grandparents here, too. I love my grandparents' home. I like to be with them.

Peter:

You see, there are only three bedrooms in my grandparents' home. There isn't enough room for us. So I have to share one bedroom with my brother, Paul. But it's OK to share with him. Because I like the time that we spend together with my grandparents. I can chat with them and I can eat the nice food that my grandma makes. It's always a good time with them. I love my grandparents' home.

【设计说明】 教师通过自制视频,引导学生对比 the Chens 又大又漂亮的新家和 grandparents 又小又旧的家,深入思考"家"含义,进而确保育人目标在课堂教学中的有效落实,并为学生进一步提炼和概括信息做好铺垫。

【效果评价】 教师观察学生能否通过交流与讨论,树立正确的对"家"的态度。

步骤三　创编对话,升华情感(8 分钟)

Activity 1: Draw and display (6 mins)

Students draw the pictures of their own homes before class. They display the pictures and introduce their homes in groups. Then they make a dialogue according to the given expressions in pairs. At last, some students will be invited to show in front of the class.

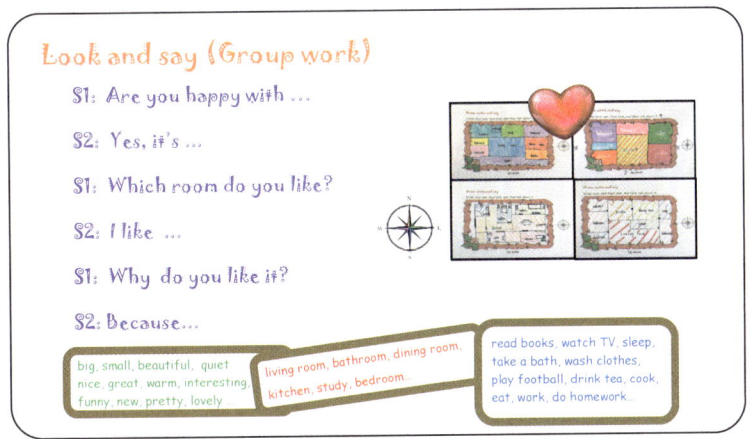

图 10

【设计说明】　通过向小组伙伴描述自己温馨的家,并创编对话(见图 10),学生能在完成交际任务的过程中深化对主题意义的认知,内化核心语言,进而提升在真实情境中运用所学语言和文化知识解决问题的能力。这是在真正鼓励学生的个性化发展,培养其优良的个性品质。

【效果评价】　教师观察学生整合运用相关语言创编对话的情况,确保学习真正发生并取得成效。

Activity 2: Enjoy a video (2 mins)

Students enjoy a warm and sweet video about their home life.

图 11

【设计说明】 教师通过引导学生欣赏在家的温馨画面(见图11),增强其参与感和体验感,使其在熟悉的场景、轻松的状态下内化知识,接受德育,从而强化课堂效果,升华课堂主题。

(六) 作业设计

★1. Listen to the dialogue on Page 27 and read it aloud.

★★2. Draw a picture of your home and describe it under the topic of "I love my home".

【设计说明】 本作业通过设计有梯度的星级任务,让学生在学习后进行巩固、应用与提升。一星作业为基础性作业,旨在使学生巩固知识,内化语言;二星作业为实践性作业,旨在鼓励学生发散思维,迁移并拓展所学知识,实现深度学习,将能力转化为素养。

(七) 板书设计

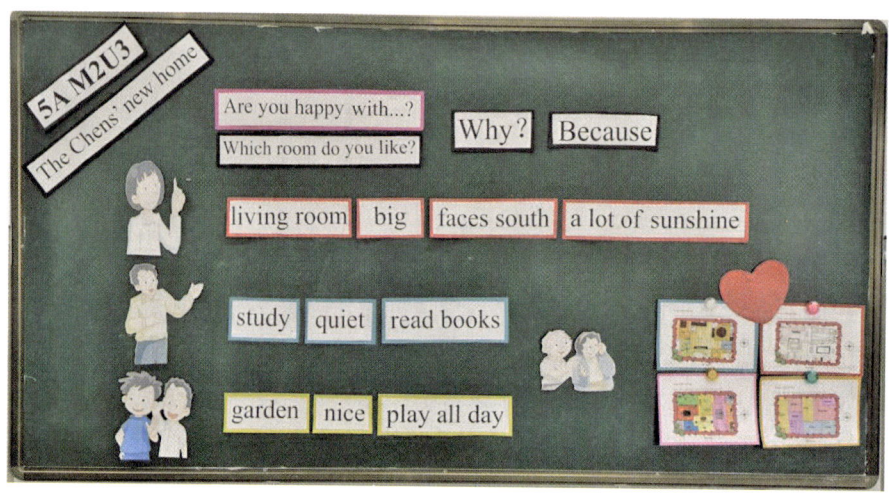

图 12

【设计说明】 板书包括课题名称和课堂要点。板书的上方是涉及本节课核心语言的问题部分,本课紧紧围绕"Are you happy with our new home?""Which room do you like?""Why?"这三个核心问题展开。其下是问题的回答部分,它清晰地呈现了本节对话课的发展过程。最后,板书的右侧展示了本节课的主题意义。该板书逻辑清晰,结构明了,呈现出了教师有意识地引导学生进行逻辑思考的动态过程。

(八) 教学反思

在本节课中,教师对课时内容进行了有机拆分与整合,生成多重对话语境,引导学生在真实语境和交际中学习目标语言,体会家人在一起的重要性。此外,教师还设立了多轮自主评价的活动,激发学生学习的主动性,提升自主学习能力。

1. 创设多重对话语境,发展真实性交际

本节课教师对教材语篇的情境进行了合理拆分、调整及补充,引导学生逐步由"基于语篇的学习"走向"超越语篇的学习",发展真实交际能力。教师将原情境拆分为三个子情境:第一个子情境为 Sally 和 Dad 相互分享各自喜欢的房间并说明理由;第二个子情境为 Sally 和 Dad 讨论 Peter 和 Paul 喜欢的房间并阐明理由;第三个子情境为 Sally、Peter 和 Paul 描述 grandparents 的房子。前两个教学情境皆是基于语篇拆分而成,第三个情境则是教师依托语篇主题意义创造的。学生在本节课中先进入"Sally 和 Dad 互相分享喜欢的房间"这一情境,提升分析推理的能力。随后进入 Peter 和 Paul 的情境,对此前学习的核心语言点展开应用实践。在此基础上,学生进入第三个子情境,通过对比不同住所加深对"家"的认识,发现家的温馨和家人之间相互关爱与照顾的温暖,进而更加爱护自己的家人与家庭。各个对话情境环环相扣,为学生的真实语用创造机会,也确保了学科育人目标在课堂教学中的有效落实。

2. 设置多轮评价,助力个性化学习

在本节课中,教师设置了多轮评价,并将其置于各个教学环节之中,评价目标清晰,方式多样,能有效促进教学目标的达成,满足学生的个性化学习需求。在"引入主题,激活旧知"的环节,教师以校对前置性作业的形式,引导学生自我评估对本课话题"home"已有的知识储备,激发其探索未知的兴趣。在"理解加工、初步应用"这一环节,教师主要借助问答的评价方式,围绕"Are they happy with their new home?" "Why do they like it?"这两个概括性、开放性问题,开展听一听、勾一勾、连一连等学习活动,评估学生对语篇的深度理解情况。其间,教师利用小组评价和任务分层,让每一位学生都充分参与到课堂中来,让个体的学习始终在最近发展区内稳步推进。在"创编对话、升华情感"的环节中,教师的评价不再拘泥于单一标准,而是侧重观察学生在表达与创编对话时的迁移运用能力,真正鼓励学生的个性发展,培养学生优良的个性品质。

(九) 附件

学　习　单

Activity 2: Watch, tick and match

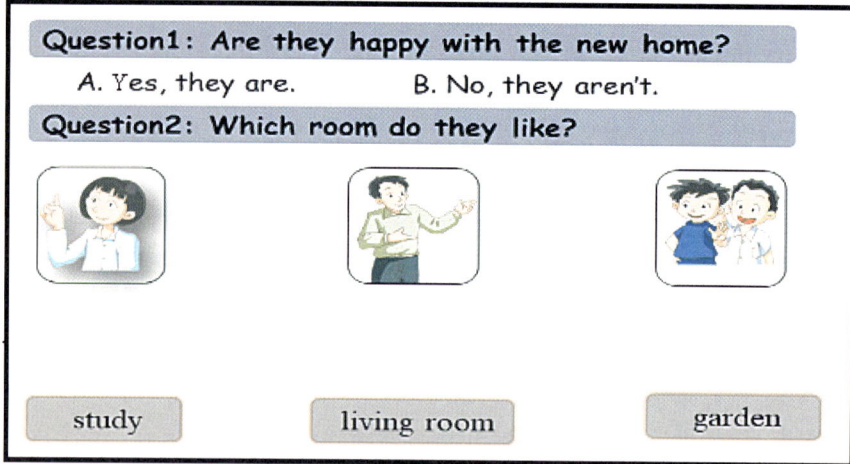

Question1: Are they happy with the new home?

　　A. Yes, they are.　　　　　　B. No, they aren't.

Question2: Which room do they like?

study　　　　　　living room　　　　　　garden

Activity 3: Read and order

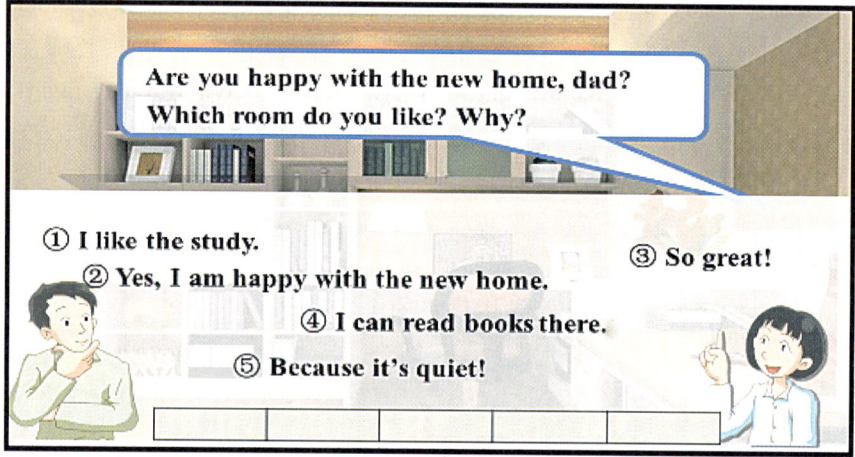

Are you happy with the new home, dad?

Which room do you like? Why?

① I like the study.　　　　　　③ So great!

② Yes, I am happy with the new home.

④ I can read books there.

⑤ Because it's quiet!

Activity 4: Read and say (Group work)

Step1: Read and find the answers 读课文，从文中找出答案

Step2: Check and say 小组讨论，并说一说

Peter and Paul are...

They like...

Because it's...

They can...

So...!

Activity 5:　Look and say (Group work)

Groupwork

Step1: Describe your home. 描述自己的家。

Step2: Share your home in groups. 小组内讨论并分享自己的家。

Step3: Show your home to us. 选一位代表上台展示你们的家。

S1: Are you happy with ...

S2: Yes, it's ... / No, it's ... Because ...

S1: Which room do you like?

S2: I like the ...

S1: Why?

S2: Because ...

... is ...
... face(s) ...
... can ...
So ...!

big, small, beautiful, quiet
nice, great, warm, interesting,
funny, new, pretty, lovely ...

living room, bathroom, dining room,
kitchen, study, bedroom...

read books, watch TV, sleep,
take a bath, wash clothes,
play football, drink tea, cook,
eat, work, do homework...

课例 **11**

Oxford English 4B M2 U3 Home Life
（*Look and say*）

说课实录①

Hello, everyone! I'm Roxanne. It's my great honor to present my lesson plan for you. Now, I'd like to introduce it from three aspects, learning objectives, learning process and learning effects.

Learning objectives

First, let's pay attention to learning objectives, which are based on the analysis of learning materials and learners. Let's take a look.

The learning material is from Oxford English 4B Module 2 *My favorite things* Unit 3 *Home life,* Look and say, which is the first lesson of this unit. The theme of this text is *man and self*, concerning *family and family life*.

What

As for the main content, it tells that Kitty's father comes back home after work, gets together with his family and asks Kitty, Ben and Maggie where they are and what they are doing. This dialogue depicts the scene where Dad and his family help each other to make dinner and shows us that the family members love and help each other.

Why

The dialogue not only presents information about where the family members are and what they are doing, but also reflects how much they care for each other. Therefore, students' awareness of the importance of caring for family members can be developed.

How

This dialogue includes two parts. In the first part, Dad asks Kitty, Ben and Maggie where

---

① 本说课稿由温州市瓯江小学李莞尔撰写。

they are by using the sentence patterns "Where are you?", "I'm in the …", "I'm … (doing)", the words like "bedroom", "living room", "bathroom", "kitchen", and phrases like "doing homework", "making a model plane", "washing hair" and "cooking dinner" to describe what they are doing. In the second part, Maggie and Dad ask for help in a polite way, using the sentence pattern "Can you …, please?".

After the analysis of learning materials, now let's turn to the analysis of learners.

My students are in Grade 4. They are familiar with the topic of family life and are also curious about others' family life, so they have a strong learning motivation.

Also, after 3 years of English learning, students already have a large vocabulary of family activities and are able to carry out conversations in the simple present tense. However, they are unfamiliar with the present continuous tense, so they are unable to recognize the differences between the two tenses. Therefore, it is necessary for me to guide them to perceive, judge and generalize the use of the present continuous tense in the context.

In addition, my students are able to predict and infer. Also, they can grasp the main idea and extract key information through listening and watching. However, it is difficult for them to understand the thematic meaning of the dialogue, so they need to be provided with supplementary story plots to enhance their understanding of the content.

Based on the above analysis, the following learning objectives are set. By the end of this lesson, my students will be able to:

1. extract and sort out the information about characters, places and activities and understand the importance of caring for their family members.

2. use the sentence patterns "Where are you?", "I'm in the …", "I'm … (doing)" to describe what they are doing and where they are, and then act out the dialogue under my guidance.

3. discuss and talk about their family activities in groups, briefly comment on their daily activities, and appreciate the warmth of family love.

Learning process

Now let's move on to the learning process. In this lesson, students will go through four learning stages.

The first stage is Foreshadow New Knowledge and Perceive Language Structure.

In the first activity, students will sing the song "What are you doing?" with actions and think about the activities they see in the song. This activity can not only activate the classroom's atmosphere, but also let students learn with multiple senses, and perceive the topic and the target language of this lesson.

In the second activity, students will listen to the sound effects and observe the GIF images to guess what the girl is doing. When checking the answers, they will think about the grammatical structure of the present continuous tense and finally make a conclusion. In this way, they will be familiar with the grammatical structure of this tense and have a basic understanding of its meaning. I can observe whether students can explain the rules correctly to know if they perceive the grammatical structure.

Entering the second stage, I designed a situation of the father's birthday to expand the story of the textbook to help students better understand the thematic meaning of the dialogue.

In Activity 1, students will listen to the recording which was made by me. While listening, they will hear the words like "sofa", "TV", "bed", "cook", etc. By relating these words to different living places, students can infer the meaning of "living room", "bedroom", "kitchen" and "bathroom". Then they will number the rooms on the worksheet orderly and use phonics to spell the words independently when checking the answers. This activity aims to improve students' ability to infer the meaning of words and enhance their spelling ability. I will check whether they can number the word correctly to see if they understand the meaning of the objective words.

After that, students will listen to the original dialogue and match the rooms with family members. To check the answers, they need to use the sentence patterns "Where are you?", "I'm in …" and "I'm … (doing)" to reproduce the dialogue. Through listening and matching, students can extract key information and understand the main idea of this dialogue. Also, the reproduction of the dialogue helps lay a foundation for the later application of the target language. I will check their answers to see if they understand the main idea of the dialogue.

In Activity 3, students will observe the pictures and use the new expression "Maybe … is (doing) in the …" to predict family members' activities. It will not only help students to recall the verbs they know and use the target language, but also cultivate their ability to view and infer with illustrations. If they can make reasonable predictions with the above expression, then we can move on to the next activity.

So far, Dad has been very happy to think that everyone is busy preparing a birthday surprise for him. So in Activity 4, students will figure out what everyone is doing. They need to listen to the dialogue and tick the answers on their worksheets. Before listening, students will follow me to pre-read the options to perceive the pronunciation of new words: "model plane" and "homework". After that, they will read the dialogue and use the sentence pattern "I'm … (doing)" to check the answers. Through this activity, students can have a better understanding of the learning material. By observing whether the students can tick the correct answers, I can determine whether they can extract the information accurately. Therefore, I can judge whether the first and second learning objectives have been achieved.

Here, as the story progresses, Dad is heartbroken when he finds no one has prepared a birthday surprise for him, which naturally introduces the question in Activity 5—"Does Dad help Maggie while feeling sad? Why?". Students will have an open discussion on this question. After that, they will watch the video and revise their opinions. This enables students to understand the value orientation behind the text so that they can realize the importance of family love. I can observe whether their opinions are reasonable to judge whether they have formed the correct values.

Now, let's move on to the third stage, Apply the Knowledge: Do a Role-play. In Activities 1 and 2, students will listen to the recording and repeat it. Then they will act out the dialogue in groups of four. In this way, they can not only perceive and imitate the pronunciation, intonation and tones, but also internalize the target language. If they can pronounce correctly and act emotionally, I can tell the second learning objective has been fully realized.

Now let's come to the last stage. In this stage, students will make new dialogues based on what they have learnt.

The first activity is Think and act. Students will talk about Kitty's home life. I divide this activity into 3 parts. Part A is Choose the character. Students view the pictures and think about what Kitty, Maggie and Ben are doing actually. Then they work in four, and each of them chooses one character to act. Part B is Complete the dialogue. According to the text information, students come up with appropriate verbs to complete the dialogue. Part C is Act out. All the students need to act emotionally. This activity guides the students to think about how family members should get along with each other, and understand the importance of caring for family members. What's more, it helps students to improve their imagination, cultivate logic thinking and language organization skills. Meanwhile, through group work of creating dialogues, students are guided to use the language they have learnt to depict the roles' acts and their status according to the story, so as to enhance their interpersonal skills and teamwork spirit. The teacher observes whether the verbs they use are reasonable and whether the grammar is correct to judge the accuracy of their language expression.

The second activity is Think and share. Students will talk about their home life. Three parts are included. Part A is Think and write. Students will write down what they are doing and where they are in the photos and how they feel. Part B is Share in groups. They will make up a new dialogue with the expressions "I'm in the …", "I'm … (doing)" and "It's so …!" to talk about their family life and express their feelings about family activities. Part C is Show and talk. Students show the new dialogues in the class. This activity encourages students to express themselves in the real situation, deepens their understanding of the theme of this lesson, and helps them form a correct attitude towards and value of family love. I will evaluate the effectiveness of teaching and learning by observing whether students can accurately use the tense and language in the dialogue they create, and whether the dialogue can reflect the theme of caring for family members.

After the class, there are two assignments for students. First, they are required to listen to the dialogue on Page 27 and read it aloud, so they can review what they have learnt in the class. The second one is an optional task, which asks them to share their family life with other classmates.

As for blackboard design, the sentence patterns and the key information are presented clearly, from which students can better memorize and recall what they have learnt.

Learning effects

At the end of my presentation, I'd like to stress the uniqueness of my lesson.

Firstly, to help students have a deep insight into the thematic meaning, the listening and speaking contexts are expanded. Although the original dialogue presents detailed information, it doesn't clearly reflect the value of caring for one's family. For example, Maggie asks Dad to cook dinner even though he has just returned from work. So, based on the original dialogue, I add a surprising plot where family members prepare a birthday party for Dad to enable students to notice the change in Dad's feelings, think about how family members should get along with each other, and understand the importance of caring for family members. Then, based on their further understanding of family love in the original dialogue, students are asked to share family love in their own lives, thus deepening their understanding of the thematic meaning.

Secondly, to assist students to improve their ability to use the target language, multilevel activities are carried out. During the class, I use GIF images, videos, and audio to create an intuitive situation and stimulate students' multi-sensory experience, so they can perceive the target language. Then, through speaking and role-play, students can use and master the target language. Finally, through talking and role-play, students are able to transfer the language into reallife situations and express creative ideas, thus improving their ability to use the language.

That's all about my presentation. Thanks for watching!

试课实录①

试课视频

步骤一 铺垫新知,感知语言结构(5分钟)

Activity 1: Sing and act

T: Class begins! Good morning, boys and girls.

Ss: (Good morning, Miss Li!)

T: Sit down, please. Now, let's enjoy a song, and then sing and act. Ready? Go!

Ss: [sing the song with actions]

Activity 2: Listen and guess

T: Wow! Boys and girls, you all sing really well. In the song, what is the girl doing? She is …? [play the sound of running water]

S1:   (She is washing.)

---

① 本试课稿由温州市瓯江小学李莞尔撰写。

T:　　Yes! She is washing her face. So clean! Listen! What is she doing? [play the sound of chewing]

S2:　(She is eating.)

T:　　Yes! She is eating breakfast. So yummy! Listen! What is she doing now? [play music]

S3:　(She is dancing.)

T:　　Yes! She is dancing. So fun! Now, please look at these three sentences. What rules can you find?

S4:　(I can see "ing".)

T:　　Oh! You see "ing". And you?

S5:　(I can see she is doing something.)

T:　　Great! She is doing something, right? When you want to say you are doing something right now, add "ing" after the verbs. Clear?

Ss:　(Yes.)

步骤二　**理解语篇,探究主题意义**(13 分钟)

Activity 1: Listen and number

T:　　Now, look! Who's coming?

Ss:　(He's Mr Li.)

T:　　Yes, Mr Li. Is he happy?

Ss:　(Yes!)

T:　　Great! Today is his birthday. Maybe he can get … ?

S6:　(Maybe a birthday cake.)

T:　　Oh, a cake? Look, maybe he can get a … ?

Ss:　(A gift!/A birthday cake!/A birthday card!/A hug!/A birthday party!)

T:　　Wow! He is very excited right now. He can't wait to go home. Look, this is his home. Mr Li has a very nice home. Do you want to take a look?

Ss:　(Yes!)

T:　　Let's follow him. Now please take out your worksheet. Let's listen and number the rooms you hear. Go!

Ss:　[listen to the recording]

T:　　OK, now let's check. Tell me. This is room number … ?

Ss:　(Room number one.)

T:　　Great! Can you try to read it?

Ss:　(Living room.)

T:　　Yes, follow me, li-ving room. Living room. This is room number … ?

Ss:　(This is number three.)

T: Yes! Number three! Who can read it? You please.

S7:   (ba-th-room, bathroom.)

T: Yes! Follow me, ba-th-room. Bathroom. This is room number … ?

Ss: (It's room number two.)

T: Yes! Can you read it?

S8:   (Bedroom.)

T: Nice! How about the last one?

Ss: (Four!)

T: Yes! Who can try to read it?

S9:   (Let me try! kit-chen, kitchen.)

T: Very good! Please pay attention to the silent "t" here. Follow me, kitchen.

Ss: (Kitchen.)

T: Excellent! Look, Mr Li is at home now. He is looking for his families. They are … ?

Ss: (Kitty, Ben and Maggie.)

Activity 2: Listen and choose

T: But where are they? Let's listen and choose. Ready? Go!

Ss: [listen to the recording]

T: OK, now let's check. Tell me. What does Dad ask?

S10: (Kitty, where are you?)

T: Yes, follow me. Kitty, where are you?

Ss: (Kitty, where are you?)

T: Who can try to be Kitty? You try, please. Boys and girls, let's ask her together.

T & Ss: (Kitty, where are you?)

S11: (I'm in the living room.)

T: Great! Kitty says, "I'm in the living room. " How about Ben? You try, please. Let's ask together.

T & Ss: (Ben, where are you?)

S12: (I'm in the bedroom.)

T: Yes. Ben is … ?

Ss: (Ben is in the bedroom.)

T: Who can be Maggie? You try, please. Let's ask her together.

T & Ss: (Maggie, where are you?)

S13: (I'm in the bathroom.)

T: Yes. Maggie is in the bathroom.

Activity 3: Look and guess

T: Look, Kitty is in the living room. What is she doing? Now let's look at the picture. Maybe Kitty is reading books in the living room. How about Ben and Maggie? Work in pairs and use the sentence pattern.

Ss: [guess in pairs]

T: Now, which pair can have a try? You two please.

S14: (Maybe Ben is sleeping in the bedroom.)

S15: (Maybe Maggie is brushing teeth in the bathroom.)

Activity 4: Listen and tick

T: Well, good guess! So what are they doing exactly? Now, take out your worksheet again. Listen and tick. Maybe Kitty is drawing Dad's picture or doing her homework. Maybe Ben is making a model plane or singing a birthday song. Maybe Maggie is dressing beautifully or washing hair in the bathroom.

Ss: [follow the teacher and pre-read the options]

T: Now, listen.

Ss: [listen to the recording]

T: Now, let's check. Who can be Kitty? You try, please. Let's ask her.

T & Ss: (Kitty, where are you?)

S16: (I'm in the living room. I'm doing my homework.)

T: Great! Boys and girls, don't forget the "ing". Look at Dad. He is unhappy now, because there is no birthday surprise from Kitty. How about Ben? You please. Let's ask.

T & Ss: (Ben, where are you?)

S17: (I'm in the bedroom. I'm making a model plane.)

T: Oh, no. There is no birthday song for dad. He is sad now. How about Maggie? You try. Let's ask.

T & Ss: (Maggie, where are you?)

S18: (I'm washing my hair.)

T: Yes. Maggie is washing her hair. Boys and girls. How does Dad feel now?

Ss: (Sad!)

T: Oh, he is really sad! Because no one remembers today is his birthday. Poor Dad!

Activity 5: Discuss and watch

T: Look, Maggie comes. She says, "Can you cook dinner, please?" Look at dad. Will he say yes?

Ss: (Yes./No.)

T: Why/Why not?

S19: (Yes. Because he loves Maggie.)

S20: (No. Because they forget it's his birthday today.)

T: Yes or no? Now let's watch the video and find out.

Ss:　[watch the video]

T:　OK, tell me together. Does Mr Li cook dinner finally?

Ss:　(Yes!)

T:　Great! Yes! Dad is cooking dinner in the kitchen. Why does dad help Maggie? What's your idea?

S21:　(Because Dad loves and helps his families.)

步骤三　角色扮演,应用目标语言(7分钟)

Activity 1: Listen and imitate

T:　Yes! So do we, right? It's time for you to listen and imitate. Please pay attention to the intonation.

Ss:　[listen and imitate]

T:　Great! You can read really well!

Activity 2: Do a role-play

T:　Now, it's time for you to act. Let's act in groups of four.

Ss:　[act it out and evaluate]

步骤四　创编对话,灵活运用语言(10分钟)

Activity 1: Think and act

T:　Look, Ben comes. He says … ? [plays the recording] But, look! Is this a basketball?

Ss:　(No.)

T:　So, what happens? Let's watch and find out.

Ss:　[watch the video]

T:　Wow, there is a surprising birthday party for dad. How nice! They love dad very much. Look, Dad is very … ?

Ss:　(Happy!)

T:　Great! What can we do to surprise Dad? Can you be happy Dad? Let's act.

S22:　(Kitty, where are you?)

T:　I'm in the living room. I'm making a birthday card. I'm cutting. This is my birthday gift for dad. How about you? Now you can choose one character to act and use the verbs here to complete your dialogue, then come and act in four. When acting, please speak correctly, fluently and act emotionally. Ready? Go!

Ss:　[choose character and act in four]

T:　Time's up! Which group can try?

S23 & S24 & S25 & S26:　[act out]

T:　Thank you! Do they act well? How many starts can they get?

Ss: 　(Three!)

T: 　Thank you! Now families, I'm gonna take a photo for you. Come closer, and say cheese!

S23 & S24 & S25 & S26:　(Cheese!)

Activity 2: Think and share

T: 　Now, there is a new family photo on the wall. Look, I have some family photos too. Look at this one. [introduces teacher's family photos] How about you? You can share your family moments too. Step 1, think and write what you were doing in the photos. Step 2, share in group. Step 3, come to the front and share group by group. Which group is ready?

S27 & S28 & S29 & S30:　[share and talk]

T: 　Thank you, boys and girls. Family members always love and help each other.

作业布置

T: 　Here is your homework. The first one is to listen to the dialogue and read it aloud on Page 27. The second one is to share your family lives with other classmates. That's all for today. Bye.

教学设计①

配套课件

（一）语篇研读

本课语篇选自沪教版牛津英语四年级下册第三单元 Home life 的 Look and say 板块,属于"人与自我"主题范畴,内容涉及"家庭与家庭生活"。

What

本课语篇描述了 Dad 下班回到家后,与家庭成员 Maggie、Kitty 和 Ben 展开的对话。对话中,Dad 询问各个家庭成员在哪个房间、正在做什么,成员们依次作出回应。其间,Maggie 表示自己在洗头,询问 Dad 能否负责做晚餐。此时,Ben 邀请 Dad 一起打篮球,被 Dad 邀请共同烹饪晚餐。对话中,一家人关爱彼此,互帮互助。

Why

Dad 与每位家人的对话语篇不仅直观呈现了家庭成员所在场所及与之匹配的活动信息,也间接体现了 Dad 对 Maggie、Kitty 和 Ben 日常活动的关心和家人相互之间的关爱。该语篇意在让学生了解起居室、卧室等个人家庭生活空间及其功能,并形成主动询问家人日常活动的意识,懂得关爱家人,营造温馨的家庭氛围。

---

① 本教学设计由温州市瓯江小学李莞尔撰写。

How

本课的语篇内容是 Dad 和 Maggie、Kitty、Ben 之间的对话，对话内容主要分为两个部分。一是 Dad 依次询问家人在哪个房间、在做什么，家人们用现在进行时描述自己正在做的事情。这部分内容涉及描述生活场所的核心词汇，如 bedroom、living room、bathroom、kitchen；介绍家庭活动的词组，如 do homework、make a model plane、wash hair、cook dinner 等；询问并回答涉及地点及当前行为信息的句式表达，如"Where are you?""I'm in the …""I'm …（doing）"。二是 Dad 与家人互帮互助，制作晚餐。Maggie 和 Dad 在寻求他人帮助时，使用了"Can you …，please?"等寻求帮助的礼貌用语。

（二）学情分析

本课授课对象为 Z 省某小学四年级学生，他们对"家庭生活"这一话题较为熟悉，好奇彼此间的家庭活动，具有较强的学习动机。先前的英语学习使本班学生已具备大量关于家庭活动的词汇储备，并能用一般现在时开展对话。但本节课新授现在进行时，学生对该时态的形式、意义、用法较为陌生，尚不能识辨出两种时态的语用差异。因此，教师有必要引导学生在不同的语言使用情境中感知、判断和概括现在进行时的用法，并在真实交流与表达中熟练掌握这项语法。此外，本班学生能简单预测与推断，理解听力语篇大意与表面细节。但他们很难独立推断出语篇传递的主题意义，需要教师补足故事情境，提供角色扮演任务，增进其对语篇内容的深层理解。

（三）教学目标

通过本课时学习，学生能够：

1. 在听、看、说的活动中，获取和梳理家庭成员谈话中提到的人物、场所和活动信息，理解对话内容；

2. 运用核心句型"Where are you?""I'm in the …""I'm …（doing）"描述个人正在进行的活动，分角色表演对话；

3. 小组内谈论与展示个人在不同房间内的活动，简要评价其他家庭成员的日常活动，感受家人带来的温暖。

（四）教学流程

在本节课中，学生将经历四个学习阶段。第一阶段为铺垫新知，感知语言结构。教师边跟唱歌曲边表演动作，学生听音猜词和总结规律，初步感知现在进行时的语言结构。第二阶段重在探究、提炼语篇的主题意义。学生在教师创设的情境引导下，梳理文本信息，解读人物情感，提炼主题意义，理解现在进行时的语法意义。第三阶段为角色扮演，应用目标语言。学生由模仿与跟读对话逐步走向小组合作表演，有意义地操练所学语言。第四阶段为创编新对话，迁移运用语言。学生在教师的鼓励下发散思维，联系生活实际拓展对话内容，描述个人家庭活动，进而抒发个人情感，深刻体会语篇传递的主题意义，即采取主动对话与行动的方式，关爱家人，建设和谐家庭。

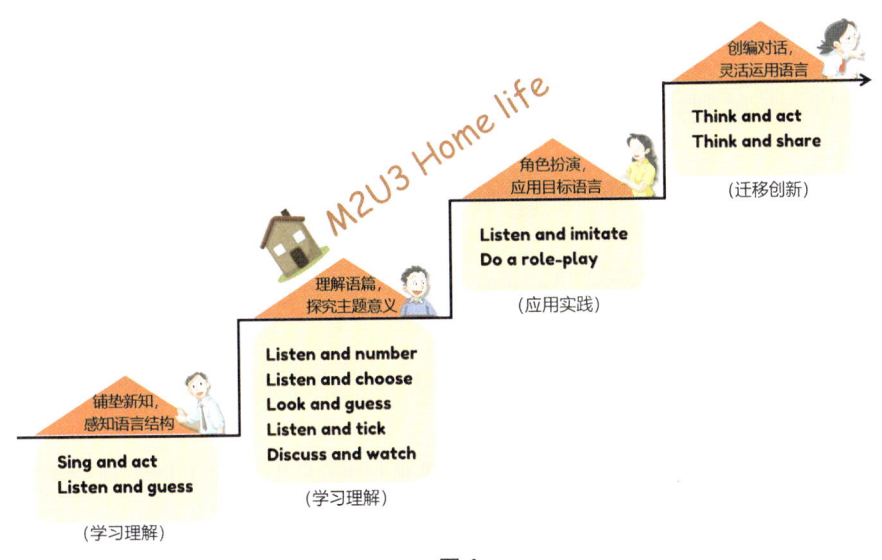

图 1

（五）教学过程

步骤一　铺垫新知，感知语言结构（5 分钟）

Activity 1: Sing and act (2 mins)

Students enjoy and then sing the song "What Are You Doing?" with actions, and think about what activities there are in the song.

Lyrics

What Are You Doing?

What are you doing? I'm washing, washing. What are you doing? I'm eating, eating. What are you doing? I'm dancing, dancing. I'm dancing. I'm dancing now!

What is he doing? He's running, running. What is he doing? He's drawing, drawing.

What is she doing? She's sleeping, sleeping. She's sleeping. She's sleeping now. Shh!

【设计说明】　通过节奏欢快的歌曲，活跃课堂氛围，调动学生的多种感官，激发学生的学习积极性，引出本课时的话题，并让学生感知本课时的核心语言与教学情境。

Activity 2: Listen and guess (3 mins)

Students look at three Gif pictures and listen to the sound effects to guess what the girl is doing. Then students think about the grammatical structure of the present continuous tense and finally make a conclusion under teacher's guidance.

图 2

【设计说明】 教师通过标红动词"ing"的部分,引导学生观察和初步感知现在进行时的语言结构。(见图 2)

【效果评价】 教师观察学生回答内容的准确度,判断学生是否理解现在进行时的语言结构,并及时给予提示和讲解。

步骤二 理解语篇,探究主题意义(13 分钟)

Activity 1: Listen and number (3 mins)

Students listen to the recording made by the teacher, distinguish the rooms according to the key words, and number the rooms on the worksheet. When they check the answers, they use phonics to spell the target vocabulary.

图 3

Transcript

Welcome to my home! This is our living room. It's big and bright. There is a sofa in the living room. You can watch TV on it. Come and sit, please. Oh look! That is Ben's bedroom. It has a big window. Ben's bed is soft and smooth. He likes sleeping in his bedroom. What's next to it is our bathroom. It's very warm. We like having a bath there in winter. And this is our kitchen. Maggie usually cooks nice food in it. She likes cooking very much.

【设计说明】　教师通过听力任务,锻炼学生的逻辑思维能力。通过校对答案,引导学生借助拼读活动,初步学习核心词汇的发音。

【效果评价】　教师通过检查学生的排序情况,判断学生梳理信息的能力,同时通过检查学生的发音,判断学生是否掌握并熟练运用拼读法。

Activity 2: Listen and choose (2 mins)

Students listen to the dialogue and match the rooms with family members. Then students use the sentence "Where are you?" to make a dialogue and check the answers.

图 4

Transcript

Dad:　Kitty, where are you?

Kitty:　I'm in the living room. I'm doing my homework.

Dad:　Ben, where are you?

Ben:　I'm here, Dad. I'm in my bedroom. I'm making a model plane.

Dad:　Where are you, Maggie?

Maggie: I'm in the bathroom. I'm washing my hair. Can you cook dinner, please?

Ben:　Dad, where are you? Let's go and play basketball.

Dad:　I'm in the kitchen. I'm cooking dinner. Come and help me, please.

【设计说明】　教师通过听力任务,让学生将人物与场所的信息配对,使学生感知语篇主题内容。同时,教师通过强调"Where are you?",引导学生关注 Dad 主动关心家人的行为,感受 Dad 对家人的关爱,引发学生对语篇主题意义的关注(见图4)。

【效果评价】　教师观察学生在听力中获取信息的全面性和准确度,根据学生的表现给予必要的提示和反馈。

Activity 3: Look and guess (2 mins)

Students observe the pictures and use the given sentence pattern to guess what the family members are doing.

图5

【设计说明】 教师引导学生观察图片,猜测并运用核心句型描述 Ben 和 Maggie 正在做的事情,在情境中学习并使用核心语言(见图5)。

【效果评价】 教师根据学生对活动的猜测,评价其利用图片推断信息的能力;观察学生对语言的使用是否正确,了解学生对核心语言的掌握程度。

Activity 4: Listen and tick (2 mins)

Before listening, students follow the teacher to pre-read the options so that they can learn the pronunciation of new words: "model plane" and "homework". And then they listen to the dialogue and tick the answers on the worksheet. After that, students use the sentence pattern "I'm … (doing)" to check the answers.

图6

【设计说明】　教师通过听力任务,培养学生捕捉关键信息的能力。校对答案时,通过解读教材,加深学生对文本的理解,巩固学生对时态结构的认知,并营造"There is no surprise for Dad. He is sad."的情境氛围,助力语篇的情感升华(见图6)。

【效果评价】　教师观察学生能否勾选出正确答案,判断其能否准确获取信息。

Activity 5: Discuss and watch (4 mins)

A: Let's discuss

Students have an open discussion on the response Dad might have to Maggie's request, and give the reason.

【设计说明】　在观看视频前,教师请学生猜测爸爸可能会有的行为。同时通过追问原因,鼓励学生表达个人看法,培养学生独立思考的能力。

【效果评价】　教师根据学生的答案,了解学生的真实想法,观察学生是否具有关爱家人的意识,并给予评价。

B: Watch and tick

Students watch the video and answer the question "Does Mr Li cook dinner finally?".

【设计说明】　教师引导学生通过观看视频,理解人物行为,体会父母对子女的关爱,为实现本课时的情感价值目标做铺垫。

【效果评价】　教师观察学生给出的原因是否合理,判断学生是否体会到家人相互关爱的重要性。

步骤三　角色扮演,应用目标语言(7分钟)

Activity 1: Listen and imitate (2 mins)

Students listen to the recording and repeat with the correct pronunciation, intonation and tones.

【设计说明】　通过听音跟读,教师引导学生关注语音、语调与节奏,培养学生"听"的能力和语言感受能力。通过引导学生模仿跟读对话的内容,帮助学生内化所学语言。

Activity 2: Do a role-play (5 mins)

Students act out the dialogue from the text in groups of four: Mr Li, Kitty, Maggie and Ben. They evaluate each other's performance with three questions in mind: Do they speak correctly? Do they speak fluently? Do they act emotionally?

【设计说明】　教师鼓励学生运用所学时态,演绎家庭成员各自进行的活动,感受家庭成员的性格与家庭成员间的亲情。

【效果评价】　教师观察学生能否借助板书呈现的语言支架完成角色扮演,并根据学生的表现给予必要的提示和指导。

步骤四　创编对话,灵活运用语言(10分钟)

Activity 1: Think and act (5 mins)

Students watch the video made by the teacher and understand that all the family members are preparing for the party secretly. In this way, students will be more prepared to make the new dialogue.

A: Choose the character

Students look at the pictures and think about what Kitty, Maggie and Ben are doing actually. Then they work in groups of four, each student chooses one character to act.

B: Complete the dialogue

According to the text information, students come up with appropriate verbs to match their activities.

C: Act out in groups

According to the story situation, students who act as Dad, should think about the question "How does Dad feel now?" and act joyfully. The other actors also need to act emotionally.

【设计说明】 学生通过观看教师自编的视频,得知大家其实都在为爸爸的生日做准备,发现故事的情境发生了转折。教师让学生关注 Mr Li 的心情变化,体会亲情的温暖,引导学生思考家人之间应该如何相处,从而明白关爱家人的重要性,深刻理解本节课的主题意义。同时,通过分析人物活动,让学生思考如何使用合适的动词来拓展对话,锻炼学生的想象力,培养其逻辑思维能力和语句组织力。通过小组合作创编对话,引导学生根据故事情境运用所学语言表达人物的活动状态,增强人际交往能力和团队合作精神。

【效果评价】 教师观察学生所使用的动词搭配是否合理,判断其语言表达的准确性。

Activity 2: Think and share (5 mins)

A: Think and write

Students take out their family photos, and then write down what they were doing in the photos, where they were and how they felt.

B: Share in groups

Students make up new dialogues with the expressions "I'm in the … I'm (doing). It's so fun!" to talk about their family life and show their feelings about family activities.

C: Show and talk

Students show the new dialogue in the class group by group.

图7

图 8

【设计说明】　教师引导学生联系实际生活,创编对话,培养学生在真实情境中准确运用时态、语言进行表达的能力,深化学生对主题意义的认识,让其意识到应关爱家人、与家人互爱互助(见图7、图8)。

【效果评价】　教师观察学生所创编的对话是否运用了正确的时态、词语,能否体现关爱家人的主题,由此评价教与学的成效。

(六) 作业设计

*1. Listen to the dialogue and read aloud on Page 27.

**2. Share your family moments with your classmates after class.

【设计说明】　本作业根据星级,进行了难度递增的分层设计:一星作业为基础性作业,旨在引导学生及时巩固核心语言;二星作业为实践性作业,引导学生回想家里的快乐时光,并运用所学语言进行真实的交流。

(七) 板书设计

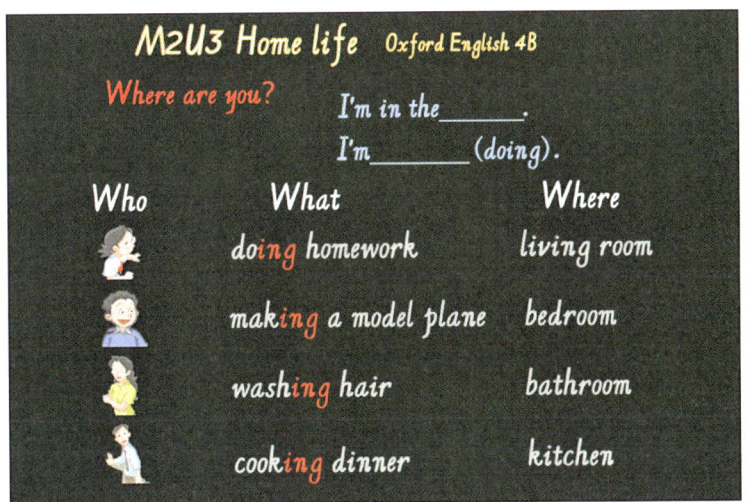

图 9

【设计说明】 板书包括课题名称与课堂要点。课堂要点可分为四个部分：首先，板书上方呈现本课时核心句。其次，板书下方从左到右依次呈现人物、活动、地点（及图片）三类细节信息。板书整齐美观，清晰地展现了本节课所包含的所有信息，借助板书的提示，学生能自主地进行课文的回顾和复述。

（八）教学反思

本节课教师围绕主题意义，主要采用情境拓展与活动分层两项策略，使对话文本和学生的真实生活建立联系，引导学生掌握目标语言，提升思维品质，发展语用能力。

1. 拓展听说情境，深度理解主题意义

本节课的听力语篇主要描述了 Mr Li 下班后与家人相聚的场景，他询问家庭成员在哪个房间以及正在做什么，家人依次作出回应。对话内容虽直观呈现了细节信息，但没有明确体现关爱家人的价值观导向，未能体现温馨的家庭氛围，如在 Dad 非常疲惫的情况下，Maggie 仍要求 Dad 帮助其烹饪晚餐。因此，学生不易在文本中直接感知关爱家人的主题意义。鉴于此，教师通过视听任务，引导学生在获取细节信息的同时，挖掘、提炼语篇主题意义。而且，教师在完成原教材的学习后，创设"Mr Li's birthday surprise"这一情境，利用自编视频，呈现家庭成员秘密谋划惊喜派对的故事情节，引导学生解读 Mr Li 的心态变化、评价人物行为、探究人物情感。最后，学生通过介绍各自家庭照片的小组活动，运用所学语言描述个人家庭生活，抒发个人对家庭的情感，思考自己的家庭生活方式，从而形成对主题意义的深层认知和价值判断。

2. 开展多元活动，逐步升级真实语用

本节课教师基于英语学习活动观，设计了看、听、说、演等学习理解、应用实践、迁移创新类活动，旨在促进学生认知与思维的多层次体验，逐级发展其真实语用能力。教师首先借助 Gif 动图、视频、音效等创设直观语法情境，带动学生进行多感官体验，初步感知现在进行时的语法结构。通过 Listen and number 和 Listen and choose 环节，学生学习词汇，获取语篇大意与细节信息。在 Look and guess 环节，学生观察并猜测家人们的活动，在语篇理解的过程中学习语法、模仿操练。随后在 Listen and imitate 和 Do a role-play 环节，教师引导学生进行应用实践，由模仿跟读对话逐步升级为小组合作表演，在课文情境下运用、内化所学语言。最后，教师鼓励学生发散思维，实现迁移创新。学生通过 Think and act 活动进行角色代入，拓展对话并进行演绎。在 Think and share 环节，学生联系实际生活，使用现在进行时描述家庭照片，在真实的语境下运用目标语言，提升语用能力。

（九）附件

Oxford English 4B   M2U3 Home life

Name_____   Class_____

Ⅰ.Listen and number: 听录音，将听到的房间按顺序排号，将数字填在框内。

II.Listen and choose: 听录音，将人物选入所在的房间，填字母代号。

A. Kitty

B. Maggie

C. Ben

Ⅲ.Listen and tick: 听录音，勾出 Kitty,Ben,Maggie 正在做的事情。

	A. drawing Dad's picture	B. doing homework
	A. making a model plan	B. singing a birthday song
	A. dressing beautifully	B. washing hair

Ⅳ.Group work: 思考 Kitty,Maggie,Ben 正在准备哪些礼物、小组表演、说一说。

Ⅴ.Group work:分享你的家庭生活。

课例 **12**

Starting Line B8 U1 My neighbourhood
（Lesson 3 Read and draw the route）

说课视频

说课实录①

Hello, everyone. I'm Celine from Wenzhou Dalton Elementary School. It's my great honor to present my lesson plan here. This is a reading for writing lesson. My lesson plan consists of three parts, namely, learning objectives, learning process and learning effects.

Learning objectives

In order to set clear and reasonable learning objectives, the analysis of learning materials as well as learners shall be conducted before the statement of learning objectives.

This reading material is extracted from Starting Line Book 8 Unit 1 *My neighbourhood*. The theme of the passage is *man and self*, concerning *difficulties, problems and solutions in life*.

First, let's look at the material.

What

It's a fictional story about a pet dog called Lucky, who is usually happy to do various tasks for his owner, Bill. However, he fails to properly plan his route and time this time because he does many other things on the way. As a result, he is unable to deliver the book to the post office for mailing on time.

Why

The locations of the different places in this story provide opportunities for students to think about and understand coordinates and review target words and sentences. Based on Lucky's failure, the passage tells us that we should focus on the goal of the task, even if we are familiar with the task. Also, it's better to plan our route in advance and stick to it determinedly. The story enables students to understand the necessity of planning, thus developing their awareness of

---

① 本说课稿由温州道尔顿小学王俊之撰写。

planning and improving their ability to solve real-life problems. In this way, students can also develop a sense of self-management and regulation.

How

This text is a narration which tells a story in a neighborhood in the order of time and space. With the help of the map in the story, students can review the expressions of some places in a neighbourhood such as "the hospital", "the restaurant" and "the post office" and the sentence structures like "I can go straight and turn right …". In the story, the route is clearly depicted by means of the direction phrases and the adverbs of sequence such as "then" and "finally". All these set good examples for asking and answering directions in daily life.

Now, it's time to take a closer look at the learners. The students are in Grade 4 and they have been learning English for more than three years. They are interested in the topic of "planning a route", and are willing to express and share their own plans.

What's more, students have learnt about the expressions of places in the neighbourhood and have known how to ask for and give directions to specific places. After learning English for more than three years, most students can sort out information they need and retell the story with the mind map. However, they may have difficulty in visualizing the route through drawing the route on the map after reading. Besides, they may find it difficult to infer the theme of the story and give reasonable advice. Therefore, some corresponding activities should be designed to enhance their analytical and creative thinking skills. In addition, some scaffolds and checklists should be provided to meet different needs of all students, especially those who are comparatively weaker in English.

Based on the above analysis, I have set the following learning objectives. By the end of this lesson, students will be able to:

1. understand the story and find out Lucky's walking route.

2. retell the story with the help of the mind map and language scaffolds, analyze the changes in Lucky's emotion, and find out the unexpected situation in the story.

3. write advice cards for Lucky to help him find the best route.

4. infer and understand the theme of the story and try to solve real-life problems.

Learning process

Now let's move on to the learning process.

In this lesson, three steps are designed: Pre-reading (daily life before the story), While-reading (the unexpected situation in the story) and Post-reading (reflection after the story). In the process, I will design 12 activities and create many real-life situations for students to "experience" Lucky and Bill's life, "taste" their feelings, "understand" the theme of the story and "apply" the target language to communicate and solve real-life problems.

Let's take a look.

For the first objective, I have designed six activities from Step 1 to Step 2.

There are three activities in Step 1, Pre-reading. Students will review the key words and phrases about places in the neighbourhood in Activity 1, Enjoy a song. Then in Activity 2, Look and say, they will guess the places, describe their locations in Lucky's neighbourhood and create a map of it. What's more, in Activity 3, Predict and do a role-play, students will see the pictures and predict what Bill will ask Lucky to do and how Lucky will help him by using the sentence structures in this unit to do a small role-play. In this process, I can evaluate students' ability of using pictures to infer information based on the reasonableness of their guesses about the content. Meanwhile, I will observe their ability to use vocabulary and sentence patterns accurately in role-play to determine whether they have internalized the core language. This removes the barriers before reading, and develops students' ability to "view" and understand the story.

There are also three activities in Step 2, While-reading. First, Skim for the main idea, students will be guided to check their predictions by skimming the story and answering three questions. Then, they will Scan the story and draw the route to solve the problem "How does Lucky get to the bank?". Lastly, some follow-up questions are designed to develop students' ability to grasp key details, and they will read again to answer these questions and learn to describe Lucky's route with language support.

Drawing the route is also one of the difficult points of this lesson. To deal with it, I will walk around the classroom to see students' works, invite one who has made an error in drawing the route to draw on the blackboard, and then check his/her work together with the whole class, ensuring that most students can achieve the first objective.

As for the second objective, the following activities from Step 2 are designed.

First, students are guided to listen to the tape and imitate the pronunciation and intonation of the material to experience Lucky's emotional changes. Then they will sort out the information from the text to form a mind map under the teacher's guidance, which is helpful for them to analyze Lucky's emotional changes, and find out the special case in the story.

Afterward, they will act as Lucky to retell the story with the mind map and the given language support. Experiencing and discussing Lucky's inner emotional changes deepens their understanding of the story and promotes the application of the target language. Their role-play and answers reflect whether they have succeeded in achieving the second learning objective.

Moving on to the third learning objective, two activities in Step 3 Post-reading are designed for it.

First, in Activity 1, Discuss and say, students will discuss in groups about "What will Bill say to Lucky?". This activity will stimulate students' thinking and their desire to express themselves and develop their ability to extract key information in reading, thus deepening their understanding of the text and promoting their internalization of the core language. I will help students develop the right attitude towards friendship if necessary. And then in Activity 2, Give advice and write, students are asked to provide advice to Lucky. It requires students to help Lucky find the best route. This activity is also the key of this class. In order to deal with it, I will provide a checklist focusing on their handwriting, spelling, meaning and creativity. Thus, self-evaluation, peer evaluation, and teacher evaluation can all be achieved. It also helps to fulfill the third learning objective.

To achieve the last objective, the last activity in Step 3 is designed.

In Activity 3, Think and share, students will analyze the theme of the story through thinking, discussing and sharing what they have learnt from the story. It is another difficult point in the class. To deal with it, I will provide them with some useful pictures and language scaffolds, give necessary guidance and feedback, as well as share the correct values. I will observe whether students can draw the conclusion that "focus on what you should do and must do" during the group discussion, and give necessary guidance and feedback as needed to guide them to form correct attitudes and value judgments.

At the end of this class, I will assign the homework. First part is required, that is, listen to the passage on Page 6 and imitate it as well as retell Lucky's story with the mind map. Must-do homework helps students consolidate what they have read and learnt in this class. The second part is optional, and it can be challenging for some students. They can continue to make up the story and write it down. It is a good complement to the last objective, which is part of transferring and innovating.

As you can see from the blackboard, there is a map of a neighbourhood that contains the key words and phrases in this lesson. Also, the development of the story is presented, showing the route, as well as the time, the roles, etc., which is helpful for students to review and retell the passage. It also serves as a scaffold when students write a new ending.

Learning effects

Speaking of the highlights in the achievement of all the learning objectives, this lesson has clear lines, and it has three steps (their daily life before the story — the special case in the story — the reflection after the story), which form a logical connection. The real-life situations pave the way for students to develop their thinking and feel the warmth of the class.

The students are guided to predict the story through role-play in the first situation, which improves their thinking to make reasonable predictions. The image of "Helpful Lucky" is set up for students to appreciate the warmth between the dog's owner Bill and the dog Lucky before the story.

After that, with a mind map and another image of "Naughty Lucky", students are guided to explore the conflict in the story. In this process, the conflict, Lucky's self-telling and Bill's feeling can fully develop students' analytical thinking as well as inspire them to imagine the following story. Moreover, through reading and thinking, Lucky's apology and Bill's response also allow students to feel the warmth between the characters.

Finally, Lucky's reflection triggers students' creative thinking. They are going to give advice and solve the problem together through discussion. The heated discussion is not just about the analysis of the story, but also the perception of the warmth between the roles.

Throughout the whole class, students' thinking is constantly activated and developed. In the process of thinking, students feel the warmth of the story, which helps to create a warm atmosphere in the class and achieve the educational goal.

That's all for my presentation. Thanks for watching.

试课实录①

试课视频

步骤一　读前——创设"情境"，激活旧知，预测故事（5 分钟）

Activity 1: Enjoy a song

T:　Class begins! Good morning, boys and girls.

Ss:　(Good morning, teacher!)

T:　Sit down, please. Today, we are going to learn Lucky's Story. First, let's enjoy a song.

Ss:　[enjoy a song]

Activity 2: Look and say

T:　Wow! There are many places in this neighbourhood. What's in Lukcy's neighbourhood? [points to the map] Can you guess? Maybe … ?

S1:　(Maybe there is a park.)

S2:　(Maybe there's a supermarket.)

T:　Good guess! Let's check and say! [turns over one of the place cards on the blackboard] What's in Lucky's neighbourhood?

Ss:　(A school.)

T:　Group one. Let's say together.

G1:　(A park.)

T:　Group two.

G2:　(A cinema.)

T:　Where is the Toy Shop? [takes out a picture of Toy Shop with some words on the back] Who can read?

S3:　(The Toy Shop is next to the school and opposite to the restaurant.)

T:　Who can help me put the picture in the right place?

---

① 本试课稿由温州道尔顿小学王俊之撰写。

Ss: (I can help.)

T: You please.

S4: [put the picture at the right place on the blackboard]

T: Wow, you're so helpful. Where is the bookshop? [puts the picture on the blackboard]

S5: (It's between toy shop and post office.)

T: You're so helpful.

Activity 3: Predict and do a role-play

T: Lucky is also a very helpful dog. Now, I am his owner, Bill. Hi, Lucky, take my book to school.

Ss: [listen to the recording]

T: Thank you, Lucky. You're so helpful. What might Bill want Lucky to do today? How will Lucky help? Now, think about it and do a role-play. One is Lucky, and the other is Bill. Here we go!

Ss: [work in pairs]

T: Time's up! Who'd like to be Bill? Who can be Lucky?

S6: (Lucky, take my book to the library.)

S7: (OK, I'll go straight and turn left at the first crossroads. It is next to the bank.)

S6: (Nice job. Lucky, you're a helpful dog.)

T: Wow! What a helpful dog!

步骤二 读中——延续"情境",复述故事,品味情感(18分钟)

Activity 1: Skim for the main idea

T: Is Lucky really helpful today? What does Bill want Lucky to do today? Let's come to the story. Please open your book and turn to Page 6. Please skim the passage and find out what Bill wants Lucky to do today.

Ss: [skim the passage]

T: Time's up. What does Bill want Lucky to do today?

S8: (Bill asks Lucky to send a book to his friend.)

T: How do you know? Which sentence tells you that?

S8: (Lucky, get some money from the bank, and then get to the post office before 4:30.)

T: You're so helpful. That's right. Now. Let's listen and read after it.

Ss: [listen and read]

T: So first, Lucky should go to the bank to … ?

Ss: (To get some money.)

T: [writes down the key words on the blackboard] Then?

Ss: (Get to the post office before 4:00.)

T:　　[writes down the key words on the blackboard] Can Lucky finish the task in the end?

S9:　　(No.)

T:　　Why not?

S9:　　(The last sentence says, "Finally Lucky gets to the post office, but it's five. Oh, no. ")

T:　　Very good! Let's read again. Oh no!

Ss:　　(Oh no!)

T:　　So what is the main idea of this passage? Who can try? You please.

S10:　　(Bill asks Lucky to send a book to his friend in the post office, but Lucky doesn't finish the task.)

T:　　Well done!

Activity 2: Scan and draw the route

T:　　So first Lucky should go to the bank to get some money. How does Lucky get to the bank? Let's read again and draw the route on the map. [walks around to see the students' work and asks a student who draws wrong to draw on the blackboard] Can you draw on the screen?

S11:　　[draws on the blackboard]

T:　　OK! Time's up. Let's look at the screen. Is this the right way?

Ss:　　(No.)

T:　　Why? You please.

S12:　　(He goes straight and turns left at the second crossroads.)

T:　　Yes. Let's read this sentence again together.

Ss:　　[read together]

T:　　Can you come to the front and correct it on the screen?

S13:　　[corrects the wrong route]

T:　　Is this right now?

Ss:　　(Yes.)

Activity 3: Read and describe the route

T:　　This is the first crossroad, right? And this is the second crossroad. [explains if necessary] So we know Lucky is helpful this time. But why can't Lucky finish the task at last? Where does he go? Let's read again. Circle the places, and then number them. [gives an example on the screen about Bank]

Ss:　　[read, circle and number]

T:　　OK, where does he go first? Let's check together.

Ss:　　(First, he goes to the bank to get some money.)

T:　　Wow, helpful Lucky. And next, who can try?

S14:　　(Next, he goes to a restaurant to have a hamburger.)

T: But do you think that's good?

S14: (No. Naughty Lucky.)

T: After that?

S15: (After that, he goes into the Toy Shop to buy some toys.)

T: Finally?

S16: (Finally, Lucky goes to the post office to send books, but it's too late. It's 5 o'clock.)

T: Naughty Lucky. So now we know Lucky is not helpful this time.

Activity 4: Listen and imitate

T: Let's read again! And try to feel. Pay attention to "stop" at the right place in a long sentence.

Ss: [listen and imitate]

T: This is a long sentence, so we should stop here. You can draw a slash here. Let's try once again.

Ss: [listen and imitate again]

Activity 5: Form a mind map

T: Now we know why Lucky cannot finish the task. Because first, he goes …?

Ss: (He goes to the bank to get some money.)

T: Helpful Lucky. Let's say together.

Ss: (Helpful Lucky.)

T: And how does he get there?

Ss: (He goes straight and turns left at the second crossroad.)

T: So Lucky is so helpful and clever, right? Let's say together. [shows the card]

Ss: (Helpful Lucky.)

T: Then …? [put the relevant card on the right place]

Ss: (Then he goes to the restaurant.)

T: To …? [shows the card]

Ss: (To eat a hamburger.)

T: Next …? [put the relevant card on the right place]

Ss: (He goes into the Toy Shop to buy some toys.)

T: After that …? [put the relevant card on the right place]

Ss: (He goes to the post office to send the book.)

T: But …? [put the relevant card on the right place]

Ss: (But it is 5 o'clock.)

T: Yes, and also he has no money.

Ss: (Oh no, naughty Lucky.)

T: Lucky is so sad. And he goes back with the book.

Ss: [listen to the recording from Bill: What happened, Lucky?]

Activity 6: Retell the story

T: Can you help Lucky to tell Bill what happened? But pay attention: When you're telling, you should act with feelings and actions, okay? [points to the checklist] Practise by yourself.

Ss: [practise]

T: Now I'm Bill. Who can be Lucky?

S17: [puts a hand up]

T & S17: [perform the dialogue]

T: How many stars for us?

Ss: (Two.)

T: Thank you so much. Now everybody stands up. You're all Lucky. I'm still Bill. Don't forget to act with feelings and actions.

Ss: [retell the story]

T: I can feel you're sorry for Bill.

步骤三 读后——延伸"情境",提出建议,提升素养(12 分钟)

Activity 1: Discuss and say

T: After hearing Lucky's words, what will Bill say to Lucky? Discuss in groups of four.

Ss: [discuss in groups]

T: So what will Bill say to Lucky? You please.

S18: (That's all right, Lucky. You can try next time.)

T: And Bill, what will you say? [chooses one student]

S19: (Lucky, you're so naughty. Don't do that again. Come on! Don't be sad. You can post it tomorrow.)

T: You're so kind! [chooses another student] How about you?

S20: (You are a bad dog. I hate you.)

T: Yes, Lucky is very naughty and did something wrong in the story. But if Lucky wants to change, will you forgive him?

S20: (Yes.)

Activity 2: Give advice and write

T: After hearing Bill's words, what will Lucky do?

Ss: [listen to the recording from Lucky]

T: Can you give Lucky some good advice? Please discuss in groups of four.

Ss: [discuss in groups]

T: Time's up. Who can help Lucky?

S21: (First, he can go to the bank and get some money at two thirty. And next he can buy a toy and eat a hamburger. After eating the hamburger, he can go back to get more money. Then he can get to the post office at 4:30.)

T: Oh, you mean he can set out earlier, then he can get to the post office on time, right? Oh, you have a good sense of time. But maybe time is limited. It's difficult for him to do all the things and get to the post office on time. Who can give a better route to help him?

S22: (First, Lucky can go to the bank and get some money, and then just goes to the post office to send the book. After that he can buy the ball and eat a hamburger.)

T: You're so clever. He can finish the task and can also eat and play. You are good at making plans. What about you?

S23: (I think we don't need to go to the Toy Shop and the restaurants, because there is a supermarket in the neighbourhood. He can go to the supermarket to buy a ball and a hamburger together. It's more convenient and also it is 50% off!)

T: Wow, I love your plan. You are really good at making plans. [says to Lucky on the screen] Hi, Lucky, what do you think of the advice?

Ss: [listen to the recording: Thank you for your advice. Can you write it down for me?]

T: Can you?

Ss: (Yes!)

T: Please take out your Advice Card and write down your advice. According to the checklist, please write neatly on the line; spell correctly; "make sense" here means make your advice more reasonable; and if you have a creative suggestion, it will be better.

Ss: [write down their advice]

T: Most of you have finished. Let's look at one of your works. [presents one of their cards] According to the checklist, how many stars will you give?

Ss: (Three stars.)

Activity 3: Think and share

T: Boys and girls, what could you learn from Lucky's story? Can you get some good ideas from Lucky's story? Please have a discussion with your group members. The following structures may help you.

Ss: [work in groups]

T: Which group wants to share?

S24: (We learnt the following two points from the story.)

S25: (First, we need to make a plan before doing something.)

S26: (Second, "First work and then play!". I think it's the same when we are studying. We have a lot of things to do and want to do. If we finish the things we have to do first, then we can do the things we want to do happily.)

T:　Totally right! I can't agree more. You need to focus on the important things. If you're doing your homework when your friends are asking you to play with them, what will you do?

Ss:　(Finish homework first.)

T:　Yes, focus on what you should do. Focus on what you must do. That will be good for you. Do you think so?

Ss:　(Yes.)

T:　Wow, we have learnt a lot from the story.

作业布置

T:　Here comes our homework. Homework One, listen to the passage on Page 6 and imitate it. Homework Two, retell Lucky's story with the mind map. If you want to challenge yourself, you can continue to make up the story and write it down. This is Lucky's story. Class is over. Goodbye, kids.

教学设计①

配套课件

（一）语篇研读

本课教学内容选自人教版新起点（一年级起点）英语四年级下册第一单元 My Neighbourhood,该语篇属于"人与自我"主题范畴,内容涉及"生活中的困难、问题和解决方式"。

What

本课语篇讲述了 Bill 的宠物狗 Lucky 到邮局邮寄图书的虚构故事。为了给朋友邮寄图书,Bill 告知 Lucky 先去银行取钱,并在下午 4:30 前将这本书送至邮局。Lucky 于下午 3:30 出发,在银行取完钱后到附近餐馆吃了个汉堡,随即又被餐馆对面的玩具店吸引,买了一个球,最终到达邮局时已经下午 5 点,错过了营业时间。

Why

该语篇中,Lucky 的家、银行、餐馆、玩具店和邮局之间的位置关系是学生思考和理解坐标方位的概念,复习社区内表示地点的词汇和指路句型的宝贵资源。宠物狗 Lucky 由于没有合理规划路线和时间,导致未能按时将书寄走的失败结局,有助于引导学生在日常生活学习中养成提前规划的良好习惯,优先考虑重要且紧急的事情,进而专注目标任务,形成自我管理与调节意识。

How

该语篇包含一般记叙文叙事的要素,即事件发展的时间、地点、先后顺序等,清晰地描绘

---

① 本教学设计由温州道尔顿小学王俊之撰写。

出 Lucky 去邮局的完整路径。故事发生在学生熟悉的社区环境,文本中的社区插图涉及 hospital、restaurant、post office、toy shop、grocery、cinema 等日常生活场所的词汇,能为复习单元重点句型"_____ can go _____ and turn _____ at the _____ crossroads. It's _____"提供语境。故事沿着 Lucky 的行进路线推进,因而涉及"go straight and turn left at the second crossroads"等体现行走方向的表达和 then、finally 等表明先后顺序的连接词。

(二)学情分析

本课授课对象为 Z 省某小学以一年级为英语学习起点的四年级学生。在这一阶段,他们已有一定的自我行为规划意识,对"如何用英语有效规划出行路径"的话题展露出较高的学习兴趣,乐于表达和分享自己的规划。此外,通过本单元前面几课时的学习,学生已经熟记表示社区常见场所的词汇,基础扎实的同学已经掌握了用英语问路与指路的表述方式。同时,经过三年多的英语学习,本班大部分学生可以在教师的引导下,快速识别、获取、提炼,乃至概括故事的关键信息,且能借助思维导图和语言支架进行简单的原文复述。但对将表示路线的文字转换成地图上的路线这一任务还有一些陌生。另外,对他们而言,学习的难点在于洞察和感悟故事中蕴含的人生哲理,结合语篇背后的主题意义,为他人的日常出行计划安排提供建议。这需要教师适当增加应用实践和迁移创新类挑战任务,拓展学生的思维深度。

此外,班内也存在一部分语言基础较为薄弱的学生,他们需要教师为其提供充足的学习脚手架,如设置同伴互助互学的空间,提供自我诊断与评价工具等。这有助于满足不同层次学生的个性化学习需要,使其乐学、勤学、善学。

(三)教学目标

通过本课时的学习,学生能够:

1. 梳理故事情节,理解地图上 Lucky 的行走路线;
2. 借助思维导图与语言支架复述故事,分析 Lucky 的情感变化,发现故事中的意外;
3. 运用关键句完成建议卡,帮助 Lucky 设计与规划最优路径;
4. 探究故事寓意,并将这一理解迁移运用至合理规划出行路径的现实问题中,达成对主题意义的深度探究。

(四)教学流程

教师受记叙文写作中"冲突"表现手法的启迪,以"冲突"为切入点,设计了"故事前的日常""故事中的意外"与"故事后的反思"三个学习环节,帮助学生更为深刻地理解故事寓意,并运用所学解决现实生活中的问题,形成正确的态度和价值判断。教师首先创设听歌、猜词的活动,引导学生回顾本单元关键词句,再通过角色扮演演绎 Lucky 与 Bill 的生活日常,运用单元重点句型"_____ can go _____ and turn _____ at the _____ crossroads. It's _____"的活动,引导学生预测故事可能的发展,生成"故事前的日常"。随后进入"故事中的意外"环节,学生通过略读、扫读和精读获取文本信息;借助连接词梳理文章脉络;利用思维导图和语言框架复述故事;通过体会 Lucky 内心的情感变化发现"故事中的意外"。由意外产生的认知冲突将激励学生主动进入"故事后的反思"环节,通过组内讨论 Lucky 的得失,学生品味故事背后的主题意义——专注目标任务,提高自制力。在此基础上,学生还需为 Lucky 提供出行的路径建议,解决现实生活中的出行规划问题,由此真正做到学用结合,学以致用。

图 1

五、教学过程

步骤一 **读前——创设"情境",激活旧知,预测故事**(5 分钟)

Activity 1: Enjoy a song (1 min)

Students enjoy the song "What's in Your Neighbourhood?" and review the key words and phrases about places in the neighbourhood.

Lyrics

What's in Your Neighbourhood?

What's in your neighbourhood?(＊2) There's a post office. I post a letter there!

What's in your neighbourhood?(＊2) There's a supermarket. I buy food there!

What's in your neighbourhood?(＊2) There's a park. I play there!

What's in your neighbourhood?(＊2) There's a library. I read there!

…

【设计说明】 教师通过歌曲导入,激发学生兴趣,激活旧知,复习单元地点词汇与相关动词词组,引入课题。

Activity 2: Look and say (2 mins)

Students guess the places in Lucky's neighbourhood and then review the names of these places. After that, students put the places in the right place according to the information given to form the map of Lucky's neighbourhood and describe the positions of some places.

图 2

【设计说明】 学生通过猜一猜,进行头脑风暴;通过说一说,复习地点词汇并描述地点的位置;通过贴一贴,完成 Lucky 街区的地图(见图 2)。

【效果评价】 教师观察学生用词的准确性,评价其根据情境使用词汇的能力,把握学生对所学内容的掌握情况。

Activity 3: Predict and do a role-play (2 mins)

Students see the pictures and predict what Bill will ask Lucky to do and how Lucky will help him, and do a small role-play by using the sentence structures in this unit.

图 3

【设计说明】 教师创设了故事前的日常情境,通过师生互动与生生互动的方式,引导学生操练单元核心句型,巩固他们对核心语言的掌握,培养其合作学习能力。通过看图(见图3)预测的任务,引发学生思考,培养学生"看"的能力和利用插图信息进行推断预测的能力。通过预测与角色扮演,使学生体会 Lucky 与 Bill 的生活日常,感受 Helpful Lucky 的形象,为故事反转做铺垫。

【效果评价】　教师根据学生对内容猜测的合理性,评价其利用图片推断信息的能力;教师观察学生在角色扮演中能否准确使用词汇和句型,判断其是否内化了核心语言。

步骤二　读中——延续"情境",复述故事,品味情感(18分钟)

Activity 1: Skim for the main idea (2 mins)

Students skim the story to check their prediction and answer the following questions: "What does Bill want Lucky to do today?", "Does Lucky finish the task?" and "What's the main idea?".

【设计说明】　教师引导学生略读课文,快速获取相关信息,验证读前预测。同时,通过对文章几条关键信息进行提问,帮助学生快速概括文章大意,培养学生的概括能力。

【效果评价】　教师根据学生的回答,评估其通过略读迅速获取文章的主旨和概括大意的能力,并适时给予指导。

Activity 2: Scan and draw the route (3 mins)

Students scan the story, find out the answer to the question "How does Lucky get to the Bank?" and draw the route.

【设计说明】　教师通过设置关联性问题进行追问,引导学生通过扫读快速提取文本信息并将读到的信息绘制到地图上,培养学生捕捉关键细节的能力和将文字转换成图形的能力。

【效果评价】　教师根据学生的任务完成情况,判断其能否准确获取信息。画路线的任务为本课难点,教师在教室里巡查,找到画错的学生,让其在黑板上画,然后引导全班同学一起讨论分析,找出文中的关键句,修正路线,从而确保全班同学都能顺利突破难点。

Activity 3: Read and describe the route (4 mins)

Students read the story for the third time to find the answers to the following questions by circling, numbering and saying: "How many places does Lucky go?", "What places are they?", "Why does he go to these places?".

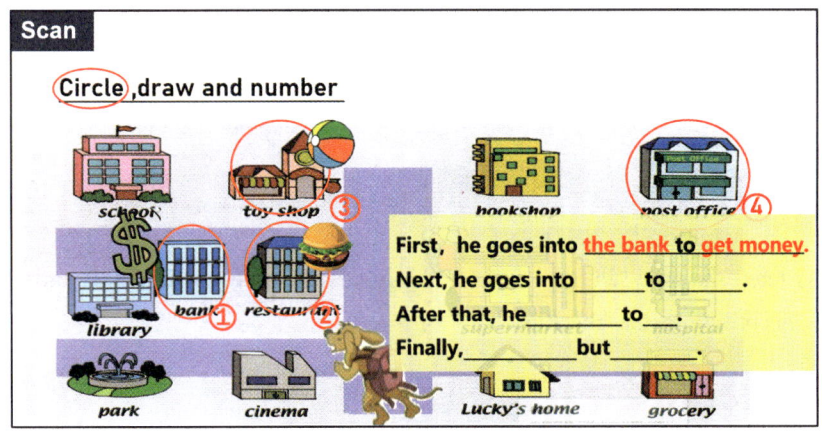

图 4

【设计说明】　教师通过设置让学生圈地点、标顺序、利用语言框架描述等活动,引导学生精读文本,最终完成路径描述(见图4),培养学生梳理和整合关键信息的能力。

【效果评价】　教师根据学生对路径的描述情况,判断其提取信息、梳理和整合信息的能力,并根据情况给予反馈与评价。

Activity 4: Listen and imitate (3 mins)

Students listen to the tape and try to repeat with correct pronunciation and intonation. They need to pay attention to the "pause" at the right place when there's a long sentence.

Listen and repeat

Lucky leaves at 3:30. He goes straight/and turns left at the second crossroads. He sees the bank/next to a restaurant. He gets some money/and then goes into the restaurant. There he eats a hamburger. Then he sees a toy shop/across from the restaurant. Lucky wants a toy, so he buys a ball. Finally, Lucky gets to the post office, but it's 5:00. Oh no!

图 5

【设计说明】　教师利用教材配套的音频资源带领学生跟读,引导学生注意意群的划分与语句中的停顿(见图5),帮助学生感知和模仿语音、语调和节奏。这有助于学生内化所学语言,把握主人公情感变化。

Activity 5: Form a mind map (3 mins)

Students answer the teacher's questions to form a mind map, which is helpful for them to retell the whole story by themselves.

【设计说明】　教师借助板书,采用问答、引导描述等活动,帮助学生运用和内化语篇的核心语言;与此同时,教师引导学生再次运用 first、next、after that、finally 等连接词,结合路线图和框架,梳理文章脉络,把握人物情感变化,为角色扮演作语言与情感的铺垫。

【效果评价】　教师观察学生能否准确地使用相关语言进行表达,从而把握学生对核心语言的学习和内化情况。

Activity 6: Retell the story (3 mins)

Students retell the story with the help of the mind map and the structures and evaluate each other's show according to the checklist.

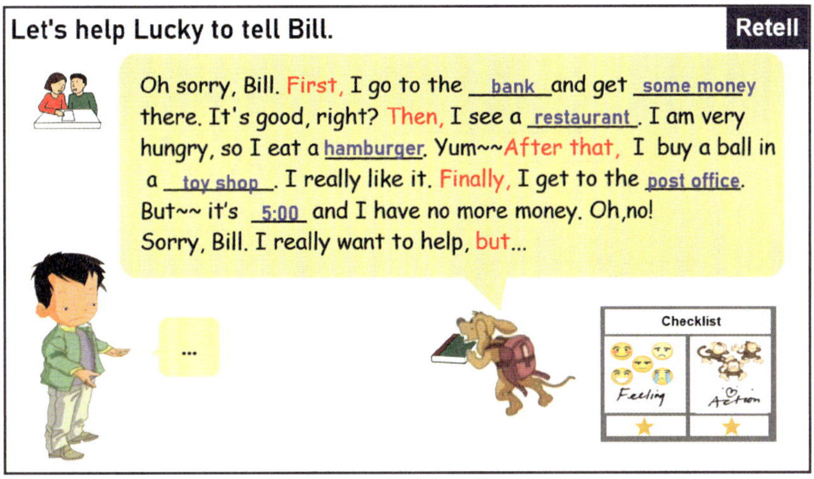

图 6

【设计说明】　教师让学生通过角色扮演体验角色的矛盾心理,理解角色的语言,探索角色的内心世界,从而发散其思维,激发其表达欲(见图6),培养学生在阅读中获取关键信息的能力,深化其对文本的理解。

【效果评价】　教师观察学生能否借助板书呈现的故事线和语言支架,深入角色进行深情演绎,根据学生的表现给予必要的提示和反馈。同时引导学生使用评价表,进行自评和互评。

步骤三　读后——延伸"情境",提出建议,提升素养(12 分钟)

Activity 1: Discuss and say (3 mins)

Students discuss in groups about "What will Bill say to Lucky?", and then say to Lucky.

【设计说明】　通过 Bill 对 Lucky 的行为评价与内心感受的表达,教师引导学生在人际交往的过程中,做出正确的价值判断,尝试理解对方的感受,学会合理调整表达方式,表现得礼貌、得体。

【效果评价】　教师观察学生是否能深入理解人物性格,代入角色,并根据学生的表现给予必要的提示及价值观上的引导,帮助学生树立正确的价值观,进行友善的沟通表达,培养其待人处世的能力。

Activity 2: Give advice and write (7 mins)

Students give Lucky some good advice according to the situation with the help of the given structures. After giving the advice, students write down their advice on the Advice Card and evaluate them according to the writing checklist from four aspects "Can you write neatly?" "Do you spell correctly?" "Does your plan make sense?" and "Is your idea creative?".

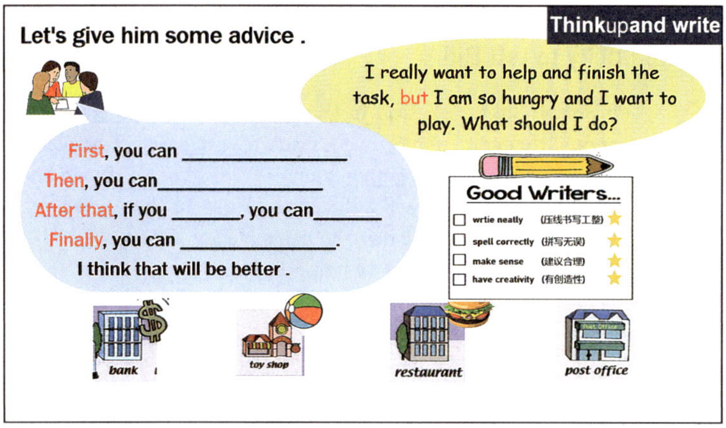

图 7

【设计说明】 教师借助故事情节,给学生们创设了一个思维碰撞的场景,让学生联系生活,创造性地运用所学语言,优化路径,帮助 Lucky 解决问题。教师引导学生从课本走向现实生活,在为 Lucky 制订计划的过程中,发展其语用能力,使其深入认识到合理规划的意义和价值,并引导学生通过评价表及时调整建议卡内容(见图7)。

【效果评价】 教师观察学生能否运用所学内容给出合理的行程规划,根据需要给予必要指导和反馈,并适时引导学生树立正确的价值观。同时,教师观察学生能否有效使用评价表完善建议卡,将评价贯穿于写的全过程。

Activity 3: Think and share (2 mins)

Students think, discuss and share their opinions about what they can learn from the story in groups. With the help of classmates and the teacher, students can get the idea of "Focus on what you should do. Focus on what you must do."

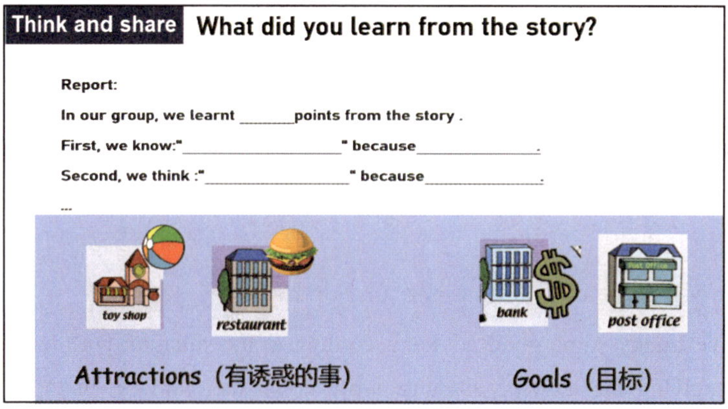

图 8

【设计说明】 教师给出一些图片与语言的帮助(见图8),组织学生进行小组讨论,引导学生超越语篇,联系实际生活,运用所学语言和文化知识解决实际问题,深化其对本课主题意义的认识,以达到育人的目的。

【效果评价】 教师观察学生在小组讨论和小组展示中的表现,根据需要给予必要指导和反馈,引导学生形成正确的态度和价值判断。

(六) 作业设计

★1. Listen to the passage on Page 6 and imitate it.

2. Retell Lucky's story with the mind map.

★★ 3. Make up a story and write it down.

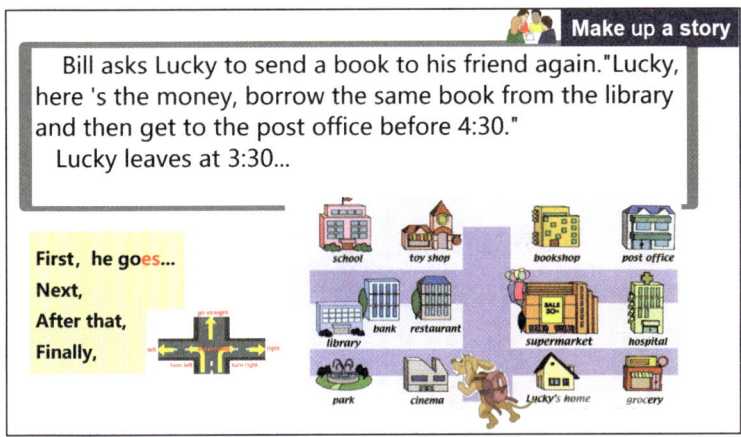

图 9

【设计说明】 本课作业分为必做和选做(见图9),必做作业为基础性作业,旨在引导学生及时巩固学习核心语言;选做作业为实践性作业,引导学生超越语篇,联系实际生活,用所学语言续编故事,实现迁移创新的目标。

(七) 板书设计

图 10

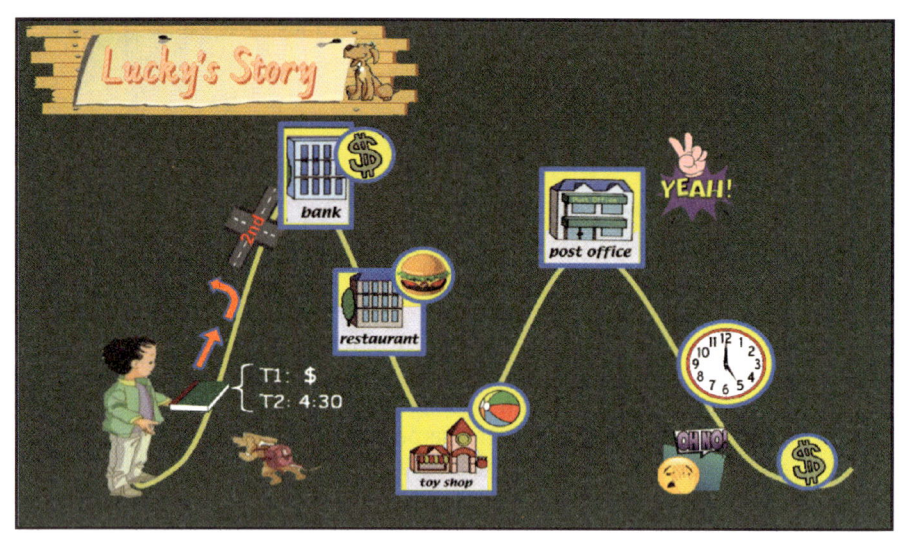

图 11

【设计说明】 板书左边是本课书上的一个街区图的放大版(见图10),它展示了本单元的地点词汇、描述位置的词组和寻求帮助的句型。板书的形成过程让教学过程更有情境感,使学生乐学、善学,同时可夯实其基础。板书右边是教师在引导学生梳理文章脉络与情感变化的过程中形成的一个思维导图(见图11),清晰地呈现了本节阅读课的故事发展,包括时间、人物、地点、事件、结果和情感变化等要素。学生借助课堂生成的板书,能自主地进行课文的回顾和复述。

(八) 教学反思

本节读写课围绕 Lucky 与 Bill 的故事展开。教师设置"故事前的日常""故事中的意外""故事后的反思"三个关联性的情境,构成具有逻辑联系的学习环节。学生在主题情境的感染下,通过思维的张力和学法的运用,品味文本的内涵。从已有经验出发,逐级完成"阅读故事——产生共情——主动思考——完善生活认知"的目标,提升了交流与解决问题的能力。这是一节由"情"与"境"带动,思维流动,温情流淌,有助于素养提升的活力课堂。

1. 思维在"情境"的转换与冲突中流动

在本节课中,教师首先创设了 Bill 让 Lucky 帮忙送东西的"情境",引导学生通过角色扮演预测故事的常规发展走向。然后,教师借由"故事中的意外",即 Lucky 本可以将书寄出的"日常情境"与结果未能按时寄出的"意外情境"之间的冲突,打开学生们思维的"黑匣子",并在 Lucky 向 Bill 道歉的"情境"中,生成反思空间,激活学生的分析性思维。随后,教师用 Lucky 求助的"情境"点燃学生提出创造性建议的热情,使他们在讨论中体会到思维碰撞的快乐。在整节课的教学过程中,学生的分析性思维和创造性思维不断被激活,流动于课堂。学生在思维的流动中,感悟故事背后的主题意义,从而形成正确的价值判断和人生态度。

2. 温情在"情感"的品味与互动中流淌

在本节课中,教师设计了多样的品读与迁移应用语篇的活动,通过角色代入,学生感受故事前的"Helpful Lucky"的形象与故事中"Naughty Lucky"的形象的冲突,理解 Bill 与

Lucky 的情感变化,品味故事中的温情。在读中环节,利用思维导图引导学生分析语篇、挖掘角色情感,产生同理心。随后的 Lucky 对 Bill 的道歉独白,更是让学生在真实情境中展开迁移创新,感受角色之间的浓浓温情。最后的小组讨论,让学生再次品味语篇内容及主题意义,从而树立正确的价值观和积极向上的情感态度。教师引导学生在品与用的交替中,在读与写的互动中,通过多次角色扮演,真实体验故事中的喜怒哀乐,感受角色情感的起伏变化,由此确保课堂的情感温度,达到育人的目标。

课例 **13**

Starting Line B4 U3 Seasons
(Lesson 2 Look, listen and repeat)

说课视频

Hello, everyone! I'm Lena from Wenzhou Qinyuan Primary School. It's my great honor to present my lesson plan for you. I'd like to introduce my teaching from five aspects, namely, learning material and learners, learning objectives, learning process, homework and blackboard design, and learning effects. Now, let's come to the first part.

Learning material and learners

Generally speaking, the analysis of learning material and learners are the basis for the establishment of learning objectives. So first, let's take a close look at the learning material.

The learning material is from Starting Line Book 4 Unit 3 *Seasons* Lesson *2 Look, listen and repeat*. The theme of this dialogue is *man and nature*, involving *the characteristics and changes of seasons*.

What

It's a daily dialogue among students. In this dialogue, Lily and her friends are talking about their favourite seasons and why, while they are playing in the park.

Why

By learning this dialogue, students will understand the changes of seasons, find the unique charm of them, and get interested in describing their favourite seasons and giving reasons in English, finally fostering a positive attitude of loving nature and life.

How

It's a typical dialogue of students' daily life. The plot is simple and easy to understand with practical significance and educational value. Also, Lily and her friends talk about seasons in the

---

① 本说课稿由温州市沁园小学陈丽娜撰写。

present tense by using the sentence pattern "What's your favourite season? Spring. /Summer. / Autumn. /Winter. ", as well as words and phrases like "warm", "windy", "fly a kite", etc.

Now, let's focus on the analysis of learners. Students are in Grade 2. They are familiar with seasons and are willing to express and share their preferences, but they haven't learnt the relevant expressions on seasons systematically yet. Also, after learning English for some time, students have learnt some words and phrases about weather and activities, and can communicate with others in present tense. However, they still have some difficulties in mastering the pronunciation and pragmatic rules of some words like *favourite, season* and *spring*. Thus, the teacher needs to create an authentic situation and design interesting activities to stimulate students' learning motivation and the desire to express their opinions about seasons so that students can acquire the language naturally.

Due to the fact that the second graders lack abstract thinking ability, it's difficult for them to discover the structural characteristics of the content by themselves and think about the theme of the content. Therefore, the teacher needs to use songs, pictures, videos and other multimodal resources to guide students to pay attention to the internal logic of the content, perceive the correlation between seasonal change and daily activities, and actively express their preferences with the mind map.

Learning objectives

Based on the above analysis, the following learning objectives are set. By the end of this lesson, students will be able to:

1. get the information about children's favourite seasons and the reasons from the dialogue, and understand the content through viewing, listening and speaking.

2. use the sentence pattern "What's your favourite season? Spring. /Summer. /Autumn. / Winter. It's … I can … " to ask and answer questions about seasons and then act out the dialogue with the help of the teacher.

3. investigate each other's favourite seasons in groups, then present the results to the whole class with a new dialogue. By doing so, students will feel the unique charm of four seasons and deepen their love for nature and life.

Learning process

Now let's move on to the description of learning process. This class is designed based on the Activity-based Approach to English Learning and divides the whole process into four stages: Involve, Interpret, Inspire, and Innovate.

In the first stage, Involve, there are four activities designed.

In the first activity, students will sing the song and talk about what they hear in the song. This activity can not only activate the classroom's atmosphere, but also let students perceive the target language of this lesson.

In Activity 2, students will play a jigsaw game about four seasons. They will look at the pictures and talk about them, and then the teacher will put the pictures all together and let students guess what season it is. This activity will stimulate students' interest in learning, give them a chance to describe the details of the pictures and help them review the expression of seasons.

The next activity is Look and say. Students will choose a picture of one season, and talk about the weather with their partners by using the sentence pattern "What's the weather like in …? It's …". I will observe whether students can talk about the weather with their partners with the given sentence patterns to find out how well they know the words of climate features.

In the last activity of the first stage, students will listen to the chant on Page 55 to review the words of seasons and weather.

In the second stage, Interpret, there are five activities.

Activity 1 is Listen and tick. Students will look at a picture from the book and predict what the characters in the picture are talking about, which will develop students' ability of "viewing" and inferring. I can evaluate their ability to infer information from pictures according to their guesses. Then students are required to listen to the tape and tick the right answer on the learning sheet. By listening, they can get a general idea of the dialogue and develop their ability to extract key information. Meanwhile, I can check their answers to judge whether they can correctly extract the key information.

The next activity is Watch and match. Students will watch the video and match each character with his/her favourite season. Then they will learn and practise the sentence pattern "What's your favourite season? Spring. / Summer. / Autumn. / Winter. " by making dialogues. Through observing their dialogues, I can know whether students have mastered the sentence pattern. I will give them guidance and assessment if necessary.

After that, students will watch the video twice more. They need to find the weather and activities children like to do in different seasons, and then stick their names in the blanks. The above activities are designed to help students understand the whole dialogue, perceive the new sentence pattern, and develop their ability to extract information about seasons, weather and activities. I will determine whether students can accurately obtain detailed information based on the accuracy with which they fill out the form.

In Activity 5, students will listen to the tape and repeat with correct pronunciation, intonation and stress, so as to lay a foundation for their language output.

In the third stage, Inspire, there are two activities.

The first one is Role-play. To help students apply the language and understand the meaning of the dialogue better, I will let them act out the dialogue in groups of five. Then, students will evaluate each other's performance according to the checklist from three aspects. I will observe whether students can role-play vividly and whether they can evaluate others' performance using the checklist.

After that, students are asked to read the sentences given, think about Binbin's favourite season, and tell the reasons. In this way, students will think about their favourite seasons from more aspects.

In the last stage, Innovate, there is one activity, Make a new dialogue, which is divided into 3 parts. Part A is Look and enjoy. Students will enjoy the pictures drawn by themselves in groups and guess whose pictures these are. Part B is Do a survey. Students will think about their favourite seasons, and get to know their friends' favourite seasons in groups by doing surveys, and then write the names down in the table on Page 21 of the book. I will observe the language they use to discuss with their group members, and give guidance and encouragement if necessary. Part C is Find the picture. Students will show the dialogue they make up in front of the class. Then, they will find the right pictures drawn by their partners according to the dialogue. I will evaluate the effectiveness of teaching and learning by observing how well students can use the language they have learnt to complete the interview and present the results to the class. In this way, I can cultivate students' ability to use the language they have learnt to solve practical problems based on real situations, and perceive the unique charm of four seasons.

Homework and blackboard design

After class, there are two assignments for students. First, they are required to listen to the dialogue on Page 21 and read it aloud. So they can review what they have learnt in this lesson. The second one is optional. They need to do a survey and know more about their classmates' favourite seasons, which can encourage them to use the language they have learnt to communicate with others.

As for blackboard design, the key sentence and a mind map are presented clearly, from which students can better memorize and recall what they have learnt in this lesson.

Learning effects

To sum up, there are two highlights I'd like to point out.

The first one is the "4I" learning stages, that is Involve, Interpret, Inspire and Innovate. These stages are closely related to the Activity-based Approach to English Learning and the activities of each stage match the learning conditions and expectations of students. From perceiving the weather of four seasons and key sentence pattern initially, to learning the core sentence pattern and understanding the content of the dialogue and the basic characteristics of each season, then to using language to express personal opinions actively, and finally to transferring and innovating what they have learnt, the "4I" learning stages pave the way for the implementation of Activity-based Approach to English Learning in lower grades teaching in primary schools.

The second highlight is the various learning activities designed according to students' cognitive style, so as to ensure the efficiency of learning. The activities include an interesting jigsaw game to help students recall the words about seasons, acting out the dialogue with the actions, like "Fly, fly! Fly so high!" to strengthen the understanding and learning of the key sentence pattern, a role-play to apply the key sentence pattern they have learnt, and finding the authors of the pictures by doing a survey as well as sharing their preferences for four seasons. These learning activities in four stages are closely linked around the main teaching line of "know the change — find the unique charm — express preference". It can not only stimulate students' learning motivation, but also create an opportunity for students to acquire the language naturally.

That's all for my presentation. Thank you for your watching!

试课实录①

试课视

步骤一 卷入——感知语言(7分钟)

Activity 1: Enjoy a song

T: Class begins! Stand up! Good morning, boys and girls.

Ss: (Good morning, teacher!)

T: Look outside. What's the weather like today?

Ss: (It's sunny.)

T: Good! Let's enjoy and sing a song together. Are you ready? Go!

Ss: [sing the song]

T: Nice voice! The song is about … ?

Ss: (Seasons.)

T: Yes! Boys, read after me, seasons.

Boys: (Seasons.)

T: Girls, seasons.

Girls: (Seasons.)

Activity 2: Jigsaw game

T: Now, let's play a jigsaw game about seasons. Please look at the pictures quickly and tell me what you can see.

S1: (Grass.)

S2: (A girl and a kite.)

S3: (A tree and a bird.)

S4: (I can see flowers.)

T: Great! Let's put them all together. What season is it?

Ss: (Spring.)

---

① 本试课稿由温州市沁园小学陈丽娜撰写。

T:　　Bingo! What season is it?

Ss:　(Summer.)

T:　　How about this one?

Ss:　(Autumn.)

T:　　The last one is … ?

Ss:　(Winter.)

Activity 3: Look and say

T:　　So there are four seasons in a year: spring, summer, autumn and winter. Let's look at "spring" first. What's the weather like in spring?

S5:　(It is warm.)

T:　　Good job! Now, please work in pairs and talk about summer, autumn and winter.

Ss:　[work in pairs]

T:　　Time's up! Who can try? You please.

G1:　(What's the weather like in summer? It's hot.)

G2:　(What's the weather like in winter? It's cold.)

G3:　(What's the weather like in autumn? It's cool.)

T:　　Great! Big hands for them.

Activity 4: Listen and chant

T:　　We know, warm in spring, hot in summer, cool in autumn, cold in winter. Let's enjoy a chant. You can clap your hands.

Ss:　[chant together]

步骤二　阐释——理解语言(15 分钟)

Activity 1: Listen and tick

T:　　Now, boys and girls, who can you see in the picture?

Ss:　(Yaoyao, Bill, Lily and Joy …)

T:　　Where are they?

Ss:　(They are in the park.)

T:　　Yes! They are flying kites and playing football in the park. Can you guess what they are talking about? Maybe …

S6:　(Weather.)

S7:　(Seasons.)

T:　　Nice guess! I have two choices for you. Maybe they are talking about seasons, or maybe they are talking about friends. Please take out your learning sheet. Let's do Activity 1, Listen and tick. Pencils ready? Go!

Ss:　[listen to the recording]

T:　　Let's check. Which one do you choose?

Ss: (Seasons.)

T: Good job!

Activity 2: Watch and match

T: These four pictures are from our friends. Whose pictures are these? Who likes spring? Let's watch the video and match the pictures with children.

Ss: [watch the video]

T: Let's ask Lily first. What's your favourite season, Lily?

S8: (Spring.)

T: Good! What's your favourite season, Yaoyao?

S9: (Summer.)

T: Good job! How about Joy? Who can ask?

S10: (Joy, what's your favourite season?)

T: Excellent! Please read after me: "What's your favourite season?".

Ss: (What's your favourite season?)

T: Pay attention to this word, "favourite". Clap your hands with me, "fa-vou-ri-te".

Ss: (Fa-vou-ri-te.)

T: Train, train, train.

Ss: (Go, go, go!)

T: This train, go!

S11: (Favourite.)

T: Good!

S12: (Favourite.)

T: Nice!

S13: (Favourite.)

T: Excellent! Now, let's read the whole sentence: "What's your favourite season?".

Ss: (What's your favourite season?)

T: So, what's your favourite season, Joy?

S14: (Winter.)

T: How about Bill? Please talk in pairs. One asks and one answers. Who can try?

S15: (Bill, what's your favourite season?)

S16: (Autumn.)

T: Good! What's Binbin's favourite season?

S17: (I don't know.)

T: The wind blows too strong, so we can't hear it clearly. Maybe we'll find it later.

Activity 3: Watch and choose

T: Lily's favourite season is spring. Do you know why? Let's listen.

Ss: [listen to the recording]

T:　　Who can tell us?

S18:　(It's warm and windy.)

T:　　Yes. Lily likes spring because of the nice weather. What else?

S19:　(She can fly a kite.)

T:　　Great! She likes spring because of the interesting activity. But first, let's focus on the weather. Lily, what's your favourite season?

Ss:　　(Spring. It's warm and windy.)

T:　　So we choose C. How about Yaoyao, Bill and Joy? Please take out your learning sheet again, let's watch the video and choose.

Ss:　　[watch the video]

T:　　Who can come to the blackboard and stick the words? The boy, you try.

S20:　[stick the words]

T:　　Let's check. Is he right?

Ss:　　(Yes.)

T:　　Are you right?

Ss:　　(Yes!)

T:　　Big hands!

Activity 4: Watch and stick

T:　　Next, let's focus on the interesting activity. Lily can fly a kite. Do you like flying a kite? Everybody, stand up. Let's fly a kite together. Fly, fly! Fly so high!

T&Ss:　(Fly, fly! Fly so high!) [do the action]

T:　　Good job! Sit down, please. So, we stick "Lily" in this blank. How about others? Please take out your learning sheet again. Let's watch the video and stick their names in the blanks.

Ss:　　[watch the video]

T:　　Do you find the answers? Don't worry. Let's check in pairs first. One asks "What's your favourite season?", and the other answers " Summer. / Autumn. / Winter. I can … ". You have one minute, go!

Ss:　　[work in pairs]

T:　　Time's up! Who can show us?

G4:　　(What's your favourite season, Yaoyao? Summer. I can swim in summer. Swim, swim! Swim very fast.)

G5:　　(What's your favourite season, Bill? Autumn. I can ride a bike in autumn. Ride, ride! Ride my bike.)

G6:　　(What's your favourite season, Joy? Winter. I can make a snowman in winter. Look, look! Look at my snowman!)

T:　　Now, let's look at the blackboard. In spring, I can fly a kite. Fly, fly! Fly so high!

Ss:　(Fly, fly! Fly so high!) [act it out]

T:　I can swim in summer. Can you swim? Everybody, let's swim together. Swim, swim! Swim very fast! [do the action]

Ss:　(Swim, swim! Swim very fast!) [act it out]

T:　I can ride a bike in autumn. Can you ride a bike? Let's ride bikes together. Ride, ride! Ride my bike! [do the action]

Ss:　(Ride, ride! Ride my bike!) [act it out]

T:　The last one is "I can make a snowman in winter". Look, look! Look at my snowman! [do the action]

Ss:　(Look, look! Look at my snowman!) [act it out]

Activity 5: Listen and imitate

T:　This time, let's listen to the tape and imitate.

Ss:　[read the dialogue]

T:　Wow! You can read it very well.

步骤三　启发——应用语言(6分钟)

Activity 1: Role-play

T:　Now, let's make a role-play. I'll be Lily, who can be Joy, Bill, Yaoyao and Binbin? Here is the checklist. All of you are judges. You need to judge how many stars we can get, OK? Ready? Action!

T & S21 & S22 & S23 & S24: [act out the dialogue]

T:　How many stars can we get? Show me your fingers.

Ss:　(Three stars.)

T:　Thank you! Now, it's your turn. Five students in a group, and make a role-play.

Ss:　[act out the dialogue]

T:　Time's up. Which group can come here and show us? Your group. Ready? Action!

G7:　[act out the dialogue]

T:　How many stars for them?

Ss:　(Three stars.)

T:　Hey, hey, great!

Ss:　(Hey, hey, great!)

Activity 2: Think and say

T:　We know their favourite seasons. How about Binbin? I wonder, "What's your favourite season, Binbin?" Now, all of you are Binbin. Let's read it together.

Ss:　(It's warm and sunny. I like green trees and green grass. I can play football. Goal, goal! Goal my football!)

T:　Do you find it?

S25: (Spring.)

T: Good! How do you know that?

S26: (It's warm and sunny.)

T: Yes! What else?

S27: (I like green trees and green grass.)

T: Very good! So, when we talk about seasons, we can also talk about colours! Spring is green, and …?

Ss: (Summer is red. Autumn is yellow. Winter is white.)

步骤四 创新——活用语言(7 分钟)

Activity：Make a new dialogue

T: Do you want to know your classmates' favourite seasons? Here comes the final task. Step one: Look and enjoy the pictures in your group and think about "Whose pictures are these?" Step two: Do a survey in groups of four. You can use the sentence "What's your favourite season? Spring. /Summer. /Autumn. /Winter. It's … I can …". Don't forget the weather, the interesting activity or colour. Please open your book, turn to Page 21, then write down his or her name on the table. Step three: find the picture according to your table. Clear? Here you go!

Ss: [work in groups]

T: Which group can show us? Your group, please.

G8: [group performance]

T: Big hands for them.

Ss: [clap hands]

作业布置

T: So much for today's lesson. Here's today's homework. Homework one, listen to the dialogue and read it on Page 21 aloud. Homework two, do a survey and know more about your classmates' favourite seasons. Class is over. Goodbye, boys and girls.

Ss: (Goodbye, teacher!)

教学设计①

配套课件

(一) 语篇研读

本课教学内容选自人教版新起点(一年级起点)英语二年级下册第三单元 Seasons 第二

---

① 本教学设计由温州市沁园小学陈丽娜撰写。

课 Look，listen and repeat 板块,该语篇属于"人与自然"主题范畴,内容涉及"季节的特征与变化"。

What

本课是一节对话课,语篇为小学生日常对话,内容围绕学生与同伴谈论季节及其相关天气和活动展开。Lily、Yaoyao、Joy 等同学在公园里一边玩耍,一边讨论各自最喜爱的季节及其原因。

Why

语篇描述了 Lily、Yaoyao、Joy 等同学在公园里讨论各自最喜爱的季节这一情景。教师引导学生了解季节的更替,发现四季独特的魅力,使学生有兴趣用英语描述自己喜爱的季节及其原因,从而形成热爱自然、热爱生活的积极态度。

How

该语篇是 Lily、Yaoyao、Joy 等同学间的对话,他们结合天气和相关活动,采用一般现在时描述自己最喜爱的季节。对话情节简单,富有逻辑,具有现实意义和教育价值。对话中涉及天气和活动的词汇与短语有 warm、windy、fly a kite 等,学生在交流时使用的核心句型有"What's your favourite season? Spring. / Summer. / Autumn. / Winte. It's … I can … "。

(二)学情分析

本节课授课对象为 Z 省某小学二年级学生,他们对"季节"这一话题较为熟悉,也乐于分享自己的喜好,但尚未系统学习如何用英语介绍自己最喜爱的季节并说明原因。此前的英语学习使得学生已有一定的单词和短语储备,如用于描述天气的简单形容词和表达日常活动的动词短语。他们能够运用一般现在时与他人进行简单的交流,但在使用核心句型展开对话,掌握 favourite、season、spring、summer 等词的发音与语用规则上还存在一定困难。因此,教师需要设计真实、连续的语用情境,开展拼图游戏、角色扮演等寓教于乐的趣味活动,激发学生的学习动机和语言表达欲望,使其自然习得语言。同时,二年级学生多运用具象思维思考语篇内容,较难自主发现语篇的结构特征,独立思考语篇主题意义。因此,教师需要借助歌曲、图片、视频等资源,引导学生关注语篇内在逻辑,感知季节更替与日常活动的关联,并利用思维导图积极表达自己的观点。

(三)教学目标

通过本课时的学习,学生能够:

1. 在看、听、说的活动中,理解语篇对话内容,获取和梳理对话中小朋友们各自最喜爱的季节及其原因;

2. 运用核心句型"What's your favourite season? Spring. / Summer. / Autumn. / Winter. It's … I can … "进行同伴询问和回答,并分角色表演对话;

3. 在小组内调查同伴最喜爱的季节,以对话的形式向全班呈现交流结果,感受四季独特的魅力,表达对生活和自然的热爱。

（四）教学流程

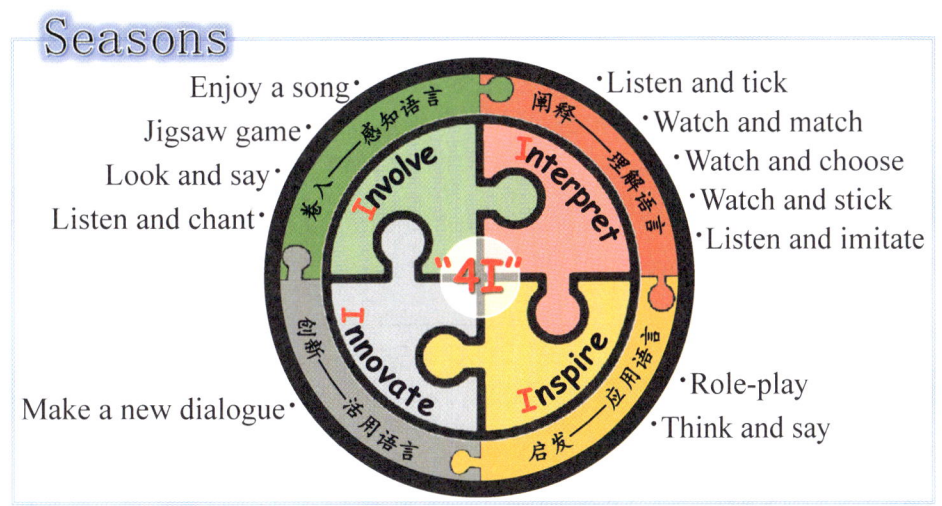

图 1

　　学生在本节课共经历"Involve — Interpret — Inspire — Innovate"四个学习阶段。第一阶段为"卷入"(Involve)——感知语言阶段。教师设计唱、拼、说、诵四种类型的趣味活动，快速调动学生的学习热情，让学生不自觉地"卷入"主题情境之中。第二阶段为"阐释"(Interpret)——理解语言阶段。这是学生能否最终走向应用实践和迁移创新的关键阶段。学生将经历看图推测、听音频、看视频、听音模仿等环节，提炼关键信息，操练核心语言，梳理关键信息，把握语篇结构。第三阶段为"启发"(Inspire)——应用语言阶段。语言应用是检验学生是否真正理解并掌握核心语言的重要依据。教师将引导学生通过角色扮演，内化所学语言，并运用核心语言进行推断与表达。第四阶段为"创新"(Innovate)——活用语言阶段。学生联系个人实际情况，以小组合作的形式采访小组成员最喜爱的季节，完成核心语言的真实运用，实现语言输出。

（五）教学过程

步骤一　卷入——感知语言(7 分钟)

Activity 1: Enjoy a song (1 min)

Students enjoy and sing the song "The Seasons Song" with actions.

Lyrics

The Seasons Song

What's your favourite, what's your favourite season, season? (*2)

I like spring. (*2) The flowers bloom. (*2) I like summer. (*2) It's hot outside. (*2)

What's your favourite, what's your favourite season, season? (*2)

I like fall. (*2) The leaves change colour. (*2) I like winter. (*2) I love the snow. (*2)
Spring, summer, fall, winter. (*3)

【设计说明】 教师通过节奏欢快的歌曲,营造活跃的课堂氛围,调动学生多感官参与学习,使学生初步感知本课时的核心语言。

Activity 2: Jigsaw game (2 mins)

Students look at the parts of a jigsaw and talk about them. Then the teacher will put the parts all together and let students guess what season it is.

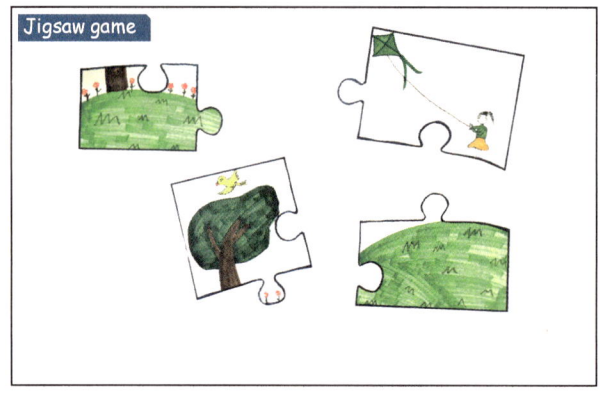

图 2

【设计说明】 教师通过展示零散的拼图图片(见图2),激发学生学习兴趣,引导学生描述图片信息,猜测拼图所代表的季节,从而达到复习季节相关词汇的目的。

Activity 3: Look and say (3 mins)

Students choose one picture to talk about the weather with partners by using the sentence pattern "What's the weather like in …? It's …".

图 3

【设计说明】 拼图组成四个季节后(见图3),教师引导学生用已知句型"What's the weather like in …? It's …"谈论相关气候,激活学生旧知,为后文描述自己最喜爱的季节做铺垫。

【效果评价】 教师观察学生是否能与同桌一起利用已知句型和相关词汇谈论天气,了解其对气候特征词汇的掌握情况,并适时进行补充和提示。

Activity 4: Listen and chant (1 min)

Students listen to the chant from the book, and review the weather in different seasons.

Chant

Four seasons in a year. Spring, summer, autumn, winter.

Warm in spring. Hot in summer. Cool in autumn. Cold in winter.

Four seasons in a year. Spring, summer, autumn, winter.

【设计说明】 通过教材里的 Chant 活跃课堂氛围,综合复习季节和气候相关知识。

步骤二 **阐释——理解语言**(15 分钟)

Activity 1: Listen and tick (2 mins)

Students look at the picture from the book and predict what they are talking about. Then they get the general idea by listening to the recording and tick the right answer on the learning sheet.

Transcript

Narrator: The children are playing in the park. They are talking about their favourite seasons.

图 4

【设计说明】 通过看图预测的活动,引导学生仔细观察图片(见图4)并主动思考,培养其"看"的能力;通过听录音的活动,引导学生获取关键信息,验证预测,培养其"听"的能力。

【效果评价】 教师根据学生对话题内容猜测的合理性,判断其能否准确获取信息,观察学生的作答情况,评价其看图推断信息的能力。

Activity 2: Watch and match (5 mins)

Students watch the video and match the child with his or her favourite season. Then they learn and practise the key sentence pattern "What's your favourite season? Spring. /Summer. / Autumn. /Winter. ".

Transcript

Joy: What's your favourite season?

Lily: Spring. It's warm and windy. I can fly a kite in spring. Fly, fly. Fly very high!

Yaoyao: Summer. It's hot and sunny. I can swim in summer. Swim, swim. Swim very fast!

Yaoyao: What's your favourite season, Joy?

Joy: Winter. It's cold and snowy. I can make a snowman in winter. Look, look. Look at my snowman!

Binbin: What's your favourite season, Bill?

Bill: Autumn. It's cool and windy. I can ride a bike in autumn. Ride, ride. Ride my bike!

Bill: And you?

Binbin: …

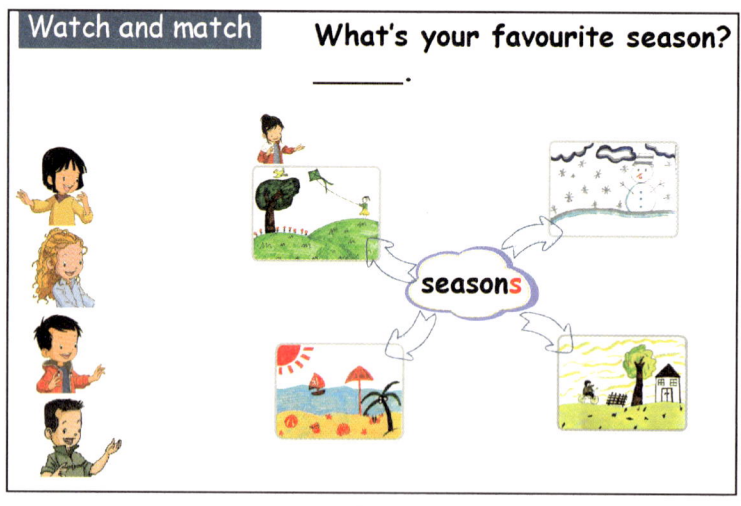

图 5

【设计说明】 通过观看教师改编的视频资源(见图5),学生获取视频中小朋友们各自最喜爱的季节信息,将人物与季节相匹配,在语境中完成对核心语言的识记和理解。

【效果评价】 教师根据学生的对话情况,判断学生是否掌握核心语言"What's your

favourite season? Spring. ／Summer. ／Autumn. ／Winter. ”，并根据学生的表现给予指导和评价。

Activity 3: Watch and choose（3 mins）

Students watch the video again and choose the weather for different seasons.

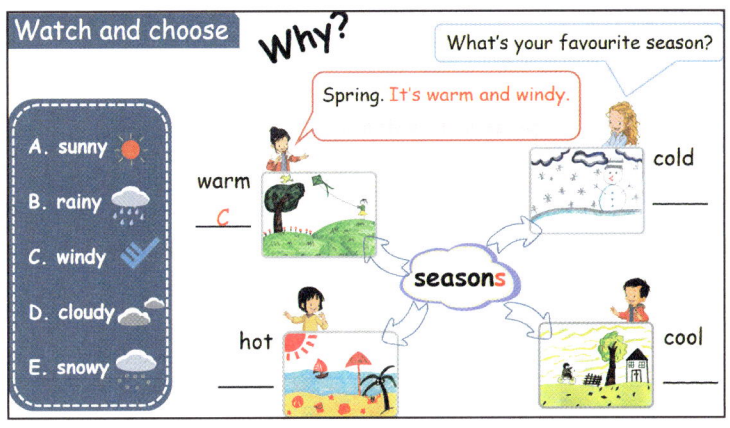

图 6

【设计说明】　教师引导学生再次观看视频，获取小朋友们喜爱的不同季节的天气特征（见图 6），将相关天气的选项匹配至对应的季节，帮助加深学生对文本内容的理解。

【效果评价】　教师根据学生的选项反馈，判断学生是否能准确获取细节信息，并及时进行评价。

Activity 4: Watch and stick（3 mins）

Students watch the video again and find the activities they like to do in different seasons, then stick their names in the blanks.

图 7

【设计说明】　教师引导学生再次观看视频，获取关于不同季节典型活动的细节信息（见图 7），并将人物名字贴在表格相应的空格里，帮助学生进一步理解对话内容。

【效果评价】　教师根据学生填写表格的准确度，判断学生是否能准确获取细节信息。

Activity 5: Listen and imitate (2 mins)

Students listen to the tape and repeat with correct pronunciation, intonation and stress.

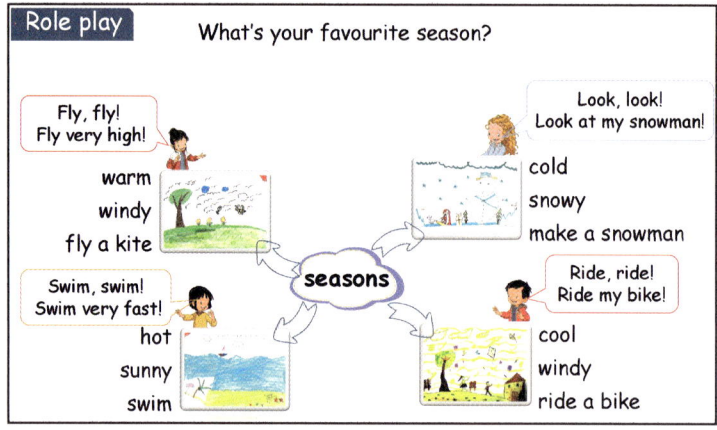

图 8

【设计说明】 通过跟读对话内容,学生感知和模仿语音、语调和重读,为语言输出奠定基础。

步骤三 启发——应用语言(6分钟)

Activity 1: Role-play (5 mins)

Students act out the dialogue in groups of five, and evaluate each other's performance from three aspects: loud voice, good action, eye contact.

【设计说明】 通过角色扮演,学生深入角色,运用语言并理解其意义(见图8),为后续在真实语境中进行表达做准备。教师引导学生从三个方面对同伴的表演进行评价。

【效果评价】 教师观察学生能否借助板书中的语言支架完成角色扮演,根据学生的表现给予必要的提示和指导。

Activity 2: Think and say (1 min)

Students read the sentences, think about Binbin's favourite season, and then tell the reasons.

图 9

【设计说明】　对 Binbin 最喜爱的季节的猜测能够发散学生思维,激发学生的表达欲望。通过阅读(见图9),学生多角度提炼并陈述最喜爱季节的理由,如天气、活动、颜色等,为最后一个活动的输出拓展语言支架。

步骤四　**创新——活用语言(7分钟)**

Activity: Make a new dialogue (7 mins)

A: Look and enjoy

Students enjoy the pictures drawn before the class by their group members.

B: Do a survey

Students think about their favourite seasons, and survey their group members' favourite seasons, then write the names down in the table on Page 21 of the book.

C: Find the picture

According to the dialogue, students match the right pictures to their group members.

图 10

【设计说明】　采访小组中其他人最喜爱的季节的活动(见图10),然后根据采访结果猜测图画作者。教师引导学生基于真实情境运用语言,培养学生解决实际问题的能力,感受四季独特的魅力。

【效果评价】　教师观察学生能否运用所学语言完成采访并向全班展示结果,评价教与学的成效。

(六) 作业设计

*1. Listen to the dialogue and read it on Page 21 aloud.

**2. Do a survey and know more about your classmates' favourite seasons.

【设计说明】　本作业依据学生的特点而分层布置:一星作业为基础性作业,旨在引导学生通过听读模仿,巩固核心语言知识;二星作业为实践性作业,鼓励学生运用所学知识进行真实的调查采访,达到学以致用的目的。

(七) 板书设计

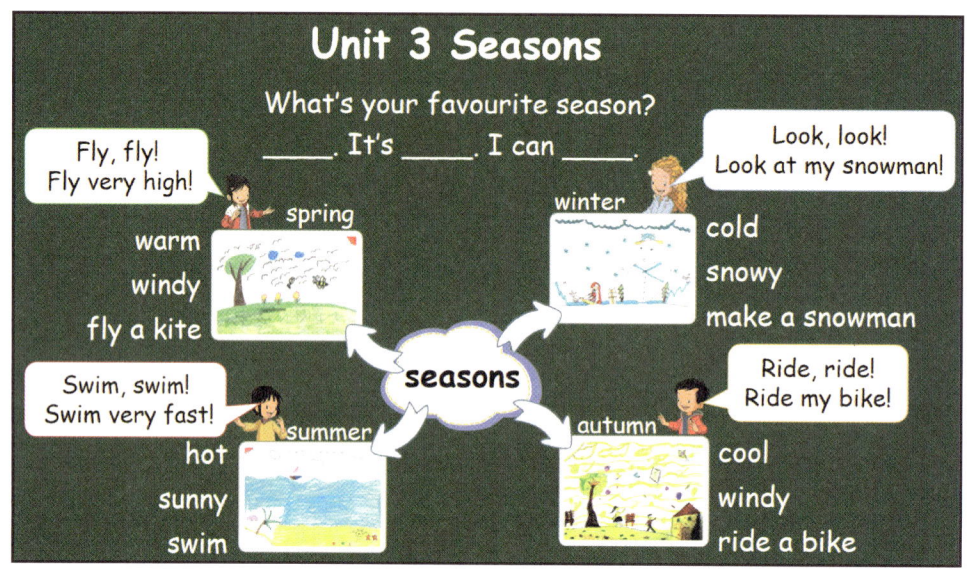

图 11

【设计说明】 板书包括课题与课堂要点。板书上方是本节课的核心句型;板书下方以思维导图的形式呈现了课堂要点,包括季节、天气、活动等内容。板书随教学进程动态生成,学生能借助板书进行课文的回顾和角色扮演。

(八) 教学反思

本课是一节对话课,教师围绕单元主题,借助学习单、自主学习、同伴互学、小组合作等形式,以多样的语用任务,循序渐进地发展学生的语言运用能力,训练学生的逻辑性思维。纵观整节课,教师作如下反思:

1. "4I"联动,层层递进,落实英语学习活动观

教师根据英语学习活动观,将本节课划分为"Involve""Interpret""Inspire""Innovate"四个阶段,有侧重地设计各阶段的活动,以更好地匹配低段学生的学情。其中,"Involve"阶段主要指向"学习理解"层级的目标。但与初高中英语教学快速引导学生进入主题语篇的做法不同,本课的"Involve"首先通过 Jigsaw game 和 Look and say 两项趣味性活动让学生卷入学习,调动其学习理解的积极性,初步感知四季的气候特征及相关核心句型。第二阶段"Interpret"重在帮助学生从 weather 和 activity 这两个上位概念出发理解语篇,通过核心句型"What's your favourite season?"进阶学习"Why does he/she like spring/summer/…?"的部分,掌握描述各个季节具体特征的行文逻辑。第三阶段"Inspire"重在通过 Role-play 和 Read and think 两个活动,引导学生在语境中积极发散思维,表达个人观点,从而实现"应用实践"层级的目标。最后"Innovate"阶段指向"迁移创新"层级的目标。教师通过 Make a new dialogue 的活动引导学生以小组合作的形式描述各自喜爱的季节,实现目标语言的真实运用。因此,教师所提炼的"4I"教学步骤与英语学习活动观具有共同的育人内核,为小学低段教学落实英语学习活动观提供了实用参考。

2. 基于主线,趣学趣演,保障低段学习有效性

在本节课中,教师充分考虑低段学生的认知风格,围绕教学主线设计了拼图游戏、听音诵读、看图猜画、模仿朗读、角色扮演、调查报告等丰富多彩的学习活动,确保低段英语学习趣味、高效。其中,"Involve"阶段利用拼图片猜季节的游戏导入"四季"相关的词汇,富有趣味性;"Interpret"阶段利用"Fly, fly! Fly so high!"等句子让学生边对话边表演,强化了学生对核心句型"What's your favourite season? Spring./Summer./ …"的理解和学习;"Inspire"阶段的角色扮演意在复现核心语言,并启发学生感受四季的独特魅力;"Innovate"阶段通过调查报告的形式,引导学生利用信息差寻找图画作者,并与同伴分享对四季的喜爱偏好。四个阶段的教学活动实际是围绕"了解季节的更替——发现四季的独特魅力——表达对四季的喜爱与偏好"这一教学主线紧密联系在一起的,且共同依托"四季与人们的日常生活"这一大情境展开,这不仅能激发学生的学习动机,还能让学生在更为自然的状态下高效习得语言。

（九）附件

学　习　单

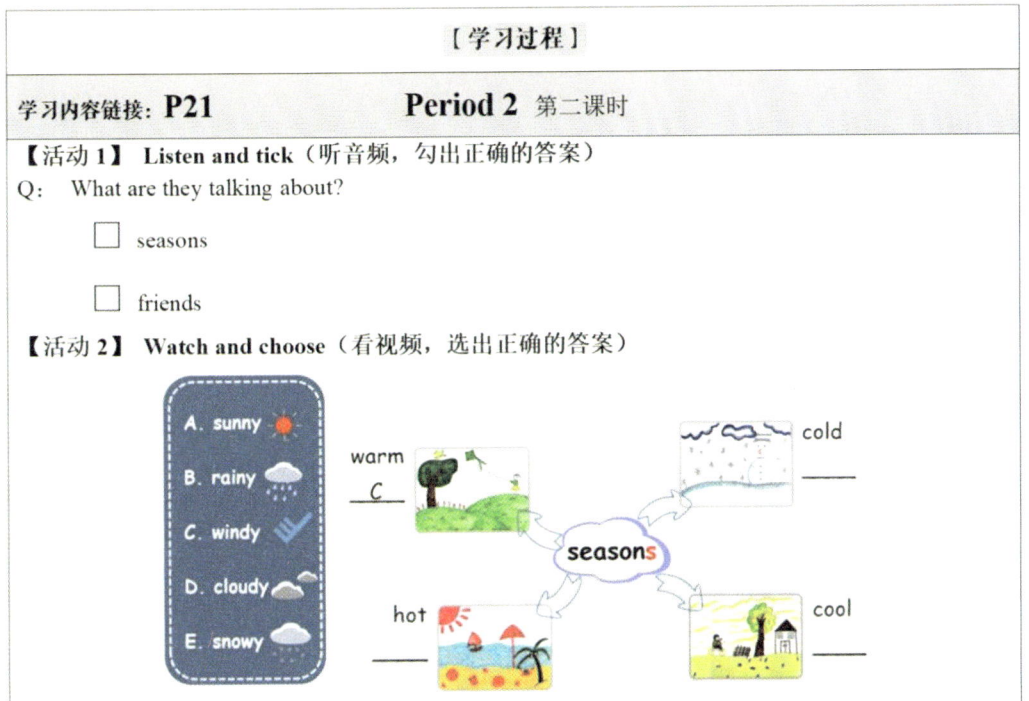

【学习过程】

学习内容链接: **P21**　　　　**Period 2** 第二课时

【活动1】　**Listen and tick**（听音频,勾出正确的答案）

Q:　What are they talking about?

☐　seasons

☐　friends

【活动2】　**Watch and choose**（看视频,选出正确的答案）

【活动3】 **Watch and stick**（看视频，将名字贴在方框里）

课例 **14**

PEP B6 U6 Work quietly
（Part B Read and write）

说课视频

说课实录①

Hello, everyone! I'm Nicole. It's my great honor to present my lesson plan to you. Now, I'd like to introduce my teaching from learning material and learners, learning objectives, learning process, homework and blackboard design, and learning effects. Now, let's come to the first part.

Learning material and learners

So first, let's take a close look at the learning material.

The learning material is from PEP Book 6 Unit 6 *Work quietly* Part B *Read and write*, which is the sixth lesson of this unit. The theme is *man and society*, dealing with *science and technology changing daily life* and *typical cultural icons at home and abroad*.

What

The title of the text is "The world robot exhibition". As for the main content, Sarah and Robin are visiting the world robot exhibition, during which they see robots from Canada, Japan, Spain, China and the USA. The cultural characteristics of these five countries including national flags, clothes, food, sports and music are subtly hidden in the robots, showing the unique culture of each country.

How

The text is constructed by some dialogues among Sarah, Robin and robots from different countries. Using some simple words, they talk about the activities in the present continuous tense, such as "What are you doing?", "Are you *v*. -ing? I am+*v*. -ing. ". Some words like "exhibition" "Canadian" "Spanish" and phrases of rules like "take turns" are also employed to

———————————————

① 本说课稿由金华市湖海塘小学刘晨撰写。

describe the world robot exhibition.

Why

The world robot exhibition is advanced and interesting, showing the leading status of our country's artificial intelligence and providing a good opportunity for students to think about robots' contribution to human civilization. Through this experience, students will taste the glamour of culture, build up cultural confidence and learn to appreciate and respect multi-culture.

Now, let's turn to the analysis of learners.

My students are in Grade 5. They are familiar with the topic "robots" and are curious about the different types and functions of robots. They have already learnt the grammar knowledge of *v.* -ing and can use it to describe what is happening in simple present continuous tense. But the text is about a world robot exhibition, in which students need to identify robots with different cultures as well as understand the text. So I need to provide supplementary background information of multi-culture and the exhibition by means of pictures and videos. Also, they have not yet used the present continuous tense to describe robots with various actions and cultural characteristics. Therefore, in order to reduce the difficulty of writing and broaden their mind, I need to provide students with sufficient and comprehensible topics and language input to build a framework for imitative writing.

What's more, my students are able to predict and infer according to the pictures quickly. But they lack creative and logical thinking, which requires various learning activities to help them analyze the text and generate creative output.

Learning objectives

Based on the above analysis, the following learning objectives are set. By the end of this lesson, students will be able to:

1. extract basic information about robots, such as nationalities, cultural characteristics and activities, understand what Sarah and Robin are doing and form a knowledge structure map.

2. use the core language to describe robots of various characteristics and activities in different halls based on the knowledge structure map, think about the contribution of robots to human civilization, build up cultural self-confidence and learn to respect cultural diversity.

3. evaluate the functions of robots, describe the robots in Robin's hall and write it down with a few coherent sentences.

Learning process

Now, let's move on to the learning process. In this lesson, the Activity-based Approach to English Learning will be adopted, which divides all the learning activities into three categories: learning and understanding, applying and practicing, as well as transferring and innovating. Based on the approach, the whole teaching process is divided into four stages: Review,

Elementary Reading, Analytical Reading and Developmental Thinking. Stages 1 and 2 are designed to help students read the lines and read between the lines, stage 3 is designed to help them read between the lines and the last stage helps students read beyond the lines.

Now, let's move on to the description of teaching process.

In the first stage, Review, there are two activities designed.

These two activities are Free talk and Let's sing. Firstly, students will greet the robot teacher and talk about their old friends Robin and Sarah. Then, they watch a video of Robin and Sarah, and try to sing it together. In the song, Robin and Sarah are talking about going out. This paves the way for the next activity, which explains that the two go to the exhibition. These activities can not only stimulate students' interest and create a cheerful atmosphere, but also help them review the *v.* -ing form. During this process, I will observe what words the students use to complete the song and give tips and comments based on their performance.

In the second stage, Elementary Reading, there are six activities.

The first and the second activity are Look and infer and Look and ask. Firstly, students learn the new word "exhibition". Then they look at pictures and infer what kind of exhibition it is. After that, students count the number of robots and raise questions about the robot exhibition based on the pictures and their experience. These two activities aim to help students perceive the new word and view these pictures carefully. In the process, I will evaluate students' pronunciation and give feedback based on the questions they raise.

Activity 3 is View and guess. Students view the robots and guess where they are from by circling the key information in the pictures. They answer the following questions: Where are they from? How do you know? What robot exhibition are they seeing? While guessing, some background information of *kungfu*, maple leaf, kimono, cowboy and guitar (flamenco) will be shown. At last, students will get to know that the robots are from different countries. This part helps develop the student's ability to view and to infer through extracting detailed information from the pictures, and understand the different cultural characteristics of each country. I give guidance and explanation according to students' answers during this process.

After that, the fourth activity, Read and underline, is set. Firstly, students read the text to find out answers to "What are they doing?". Then they underline the verbal phrases in the text according to the example given, such as "speaking Chinese", "drawing a picture", "cooking rice", "making sushi" and "doing *kungfu*". This activity enables students to understand the content and review the present continuous tense. I observe whether students can find out the key information and evaluate their ability of extracting detailed information from the text, and offer guidance and encouragement accordingly.

The last two activities are Write, check and answer and Shadow reading. Students fill in the blanks. Then, they check the answers and answer seven questions. In the last activity, students watch the video and repeat with correct pronunciation and intonation. These activities can help students understand the content in depth, realize the significance of robots in human civilization and have an overall perception of the text again. According to students' writing, answers and imitation, I offer guidance, feedback and correction if necessary.

In the third stage, Analytical Reading, there are two activities contained.

Activity 1 is Do a role-play. Students choose one robot and do a role-play in pairs after my demonstration. They evaluate each other's performance according to the checklist in four aspects. It aims to help students practise oral English and internalize the language they have learnt, laying a foundation for the language application. Next, in Activity 2, Think and say, students voice their opinions about which robot they like best and share their reasons. In this part, students learn to understand the thematic meaning of the text, build cultural confidence, as well as realize the significance of loving our own culture and respecting other cultures. Meanwhile, I observe students participate in the interaction, and offer demonstration, guidance, encouragement and evaluation according to their performance.

In the last stage, Developmental Thinking, there are three activities in total.

The first one is Read and choose. Students get the news that Sarah is lost. After that, they read Sarah's WeChat message and choose where she is. Then, in Activity 2, Let's talk, they talk about Robin's location based on the words given in the worksheet. In the last activity, students write down Robin's location based on the talk. In this way, students are encouraged to think divergently, express boldly and use the target language expertly to solve practical problems. I evaluate the effect of learning according to students' choice and writing, and give timely guidance and evaluation.

Homework and blackboard design

After the class, there are two assignments for students. First, they are required to listen and read the dialogues on Page 63 aloud. So they can review what they have learnt in this lesson. The second one is polishing writing according to the checklist, which can enhance students' general tinguistic competence and promote learning through evaluation.

As for the blackboard design, the countries, the present continuous tense verbs and thematic meaning are presented clearly, from which students can better memorize and recall what they have learnt in this lesson.

Learning effects

Now, here comes to the learning effects. To sum up, there are two highlights.

The first one is the promotion of thinking quality. Based on the original situation of seeing the exhibition, I create a continuous situation and assign tasks of different thinking levels, aiming to develop students' thinking quality. Firstly, students extract elementary information of robots by some comprehensive or simple analytical questions. Then, students learn and understand the significance and contributions of robots through answering some analytical or evaluative questions. Lastly, in the created situation that Robin is lost, students creatively use the target language to describe robots' appearances, activities and halls so as to solve the problem. Then, the analytical and creative question has been answered. Throughout the teaching process, many questions of different thinking levels are connected, which can train students' core competence.

The second highlight is the enhancement of cultural awareness. In this lesson, students are guided to view the illustrations to find different cultural characteristics, which are scattered on the robots. Therefore, students are provided with some explanatory information, such as the long history of Chinese martial arts, and the Japanese kimono culture. Some supplementary information about the cultural background is also mentioned, which makes the text more readable and logical. Throughout the learning process, students can not only get a deeper impression of the world robot exhibition through decoding the illustrations, but also realize the diversity of cultures, and learn to respect and appreciate multi-culture in depth.

That's all for my presentation. Thanks for your attention.

试课实录①

试课视频

步骤一　复习巩固(4 分钟)

Activity 1: Free talk

T:　Hello, everybody! I'm your robot teacher Nicole. Good morning, boys and girls.

Ss:　(Good morning, teacher!)

T:　Do you like robots?

Ss:　(Yes.)

T:　Look, who are they?

Ss:　(Robin and Sarah.)

T:　Yes. They are our old friends, Robin and Sarah. Robin is a robot, too. He can do many things.

Activity 2: Let's sing

T:　Let's know more about Robin and Sarah. Here is a song. Let's watch and sing together. Here we go.

Ss:　[watch the video]

T:　What is he doing?

T & Ss:　(He is cooking, cooking.)

T:　What is he doing?

T & Ss:　(He is singing, singing.)

---

① 本试课稿由金华市湖海塘小学刘晨撰写。

T: What is he doing?

T & Ss: (He is dancing, dancing. He's dancing. He's dancing now.)

T: What is she doing?

T & Ss: (She is eating, eating.)

T: What is she doing?

T & Ss: (She is cleaning, cleaning.)

T: What are they doing?

T & Ss: (They are talking, talking. They're talking. They're talking now.)

T: Wonderful! What are they talking about? Let's listen.

Ss: [listen to the record]

T: They are going to the … ?

T & Ss: (They are going to the exhibition.)

T: Good!

步骤二 基础阅读(15分钟)

Activity 1: Look and infer

T: Now they are seeing the exhibition. Let's spell together, exhi-bi-tion, exhibition.

Ss: (Exhi-bi-tion, exhibition.)

T: Follow me, exhibition, exhibition.

Ss: (Exhibition, exhibition.)

T: What is an exhibition?

S1:   (展览。)

T: So, in English, an exhibition is a public show. We can see many things in the … ? [points to the "exhibition" on the blackboard]

Ss: (Exhibition.)

T: Look! What exhibition are they seeing?

Ss: (The robot exhibition.)

T: Good job!

Activity 2: Look and ask

T: In the robot exhibition, there are many robots. How many robots do they see? Let's count together.

Ss: (One, two, three, four, five, six.)

T: There are six robots. What do you want to know about them? Try to ask some questions.

S1:   (Where are the robots from?)

T: Good question! You try!

S2:   (What is the Chinese robot doing?)

T: Yes, the Chinese robot. I like this point. You please!

S3:   (What are the robots doing?)

T: Wonderful! I want to know it, too.

Activity 3: View and guess

T: Now, look at the pictures and try to guess. Where are the robots from? And how do you know? Please discuss in pairs and circle the key information. [pastes different robots' pictures on the blackboard]

Ss: [discuss in pairs and circle the key information]

T: Time is up! This robot is from … ?

S4:   (Canada.)

T: [pastes "Canada" on the blackboard] Canada. How do you know?

S4:   (Because there is a maple.)

T: Nice. This robot is from Canada because there is a maple leaf. Canada is "the country of Maple". How about these two robots?

S5:   (These robots are from Japan because of the clothes.) [pastes "Japan" on the blackboard]

T: Japan. Yes. Wonderful! The robots are from Japan because they are wearing the Japanese clothes, or we can say "Kimono". This one?

S6:   (This robot is from Spain because there is the word "Spain".) [pastes "Spain" on the blackboard]

T: Yes, Spain. Good job! What's he playing?

S6:   (Guitar.)

T: The guitar is from Spain. And he is wearing Spanish clothes like a bullfighter. This one?

S7:   (This robot is from China, because he is doing *kung fu*.) [pastes "China" on the blackboard]

T: Yes, China, because he is doing *kung fu*. Look, it's cool. The last one?

S8:   (This robot is from the USA, because there is the word "USA".) [pastes "USA" on the blackboard]

T: The USA. Yes. You are right. He looks like a cowboy. Look, robot 1 is from?

Ss: (Canada.)

T: Robots 2 and 3 are from?

Ss: (Japan.)

T: Robots 4, 5 and 6 are from?

Ss: (Robot 4 is from Spain. Robot 5 is from China. Robot 6 is from the USA.)

T: Wow! There are so many robots from different countries. So what robot exhibition are they seeing?

S9:　(World robot exhibition.)

T:　　Good! They are seeing?

T & Ss:　(The world robot exhibition.)

Activity 4: Read and underline

T:　　In the world robot exhibition, robots are doing different activities. [pastes activities on the blackboard] What are they doing? Please read and underline the verbal phrases. Go.

Ss:　 [read and underline the verbal phrases in the sentences]

T:　　Time is up! The Canadian robot is?

S10:　(The Canadian robot is drawing a picture.)

T:　　Yes, drawing a picture. The Japanese robots are…?

S11:　(They are cooking and making sushi.)

T:　　Wonderful! The Spanish robot is…?

S12:　(The Spanish robot is playing music.)

T:　　Good job! The robot from China is…?

S13:　(He is doing *kung fu*.)

T:　　You are so smart! What about the robot from the USA?

S14:　(He is talking to Robin.)

T:　　Talking to Robin? Yes or no?

Ss:　 (Yes!)

T:　　Yes. Pay attention to the verbal phrases. What tense is used here?

S:　　(Present continuous tense.)

T:　　What's the rule of this tense?

Ss:　 (Be plus v-ing form.)

T:　　Good job! All of you are good learners.

Activity 5: Write, check and answer

T:　　Look, boys and girls, the Canadian robot is the robot from?

T & Ss:　(Canada.)

T:　　The Spanish robot is the robot from?

T & Ss:　(Spain.)

T:　　Good job! It's time for you to fill in the blanks, to write it down. Go.

Ss:　 [fill in the blanks]

T:　　Now let's check it. [checks one student's answer on the projector] This one. Drawing?

Ss:　 (Yes.)

T:　　What is he drawing?

S15:　(Maple tree.)

T:　　He is drawing the maple tree. The second one, making?

Ss:　(Yes.)

T:　Is Asako a Chinese name?

Ss:　(No.)

T:　It's a Japanese name. This one, playing music?

Ss:　(Yes.)

T:　Nice job! Robin is?

Ss:　(Doing *kung fu*.)

T:　Can Robin do *kung fu* in Picture 1?

Ss:　(No!)

T:　Can Robin do *kung fu* in Picture 2?

Ss:　(Yes!)

T:　Robin can learn so quickly! What do you think of Robin?

S16:　(He is very clever.)

T:　Yes, clever. What do you think of other robots? They are very … ?

T & S17/18/19:　(Interesting/Cool/Helpful.)

T:　Great! Robots are very helpful. They can do many things. And Sarah and Robin are talking to the Spanish robot. Yes or no?

Ss:　(Yes!)

T:　What are they talking about? Let's read it.

Ss:　[read the dialogue among Sarah, Robin and the Spanish robot]

T:　What does "take turns" mean?

S20:　(按顺序来。)

T:　Excellent! It means one by one.

Activity 6: Shadow reading

T:　Now let's watch and imitate. Please read and pay attention to the pronunciation and intonation.

Ss:　[read and imitate]

步骤三　分析阅读(6分钟)

Activity 1: Do a role-play

T:　Now it's our showtime. I'm Robin, who can be the Canadian robot?

S21 & S22:　[put hands up]

T:　Good! All of you can evaluate our performance according to the checklist. Here we go.

T & S21 & S22:　[act out the dialogue]

T:　How many stars for us?

Ss:　(Four stars.)

T:　Thank you so much. And it's your turn. Choose one robot and work in pairs, OK?

Ss:　[act out the dialogue]

T:　Time's up. Who can show us? OK, you two.

S23 & S24: [act out the dialogue]

T:　Wow, big hands for them. How many stars for them?

Ss:　(Four stars.)

T:　Yes, I think so. Good job, kids!

Activity 2: Think and say

T:　Look! Robots from different countries are doing different activities, which robots do you like best? And why?

S25:　(I like the robot from Spain because I like playing music.)

T:　Wow, sounds good. You please!

S26:　(I like the robot from China because I like doing *kung fu*.)

T:　Yes, it's very cool.

S23:　(I like the robot from Japan because I like eating sushi.)

T:　Me, too. I like eating sushi. It's yummy. Boys and girls, there are so many different cultures in the world, and we can see their differences in many ways, for example, food, clothes, sports, music and so on. Robots from different countries are doing different activities, because they have different cultures. As for us, we should love our country's culture and respect different cultures.

步骤四 思维拓展(10分钟)

Activity 1: Read and choose

T:　Oh! Look at Robin. He cannot find Sarah! Where is Sarah? Sarah is lost. Let's help Robin. There are three halls in the exhibition. The Home Robots Hall, the Sports Robots Hall, and the Artist Robots Hall. Now take out your worksheet. Read Sarah's WeChat message and find out where she is. Go!

Ss:　[read Sarah's WeChat message]

S24:　(Sarah is in the Artist Robot Hall.)

T:　Yes or no?

Ss:　(Yes!)

T:　How do you know?

S27:　(Spainish robots are singing; The USA robots are dancing … So Sarah is in the Artist Robot Hall.)

T:　You are so smart!

Activity 2: Let's talk

T:　We find Sarah. Where is Robin? Here is a message from him.

Ss:　[read the message]

T:　Work in pairs and find out where he is.

Ss:　[work in pairs]

T:　Time is up! Who wants to show your message?

S28: [personal performance]

T:　Wow! Big hands! You try!

S29: [personal performance]

T:　Yes. You did a good job!

Activity 3: Let's write

T:　Now let's write it down. Some words in the worksheet can help you, here we go.

Ss:　[write it down]

T:　Now let's share. [shares and evaluates one student's worksheet on the projector]

Ss:　[listen to the teacher and read the student's worksheet]

T:　I like your writing. Thank you, boys and girls. Robots are helpful. While facing different cultures, we should love our culture and respect other cultures.

作业布置

Here comes our homework. First, listen and read the dialogues on Page 63. Second, polish your writing according to the checklist. So much for today's class. Bye, kids.

教学设计①

配套课件

（一）语篇研读

本课教学内容选自人教版英语五年级下册第六单元 Work quietly B 部分 Read and write 板块,该语篇属于"人与社会"主题范畴,内容涉及"科学技术改变生活"和"中外典型文化标志物"。

What

本课语篇标题是"The world robot exhibition",文中 Sarah 和 Robin 与各国机器人进行了简单对话。具体内容为 Sarah 和 Robin 一起参观世界机器人展,看到了来自加拿大、日本、西班牙、中国和美国五个国家的机器人。五个国家的国旗、服饰、饮食、运动及音乐等文化特征,都巧妙地隐藏在机器人身上,隐含了不同的文化体验。

Why

语篇通过世界机器人展这一情境,说明我国人工智能已达到了世界先进水平,促使读者

---

① 本教学设计由金华市湖海塘小学刘晨和杭州市福山外国语小学董方圆撰写。

思考机器人在人类文明中的贡献。引导读者在感受科技发展的过程中品味并体验不同国家的文化魅力,在建立文化自信的基础上,尊重和欣赏多元文化。

How

该语篇为 Sarah、Robin 和各国机器人之间的对话,情节较为简单,易于理解。语篇使用现在进行时描述各个机器人的动作,涉及的核心语言有"What are you doing? Are you *v.* -ing? I am+*v.* -ing."等;介绍世界机器人展的词汇有 exhibition、Canadian、Spanish 等;介绍规则的短语有 take turns 等。

(二) 学情分析

本课授课对象为 Z 省某小学五年级学生,在日常生活中常有机会接触机器人,对不同类型的机器人及其功能充满好奇,因此具有较高的学习动机。

经过两年半的英语学习,学生已有关于动词-ing 形式的词汇储备,能运用现在进行时谈论和描述日常生活中正在发生的事情。本课围绕世界机器人展的话题情境展开,学生在理解语篇的同时,还需鉴别那些文化各异的机器人。因此教师需要借助图片、视频等工具,为其提供多元文化和展览的相关背景知识,引导学生通过多种阅读策略,突破阅读重难点,发展文化意识。另外,学生尚未尝试运用现在进行时介绍和描述不同功能场馆内不同动作、不同国家文化特征的机器人以及他们正在做的工作。因此,教师需要在学生写作前提供大量可理解的话题、语言输入,搭建仿写的支架,帮助学生开拓思路,以提升其文本创新和组织能力,降低写作难度。

本班学生思维敏捷、灵活,能根据图片推理信息,具有一定的猜测和推断的能力。但其思维的创新性和逻辑思维能力还有待提升,这需要教师设计各种学习活动来帮助他们分析文本并产生创造性的输出。

(三) 教学目标

通过本课时的学习,学生能够:

1. 借助视觉化、预测、启动先备知识、问题化、连结等阅读策略,获取并梳理机器人的基本信息(国籍、文化表征、活动),理解 Sarah 和 Robin 的所见所闻,形成知识结构图;

2. 借助视觉化和自我监控的阅读策略,基于知识结构图,用核心语言连贯描述不同功能场馆内机器人的文化表征与活动,尊重文化多样性,思考机器人在人类文明中的贡献,树立起文化自信;

3. 借助视觉化和整合的阅读策略,评价机器人的功能,并运用连贯的几句话描写 Robin 所在场馆的机器人。

(四) 教学流程

学生在本节课将经历"R－E－A－D"四个学习阶段。第一阶段为"review",教师借助自制歌曲,创设两位主人公 Robin 和 Sarah 去参加 exhibition 的情境,引导学生复习旧知,快速进入本课主题,实现"看"以入境。第二阶段为"elementary reading",学生利用图片预测文

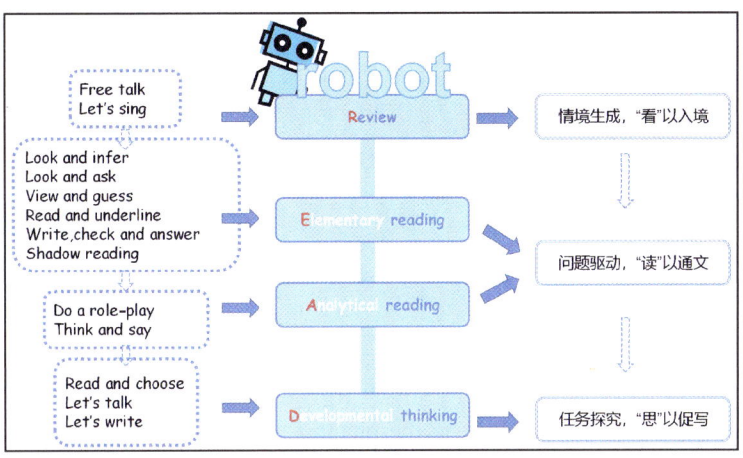

图 1

本,推断主旨大意;通过细读文本,获取、梳理信息,形成由基本信息组建的知识结构图。第三阶段为"analytical reading",学生在教师引导下,对主题语境有了更深入的理解,进一步内化语言。他们需要进行角色扮演,进而对各国机器人开展多元评价,拓展对多元文化的认识。在上述两个教学阶段,教师设置了具有连续性、进阶性的问题链,提升学生的文化意识,帮助学生实现"读"以通文。第四阶段为"developmental thinking",教师转换情境,邀请学生完成一项任务:描述 Robin 所在的场馆,从而帮助 Sarah 找到 Robin。此时,学生需要发散思维,以写作的方式解决问题,从而真正内化本节课的目标语言,达成以"思"促写的学习目标。

(五) 教学过程

步骤一　**Review**(4 mins)

Activity 1: Free talk (2 mins)

Students greet the robot teacher and talk about their old friends Robin and Sarah.

【设计说明】　教师模仿机器人和学生打招呼,激发其对机器人的探究兴趣,在热烈、欢快的氛围中引出机器人朋友 Robin 和 Sarah。

Activity 2: Let's sing (2 mins)

Students watch the video of Robin and Sarah, fill in the lyrics and try to sing along with the teacher.

Lyrics

What Is He Doing?

What is he doing? He's <u>cooking</u>, <u>cooking</u>. What is he doing? He's <u>singing</u>, <u>singing</u>. What is he doing? He's <u>dancing</u>, <u>dancing</u>. He's <u>dancing</u>. He's <u>dancing</u> now.

What is she doing? She's <u>eating</u>, <u>eating</u>. What is she doing? She's <u>cleaning</u>, <u>cleaning</u>. What are they doing? They're <u>talking</u>, <u>talking</u>. They're <u>talking</u>. They're <u>talking</u> now.

【设计说明】 通过自制歌曲,学生既复习了核心语言动词-ing 形式,又熟悉了课文的两位主人公 Robin 和 Sarah,知晓了两人要出去游玩的背景,这为下一环节交代两人去看展览做铺垫。

【效果评价】 教师观察学生对歌曲下划线部分回答的正确性,了解其对动词-ing 形式的掌握情况,根据学生的表现给予提示和评价。

步骤二 **Elementary reading**(15 分钟)

Activity 1: Look and infer (1 min)

After singing, students listen to know what they are talking about. They firstly learn the new word "exhibition". Then they look at the pictures and infer what kind of exhibition it is.

图 2

图 3

【设计说明】 学生学习新单词"exhibition"(见图 2),并在教师的引导下观察图片(见图 3),整体感知语篇内容。

【效果评价】 教师观察学生使用的语言是否正确,把握学生对所学内容的感知情况;教师根据学生对展览类型猜测的合理性,评价其根据图片推断信息的能力。

Activity 2：Look and ask（2 mins）

Students count the robots first, and then raise questions about the robot exhibition based on the pictures and their experience.

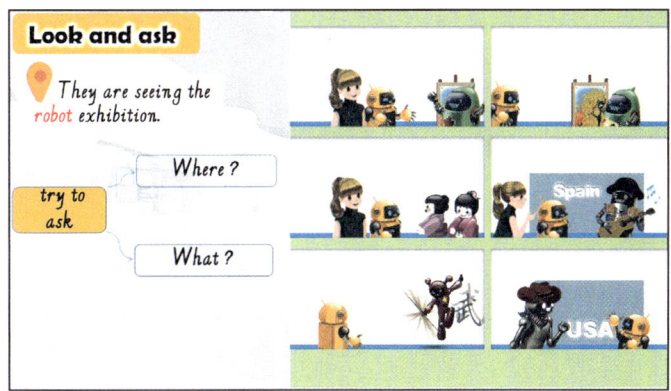

图 4

【设计说明】 学生利用教材图片作为信息源,尝试对语篇内容自主提问(见图4),初步掌握整合资源的阅读策略,产生深入阅读的动机。

【效果评价】 教师根据学生提出的问题的合理性,评价其根据图片推断信息的能力,必要时给予提示和指导。

Activity 3：View and guess（3 mins）

Students view the robots and guess where they are from by circling out the key information in the pictures.

Q1: *Where are they from?*

Q2: *How do you know?*

Then students put up the magnets of countries on the blackboard. While guessing, some information on the blackboard of *kung fu*, maple leaf, kimono, cowboy and guitar (flamenco) will be shown. After that, students answer the question.

图 5

Q3: *What robot exhibition are they seeing?*

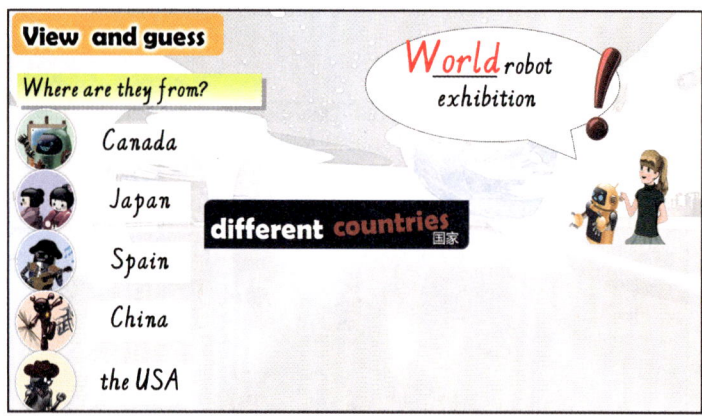

图 6

【设计说明】 学生通过捕捉细节,使用答题模板完整地回答问题(见图5),发展"看"的能力,强化对各个国家文化特征的理解,在问与答中提升文化意识。第一个问题属于理解类问题,难度较低;第二个问题为分析类问题,学生需要分析机器人身上的国旗、服饰、所拿的食物或所做的动作才能回答。第三个问题属于分析类问题,学生更加深刻体会机器人展的规模。两类问题的搭配使用将帮助学生更好地理解图片所传递的信息,提升其阅读能力和利用插图信息进行推断预测的能力。

【效果评价】 教师根据学生对国籍的回答,判断其信息获取的准确性,并评价其对阅读策略掌握的水平(对重点信息、图片的标记和理解),并根据需要给予解释和指导。

Activity 4: Read and underline (3 mins)

Students read the text to find out answers to "*What are they doing?*". They underline the verbal phrases in the text according to the example given (*speaking Chinese, drawing a picture, cooking rice, making sushi, doing* kungfu). Then they review the rules of present continuous tense.

图 7

【设计说明】　通过阅读了解 robots 正在进行的活动,学生进一步整体感知对话内容;通过画线(见图7),学生在教材对话语篇里学习理解现在分词词形变化的意义,运用和内化核心语言,为最终完成写的任务打好基础;通过复习现在进行时的语法规则,强化核心语言,实现音、形、义的整合。

【效果评价】　教师观察学生能否正确填空,判断其获取信息的能力;根据学生能否在语篇中找出动词现在进行时的词组,评价其对核心语言的内化程度,并及时提供帮助。

Activity 5: Write, check and answer (4 mins)

Students fill in the blanks. Then, they check the answers according to the writing. While checking, they answer the following questions one by one:

Q1: What is the Canadian robot drawing?

Q2: Is Asako a Chinese name?

Q3: Can Robin do kung fu *in Picture 1/Picture 2?*

Q4: What do you think of Robin?

Q5: What do you think of other robots?

Q6: What are Sarah, Robin and the Spanish robot talking about?

Q7: What does "take turns" mean?

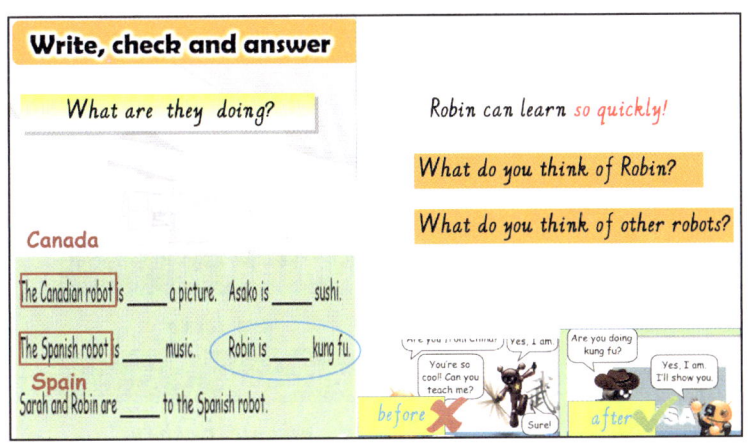

图 8

【设计说明】　通过书写,强化对核心语言的掌握,实现音、形、义的整合。核对答案过程中,教师采用追问的方式,引导学生挖掘更多的文化特征,进一步解读文本,理解人物。通过评价机器人(见图8),学生思考机器人对人类文明的影响。

【效果评价】　教师根据学生能否正确填写信息,判断其核心语言的内化程度,给予必要指导和反馈;在核对的过程中,教师观察学生参与互动和交流的情况,必要时调整提问方式,进行追问或给予鼓励。

Activity 6: Shadow reading (2 mins)

Students watch the video and repeat with correct pronunciation and intonation.

【设计说明】　通过看视频模仿的活动,帮助学生再次整体感知文本情境,熟悉文本结构。教师提醒学生在模仿跟读时,关注语流、语速、语气,并进行模仿。

【效果评价】 教师根据学生的语音、语调,判断其对核心语言的掌握程度,并根据学生的表现给予反馈。

步骤三 **Analytical reading**(6分钟)

Activity 1: Do a role-play (3 mins)

After the teacher's demonstration, students choose one robot they like and do a role-play in pairs. One will be Robin or Sarah and the other will be a robot. The students will evaluate their performance according to the checklist.

图9

【设计说明】 通过角色扮演,学生能在有限的课堂时间内得到口语练习的机会,并在练习过程中熟悉文本内容、语言结构、阅读重点,为之后的语言运用打下基础。

【效果评价】 教师观察学生能否使用正确的语言、语音、语调演绎出 Sarah、Robin 和机器人的对话,根据学生的表现给予反馈和指导。教师观察学生能否借助评价核查表(见图9),从四个方面对其他小组的表演进行评价。

Activity 2: Think and say (3 mins)

Students voice their opinions about which robot they like best and share their reasons. After that, they realize the importance of respecting and appreciating different cultures.

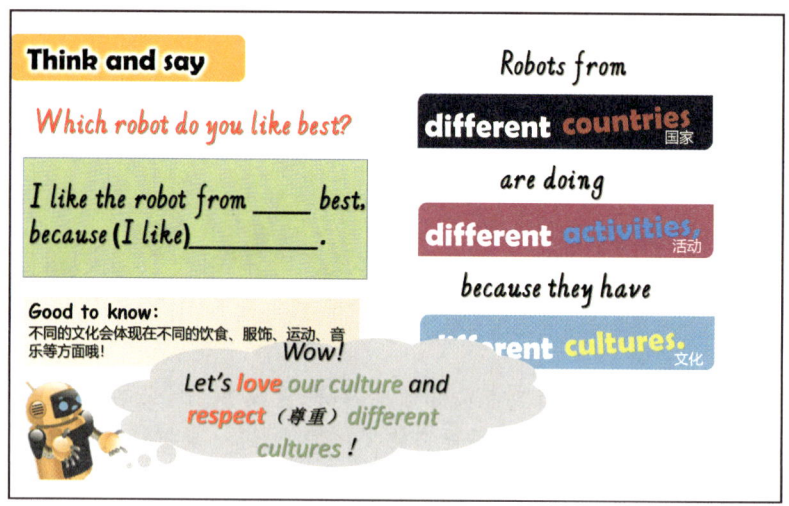

图10

【设计说明】 学生通过谈论自己喜欢的机器人并给出理由(见图10),感悟语篇背后隐含的意义,建立文化自信,尊重和欣赏多元文化。

【效果评价】 教师观察学生参与互动和交流的情况,并根据需要进行追问或给予鼓励。

步骤四　**Developmental thinking**（10 分钟）

Activity 1: Read and choose (1 min)

Students get the news that Sarah is lost and there are three halls. Then, students read Sarah's Wechat message and answer where she is.

图 11

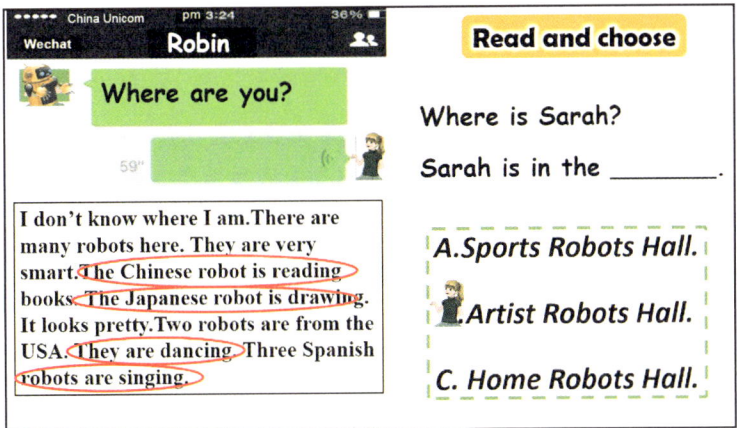

图 12

【设计说明】　学生在 Sarah 走失的新情境中（见图 11），通过阅读关键信息定位 Sarah 的位置（见图 12）；通过查找、理解与分析拓展文本中的关键信息，进一步发展阅读能力，为接下来的写作打好语言基础。

【效果评价】　教师观察学生能否勾选正确答案，评价其获取关键信息和理解文本的能力，并根据需要给予必要的帮助和指导。

Activity 2: Let's talk (2 mins)

Students talk about Robin's Wechat message based on the helpful words given in the worksheet.

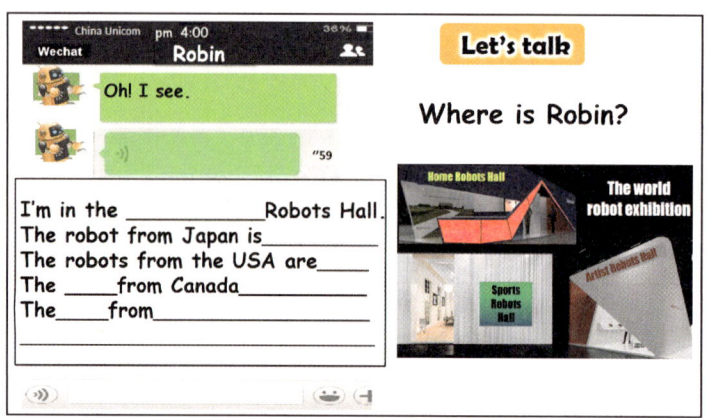

图 13

【设计说明】 通过对 Robin 位置的猜测(见图 13),学生在情境中发散思维,运用所学解决实际问题,提高语言的迁移运用能力。

【效果评价】 教师观察学生能否参与互动和交流,是否有描述机器人的动作或给出其他信息,根据需要进行追问或给予鼓励。

Activity 3: Let's write (7 mins)

Students fill out Robin's Wechat message based on the talk. After that, they share the message with deskmates.

【设计说明】 通过参考 Sarah 的 Wechat message,学生借助语言提示,综合所学内容,判断 Robin 的位置并分享,实现以读促写。

【效果评价】 教师观察学生写作的情况,给予必要指导和反馈;观察学生是否能向全班介绍 Robin 的位置,评估教与学的成效,并根据学生的表现给予反馈与引导。

(六) 作业设计

*1. Listen and read the text aloud on Page 63.

**2. Polish your writing according to the checklist.

评价核查表	是	否
1. 短文的内容是否完整?		
2. 短文是否包含了正确的动词-ing 形式?		
3. 短文的书写、拼写、标点是否正确规范?		

【设计说明】 本作业根据星级,进行了难度递增的分层设计:一星作业"课后听读"为基础性作业(学生必做),旨在引导学生进一步理解文本,巩固所学;两星作业"Where is Robin?的写作"为实践性作业(学生选做),旨在提升学生综合语用能力。学生依据评价核查表的每个问题进行自查,反复修改、完善文章,提升写作质量,实现以评促学。

（七）板书设计

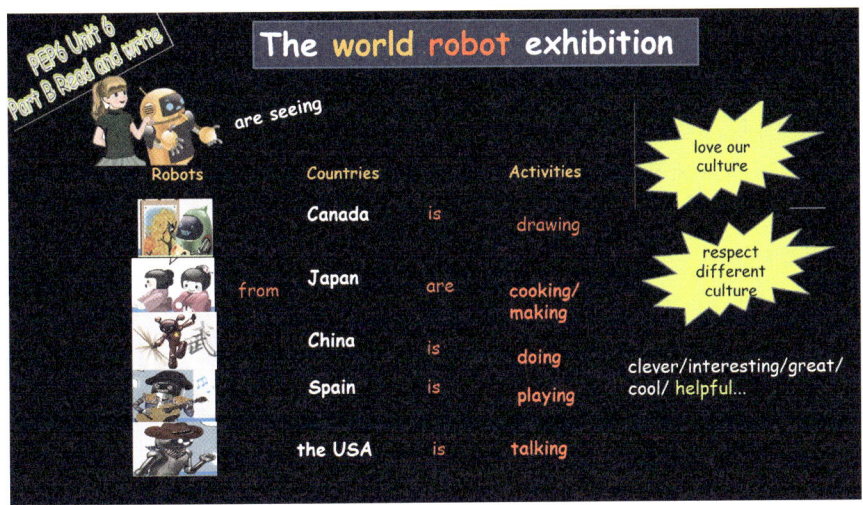

图 14

【设计说明】　板书包括课题名称与课堂要点。首先,板书左边和中间部分呈现了本节课的核心句型,借助关键词和图片,让学生关注阅读文本的重要信息。其次,板书的右边部分清晰地呈现了本节课的主题意义——爱本国文化,尊重不同文化。通过生成的板书,学生能自主地进行文本内容的回顾和复述。

（八）教学反思

　　本课是一节读写课,教师围绕"机器人"这一主题,基于英语学习活动观,依托语篇设计了一系列循环递进和整合关联的学习活动,引领学生在语境中发展学科关键能力,并体会到尊重不同文化的重要性。

　　1. 创设连续情境,设计进阶问题,提升思维品质

　　教师在 Robin 和 Sarah 周末观看展览的教材原情境基础上,创设了后续情境及相应任务,为提升学生的思维提供机会。教师首先借助语篇原本提供的展厅内不同机器人,设置"What kind of exhibition? Where are they from?"等理解性与简单分析性问题,引导学生利用已有经验挖掘文本表层信息,观察与分析不同机器人的外观;在分析文本的过程中,教师提出"Which robots do you like best? Why? What do you think of robots?"等分析性和评价性问题,引导学生思考机器人的不同功能,感受人工智能的力量;最后,教师创设 Robin 与 Sarah 在展馆走失的情境,提出"Where is Sarah? Where is Robin?"等分析性与创造性问题,引导学生综合运用本课所学(机器人外观、功能、所在场馆等信息)给出答案。在整个教学过程中,诸多不同思维层级的问题环环相扣,各有侧重地训练了学生思维的灵活性、深刻性、系统性和独创性。

　　2. 基于文本插图,拓展文化知识,培养文化意识

　　文化意识培养是小学英语教学的关键一环。考虑到教材原语篇内容简单,没有直接提

及或具体说明文化元素,教师围绕语篇提供的插图信息进行拓展,助力学生发展跨文化理解与鉴赏能力,增强对中华民族的文化自信。教材中加拿大的 maple leaf、日本的 kimono 和 sushi、西班牙的斗牛士服装和 guitar(flamenco)、美国的 cowboy 和 national flag、中国的服装和 kung fu 等元素皆以语篇插图的形式零散分布在各段对话之中,不太能引起学生的关注。因此,教师在课堂中对语篇与插图所涉及的文化提供了诠释——中国武术悠久的历史、日本的和服文化、美国西部牛仔和西班牙斗牛士的典型形象,补充说明加拿大为枫叶之国,flamenco 吉他源于西班牙等背景文化信息,使原语篇内容更为丰满,编排更有逻辑。与此同时,学生通过仔细观察插图,找出各个国家的文化标志,不仅提升了文本解码能力,在脑海中形成完整的语篇概念——they are seeing the world robot exhibition,也体会了文化的多样性,更能深刻感受文化自信,学会尊重和欣赏多元文化。

(九) 附件

学 习 单

【活动 1】Read and choose

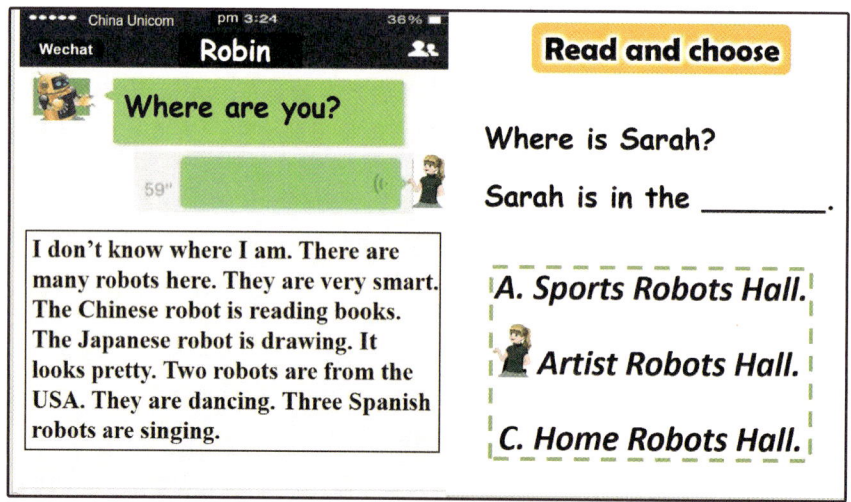

【活动 2】Let's write

> I'm in the _____ Robots Hall.
>
> The robot from Japan is _____
>
> The robots from the USA are _____
>
> The _____ from Canada _____
>
> The _____ from _____
>
> _____

Helpful words:
HOME ROBOT

wash dishes　　water the plants　　sweep the floor　　tidy the living room　　clean the window

sweep the floor　　wash clothes　　hoover the floor（用吸尘器清洁地板）　　feed the pet　　walk the dog

throw trash away make the bed　　mop the floor　　put books on a shelf　　set the table

SPORTS ROBOT

play basketball / football / volleyball / badminton / tennis / table tennis / baseball　　box（拳击）bend（伸展）

run　　jump　　jog　　swim　　skip　　hop　　ride a bike　　skate　　roller skate　　ice skate（滑冰）

wrestle（摔跤）　　dive　　fence（击剑）

ARTIST ROBOT
dance　　sing　　draw pictures　　listen to music　　play the piano（钢琴）

图书在版编目(CIP)数据

小学英语说课与试课:视频课例/罗晓杰,张璐,牟金江主编.—上海:复旦大学出版社,2024.4
(中小学英语说课与试课丛书/罗晓杰,牟金江总主编)
ISBN 978-7-309-16961-4

Ⅰ.①小⋯　Ⅱ.①罗⋯ ②张⋯ ③牟⋯　Ⅲ.①英语课-课堂教学-教学研究-小学　Ⅳ.①
G623.312

中国国家版本馆 CIP 数据核字(2023)第 157008 号

小学英语说课与试课(视频课例)
罗晓杰　张　璐　牟金江　主编
责任编辑/方　君

复旦大学出版社有限公司出版发行
上海市国权路 579 号　邮编:200433
网址:fupnet@ fudanpress.com　http://www.fudanpress.com
门市零售:86-21-65102580　　团体订购:86-21-65104505
出版部电话:86-21-65642845
上海四维数字图文有限公司

开本 787 毫米×1092 毫米　1/16　印张 21.25　字数 503 千字
2024 年 4 月第 1 版第 1 次印刷

ISBN 978-7-309-16961-4/G · 2520
定价:88.00 元